Old Lady on the Trail

Triple Crown at 76

Mary E. Davison

Old Lady on the Trail

Triple Crown at 76

Copyright © Mary E. Davison 2018

ISBN-13: 978-0-9885186-7-4

Published: 15 October, 2018 Vandeleigh Publishing

Cover Photo courtesy of Karen "RockStar" Keller

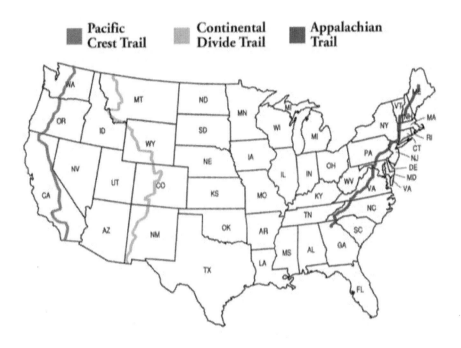

■ Pacific
Crest Trail

■ Continental
Divide Trail

■ Appalachian
Trail

This book is dedicated to the unsung heroes of the trails, those who volunteer their time and effort to maintain them. Without maintenance, trails disappear into wilderness. Without maintenance there would be no trails to walk.

TABLE OF CONTENTS

Chapter 1 September 8, 2017

The End

Shoot. There's still smoke. Disappointed, I started the descent from Swift Current Pass. I'd hoped the smoke would be cleared. Other hikers had told me it was clear from Many Glacier to the top of the pass, but they'd left Many Glacier two days earlier. Today, smoke from the fire that had consumed the Sperry Chalet had spread even past Swift Current Pass. It had joined with smoke from the Canadian fire near Waterton. Still, the haze was slightly less than the day before. I wanted to take it all in, intentionally observing everything, trying to soak it all into my vision and memory.

In spite of the smoke, the high country was still beautiful, all shades of brown, yellow and red ground cover in this very dry September. (The ranger on the border had said no measurable precipitation had fallen for 90 days.) The few remaining banks of snow amid rocky crags gradually became more visible as I neared them, smoky haze not obscuring everything, though no pictures I took would show the clear beauty of a blue sky. Green trees, bushes, ground cover and rocky crags were all grayed with smoky haze.

This was my last day to complete the Continental Divide Trail for my Triple Crown, no putting it off until another year. At age 76 I couldn't be sure I would *have* another year with the ability or opportunity for a multi-day backpack. This was the year to complete my goal, a journey begun fourteen years ago, before I knew a Triple Crown existed. I'd walked nearly 8,000 miles for the Triple Crown and 2,000 miles more on other long trails. Who knew how many more trails I would be able to walk?

As I descended, I could see two moving white dots on the opposite hill. Goats. Mountain goats. Walking a little closer I could make out heads, too, reaching down to graze, and barely seen legs moving white dots across dry forage between rocky cliffs. I was excited and happy to see the goats.

The best was yet to come. I turned a corner around the shoulder of a ridge, singing old Girl Scout songs at the top of my lungs as a warning to bears that I was on the trail. And, WOW! A grizzly bear popped out of the trees on the lower side of the trail, 50 to 75 feet in front of me. The grizzly didn't even glance at the walking singer, just lumbered gracefully across the trail and up the gulley. Stunning!

I watched in awe, but the bear was not interested in me or a threat to me. I also saw another bear up the gully. These were mature grizzlies. I'd been walking in grizzly country since northern Colorado five years ago, but I'd never seen a grizzly before. I was thrilled.

How quickly the grizzly covered ground, even though he seemed in no particular hurry. Big boulders and a few trees kept getting in the way of a clear view. I didn't want to spend precious moments trying to focus a camera. I only wanted to watch the grizzlies until they turned the corner out of sight in a rocky cleft above the trail.

What an amazing gift for my last day on the Continental Divide Trail.

After the grizzlies disappeared, I continued down the trail and turned another corner. Swift Current Basin opened up. The trail was cut along cliffs, switchbacking down to the valley below. Four thin waterfalls plunged hundreds of feet into the high mountain bowl. Even through smoky haze I could look above the waterfalls to glaciers. Yes, there was smoke. No, the pictures wouldn't be as spectacular as they would have been without the smoke. But even a smoke-filled valley couldn't completely obscure the grandeur of the view as I made out the outline of Bullhead Lake far below me.

It was an awesome way to end the Continental Divide Trail. On a personal high, I walked the rest of the way to Many Glacier. Last day on the trail and two magnificent grizzly bears.

Pretty hard for a 76-year-old lady to beat that.

There were lots of day hikers from Bullhead Lake to Many Glacier. Several spoke to me. I was the one with a big smile on my face, carrying a backpack. I was only too happy to announce that I thought I might be the oldest hiker to complete the Triple Crown.

Several of them said I was an inspiration as they, in their 50s and

60s, were thinking their hiking days might be over. They said if I could complete a Triple Crown at 76, perhaps they could continue to hike. I recommended they recognize their limitations, not try to do what young hikers do in exactly the same way, or even what they themselves *used to do*, but plan their hikes according to what they *could* do now, get light-weight equipment and keep on hiking.

It can be done. I know. I am an old hiker. I have three joint replacements and the usual assortment of conditions common to those in their 70s. Yet I completed the Triple Crown of Long Distance Hiking at age 76.

Some people I have met along the trails and years, as well as on that day, suggested I write a book. I hope they and others will enjoy reading this book. It is not a how-to book. It is the story of my journey to the Triple Crown, the story of an aging hiker completing the Triple Crown in spite of problems common with advancing age. Come, adventure with me. Discover the joys and challenges of three of our National Scenic Trails.

With light-weight equipment, a love of walking through wilderness, a certain skillset for living outdoors and moving safely on the trail, and creativity in adapting expectations to abilities, older hikers can hike long trails.

If you are one of those older hikers, Huzza for you. If you are an armchair reader, may you enjoy the trails vicariously as you meet your own challenges, discover your own possibilities, and celebrate your age.

"Congratulations. But what Is a Triple Crown?"

When I reached Many Glacier that last day of my trek, I found my friend and hiking companion, RockStar, in our room in the Many Glacier Hotel. A Congratulations Banner hung on the wall, and the room was draped with crepe-paper streamers and trimmed with a paper border depicting balloons. With glitter paper and poster board she'd also made me a crown shaped like a bishop's miter. And she'd carefully drawn the trail symbols for the Appalachian Trail, The

Pacific Crest Trail, and the Continental Divide Trail on the crown.

She and I both thought I should celebrate such an achievement. So I gleefully wore the crown to dinner in the hotel and around the lobby afterward. No one else had a crown, so of course it was a conversation starter. Some knew what the Triple Crown was, and others did not. People came up to me, shook my hand and said, rather tentatively, "Congratulations." (I was obviously celebrating something with a crown on my head.) "But what is a Triple Crown?" Their question gave me an opportunity to tell them about the three long trails that make up the Triple Crown of long-distance hiking.

The Appalachian Trail (AT)

The Appalachian Trail stretches from Springer Mountain, Georgia to Mt. Katahdin, Maine.

Benton MacKaye, born in Stamford, Connecticut in 1879, is credited with conceiving a trail connecting the ridge tops of the Appalachian Mountains from New England to the South. There are a host of other names and countless volunteers, who brought the Appalachian Trail to reality and maintain it.

The trail was completed in 1937, although completion is perhaps too strong a word as the trail changes slightly over the years. My earliest readings listed it as 2,247 miles, but more recent resources record it at 2,184 miles. The Appalachian Trail Conservancy's mission is "to preserve and manage the Appalachian Trail, ensuring its vast natural beauty and priceless cultural heritage can be shared and enjoyed today, tomorrow, and for centuries to come."

The AT crosses 14 states and is the oldest of the three trails that comprise the Triple Crown. Each year tens of thousands of hikers start from Springer Mountain, Georgia, hoping to walk the entire distance in one season, to be thru-hikers. Many thousands more, perhaps even millions, hike sections ranging from a day hike to a weekend or weeks at a time.

This trail winds its way from mountain to mountain in a narrow strip of wilderness, sometimes near large population centers. Depending on the time of year and the section of trail, you may meet many hikers on the AT or take a walk in complete solitude. The AT goes up and down many mountains and wasn't built to accommodate horses. Some steep and rocky sections require hikers to use hands as well as feet. The lush growth over most of the trail has given it the nickname of "The Long Green Tunnel."

The Pacific Crest Trail (PCT)

By 1920 the Forest Service created a trail called the Oregon

Skyline Trail, winding from Mt. Hood to Crater Lake in Oregon. To that was added the Cascade Crest Trail in Washington State from Canada to the Columbia River. It wasn't until the 1960s that a commission appointed by the Bureau of Outdoor Recreation recommended that Congress establish scenic trails. In 1968 Congress passed the National Trails System Act and the AT and the PCT were named the first two National Scenic Trails. The PCT Association's mission is "to protect, preserve, and promote the Pacific Crest National Scenic Trail as a world-class experience for hikers and equestrians."

The 2,654 miles of the Pacific Crest Trail extend from the Mexican Border below Campo, California to the Canadian Border near Manning Park, Canada. This trail does not go over every possible mountain on its route in the manner of the AT, but traverses close to many high mountain peaks while following, more or less, the crest of the Sierra and Cascade Mountains through California, Oregon and Washington. One can summit many peaks while walking the PCT, but most of them require a side trip from the trail itself.

At the time I began walking on the Pacific Crest Trail, hundreds of hikers started at the Mexican border each year hoping to thru-hike the PCT in a single season. Over the years I have been working on the Triple Crown, the number of thru hikers has increased into the low thousands. And, like the AT, many more hikers walk parts of this trail as section or day hikes.

Passing through a wide variety of terrain, the PCT moves from high desert, to alpine areas in the rocky Sierra to the mountain hemlock forests of the Cascades and many variations along the way.

The Continental Divide Trail (CDT)

The last trail, which makes up the Triple Crown is the highest, most challenging and most remote, according to the Continental Divide Trail Coalition. (Really, each trail in the Triple Crown deserves respect. Completing any of these trails is an achievement with its own unique challenges.) The CDT is not entirely complete, requiring the hiker to bushwhack (walk without trail or road) or road walk in a few sections, requiring backcountry navigation skills.

Traditionally, the CDT begins from the Mexican border in three possible places: the official start from Crazy Cook, farthest south point of New Mexico on the *boot heel* at Antelope Wells or at the border below Columbus. It then travels through states containing the Continental Divide to end at the Canadian border at Glacier/Waterton National Park, either at Waterton or Chief Mountain. At the time I began this journey there were probably only 50-100 hikers to be found thru-hiking this trail each year, although more people hiked sections or day hikes, particularly when close to populated areas or near specific attractions. The number of hikers on this trail is also increasing year by year. In 2017 the hiker grapevine said that 500 hikers left Crazy Cook headed north, and I saw another 50 to 75 southbound hikers in Montana.

The CDT was suggested when the National Trail Systems Act was passed by Congress, but it wasn't yet a real trail. The potential of such a trail arose from a study of the Department of the Interior in 1977, and in 1978 it was recognized as a National Scenic Trail.

Jim Wolf served on the early advisory board for the CDT. The US Forest Service, The Bureau of Land Management and the National Park System were all involved in the CDT, but funding wasn't robust. The early management plan called for a trail within a 50-mile corridor on either side of the Continental Divide. Forming the Continental Divide Trail Society, Jim Wolf wrote the CDT Guide Books and advocated for the CDT.

The Continental Divide Trail Association was created as a broader organization to advocate for the trail, and it united a number of smaller groups, but lacked finances to continue. While the CDTA existed, Jerry Brown (Bear Creek) mapped the official trail.

Today the Continental Divide Trail Coalition, CDTC, advocates for and contributes volunteers to the maintenance of the CDT. Jim Wolf, Jerry Brown, and numerous volunteer groups have joined forces in this organization. Its "mission is to complete, promote, and protect the Continental Divide National Scenic Trail by building a strong and diverse trail community, by providing up-to-date information to the public, and through encouraging conservation and stewardship of the Trail, its corridor, and surrounding landscapes."

From the deserts of New Mexico to 14,000-foot mountains in Colorado, through the Great Basin and the Wind River Range in Wyoming, through Yellowstone National Park, along the winding, mountainous border of Montana and Idaho to the ultimate end in Glacier National Park, the CDT presents many challenges in terrain and navigation.

Each trail is unique in philosophy, history, and challenge. Together, they draw many, many thousands of hikers from the United States and other nations to their winding treads.

Triple Crown Recognition

In long-distance hiking circles, there are those who aspire to hike the Triple Crown. Many have done so, especially in the last few years. The American Long Distance Hiker Association – West (ALDHA–West) recognizes and awards a plaque to those who complete a Triple Crown and ask for recognition. Exactly how many people have completed a Triple Crown is unknown, as not all hikers ask for recognition, and ALDHA–West does not claim to keep official records.

ALDHA–West initiated recognition of those who hiked the Triple Crown in 1994. But hikers were on the trail before that date. 1977 is the earliest date of completion listed by ALDHA–West.

Chapter 2 August 2001

Getting Started

So, how did I begin this journey to complete the Triple Crown at 76? Blame it on my parents. Blame it on the Girl Scouts. Blame it on the Wonderland Trail.

Blame it on my parents: Camping and camp skills were not something new to me at 76 or 40 or even 20. I was born into a family that camped. Each year we drove to Lake Geneva, Wisconsin from Westminster, Colorado for a conference my Dad attended. As a kid, I thought motels were only for rich people. We camped. We also drove to California to visit relatives.

Ditto. We camped. In the 1940s to 1950s it wasn't that unusual to just pull over to the side of the road or down a smaller road off the highway to find a place to spend the night. One memorable (awful) night we left home several hours later than planned, and my Dad decided he was too tired to drive safely. So we *camped* in the ditch on the side of the road going over Loveland Pass with semis roaring by us.

My most memorable family camping trip was the year I was in the 7th grade. I'd taken all my finals early, weeks before the end of the school year. Dad had a week's convention in Atlantic City, New Jersey, a week's convention in Philadelphia, and a week in between. We drove and camped from Colorado to the east coast. We stayed in a campground outside of Atlantic City for a week while Dad attended his meetings. We stayed in Valley Forge for a week while he attended meetings in Philadelphia. (Valley Forge allowed camping in those days although we seemed to be the only ones doing so.) We even found a trailer park a stone's throw from the Jefferson Memorial in Washington DC that had one small square of grass for tents. That trailer park is long gone, a freeway bridge now occupying the spot where we'd put our tent.

New York City was the only place we visited during that month-long trip where we didn't camp, staying with somewhat distant relatives outside of New York and taking in the sights by riding the train into the city.

So my parents can be *blamed* for my knowing how to camp at a young age, albeit that *camping* may just have meant throwing a sleeping bag on the ground or erecting a heavy canvas tent as our traveling home. Because we camped, I was able to visit many places in the USA, appreciating many parts of this beautiful country. Travel and camping were a part of growing up in my family.

Blamed it on the Girl Scouts: From the third grade through high school, I was a Girl Scout. In the summer of 1953 I went to Girl Scout Camp. I loved it. I talked a steady stream of chatter all the way on the several hour drive home, through dinner and into the night, telling everything I'd done in great detail, from learning songs, washing dishes, how to ride, saddle and bridle a horse to the proper way to clean a latrine. From that first year as a camper through Camp Counseling during college, I lived for Girl Scout Camp. The rest of the year was very nearly irrelevant to me. The only time that really mattered was that two or three weeks, and later, as a counselor, whole summers at Girl Scout Camp.

My camping skills were honed. Hiking became my forte. After a year or two, counselors sometimes let me lead the whole unit of 20 girls on hikes. I learned how to lead others, how to set a pace so as never to leave people behind and how to help others know and enjoy the outdoors.

The most memorable experience at Girl Scout Camp was a ten-day burro trip with eight girls and two counselors. The burros carried gear and each girl carried a small daypack. We learned to care for those burros and load them up each day, tying the load with a proper diamond hitch. Each girl carried one cup, one spoon and a sheath knife. We cooked meals of Seidel's Trail Food in #10 tin cans with bailing wire handles over wood fires and slept under heavy canvas tarps rigged from trees with binder's twine and held together with Alice's gold bobby pins.

It rained every day. It hailed every other day. And we were lost much of the time. That was of no great account to us eight girls. We made up rain songs, wrote a journal and had a blast, although our two counselors probably suffered consternation about the being lost part. I'd never had so much fun in my life. This trip was formative in teaching me to enjoy the outdoors in all weathers and all circumstances, and I loved the friends I made.

Life intervened: After Girl Scouts, other life chapters passed by over the next 35-40 years: my first job as a physical therapist in Tacoma, learning to climb glaciated mountains including Mount Rainier with the Mountaineers, a stint in the Peace Corps in Turkey as a physical therapist, marriage, the birth of my two children, divorce, remarriage and ultimately another divorce, going to seminary, and becoming a pastor and serving a congregation for 15 years. All of those are stories in their own right, but not direct parts of this particular story. Yet those chapters contributed to who I was and am as an old lady on the trail.

My physical-therapy background gave me knowledge of body mechanics. The Mountaineers taught me basic wilderness and mountaineering skills. The Peace Corps encouraged my adventurous spirit and a desire to see new things and meet new people. Marriages and divorces, and the counseling that accompanied them, taught me to be comfortable *in my own skin*, comfortable with who I am. My children and grandchildren brought and bring me joy. Seminary and the struggle to become a pastor when woman pastors were few, taught me to walk each forward step even without certainty of completion. Serving as a pastor I was called to share the love of God with others.

Every hiker is unique in who they are and what they bring to long-distance hiking. Individual backgrounds add different textures to our experience. Passing years and life chapters added depth to my being and influenced my approach to hiking long trails. An older hiker may bring to the trail multiple viewpoints accumulated over years and life chapters.

Younger hikers, too, come to the trail with different points of view and backgrounds. Whether young or old, we encounter each other in a kaleidoscope of personalities on two-foot- wide paths winding through the wonders of the natural world.

Blame it on The Wonderland Trail: *"Oh, we're done."* **(Spoken with great regret.)** Before I began long distance hiking, I had occasions to hike and take short backpack trips, taking my children and both husbands. My son was in the Boy Scouts, and he car camps and hikes with his two children now.

But my daughter was the child who liked hiking the most. We took three backpack trips together, up to five or six days each. I also took members of the congregation I served on hikes, and led a few parishioners on short backpack trips as a church activity complete with Bible study at rest stops.

In 2001, my daughter and I decided to hike the Wonderland Trail before I got *too old* to backpack. It was the year I turned 60.

The Wonderland Trail is a 90-to-100 mile trail around Mount Rainier in Washington State. Although I have hiked some 10,000-long distance miles finding beauty everywhere I go, foot for foot, the Wonderland Trail is the most beautiful trail I have ever hiked.

We hiked through meadows filled with wildflowers, past beautiful waterfalls and every step of the way there was another view, another face of Mount Rainier and its glistening glaciers. The Wonderland Trail is also almost never level. Going around Mount Rainier, one climbs up and over ridges, down into glacier-carved valleys and then up the next ridge and down the next valley, repeated all the way around the mountain, 22,000 feet of elevation gains and losses in those 90+ miles.

When we hiked the Wonderland, I knew nothing about long-distance hiking. Our packs were huge as we set out from Longmire clockwise around the mountain. Our friend Jo accompanied us. She packed way too much stuff and couldn't carry it all. I added more to my already over loaded pack to help her out. I was probably carrying 50 pounds for the first six days. The miracle was, at 60, I could do it; I certainly couldn't carry that load at 76.

Rainier National Park has strict rules about registering for and staying at backcountry campsites, and they were not easy to arrange. At that time, it meant phoning on an exact date months before your desired start date, at the exact time when the backcountry office opened, hoping your call was the first. I wasn't first, but I did manage to get sites, although we were forced to spend an extra day at a site we didn't care for, hiking to the next site when it became available. We took 16 days. The usual time for most backpackers to complete the Wonderland Trail is nine days. Trail runners do it in three days or less–but they are truly crazy. With my love of hiking, I only claim to be half crazy.

Mike, a member of the congregation, joined us for ten days and our group swelled to nine at White River with other members of my congregation. It was logistically complicated, but it all worked.

We had a wonderful time. We didn't mind the extra time. We enjoyed it all. We took books, a sun-shower (a black water bag with a short hose and shower nozzle that can be placed in sun to warm) and many other completely unnecessary things on this hike, but the trip lives as a highlight in all our memories.

We had amazingly good luck with the weather for 14 days. The last full day, northwest weather settled in, and it rained all day. My daughter and I were undaunted. Sending our packs out with Jo and a ranger at Narada Falls, we ended with a road walk since a hiking bridge over the Nisqually River was washed out. We sang rain songs all the way to the campground and continued on the next day in the rain to finish at Longmire.

Then we looked at each other and regretfully said, "*Oh, we're done.*" The long-distance-hiking bug had bitten.

Chapter 3 August 2003 PCT

"Pastor Mary, I don't think we should take the rest of the church on this hike."

So, I discovered I liked multi-day backpack trips. Did I then say, "Oh, I think I'll work on the Triple Crown?"

Of course not. I'd not yet heard of the Triple Crown. I knew there was something called the Pacific Crest Trail that went through Washington State, where I lived. I may have heard of the Cascade Crest or Skyline Trail when I was in my 20s. I knew of the Appalachian Trail in the eastern part of the United States. I'd never heard of a thru-hiker. I'd never heard of the Continental Divide Trail. The only Triple Crown I knew of was a horse race.

A parishioner was working on completing the Washington part of the trail. Interesting. It sounded like a fun project. When I began, I wasn't thinking beyond Washington State.

The section I chose to do first wasn't the best, the most scenic section of the PCT (Pacific Crest Trail) or the beginning or the end of the trail. It was the most convenient. My first PCT section began at Chinook Pass and ended at Snoqualmie Pass. Mike, the same young, red-haired parishioner, who had walked part of the Wonderland, was game to go, too. A pastoral colleague dropped us off at Chinook Pass, and my son picked us up after work six days later at Snoqualmie Pass.

I set out with my old REI external frame pack, a five-pound sleeping bag and a six-pound tent for the two of us. In those days I thought three pounds per person for a tent was the lightest possibility. I would never consider carrying such a heavy tent or sleeping bag now.

From my days in the Mountaineers, I remembered there was a great view from a short climb above Sour Dough Gap. Mike dutifully followed his pastor on a scramble up the rocky crag with a sheer drop on the other side, although he wasn't particularly comfortable with heights. Mike could have hiked much faster than his pastor on this trip but always let me lead, inexplicably saying going at my pace would keep him from hurting himself.

The most memorable part of the trip was the elk. We saw a herd of elk from a distance in Big Crow Basin, and the next night we heard more, although we didn't know at the time what we

were hearing was elk. It wasn't until we reached the Ulrich Cabin on the third night that we definitely identified the strange sounds as elk. We woke up the next morning in the cabin and found 30 to 40 elk outside. We crept as quietly as we could down a creaky wooden ladder from the sleeping loft, carefully opened the squeaky door and took many pictures of quiet elk life as the herd, mostly mothers and calves, grazed all around us.

Elk sound like ET. I have been amazed ever since at the sounds elk make. Males bugling in the fall rutting season is entirely different. In domestic bliss as they grazed around us in the meadow surrounding the Ulrich Cabin, elk made high pitched sounds very much resembling the sounds ET made in the movie of the same name.

Leaving Ulrich Cabin, we hiked in clear cuts most of the way to Snoqualmie Pass at the same time as an unusual 90+ degree heat wave hit the Pacific Northwest. Our packs were heavy. I was still carrying a sun-shower, a book to read, a lot of cooking equipment and heavy food for three course dinners as well as a heavy tent and bag. It was very hot, and I have never done well in heat. Hot weather turns me into a *dead daisy*. At one point, Mike and I struggled upwards to an old logging landing and collapsed on tiny wild strawberries. There was no shade, and we were really spent.

Mike said, "Pastor Mary, I don't think we should bring the rest of the church on this hike."

I laughed almost hysterically as I thought it the funniest statement ever, right when I was wondering why *we* had ever come on this hike.

We survived the heat and the hike, and at the end of our six days arrived at Snoqualmie Pass. The folks in the motel were kind enough to let us wait for pick up inside their air- conditioned lobby, even though we were not paying guests. I'd completed 69.5 miles of the 2,654 mile Pacific Crest Trail.

Chapter 4 April 2004 AT

"Hey, I could do this even solo."

In 2003 I planned a visit with my daughter, Sara, who then lived in North Carolina. Her husband had come home from the Kuwait War with severe kidney stones. As he recovered, we took a trip to the Great Smoky Mountains. I picked up a couple of books about the Appalachian Trail: *Walking the Appalachian Trail* by Larry Luxenberg and *A Walk in the Woods* by Bill Bryson. Later I found a series of books at a used bookstore in Tacoma: *Exploring the Appalachian Trail*. I read them all. I was hooked. My daughter and I planned to start at Springer Mountain, Georgia in April, 2004 for an eleven-day backpack trip.

We were still decked out with heavy gear: old external frame REI (Recreational Equipment Incorporated) packs, heavy sleeping bags, a six-pound REI tent, too much food, cooking gear and the sun shower. We carried foam pads to place under our sleeping bags, the only lightweight item in our packs. I discovered a foam pad was just not enough for my old bones, consequently I had very little sleep on this trip. We were still wearing heavy boots and I got my usual silver dollar sized blisters on my heels. We didn't make it eleven days as Sara's knee, dislocated in dancing classes in high school, started swelling about day five. Our packs were not monster- class, but heavy enough that we searched for rock formations, which we called *dismount rocks*, allowing us to more easily put on and take off our heavy packs. Lacking such rocks, we had to help each other into our packs.

On the AT we discovered a whole different way of doing a backpack.

The Appalachian Trail has shelters in which one can sometimes stay, a whole lot of people and access to towns. I'd never considered making a hike easier with town stops. I thought one just hiked from point A to point B with, perhaps, a stop somewhere for a food drop if you couldn't carry enough for the whole trip. We met many who hoped to be thru-hikers, going all the way to Maine that year. There was much discussion as to what percentage of those who started at Springer actually would make it to Katahdin. Lots of hikers were starting and hoped to

go the distance. Others were section hikers, weekend hikers, or day hikers. Some of them stopped frequently at nearby towns taking *zero* days (rest days walking zero miles) before heading on again.

We had a great trip. The weather was quite warm, sometimes hot. We made friends. We met many other hikers, some of whom I captured in photos scribbled with strange trail names on the back, like Nitro, Mr Clean and Frenchy. (Nitro and I would meet in future years on the PCT. And I saw Mr Clean years later, too, although he'd changed his trail name to Cog by then.)

Others on the AT had very heavy packs, but some had lightweight packs. Nitro had a Mountain Smith Ghost, an internal frame pack, and it wasn't as loaded as ours. I took note of it.

The climb up Blood Mountain was difficult with our overloaded packs. I struggled. Sara went ahead to find us a camping spot, not an easy task as it was a weekend and roughly a zillion people were camped on Blood Mountain, including at least two Boy Scout troops. Every available spot on that mountain had a tent on it, including many camped on rock slabs. Sara found us slanted grass hummocks just the size of our tent that others had by-passed. Those grass hummocks may have been lumpy, but they made my softest bed and provided the only night of solid sleep on that trip.

Blue Mountain and Tray Mountain were also challenges. The Appalachian Trail begins on a mountain (Springer Mountain, Georgia), ends on a mountain (Mt. Katahdin, Maine) and tries to go up and down most every mountain in between, even if the trail almost goes in circles to do so. Every state brags about its difficult trail. There may be an easy way up a mountain, but the AT, with perverse pride, will go up and down the hard way.

We had good times. We saw the views. We soaked up trail culture new to us such as trail names, which reminded me of Girl Scout camp names. We learned about *trail magic* first hand when we found a six pack of cokes at the Unicoi Gap trailhead with a note saying they were for any hiker who wanted one. We each took one, not wanting to be greedy with trail magic.

Some of the time we needed our good camping skills, but I learned there were other ways to hike. Many hikers were solo hikers. I'd never considered solo hiking. Both the Girl Scouts and the Mountaineers had always stressed safety in numbers. I'd been taught the safest minimum number was three: If one is injured that left one to stay with the injured person and one to hike for help. That is still the safest rule for hiking. Hiking with two was OK, but not as safe as three. I could organize and lead group hikes and backpack trips. I'd many skills, but solo hiking was new to me. The AT wasn't isolated wilderness hiking. There was plenty of room to hike alone, but there were also others on the trail. Friends were made as you went along. Being solo didn't mean I couldn't go. "Hey, I could do this." Even if I didn't have a hiking partner, I could do this.

In preparing for this trip, I'd read Appalachian Trail books that described the trail and interesting things along the trail. Sara and I were the only ones we knew who visited the Hickory Flats Cemetery Pavilion and its strange playground equipment where we had fun on the two- person Merry Go Round just before Hawk Mountain Shelter.

Nitro had a trail journal online on trailjournals.com, which I followed when I returned home.

Sara learned about hitchhiking etiquette on the AT when her swelling knee forced her off trail. We met hikers who hitchhiked to get to small towns along the way, and we heard some motels regularly sent vans to pick people up at trailheads. We trusted the hitchhiking lore told to us, and she left me at Dick's Creek Gap to find her own way to her car stashed with the person who had shuttled us up the road to Springer Mountain at the beginning of our hike. I continued on into North Carolina for another day and night solo. Sara picked me up at Deep Gap in her bright yellow car. I'd hiked 82.4 miles on the Appalachian Trail and gone from one state into another. Georgia was done. I only had 2,064.6 miles to go.

Chapter 5 August 2004 PCT

"Lose a pound for each year past 60."

In 2004, I split my vacation time between East and West, and started to hike the AT and the PCT together, a section on each trail each year. As far as I know, I am the only one to have hiked these trails in this way. Usually people hike one trail until finished with that trail, then, maybe later, hike another long trail. I was entranced with both.

So, in August, it was time for another section of the PCT. Although I was pretty sure I could manage the AT as a solo hiker, I wasn't so certain about doing that on the PCT. My daughter wasn't available. What should I do? I simply wrote about what I was planning to do in the church newsletter and asked if anyone wanted to come along. Two people were interested in coming with me for two different sections. Wonderful.

Gary, a younger man from my congregation, and I set out from Panther Lake Campground as a storm system moved into Washington. It poured. All day. Gary pulled out a yellow poncho from his pack and found it was his small daughter's and didn't cover much of a full sized man. At lunch, I rigged the rain fly with some cord, a good thing as Gary was almost hypothermic by then. He found something dry to wear and also found his own poncho, the right sized one. Life was better then, even in the rain. It rained the next day, too. We walked through wet foliage in the Indian Heaven Wilderness, and it left us even wetter. When the sun finally came out and we could dry out, we were overjoyed. In spite of the rain, we enjoyed walking by lakes and peeking through the trees at Mt. St Helens. Gary's family picked him up at Big Mosquito Lake. My son wondered why in the world I chose to camp at something named Big Mosquito anything. It's just how the miles worked out. Yes, there were mosquitoes.

The rain had stopped, and I braved a night alone at Big Mosquito. I hadn't camped alone before, but I thought I could manage one night. After a day of solo hiking, I met Kathy near Mount Adams. Her dog, Tasha, came with us. We loved the Mount Adams area and later the

Goat Rocks. Kathy was a kindred spirit, who loved the mountains as much as I did and also had hiking and climbing experience, making us a good team.

The flowers were in full bloom near Mount Adams and also coming to the Goat Rocks. The views were spectacular, some of the best the PCT has to offer, with high mountain crags and two glaciated mountains. Mount Adams and Mount Rainier. We camped by one of my favorite waterfalls in the Mount Adams area, not seeing the sign telling us not to camp in the overused area until the next morning as we left. Fields of lupine accented with Indian paintbrush were abundant and filled the air with perfume.

Kathy's husband, David, brought us a food drop at a road half way through and Kathy took a break as I walked an uninteresting section. She wanted to walk only the *pretty* parts; I wanted to walk it all.

Before we reached Sheep Lake we crossed Walupt Creek on an incredibly hot day. We were so glad to see water, and it was so hot that we shed all our clothes and sat in the creek. All went well until Kathy sat on my glasses, which I'd placed on the bank when taking my shirt off, her bare butt popping the lenses out. I repaired them with duct tape and looked like Mr. Magoo for the rest of the trip.

I took a short Thermarest air mattress, having learned that old bones don't do well with just a foam pad. I borrowed a two- pound down sleeping bag. I was still thinking a three-pound tent was lightweight. I still wore heavy boots that gave me blisters and used my ancient external frame REI pack. An older hiker in the Goat Rocks said he hiked stoveless to save weight and tried to cut a pound of weight from his pack for each year he hiked past 60 years of age. I took note of stoveless hiking and lightweight goals. Hmm, I was already 63. How could I lose three pounds? Or did my down sleeping bag mean I'd shed three pounds already? But I'd added the air mattress. How could I go lighter the next year?

Mountain goats grazed on a mountain below us as we went over the side of Old Snowy Mountain and Packwood Glacier. Mount Rainier stuck its lofty head above a sea of clouds before us from the knife-edge ridge. Near our highest campsite were banks of bright pink

Monkey Flower. From our tents tucked behind trees we had an incredible view.

Descending from Goat Rocks, we reached our campsite on a very hot day. Kathy and her dog were resting, and it was so hot she took off all her clothes and sat leaning against a downed log. I thought she was the funniest sight I ever saw, casually walking around stark naked except for her hiking boots. After a while, she put a shirt and shorts on, and almost immediately four guys walked into the camp. Her timing was good.

It rained again the last half-mile into White Pass, where we met Kathy's husband. I'd walked another 110 miles of the PCT.

Chapter 6 April 2005 AT

"We don't exactly hike together; we just sleep together."

I'd now *sampled* the two most famous long-distance trails in America. And I now had a goal, or, actually, two goals. I wanted to walk them both, all of them, from end to end. It was obviously going to take me a while to do that. I'd walked only 82.4 miles on the AT and my two trips on the PCT had netted 179.5 miles. I was definitely NOT a thru-hiker. I was also still working and not retired. At best I could manage a week or ten days of each trail a year until I retired. I really liked the idea of hiking on each trail each year. Each had a different flavor, and I liked them both.

Finding Trailjournals.com, I enjoyed reading other people's trail journals. I'd followed Nitro's and had found one written by Yogi. I learned a lot by reading their journals. Maybe I would have my own someday. I was beginning to learn about lightweight hiking.

In April of 2005 I flew off to the AT. I'd found someone who could shuttle me near to where I left off the previous year. I had a new pack, a Mountain Smith Ghost like Nitro's. I had a three-pound solo tent and still wore heavy boots, which still gave me blisters. But I didn't get as many blisters since I'd spent half a day at REI trying on boots and found a pair that fit much better than my older ones. But they were still boots and they still gave me blisters.

I started up the Kimsey Creek Trail to join the AT. (Section hikers sometimes have to add a few miles to meet the trail.) The Kimsey Creek Trail ended up just being Kimsey Creek, the first of many trails I've hiked that were really creeks, complete with small waterfalls. The weather that year was much different than my first trip. I didn't have hot weather and sunny skies but found rain, fog and snow.

I stopped in Franklin for motel, food, and shower. The day I hiked out of Franklin I was caught in a sudden thunderstorm. The wind of an eastern thunderstorm swept in through the leafless trees of early spring, sounding like a freight train coming up the valley. I wasn't prepared for its speed. I stood under a tree wondering if I should put on rain gear and before I could decide, I was drenched. That cotton long sleeve shirt stayed wet for days. I never took a cotton shirt on a hike again.

Later that day, at Siler Bald Shelter, hikers arrived and laid out sleeping bags in the shelter like cordwood. Everyone knew the weather was bringing more rain, and we squeezed in everyone who came, which was quite a trick. I think 11 people were on the floor of that shelter that night. Rain pounded and lightning flashed over and over. Those on the shelter ends got wet as the rain blew in. We weren't quite so tight that everyone had to roll over as one, but pretty darn close to that. The lone hiker who had set up his hammock-tent outside came running in the middle of the storm and took up residence under the picnic table, which wasn't exactly dry, but better than his hammock-tent. It was quite a storm.

I only remember a few names of hikers from that night, but one that stood out was Lightning Rod. He received his trail name because he'd been hit by lightning hiking the AT as a boy with his parents and lived to tell about it. Roller Girl and Weatherman were there, too. Roller Girl told stories about spring on the PCT and the dangerous river crossings in the Sierra. I took note of those tales also.

Hiking on the long trails, especially on the AT, you acquire *trail families*, people who are traveling at roughly the same speed. You see each other more than once and become friends very quickly. It was a somewhat changing *family* as people move into and out of the group depending on schedule and pace. I describe this as, "We don't exactly hike together; we just sleep together." You hike at your own pace but congregate at shelters or water sources for the night, hiking the same number of miles, even at different paces, you still end up in the same place and a *trail family* bond is formed.

Wayah Bald came after Siler Bald and should have had good views. But not that year.

There were too many foggy clouds reaching to the ground with accompanying rain or drizzle. I gratefully ate lunch in a restroom overhang. My destination for the night was Cold Spring Shelter, smaller than Siler Bald. The weather matched the name of the shelter.

Just before I reached the shelter, rain turned to spitting snow. Six of us were there, the shelter holding six like tightly laid cordwood. Being close together wasn't a problem. We needed the warmth of our neighbors. Quite concerned about the cold, I sacrificed my red nylon rope and a couple people sacrificed their ponchos so we could cover the front of the shelter. We were glad we did so. It was definitely below freezing that night and it snowed 4-6 inches, making great morning pictures.

Weatherman had left his water bottle just outside the shelter. We looked at it in the morning and it was water. We touched it, immediately sending crystal fractures through the water and it all turned to ice before our eyes in about three seconds. Interesting phenomenon.

People were not in a hurry to leave that morning, but the trail is the trail. After one or two left, so did I. I forgot my red rope. Perhaps it is still there. As I descended, the snow turned to rain, but not before I captured a picture of snow on struggling pink azaleas at Tellico Gap. Sun came out highlighting white dogwood blossoms. Lingering white snow on bare branches of leafless trees gleamed in the sunlight.

Before starting long distance hikes, you mail food to the places you'll pass along the way. The goal is to lighten the pack and realistically, you can't carry many days' worth of food before needing replenishment. At Nantahala Outdoor Center I picked up a food drop and purchased a rope replacement should I need to hang my food. Nantahala is a Cherokee word meaning "land of the noonday sun." The Nantahala River cuts deeply into a canyon in which the sun can shine directly only in the middle of the day. That means you descend to get there and climb to get somewhere else.

Thanks to Nitro's journal of the year before, I knew there was a good campsite with a great view on Cheoah Bald. Everyone else stayed at Sassafras Gap Shelter and missed the view and sunset I saw that night from Cheoah Bald, only lowering clouds followed by rain the next morning. They also missed a unique wildlife experience.

On the way up to Cheoah Bald I heard something behind me and turned to see baby wild piglets. I have never seen anything like them before or since. They had longitudinal dark stripes from their necks to their tails, were very cute and seemed to think I was their mother as they wanted to follow me up the trail. I was pretty sure their mother would be very big and very fierce, and I didn't want to see *her*. The piglets kept following me, and I had to scare them away with some rocks tossed in their direction. I felt mean doing so, but didn't want a wild boar sow attacking me for stealing her children. When I showed my pictures to Jeff and Nancy at The Hike Inn at the end of the trip, they showed me a picture of a dead sow filling the back of a pickup truck. I was quite glad I hadn't met the mother of those cute piglets.

Leaving my camera on the ledge at Brown Fork Gap Shelter, I did not realize the loss for a couple miles. That was a disaster. What to do? Seth, Emily and John came by and remembered seeing it but no one had picked it up. They took my air mattress with them, saying they would claim a spot for me in the Cable Gap Shelter by laying it down. We knew rain was again imminent and I was really hoping for the cover of the shelter. I went back for the camera, adding 3 to 4 miles on my day. Seth and crew left my air mattress in the shelter as good as their word even though it was a small shelter and not all the trail family could fit and they had to use their tent. I was very grateful.

An interesting couple of guys were already in residence at that shelter when my trail family arrived. We were all pretty sure they were on the lam from the law. They didn't act like hikers, staying to themselves and not talking to us as we chattered together. The rest of us had been hiking, more or less together, for a few days. The two strange guys slept with their backs to us when we arrived in the afternoon. When we were taking pictures, they carefully moved somewhere else so as not to be caught on film. We hikers talked together and made sure no one was left alone with those two guys or even went to the privy alone. We looked out for each other and didn't trust these characters. In the morning we all walked on, and they stayed. They were not hikers. Was the AT their hideout?

Cable Gap was my last night on the AT for the year but not my last moment with my trail family. Stopping at Fontana Dam Marina, I took one last picture of Scared of the Dark, Weatherman, John, Emily, Seth, Roller Girl and Lightning Rod. I sang them a blessing before I left to connect with Jeff and Nancy from the Hike Inn, who would shuttle me to the airport in Asheville.

And I'd walked another 75.9 miles on the Appalachian Trail.

Chapter 7 August 2005 PCT

"Two more days and, oh dear, we will be done just when we are getting in the groove."

The three books titled *The Pacific Crest Trail* by Jeffrey P. Schaffer, Ruby Johnson Jenkins, Ben Schifrin, Jeffrey Schaffer, Andy Selters and Thomas Winnett were the classic guidebooks for the PCT when I started my PCT hikes. Two were for California and one for Oregon and Washington. Wilderness Press Books, and the narrow strip map of the trail were the main tools to get you where you were going, along with compass and common sense. I generally found them quite adequate although when near roads, I occasionally found the directions confusing when compared to the trail under my feet. Some hikers called the guidebooks "the book of lies." Perhaps all that means is that some hikers had different experiences than the authors in certain sections of the trail.

My two experiences on the AT taught me, among other things, that no two years are the same. The weather my first year on the AT was near ideal, edging to hot. In my second year there was lots of rain and even snow. Likewise, your own physical condition can vary from year to year, day-to-day or even within the same day. When the guidebook said a particular trail section was easy, it meant it was easy for *them*. You may have a different point of view. If it said a climb was difficult, perhaps on the day you made that climb, it was your best day and you felt like superman or superwoman and thought it not difficult at all.

What I especially liked about the guidebook was the description of geology, flora and fauna. Those who just want to walk from one end to the other may not be interested in the details, but I appreciated them. Today a hiker can use an AP or GPS or Half Mile maps and they need not carry guidebooks. Half Mile's maps *are* better than the guidebook maps. But I am pretty old school and liked pages in my hand. I learned from other hikers to tear out the pages for the section currently being hiked and leave the rest at home. I bought double copies of the Wilderness Press guidebooks, one to keep whole and one to tear up and take appropriately when hiking.

In 2005 I squeezed out eight days on the PCT from my vacation time in addition to the AT hike in the spring. The guidebook called the section from Snoqualmie Pass to Stevens Pass a classic, week-long backpack. Kathy was my hiking partner, and her dog Tasha came along.

It was truly beautiful from the moment we started from Snoqualmie Pass on the first day's 2,300-foot climb among rocky crags to the last day descending through banks of Pearly Everlasting like clouds covering the sides of the trail. Readily available huckleberries for snacking lined the trail most of the way to Stevens Pass.

It wasn't an easy hike as there was considerable climbing and descending. The weather was northwest sunshine combined with northwest liquid sunshine. But the scenery was spectacular: trail blasted out of rock at Kendall Catwalk, views back to Snoqualmie Pass, travel through the Alpine Lakes Wilderness, great views of Lemah Mountain with its craggy spires above Spectacle Lake, the tarn on Escondido Ridge, Cathedral Rock and the general feeling of walking on top of the world interspersed with descents into deeply cut valleys.

Kathy's husband David was our trail support, taking us to trail and picking us up. He also hiked in to meet us at Cathedral Pass with a food drop. That's true love; it wasn't a short hike. He also brought fresh grapes, baby tomatoes, red sweet peppers, oranges and nectarines. We couldn't carry all the fresh fruit and veggies, but we ate as much as we could on the spot and carried some of the treats with us for dinner at our campsite below Lynch Glacier on Mt. Daniel. I wrote in my hand written journal that night, "Two more days and, oh dear, we will be done just when we are getting in the groove."

The next morning we had the case of the disappearing stream. We had filtered our water the night before from a very nice stream, and not a small one either. In the morning, my hands had gotten muddy stowing the tent. Stepping back to the stream to wash them ... the stream was gone. I was so startled I looked around three times to make sure I hadn't gotten lost in those few steps from our campsite. Nope. This was the same place I'd gotten water the night before. Now there was just one smallish puddle.

That's what happens when a glacier stops melting in the night. We had heard varying reports from other hikers about this campsite and availability of water and had been glad to find water when we camped. Now we knew why reports varied. Streams are often higher late in the day from snow melt and lower in the morning (good to know when having to ford high mountain rivers and creeks) but this was the only time I ever saw such a stark difference between a three- to-four-foot-wide bubbly stream at night and absolutely NO water flow in the morning.

I took a picture at Deception Lakes someone told me I should sell to a puzzle company; Glacier Lake and Surprise Lake were also beautiful. My feet hurt so badly by the time we reached our last camp spot that I sat on a log five minutes before I could take off my boots and waited another five minutes before I could put on my camp shoes.

Funny, I had to read old notes from this trip to remember the feet hurting. Hikers have selective memory. What I remember most, with the aid of my pictures, is the incredible beauty of this hike and hiking it with Kathy and Tasha.

I'd walked another 74.7 miles

Chapter 8 August 2006

Transition to Retirement—PCT "We're going up that?"

Obviously, if I were only to hike for a week or ten days on a trail each year, it would take me a very long time to complete any trail. But I was about to be retired. Time rushed by, and I was doing the things needed to leave my congregation in as strong a position as I could, prepared to move into their future when I left. I didn't take a hike on the AT that year. There was too much to do in preparing to retire. But I had an opportunity to take one last church backpack trip, which would be the start of a lengthier hike on the PCT. I would officially be retired after accrued vacation time expired on day ten of the trip.

Six of us started out from Stevens Pass: Brenda, Mike, Cindy, Linda, Kathy, Tasha the dog and myself. We were supposed to be seven, but Bill had back problems and knew he shouldn't attempt coming. He looked very sad as he and David dropped us all off at Stevens Pass.

The rest of us were in fine fettle in spite of a somewhat drizzly day. We camped at Janus Lake, Pear Lake, and Sally Ann Lake, coming out Indian Pass Trail to White River trailhead. Those first four days were especially scenic hiking: lakes, high meadows filled with flowers and great views of glaciated Glacier Peak, as well as other rugged mountain ranges with enough snow for great pictures.

We had challenges in the walking and joy in the togetherness. I was still pastor, leading Holden Evening Prayer each evening along with times of reflection and prayer. We helped each other as called for and commiserated together about sore feet and blisters. The fourth day was 15 miles, a stretch for us. Since the trail was all downhill, I thought we could do it. But the trail didn't cooperate much. Overgrown, buggy and hot, we were plenty tired by the time we reached White River Trailhead, where drivers picked up the church hikers and Tasha after their four days. Kathy and I ate the fresh town food they brought us. I was interested in going a little farther, but Kathy, having decided she wasn't going one more step that day, put her tent up while I was saying good-bye to the others. Well OK, the next day we were going on—to Canada.

The bridge over the Suiattle River had washed away, and information on line strongly urged us to go on the Little Giant official detour, which we did. Slowly topping Boulder Pass, the top of Little Giant came into view. A few steps more revealed the whole mountain called Little Giant with its steep cliffs, as well as the deep Napeequa Valley. I remember thinking incredulously, "We're going up *that*?"

The Napeequa was a magnificent sight, a deep, high mountain valley with a straight-up mountain on the other side and not a road or sign of civilization anywhere except for our winding trail switchbacking down seemingly endless turns from the pass. Going down those switchbacks a short ways, we found a campsite.

A deer, completely unafraid, nibbled on huckleberry bushes next to our tent as we got up the next morning before daylight. The deer's eyes caught the light of our headlamps, glowing back at us. Descending that long series of switchbacks, we forded the Napeequa, our first major river ford, the current strong and water up to mid-thigh. We slowly climbed up Little Giant, a steep trail we were glad to be going up and not down. If going up was hard, going down would be a total nightmare. The descent on the other side was a much more reasonable grade, but by the time we reached the bottom my feet were really hurting.

The river ford felt exhilarating, cold water comforting sore feet. On the other side of the river we met David, Becky and Tasha, Kathy's dog. David whisked us to Trinity Campground, and I missed 3.5 miles of the PCT. (I completed that 3.5 miles July 9, 2018.)

Not only was I tired and my feet aching, that road was dangerous, a narrow winding dusty dirt road with cars zipping around blind corners.

We feasted that night, but didn't stop for a rest day, going on the next morning with the addition of Kathy's dog, Tasha. Kathy and I again made a good team. In the mornings I was full of energy and leading us on. When I flagged in the afternoons, especially when it was hot, Kathy seemed to get a burst of energy to get to camp and I followed. It was really HOT. We were grateful neither we nor the dog got heat stroke. We were VERY grateful for a creek in the shaded fold of the mountain we were traversing, collapsing beside it for an hour or so.

On day ten we met Scott Williamson, who was doing a yo-yo thru hike. He'd come all the way from Mexico, reached the Canadian border and turned around to go all the way back. Scott held the unsupported speed record for the PCT for years. He was a good-looking 30- something, long, lean drink of water with an absolutely miniscule pack. We wondered what he could possibly have in it.

Six Mile Camp was memorable. Both of us remarked that night that somehow we felt…nervous. We took extra care to make noise and keep a clean camp. When we reached Rainy Pass we read a notice that Six Mile Camp had been having bear problems. We'd had a kind of sixth sense about a bear there, and we were probably right, though we didn't see it.

"Aren't you afraid of the bears?"

Almost the first question asked of backpackers is, "Aren't you afraid of the bears?" Bears are not lurking in the forest waiting for people to walk by to eat them for breakfast. Bears are large omnivores, who live in the forest. Unless they have become habituated to think of people as a source of food, bears, like most wild animals, try to avoid humans. Most hikers are excited to see any large game, including bear.

We walk in bear's homes as visitors. Good visitors do not leave any sort of food or *smellables,* anything with a strong smell, within bear's reach along the trail or left about camp. The unfortunate result of leaving edibles or *smellables* for bears is that in their search for food, they become aggressive towards humans and have to be removed or shot. *A fed bear is a dead bear.* Surprising a bear on the trail or walking near cubs can also provoke an aggressive response. I don't exactly fear Black Bear, but I respect them. They are bigger than me, have claws and I would lose a fight. Avoiding provocation or temptation is key.

Bear canisters, containers bears can't open, hold food and *smellables* attractive to bears.

Our bear canister required turning the lid, as well as pushing with a thumb in a particular spot at the same time. Carrying a bear can is required in some wilderness areas, important to preserve hikers and bears. Hikers generally dislike carrying bear cans as they are heavy, adding weight to the pack.

Techniques for hanging food are used when not carrying a bear can. Some hikers sleep with their food, not a ranger-approved technique, although many thru hikers get in the habit as they begin in areas where convenient trees are not available.

"That's not a dog."

At Rainy Pass, Carol, who had volunteered to support us, took us to a cabin in Mazama. By day twelve we finally had a zero day and two nights in a bed. We also visited Winthrop for dinner at a Mexican restaurant.

Our next three days took us over Cut Throat Pass, past the Golden Horn, Glacier Pass and into Hart Pass to meet two more friends, both named Becky, who brought us dinner and a food drop, driving 25 miles over a rocky road to do so. My goodness, it's nice to have friends.

Unfortunately the Mexican restaurant in Winthrop gave me food poisoning. Anything I ingested shot right through me all the rest of the way to Canada. Kathy was amazed that I could keep going. I begged diarrhea medication from every passing hiker. I tried three different kinds but none of it really helped. (I tested negative for Giardia when I got home, and I recovered quickly when I was off trail.) I used all my toilet paper. Then I used all Kathy's toilet paper. I used the gauze pads from the first aid kit. I was about to use our bandanas before we reached Canada and found a privy with toilet paper. It wasn't the most pleasant part of the trip. On a backpack trip anything can happen and sometimes town stops contain the danger.

We did enjoy many wonderful views between Rainy Pass and

Harts Pass. And I saw the only cougar I have met while hiking. In retrospect it was actually funny. We were winding through a tall brushy area, and I'd gone ahead of Kathy and Tasha, out of sight around a corner or two. I looked up and saw the cougar on the trail right ahead of me. The cougar looked at me. I looked at the cougar. The thought in my mind was, "That's not a dog." At the time, I wasn't sure it was a cougar as I thought cougars were more of a tawny gold and the coat of this beast was darker. Later I saw the cougar picture that adorns many National Park Visitor Center walls, and it was identical to this critter. It was a cougar, for sure.

The cougar turned around and disappeared up the trail. I turned around and quickly went back to Kathy, excitedly saying, "Put your dog on the leash. Put your dog on the leash." I was afraid Tasha would think the cougar was one of those chipmunks she dearly loved to chase, and we would end up with dead dog.

We didn't see the cougar again.

After picking up our food drop and enjoying a meal and a good time with our two friends, we left Hart Pass saying good-bye to them and to Tasha. This last section would take us into

Canada, and too many days on the trail is not good for a dog, nor would the hassle of crossing borders with a dog be good for us. Tasha was heartbroken at being separated from Kathy. We could hear her howls and wails for a long time until either a mountain ridge separated us, or they drove away.

The evening we reached Hopkins Lake, I was getting clean by the lake when Kathy came running down the hill from our campsite. "Look over there." she said. *Over there* was a huge billowing cloud of smoke. Kathy wondered if we should just try to walk out in the night. That smoke cloud seemed very close. "No. I can't outrun a forest fire and this lake could save us if the fire came this way." (We found out later that the PCT was closed by this fire a few days after we went through.)

We eventually reached Canada and took our pictures at the PCT monument on the border. It was just the end of our section hike, but it was a milestone to remember for us, too, even if not as dramatic as for those who walk 2,654 miles in one year to reach it.

By the time we reached the highway, our feet were screaming at us. I spied a van with dogs taking a break in the muddy stream at the trailhead and asked for a ride to the lodge. I'd read about hikers hitch hiking and figured anyone who carried muddy dogs in their van might allow two dirty hikers in, too. They did. Kathy was impressed with my ride-finding skills. They drove us to Manning Park. The next day we caught a bus to Sumas and walked across the border back to the USA to meet Kari, another friend who drove us home.

I still had two small sections of Washington left, but I'd done the longest section and another 193.6 miles of the PCT. I was now retired and would have more opportunities for longer sections.

Retirement

Retired people often say they are so busy they do not know how they ever found time to work. That has certainly been true for me. By 2007 I had three grandchildren and another shortly to appear. I remained active in my local congregation, occasionally filled in as preacher for vacationing pastors, and planted and harvested a large garden every year, timing planting carefully before and between hikes. I'd definitely decided on a retirement goal of completing both the Appalachian Trail and the Pacific Crest Trail by age 70.

Being retired meant I could do some larger chunks of the trails as well as all my other activities. I decided 400 miles was about the right number of miles for me. Why 400? I really picked the number out of the sky. But it was a good number. It seemed like a do-able number of miles, long enough to make me feel like a thru-hiker, but short enough that I could go home and take care of my garden, see my grandchildren and have a regular life as well as a trail life. I am not a thru hiker, just a long-section hiker. 400 miles twice a year seemed enough for miles to add up over a few years to actually accomplish my goal.

I was still not thinking of the Continental Divide Trail or the Triple Crown, although by now I'd read journals of people who had done both. Accomplishing two trails seemed like plenty to bite off.

Spring and late summer/fall were my desired hiking times. Hiking in the heat of summer turned me into a dead daisy, or at least, a wilted one. I preferred to put up with cold mornings and nights to avoid being superhot in the daytime.

Chapter 9 April 10, 2007 AT

Medicare Pastor

My fourth grandchild was born on March 29, and on April 8 I flew into Asheville. Nancy Hoch picked me up and drove me to the Hike Inn near Fontana Dam. Jeff took me to the trail on April 10th, and I began my walk. That year, I too had a trail journal listed on Trailjournals.com. I wrote on paper while on the trail and transferred the journal to the internet when I could find access along the way.

As I began walking, a man in a passing car asked me what my trail name was. My trail name had morphed over the few years I'd been hiking long trails. Now I was retired and Medicare seemed to be the appropriate name. (Medicare is the health insurance for most Americans after they turn 65.) But Pastor seemed right, too. I didn't stop being a pastor by being retired. So Medicare Pastor became my trail name. No further changes have ever been required. The name basically means *old lady retired pastor*.

"How old are you?" the man in the car inquired. "You don't look old enough to be on Medicare." I guess I looked a bit younger than my age. That wasn't something I could take credit for. It was just a lucky break for me.

Walking trails *has* blessed me with keeping fit and active. An older person can't simply throw on a pack and start walking on the trail. At least I wouldn't advise that tack. As I aged, I had to work harder to keep in shape, something that took more effort each year. I had to train by walking, both in my neighborhood and going up and down the mountains and hills in Washington, so that I would be able to hike distances and continue backpacking as the years passed. The preparation necessary to hike long trails kept me active and in reasonably good shape.

"If there are not some nights when you are wearing everything you have brought, then you brought too much."

I started walking at Fontana Dam, on a record cold year at the foot of the Great Smoky Mountains. Hiker journals told me the temperature had been getting down into the single digits in the week before I started. Brrr. I was hoping it would warm up a little. I didn't like heat, but freezing to death wasn't on my wish list either.

On my very first day, I acquired blisters on both heels from the steady uphill climb to Russel Field Shelter. Bummer. I'd hoped my new boots were the perfect fit, and I wouldn't get blisters. Wrong. At the shelter that night I placed the gel strips of Second Skin over my heels, chatted with Boneless, M&M, Handyman and Tex, hung my food bag and dove for my sleeping bag to stay warm. It was so cold nobody wanted to tent. Fortunately we all fit in the shelter, which also had tarps across the front to keep inside whatever heat there was. Shelter registration was required for section hikers in the Smokies (Great Smoky Mountains National Park).

Although I'd hiked the trail from Springer Mountain, Georgia, I didn't do it in 2007, so it didn't count for the thru hiker pass in the National Park. Thru hikers have the *option* of tenting in the Park, but section hikers *must* stay in shelters.

It was bitter cold and windy for most of the next day. A side wind tried to knock me over with gusts and blew my hiking poles horizontal as they dangled on my wrist straps. At Clingman Dome, 6,643 feet and the highest point on the AT, my Frogg Toggs rainsuit was worth its weight as a wind breaker as I carefully negotiated ice in the wind to the ramp leading up to the space- age-like viewpoint.

By this time I'd already met 10 hikers. They all walked faster than me and usually passed me during the day. I was, however, often the first one up, out, and on the trail. Getting an early start helped make up for the deficiencies of age and slowness.

After my first experience on the AT, I tried to have resupply boxes as often as possible to keep my pack weight as low as possible.

Knowing I needed to catch a ride to Gatlinburg from Newfound Gap to get my first resupply box, Ghetto Blaster and two other hikers reached the Gap and lined up a ride for me before I got there. They told a day hiker about my age that I was coming right behind them and needing a ride, and she graciously waited until I arrived. Amazing. A ride I didn't even have to ask for. What a nice gift. Hitching back to the trail from Gatlinburg was my first time hitching with my thumb out. It was discouraging to see cars whip right past me, but the wait was a short ten minutes until a family stopped for me. They took me all the way to the trail, though they were only intending to go to Alum Cave trailhead. The temperature was 34 degrees at the gap, although it did warm up during the day to 50 degrees. A quarter mile of the trail, thick, solidly frozen ice didn't know it was warmer. I absolutely couldn't walk on it without falling, so I picked my way through trees along the bank of the trail on equally frozen ground. But I didn't fall.

Shelters in the Smokies were great meeting places for hikers, sharing camaraderie and fun, though we surely were cold, wet, and windblown. There is a saying on the AT: "If there are not some nights when you are wearing everything you have brought, then you brought too much." There were nights I wore everything and also played footsie with myself in the sleeping bag until my feet finally thawed out, and I could sleep.

Two nights at Peck's Corner Shelter and Cosby Knob ticked by, and I was down out of the Smokies at Standing Bear Farm Hostel. Standing Bear had hot showers and bunks for $15, and I picked up another food drop. The shower was heavenly. Then it started snowing.

Medicare Pastor Again

That night at Standing Bear, I sang Holden Evening Prayer for Papa Bear and Ferrel, while standing in the storeroom as snow turned the world outside into a winter wonderland. Papa Bear had missed church on Easter Sunday and appreciated me providing them with a *bit of church*, even while standing in a cold storeroom. I can always sing Holden Evening Prayer.

A word about being a pastor on the trail: I didn't want other hikers to freak out about me being a *Pastor*. I am not an *in your face* pastor. People on the trail hold many different religious views and come from all walks of life. I do not push my views of faith on anyone. I firmly believe that God loves and cares for each person, regardless of their religious views, and I am content to let God be at work in each person's life in God's own fashion, not mine, though I *can* talk about faith if anyone so desires.

I usually carry a pocket New Testament with the Psalms and copies of Holden Evening Prayer. I like to sing that service on weekends or as requested, by myself or with others. At times, even those not wishing to participate have told me they liked to hear me sing. Marty Haugen's beautiful Holden Evening Prayer was written to be sung in the mountains at Holden Village in Washington State so it seems natural to me to sing it on the trail.

So - I was a non-pushy pastor, who carried a New Testament and sang. I also had ears to listen, but entrusted myself and my fellow hikers to God's care. That was enough.

I left Standing Indian on a white wonderland trail following a few footprints in the snow. Three days later, including a very cold night tenting by myself, I arrived at Hot Springs having shed warm layers to hike in my sports bra. Elevation change made a difference, as did a warming trend. Taking advantage of the opportunity to slack pack, I used a shuttle service along with three other hikers. (A slack pack is hiker lingo for walking with just enough for a day, without all your gear.) I also took a zero day and soaked in a spa beside the river. Cushy. I said good-bye to Papa Bear and Ferrel and wondered who would make up my next trail family in the days ahead.

Barking Spider was moving more slowly than usual, nursing shin splints, and we took each other's pictures on White Rock Cliffs. I also met Swamp Fox and Blue Sky, a delightful couple I was to see many times in 2007.

The next day I turned a challenging 14.7 mile day into an extremely challenging 18+ mile day by leaving my water bottle at a shelter and being crazy enough to go back for it from two miles out.

Everyone else thought I was nuts to do so. My feet hurt so badly that night that I couldn't even bear wearing socks to bed as I usually do.

The temperature then climbed to 80 degrees during the day, and I missed the cold but enjoyed the flowers. Spring had definitely arrived. Spring Beauties were so thick they looked like snow under the trees. Yellow Trout Lilies, huge purple Violets and tiny yellow ones plus three or four other kinds of white and yellow flowers lined the trail or could be seen under the trees. One of my joys in hiking is the flowers. Flowers differ from coast to coast, and I find new ones on every long hike, but seeing them always raises my spirits no matter the steepness of the trail or the pain in the feet.

I have problem feet. I suppose it is somewhat crazy to do long-distance hiking with problem feet. The removal of Morton's neuromas on both feet helped, but the conversation I often had with my feet went like this:

Me: "You really hurt, right?" Feet: "Owiee Zowiee, yes."

Me: "You would like to get the weight off and get put up somewhere, right?"

Feet: Oh, please, please."

Me: "Well, if we go as fast as we can today we will get to town sooner and be able to sit down."

Feet: "Oh, OK."

No, my feet didn't talk out loud. But if they could have done so that is what they would have said.

The next day my feet were hurting so I went on a 19-mile slackpack. It seemed like a good idea when I planned it and was sure my feet would agree the following day, even if they were not too sure about it at the time. You see, by taking a 19 mile slackpack, I was able to cover 19 miles WITHOUT 34 pounds of pack on my back, and the next day I would go only go 4.5 miles to reach Greasy Creek Friendly, the hiker hostel at which I planned to stay. All the rest of *that* day I planned to rest. Have I mentioned that hikers are a little nuts? But it worked.

"Dayenu - if God had only...it would have been enough."

Greasy Creek Friendly, a little bunkhouse next to Connie's house was a positive experience and a good rest with one exception. Connie, the woman who ran Greasy Creek Friendly, had a neighbor who wasn't running on all cylinders. Really. He didn't think hikers should be in his neighborhood, so he made noise by running his lawnmower constantly, even in the snow, loudly banged on things and shouted out at all hours. After a while, it got to be pretty funny. He was my snooze alarm in the morning, running his lawnmower and banging on things at 5:10. I looked at the time, deciding it was too early to get up, I went back to sleep. He started in banging again at 6:10, when I really did want to get up. I guess he felt fulfilled each morning when the hikers left, as if his banging had caused our leaving. I felt sorry for Connie, though, who had to hear him every day.

After I left Greasy Creek Friendly, the rest of the day was wonderful. I kept thinking of the phrase from the Jewish Seder - "Dayenu - if God had only...it would have been enough."

If only the rest day had made my feet feel better - Dayenu, it would have been enough. If only large sections of trail had turned smooth and easy to hike - Dayenu - it would have been enough. If only the wildflower displays - purple, yellow and white Violets, purple and white Trillium, yellow Lilies, white Bloodroot, blue Larkspur and others were all - Dayenu - It would have been enough. If only my energy was adequate for all the climbs including Roan Mountain (6,285 feet) - Dayenu - it would have been enough. If only the spectacular views from Roan, Little Rock Knob and three lovely balds including Jane and Grassy Field were all - Dayenu - it would have been enough. If only the cool weather for hiking were all- Dayenu - it would have been enough. And I'd had *all* those blessings. It was *all* wonderful.

History lessons can be found in brief snippets along long trails. Our American history lesson that night was camping at Overmountain Trail, where 1,000 North Carolinian and Virginian militiamen crossed over the mountains to defeat the British at Kings Mountain in the Revolutionary War.

Kincora

Three long days, 14.8, 17, 14.5 miles, and I was at Kincora. I was definitely not a 20-mile- a-day thru hiker. But then, not all thru hikers are 20-mile-a-day hikers either. One of those days was quite cold, and the next warm. A surprise was the crown that fell off my tooth while eating lunch. I carefully saved it.

Kincora is another legendary AT stop, the home of Bob and Pat Peoples, trail angels and trail workers extraordinaire. I picked up another food drop, and Bob Peoples found a dentist whom he talked into an early morning appointment for me to replace my crown.

My slack pack on a hot day to beautiful Laurel Falls was followed by a huge feed put on by Pat and Bob Peoples to celebrate Beltaine, the Celtic New Year. Twenty hikers had Cock a Leekie Soup, Corned Beef, Irish Soda Bread, Beer Bread, Onion Pie, Potatoes, Cabbage, Carrots, Green Beans, Sodas and Triffle for desert. We ate like pigs or starving thru- hikers. There is not a lot of difference between the two. Although we tried to practice leave-no-trace eating, we couldn't finish it all. Three or four more hikers showed up late and had the last of the feast.

What marvelous generosity the Peoples exhibited. I have a photo of white-haired Pat Peoples smiling joyously as she observed hikers' delight in eating food she'd prepared or whose preparation she'd supervised. It will always be to me the perfect picture of the joy of serving others. Pat passed away the following year of the cancer she was fighting when I saw her. I cherish my memory of her.

I sang Holden Evening Prayer at Kincora, this time with Music Man and Wonder. Music Man was headed for seminary in the fall and Wonder professed to be a Pagan who liked music. They were both musical and could sing parts, which was great fun. The words and music spoke for themselves, no preaching necessary.

The trail held a moving community. I formed a bond with people I saw once or twice. We helped each other as we could. Yet there was always the freedom to be alone, to go ahead, or to stay behind as needed or desired. The trail grapevine, through journals, notes in shelter registers or simply word of mouth, fostered the sense of community. One day Creeper left a prayer for Medicare Preacher in a shelter register though I'd only met her twice in passing on the trail.

Amazing. It was a unique, if mobile and constantly changing, community.

The morning before Damascus, thinking how nice and comfy my tent and sleeping bag was, I made myself get up with the promise of coming to town, packing up to march up the hill from Low Gap. (Anything called a Gap means a climb up out of it.) A quarter mile past the shelter a deer stood in the path so I could take its picture. It looked pretty thin to me, as if it needed to eat more.

I, however, was eating everything in sight. Hiking for multiple days uses a lot of calories. I guessed that I'd lost weight but I still had my belly pooch. It held up my pack as the waist strap settled nicely on top of it.

"Tut, tut, looks like rain."

After uneventful and mostly unremarkable ridge walking, about six miles from Damascus the skies opened up with thunder, lightning, and a deluge of rain. I liked the rain. It was cool as I walked down small streams where the trail was supposed to be. I didn't like the lightning less than a half-mile away from my ridgeline, spurring me to walk quickly, the downpour soon soaking my shorts and filling my boots. The cool water squishing between my toes made my arthritic feet feel better.

I sang rain songs, told myself Washington rain jokes and quoted Winnie the Pooh, "Tut, tut, looks like rain." In short, my spirits were high, and I was having a soggy good time. All my gear was under pack cover, and I was headed for town and the land of hot showers and laundromats. Hiking kept me warm, so there was no danger of hypothermia. I enjoyed the rain. Coming into Damascus, the trees, shrubs and grass had that just-washed look and as the warm ground met the wet rain, it smelled wonderful.

I ate with and reconnected with trail friends, Grasshopper, Swamp Fox and Blue Sky in Damascus. Rest Step, a hiker who had signed my journal even before I left home, trail angeled me when I reached Damascus. He took me to his house, provided a computer to update my journals, and built a warm fire to dry out my boots. How wonderful to be taken care of.

Feral Horses

On a very cold night in Thomas Knob Shelter, near Mt. Rogers, I discovered that tightening the drawstring on the sleeping bag, leaving only a breathing hole, you can't see when it gets light in the morning. I woke up late to 32 degrees and gusty winds. The weather had changed from the 80s or more to freezing in a few hours.

More agreeably, the Mt. Rogers area was wide and open, with views that seemed more like the western USA than the eastern USA. There were wild horses. I suppose, technically, they were feral horses. Some came quite close. I'd heard some liked to lick hikers for the salt on sweaty bodies, though none licked me.

After descending from the area of horses, I'd one of my most dangerous moments on the trail. Was it bears? Or cougars? Or even moose? No. It was an uncontrollable pair of dogs. They were on leashes but they were very big dogs and their handler wasn't big. They dragged her toward me, and the dogs, barking furiously, looked like they wanted to have me for lunch. I was very relieved when their owner finally controlled them just a foot or two before they reached me.

I hitched a ride into Troutdale for my food drop, which had been sent to the post office, and I stayed at the church hostel, two small cabins with no bunks but spotlessly clean vinyl floors, one cabin for women, one cabin for men. Church rules. The shower was wonderful, and the weather again quite warm.

Not many days remained before the end of my AT hike, I reached Partnership Shelter, and all my regular trail buddies: M&M, Swamp

Fox, Blue Sky, and Grasshopper. Nice shelter. It even had a shower. It was also near enough to town to order pizza. Most hikers ordered a large; I ordered a medium. After we ate, a well-fed and grinning Swamp Fox carried a very large stack of empty pizza boxes to the trashcan. Very little was left for breakfasts or a lunch on the trail.

Fortunately there *was* a trashcan.

"You get 'er done."

As I passed the Settlers Museum of Southwest Virginia, I enjoyed looking at the displays of the Scots-Irish and German migration from Pennsylvania. The north-south direction of the mountains prevented an east-west migration, so the flow was southward from Pennsylvania through the Great Valley of Virginia. Daniel Boone and his family moved down this valley.

Hikers moved down *into* the valley to cross Interstate 81. Apple trees were blooming, it was a VERY hot (85) and humid day, and my feet were killing me. When I reached the road, the advertised Dairy Queen wasn't open. What a disappointment. However the truck stop *was* open.

I took a two-hour break in an air-conditioned truck stop lunch booth. Other hikers had already figured out that making rootbeer floats was a good way to beat the heat and the Dairy Queen disappointment. I agreed and purchased a pint of vanilla ice cream and a liter of root beer followed with a chicken teriyaki sandwich, another pint of ice cream and the rest of my rootbeer. That was dinner. Perfect.

I walked the next day through farmland, pastures, and a herd of cows, well, dairy steers.

There were some pretty views and more flowers were starting to bloom: phlox, lily of the valley, rhodies, laurel and azaleas. On that hot day, heat radiated up from the grass of the open pastureland.

Having lunch under an Acacia tree with Swamp Fox and Blue Sky, I managed to put an acacia thorn through my Thermarest. NOT happiness. I also got a blister on the inside of my big toe. Really? This close to the end of my walk? Those irritations were mitigated as

Swamp Fox, Blue Sky, Tim, and I found a lovely campsite that night near a slowly flowing river, green branches drooping low over the water. I couldn't have asked for better company or a more pleasant site.

Grasshopper and M&M camped with me on my last night. How fitting. M&M was with me my first night and my last on the AT in 2007.

Days earlier, hikers had been having conversations guessing who might make it all the way to Mt. Katahdin. Grasshopper, a retired judge, said that even if I was a section hiker, he thought I would come back and finish the AT. I might have been a little slower than others, but, he said, "You get 'er done." Perhaps he was a prophet.

I waited for Swamp Fox and Blue Sky to catch up with me so Swamp Fox could eat the last of my homemade jam before I walked into Bland, Virginia. Linda, a hiker and Lutheran church secretary whom I'd contacted months earlier walked in to meet me. Saying good-bye to my trail friends, Linda took me to Roanoke where her friend Shirley took me to the airport to fly home the following day.

415.9 miles had been just right. I hung out with thru hikers and felt like a thru hiker. But I got to go home.

It seemed strange to get on an airplane. The trail had become the rhythm of life. I ate, broke camp, walked, looked for water sources, ate more, walked more, looked again for water sources and a place to camp and sleep. In the morning I did the same again. And the next and the next and the next. On the way I met people and saw flowers, trees and lovely views. Yes, my feet hurt. But each night I rested and then began again. Life was simple, beautiful and good.

Chapter 10 2007 Summer

Gear Upgrades and a Surprise Step

The spring AT hike confirmed that I was definitely a long-section hiker. Although the 400- mile number had been a guess, it had been a good guess. It was the right number of miles for me.

Now it was time to think what I would do on the PCT. It seemed a good idea to do the hardest part first, as I wasn't getting any younger. That would be the Sierra. I read Splash's journal. She'd walked SOBO in approximately the same time of year I wished to go. I'd heard too many tales of woe concerning deep snow and dangerous crossings of cold, raging rivers to want to do the Sierra in the early summer. Hiking in mid-August to mid-September seemed the perfect window. Section hikers get to choose the season of the year best for the section of trail.

I made three positive changes before hitting the trail. I'd been reading hiker journals and learned that the majority of thru hikers on the PCT were not wearing real boots. Yogi swore by trail runners and thin socks. Since I always got blisters, and had for years, wearing heavy hiking boots, I was quite interested in finding a different option. Footwear is a very individual decision. I was ready to try something new if it eliminated blisters. I decided on Merrill Moab Ventilators and the thinnest socks I could find. My feet are very sensitive and those thin socks were also the smoothest socks I could find. They were really little more than black nylons. Their thinness gave a promise they would also be fast drying when I washed them on the trail. Since I planned to ford rivers with shoes and socks on, quick drying would be doubly important.

I would have company on this trip. Two friends, Kathy and Linda, would come for overlapping portions of the trip. Kathy and I purchased a three-person Tarp tent. It only weighed three pounds, the same as the one-person tent I'd been using. One pound per person. Sweet!

I also purchased a Pocketmail device, as there were no places in the Sierra to find computers to post my journal entries. This gizmo was what hikers were using to write journals on the trail. A journal written on the Pocketmail could then be sent somewhere when a phone connection was found. My cousin in San Diego agreed to be my transcriber, and I would send her journal entries each time I found a phone connection. She would then post them on my site on Trailjournals.com.

I dropped two pounds of tent and had lighter shoes, but added a little weight with the Pocketmail. In preparation, I also was taking regular day hikes with Kathy, some with pack weight, getting in good elevation gain on substantial hikes. I felt like my conditioning was coming right along. We prepared and mailed our food-drop boxes for the hike on the PCT.

Then my daughter and her husband and my grandchildren came to visit. We all had a grand time: I participated in Matthew's baptism, and we took a trip to the other side of the mountains to Richland to visit my son-in-law Andrew's parents. While there, I walked down a dark, unfamiliar hallway in their condo carrying the baby, and hit a *surprise* step. It jolted me, but I didn't drop the baby. I didn't think more about it until the next morning, when I found my knee severely swollen and walking was painful. We returned home to the west side of the mountains and my daughter and family left to return to Andrew's duty station at Ft. Brag.

I was leaving for the Sierra in two days. I strapped a compression brace on my swollen knee and finished getting ready for my hike, assuming the knee pain and swelling would be a temporary problem.

Two days later, friends Becky and Michelle picked me up, and we drove to Vancouver, picking up Linda. How wonderful to have friends, who would drive us all the way to Tahoe. We were concerned about my knee. For the two-day drive I kept it elevated with ice. The swelling went down. It was still a concern, but our food boxes were mailed, and my two friends were only going because I'd planned the hike and invited them. I, of course, was very eager to go. How bad could this be anyway? It was only a surprise step. No big deal, right? I didn't know it at the time, but it was the beginning of a whole cascade of knee problems.

Chapter 11 August 12, 2007 PCT
"America the Beautiful"

The Persons, trail angels near Donner Pass, put us up the night before we hit the trail. The next day Becky and Michelle dropped us off at the trailhead, and Linda and I headed out heavily loaded, thinking water might be a problem the first day. Finding out from passing hikers that water *was* available on the trail, we quickly dropped three and a half extra liters of water. Water weight is a killer; it always weighs 2.2 pounds per liter, no matter how often you weigh it. I'd also added an extra waist pack to carry an extra water bottle and my lunch.

Quite concerned about my knee, I walked a slow, a deliberate and careful pace. Linda had been afraid at the start she couldn't keep up. No problem there. As long as the knee got no worse, I thought all would be well.

On the second day we ran into Papa Bear, a different Papa Bear than I knew on the AT. This Papa Bear was wearing Dirty Girl gaiters, colorful sleeves of spandex above his shoe tops. Many thru hikers wore Dirty Girls, made by a woman trail runner. They keep sand and small rocks out of low shoes, and the PCT has lots of sand and small rocks. I added them to my wish list for future hikes.

Becky and Michelle were super trail angels, meeting us at Barker Pass with food and a lift to their campsite by Lake Tahoe. They fed us a steak dinner and a great breakfast, and Linda and I sang Holden Evening Prayer for them. After delivering us back to the trail in the morning, our friends returned to Washington as we continued on the trail.

The Sierra has beautiful lakes. My favorites on the way to Echo Lake were Fontanelle and Aloha. Bright-blue water contrasted with white granite lakeshores. Each lake beckoned us to stay by the shore or dip in the water for a swim on a hot day, but our schedule required we keep walking to meet our pick up above Echo Lake. Aloha's rock islands in rock-bound blue water below mountains of glacier-polished cliffs of granite made me think of an interstellar monster's bones.

I hiked reasonably well these first five days, as long as I had my hiking poles. But when we followed the PCT trail signs to the *water taxi* on lower Echo Lake, and I collapsed my poles to get in the boat, I nearly collapsed as well. My knee couldn't handle the deep step by itself. (I completed PCT north of Echo Lake August 1, 2018.)

Dan, the brother of a friend in Washington, was our next support person and trail angel. He took us to his home for a delightful evening and slack packed us the next day. It wasn't a short day, 16+ miles with 2,000 feet elevation gain. But it was beautiful. There were blue lupine, red paintbrush, and yellow daisies for color. Mountains encircled us, and the bright blue of Showers Lake was too inviting to pass; I waded in and took a quick dip. Linda said the view of the lake, flowers and mountains made her want to break out in song: *America the Beautiful.* We had to push hard to meet Dan at Carson Pass, and Linda lagged behind, but I had the afterburners on, walked fast and felt good.

Dan brought us a feast, far more than we could eat. After dinner, we staggered a half mile up the trail and put up our tent. We could hear hikers passing us in the night with headlamps on, and I was glad not to be doing the same.

The next day during a tough climb with exposure straight down to Blue Lake, my knee hurt.

Linda thought she shouldn't send a picture to her mother showing that drop off; her mother would worry. The wind howled fiercely and tried to pluck us from the trail on that high ridge. But descending, we were rewarded with a lovely campsite at Lily Pad Lake, setting our tent in a small space between wide flat rock shelves of granite. I bathed and washed clothes in our pot and Linda skinny dipped in the lake.

The next day we threaded our way around volcanic spires on sometimes very narrow tread, only a boot-print wide for a stride or two, making Linda nervous. Yet the scenery was awesome with spire after spire of rock, much of it a volcanic conglomerate that looked like rocks and boulders glued together with cement.

Dan met us with more food and water at Ebbets Pass. What wonderful trail support we had. That night the moon shone so brightly through the walls of the tent I kept thinking someone was shining headlights on us, though we had purposefully set the tent hidden behind bushes. The bright light was only the moon. We could have read a book with its light.

A day later we met section hikers, Socks, Slippery Rock and the Gimp, a youngish trio headed north from Tuolumne Meadows. Socks christened Linda with a trail name, Gray Squirrel. Linda was pleased.

We missed our planned campsite at the East Fork of the Carson River, a God-blessed error, as when we finally found a campsite it was the prettiest one yet. Linda's sharp eyes found a small bit of level grass in the midst of granite slabs overlooking a marvelous waterfall falling behind and under boulders like an indoor shower. Granite cliffs shaped like giant pillows made up the mountain across the valley.

"Animals, You're Just Animals!"

Coming out at Sonora Pass, we hitched a ride to Kennedy Meadows North for showers, a bed, town food and our food drops. We also arranged to mail home everything we could give up to make our packs lighter. I could certainly live without that extra waist pack and water bottle. Catching a ride back to the trail the next morning, we met our friend, Kathy. She wasn't as *trail hardened* as we were as we slowly went up the 2,000-foot climb. But her broad smile and obvious enjoyment added to ours as she remarked about the many colors of bare rocks and mountains around us.

We met the Saufleys. I'd read about this marvelous trail-angel couple from Agua Dulce in Southern California. They annually hosted hundreds of hikers in their home and yard. Now they were out to experience some of the PCT themselves and were headed NOBO (northbound). They promised me a bed the year I got to Agua Dulce, and I was very excited to have met them.

Winding our way uphill through granite boulders and slabs, we passed Harriet and Stella Lakes and going over Dorothy Pass, we dropped to Dorothy Lake, the prettiest one yet with Forsythe Peak behind it. Linda enjoyed a skinny dip after lunch. After she was once again clothed, we headed on for what seemed to be a very long and grueling downhill. Other than the long part, I guess it wasn't that grueling unless you were 66 with bum feet and bum knees. We followed lovely little Falls River, winding through meadows, Kathy and I walking in the stream, enjoying cold water on our feet. We followed bear tracks all afternoon.

Linda hiked at a faster pace than Kathy and I, so she hiked ahead and waited for us at trail crossings, ridges or lakes. Finding friends who hike the same pace is a difficult challenge.

Though our hiking paces differed, we filled a single tent, our home on the trail.

Though we went over three passes the next day, we failed to make our target campsite, giving us the opportunity to camp in a very beautiful spot at Seavy Pass, beside a lovely tarn (a small, high lake) snuggled between granite slabs and boulders. Hanging the food bag on the side of a cliff, I looked at the tarn and our tent site and wondered if we had become so accustomed to the incredible beauty that surrounded us that we were beginning to take it for granted.

Our campsite at Seavy Pass was beyond ordinary beauty and once again brought a sense of awe as we ate breakfast while watching the rising sun color the sky and the granite a delicate shade of pink.

We hiked through a granite world. While hanging that food bag, I'd looked down a valley whose name should have been Valley Of Granite. But *every* canyon and valley was by mountains of granite, sometimes in large rounded pillows, subtly colored with shades of gray, darker gray, white, buff, and yellowish gray. Linda was tired of granite, but Kathy and I were enthralled with its rugged beauty. There is nothing like a hike over difficult terrain to show that you are not as young as you used to be. Of course, I didn't plan to have an injured knee before starting the hike. My limitations were much more obvious in the Sierra than when I'd hiked 400 miles on the AT in the spring. Yet in spite of the injured knee, we regularly made 12 to 16 miles a day. In spite of my limitations, I did the distance and the beauty around me kept me going.

Down we went to Benson Lake, then up another granite canyon to granite-bound Smedberg Lake. Linda and Kathy pumped water, while I finished lunch and doctored abrasions on my feet caused by little rocks in my shoes, vowing to get those Dirty Girl Gaiters for my next long hike. The granite ledge into the lake on which we sat made me think *sittin' on the dock of the bay* but unlike the song, we didn't waste much time there. We had miles to walk to Matterhorn Canyon to catch up with our schedule.

As we pounded the trail to Glen Aulin, we met a day hiker, who was impressed with three older ladies hiking. He kept saying, *"Animals. You are just animals!"* which he meant as a big compliment.

Glen Aulin had a beautiful waterfall, water out of a spigot, and a solar toilet – with a seat. I especially appreciated the seat as now both knees were swollen and painful. A sliding semi-fall on small pebbles on a granite shelf on the way to Matterhorn Canyon injured my *good* knee. (When you have a *bad* knee you are favoring, the *good* knee does double duty, putting it in double danger.)

For our short day to Tuolumne Meadows, Kathy said she wanted to get up at the regular time even if we were only going six miles. In the morning, she told me she wanted to hit me when I woke her up at 5:30. Oh well, I said she would have to hit herself as I was only following her instructions.

On Linda's last day on the trail we traveled along the Tuolumne River, watching it swiftly slide over slabs and sheets of granite and many waterfalls. We had a hard time attending to hiking while taking so many pictures. A gentle rain fell on us for the last half mile. Then it rained harder as we reached the general store area, the only rain we had experienced since Donner Pass; it was hard to complain. We enjoyed hamburgers, chicken sandwiches and chili and bought a few needed items at the little store, and Kathy and I picked up our resupply boxes.

"Hikers need a ride to Mammoth"

Checking into a tent cabin gave us the privilege of a shower and a bed for the night. Kathy and I mulled over our next move. My feet had been manageable as long as I took pain meds and short breaks, but we were both tired and both of my knees were swollen. The next day was a scheduled rest day, which then morphed into more. I was hoping the swelling in my knees would go down. Before this hike, the now-swollen *left* knee had been my bad knee, but my *right* knee had become my bad knee shortly before this trip. Now my *right* knee had become my good knee once again, and my *left* knee was really bad.

Kathy asked, "How can you keep track of which is which?"

The truth was they were both bad. The right knee was a little less swollen, though it would need a doc to look at it when I got back home. The left knee was swollen up like a basketball, well, at least a large grapefruit. I sat in the tent cabin with ice on the elevated left knee, telling it to get better while Kathy was transported by Linda and Gail, Linda's partner, to do our laundry, longing to get back on the trail. The weather decided to be rainy while we were at Tuolumne Meadows, so it was good to be in the tent cabin. There were four beds and a wood-burning stove in the cabin, with rest rooms and simple showers several feet away. It wasn't palatial, but it was better than our small tent. We met interesting people at meals in the camp restaurant, a very large tent.

Gail, Linda, Kathy and I sang Holden Evening Prayer by candlelight in Linda and Gail's tent cabin before Linda and Gail headed back to Washington the next day; Kathy and I were still deciding what to do. Our tablemate at dinner was a doc, who thought I might be having trouble with Baker Cysts. I was seeking medical advice wherever I could find it.

Waiting for my knees to improve, we planned to pick up our schedule at Red's Meadow, close to Mammoth Lakes. To get to Mammoth Lakes we rode a shuttle to the main road followed by two hitches, first to Lee Vining and then to Mammoth. The folks at the Tuolumne Meadows lodge gave us cardboard and a marker to make our "need a ride" sign, and we stood in the rain flashing it to passing cars. Two bedraggled old women standing by the road wearing large packs didn't look too threatening. Even people going the other way or too full up to give us a ride smiled and waved.

Our first hitch was with young rock climbers, Washington

transplants to the Bay area. They kindly gave us a ride to Lee Vining. At the service station, I held up the sign, and a young woman who worked for the Mono Lake Committee said she was going to Mammoth and would take us there. At Mammoth, we stumbled into the Reservation Bureau, and the two women working there found us lodging at the Cinnamon Bear B&B even though the Reservation Bureau only rented condos.

We were graciously helped by so many people, tablemates at dinner, strangers who gave us rides, women at the Reservation Bureau and then people at the B&B. Being in need of assistance, we experienced the kindness of others.

I hoped my knee would respond to ice and rest, but I wasn't completely crazy. I went to the hospital in Mammoth for medical advice. This hospital was an expert place for knees as it was a ski town. The nurse practitioner said I was doing all the right things for my knees: rest, compression, elevation and ice. She nixed the idea that it had anything to do with Baker Cysts and diagnosed chondromalacia. She said if I felt like I could go on, I could. Just keep taking good care of the knee.

The problem was, I didn't even have 90 degrees in range of motion, and it didn't seem reasonable to go on. Kathy phoned to see if we could get tickets home, and I took the bus to Reds Meadow to pick up our resupply boxes. That bus ride was just what the doctor ordered. By the time I returned with the resupply boxes, my range of motion had increased, and I told Kathy I wanted to try going on. We *un-planned* the tickets home and *re-planned* the rest of the hike.

Crazy? Maybe.

Months later Kathy told me she was pretty upset with all those changes but I hadn't known that at the time. She sucked it up with a smile on her face and a great deal of skepticism that I would last longer than a day more on the trail. HA.

"There's a bear on the trail."

Wow. Wow. Wow. That summed up the next day. I was deliriously happy to be back on the trail and determined to take care of my knees, setting our pace at a slow and steady stroll. Any mileage at all for the first day from Red's Meadow was a bonus, leaving a day earlier than the original schedule.

Expansive views of high mountain ranges through burned trees gave way to living trees.

Smooth trail with a gentle uphill grade was just what I needed. We climbed 2,200 feet so gradually we were never really tired or winded.

We scraped a place to camp on a small shelf hidden above the trail with an absolutely gorgeous view of the Silver Divide, one of the two most scenic campsites on the whole hike. I knew that the morrow would be a big test of my knees with some significant downhill, but the day leaving Reds Meadow was sheer gift, going at least two miles farther than anticipated. I was incredibly thankful for trails, mountains, and my hiking partner, who put up with my changing plans.

Our trail went past Duck Lake Creek, Purple Lake, Virginia Lake, and down to Tully Hole and Fish Creek. All were beautiful, towering peaks beside us or in the distance. Kathy and I especially liked Fish Creek's merry waterfalls.

Going down to Tully Hole, I saw a bear. A ways behind Kathy, picking my way slowly downhill, I could see the trail below us through the trees and a bear *gallumphing* up the trail. I yelled to Kathy, "There's a bear on the trail"

She replied, "What?"

The second time I yelled at the top of my lungs causing the bear to leave the trail and go straight up the mountain. I didn't get a picture, but was glad the bear left the trail.

Two days out of Red's Meadow we passed Squaw Lake, Lake of the Lone Indian, and other high tarns set in the midst of rugged rock, winding our way through lakes and rocks to the top of Silver Pass, 10,900 feet.

Headed down from Silver Pass, we passed more beautiful lakes through meadows by pretty little streams through more kingdoms of granite. Descending switchbacks, every turn brought new views of granite slabs and distant rugged peaks.

My poor knees hiked down 3,000 feet, but held up pretty well. We lunched by a beautiful creek that can be a dangerous ford earlier in the year. Then we climbed back up nearly 2,000 feet to Bear Ridge where we camped for the night, tired but happy.

The morning brought more climbing. Uphill was my favorite, but not Kathy's. She was having trouble with her feet, back, and shoulder.

Beauty surrounded us. Marie Lake charmed us both. The mountains north of Marie Lake looked like pyramids transplanted from Egypt to the Sierra. Passing picturesque Seldon Pass, not far past Marie Lake, we descended a pretty winding trail to Heart Lake where we stopped for dinner. We had developed a pattern of eating, then clipping off a few more miles after dinner.

Theoretically, that left attractive food smells behind with less chance of drawing bears. Stopping in a meadow below Sally Keyes Lakes, we placed our bear cans, with food and *smellables* enclosed, a good distance from our tent.

My alarm went off three or four times the next morning, but we stayed in bed until 6:00. It had become too dark and cold to get up at 5:00, frost in the meadow and ice at the edge of a shallow stream. Arriving at Muir Trail ranch about 11:00, we picked up our buckets of food drop.

Solo

Sadly, Kathy and I then went in different directions. Her feet were really hurting. She headed down a trail for five miles toward a ferry ride, and she hoped, a hitch back to civilization on the west side of the mountains, planning to rent a car and drive to the east side of the mountains to meet me after Kearsarge Pass in six or seven days. Kathy took the Tyvek groundsheet, and I took the tent.

Yes, I was going on by myself. This section of trail, concurrent with the John Muir Trail, was well populated. The knees seemed to be slowly getting better, and I felt comfortable with my decision. We hugged and told each other to be careful.

The trail followed the San Joaquin River with its entertaining rapids and waterfalls.

Crossing Piute Creek, I wet down my shirt to keep cool as the day had turned hot. Dinner was at a bridge crossing, and I took advantage of the water to clean up. The last of the day was a steep switchbacking climb by Evolution Creek along a series of plunging waterfalls.

I found my campsite just before dark, hurriedly did camp chores, and prepared for bed. It was strange to be only one in a three-person tent. I was glad it was a light-weight tent. As I went to sleep, listening to the music of the river as it tumbled past my campsite, I missed Kathy and hoped she'd made her boat connection and was somewhere back in the civilized world.

Fording the creek in the morning was no problem at all in September. Past the ford, the gentle uphill grade gave way to some serious switchbacks. Past Evolution Lake, the scrubby trees were left behind, and the rest of the day was lake after high-altitude lake set in valleys and nooks of rock, fed and emptied by streams and waterfalls. Oh, and did I mention, there was uphill? Lots and lots of uphill, until I finally staggered to the top of Muir Pass, 11,955 feet. I took pictures of the Muir Trail hut on the pass and rugged mountains in all directions. It was 5:00 when I left Muir Pass to descend to a lower altitude on a rough, rocky trail.

As I made my way down the trail, two young women from Holland passed me, also looking for a camping spot. We camped together at the edge of tree line in a beautiful small meadow with towering peaks all around. I was grateful to Karin and Rose for finding the spot.

My knees were holding up pretty well although they were glad to stop. The swelling in my left lower leg was gone, and I took no painkillers until night when the knees were aching again.

The following day, I woke up above a high-elevation lake at 10,000 feet and went to sleep at a high-elevation lake, 10,613 feet. In between I had gone down to 8,020 feet. That summed up the day, except for the beauty. It was hard to keep coming up with adjectives to describe the glorious scenery.

At noon I sat on a big rock at the edge of a river in Grouse Meadow, towering mountains of granite surrounding me, completely alone. I was in awe, soaking in the splendor all by myself on a perfect day, the wilderness my private domain.

Well, not absolutely private. Earlier that day, I'd passed a few late-rising hikers in the morning, and a woman took my picture to show her husband proof that a woman could hike alone in the Sierra. I didn't feel particularly special, just another hiker on the trail, and a slow one at that. But it was fun to have someone else think I was special.

The end of the day was very difficult. I just barely had enough time to climb up the Golden Staircase before dark. It was often a staircase built for giants, or at least men with much longer legs than mine, steps climbing beside Palisade Creek. The Golden Staircase nearly did me in. Finally reaching Lower Palisade Lake (10,611 feet) just before 8:00, I barely had enough light to put up my tent and get water before darkness settled in. I sat in the dark on a rock beside my tent, thankful to be there looking at the stars while I ate my dinner.

Chivalry Wasn't Dead

I met Tom, Michael, and Jeff on Mather Pass. They'd started off as solo hikers but had become sort of a group by the time I met them. After he learned my trail name, Tom asked for a prayer before he descended from the pass. I was happy to oblige and glad for my trail name. That night I camped with Tom, Michael, and Jeff at Lake Marjorie.

The morning at Lake Marjorie was cold. Stuffing a tent covered with ice crystals into its tiny bag with my bare hands wasn't fun. That done, I headed up 12,130-foot Pinchot Pass.

Michael passed me on the way up, and Tom and Jeff were soon there, too. Then came a long, long downhill to 8,492-foot Woods Hole and more uphill to Rae Lakes.

Rae Lakes (10,597 feet) is a beautiful gem. I approached the lakes by a lovely high mountain stream wending through a pretty green meadow. The Painted Lady was striking, colored bands running through her rocky face. I'd seen so many beautiful vistas on this trip. As I came to each spot of spectacular beauty, I was always sure it must be the best. They were all beautiful.

I didn't pull into Rae Lakes until 7:15. The three guys had been there since 5:00. Chivalry wasn't dead. Tom and Michael took my pot and pumped water for me. I called Kathy on Tom's satellite phone telling her voicemail I was coming and hoped she got the message. Tom told me I could pay for the phone call by giving him a $2.00 blessing, so I sang *God's Family* for them. I also sang an old Girl Scout song for the guys as a bedtime serenade when they were in their tents, and I was still up. They all laughed when I ended it with "Good night, Scouts."

I felt very tired that last day to Onion Valley. An accumulation of long days, early rise times and walking until late had taken its toll. A zero day was coming, and I really needed the break. At the top of 11,978-foot Glen Pass, our little group of the three guys and me rested, said our goodbyes, and had a prayer together as I knew they would all pass me somewhere on the downhill. I would take the turnoff to Kearsarge Pass, and they would go on to Whitney. Amazing how attached you can get to a hiking group even in two and a half days. They were a nice trail family when I needed one, and Michael, from Virginia, offered to be a trail angel for me on the AT. Sweet.

At lunch on Kearsarge Pass, I looked past Bullfrog and Kearsarge Lakes, watching a storm build in the far mountain ranges. Walking slowly downhill, I reached Onion Valley by 5:00 to find Kathy and Jerry, a guy she'd found to be a shuttle driver. It was so good to see her. We chattered on the way to Independence, went to eat, and I took my heavenly shower, falling at last into a real bed. ZZZZ…

"One step at a time, silly boys. One step at a time."

We had two rest days in Independence. Yay!

Kathy decided to hire a horse packer to carry our packs over Kearsarge Pass. It was exorbitantly expensive and something I would never have done by myself. But since she was determined to do so, and pay the stiff fee, I too was the beneficiary. It was the most expensive slack pack ever, but it made the first day of our last stretch of hiking much more enjoyable. We had a total of 3,800-feet elevation gain for that day, but since 2,800 feet were without packs, it just didn't seem that much.

When we picked up our packs from the horse packer, they felt like lead with seven days' food inside. Ridding our packs of a little weight, we had dinner a quarter mile before our campsite in the Central Basin. With slightly less food and *smellables* in the bear box a hundred feet from our tent, we snuggled down into our bags with a pretty view down the valley, asleep before dark.

In the morning my water bottle in the bear box was well on the way to being frozen, not solid, but with ice crystals throughout. We had breakfast, packed up in the cold, and started up the trail, climbing 2,800 feet. And it wasn't just 2,800 feet, but 2,800 to the top of 13,200-foot Forrester Pass. It took us old ladies until almost 1:00 to summit the pass. The impressive switchbacks cut into nearly vertical rock on the south side of the pass seemed like the Kendal Cat Walk near Snoqualmie Pass times 10.

When we discovered the camelback holding Kathy's water was leaking, at the first lake below those switchbacks we emptied the pack to dry things in the sun and very strong wind. Kathy's bivy bag escaped its rock weight in the wind and started blowing toward the lake. I jumped to stop it, tripped and fell flat on top of it. If you didn't know I'd tripped, I looked like a 66-year-old lady making a diving save, *Monday-Night-Football* style. I was definitely a strong- enough weight to hold down the bivy bag, but Kathy suggested I refrain from further heroics. I agreed and put a Band-Aid ™ on the scrape on my shin, and we had a few laughs.

The next morning, moisture in the lid to the pot used to boil water for breakfast was frozen before I could dry it. That's cold. Passing Bighorn Plateau and Crabtree Meadows, we camped at Guitar Lake, a common staging area for PCT hikers, who want to go up Mt. Whitney. (The lake really does look like a guitar as you climb above it.)

Climb above it we did on the following day, leaving most of our gear at Guitar Lake as we slowly moved up and up, from 11,500 feet to 14,494 feet. It was a Sunday, and there must have been 50 people summiting, most from the Whitney Portal side, not from the PCT. Mt. Whitney is a very popular climb, and non-PCT hikers must apply for permission to climb on a lottery system.

Kathy was a funny one. She struggled going over Forrester Pass, a thousand feet lower in elevation than Whitney. But Whitney is a summit. She got *summit fever* and speeded up that trail. Once on top, she flitted around the summit like a butterfly.

I, on the other hand, was just about wiped out. I didn't want to move and felt so tired I wondered how I would ever get down. Some guys, who had hiked the John Muir Trail were properly impressed to learn that I'd come all the way from Donner Pass. But they looked at me in my exhausted state, with my complexion gone slightly green-tinged from the altitude, and asked how in the world I'd ever done that. "One step at a time, silly boys. One step at a time."

Descending to Guitar Lake, we ate dinner, and I bathed part of me, hoping to feel better. Then we packed up and zoomed to Crabtree Meadows another thousand feet lower. Arriving late, we put the tent up in the dark.

The branches of the bushes by Whitney Creek were thickly coated with ice from splashes of water in the morning. The next two days became a little easier, as the character of the mountains changed. We both were very tired with a cumulative fatigue. When we stopped to eat, one or the other of us would simply fall asleep. At Chicken Spring Lake, our last water source, Kathy pumped water, and I took a nap in the sun; I fixed dinner while Kathy napped.

We were so very tired, and we were so very, very dirty, trail dust leaving every exposed surface black. Our bodies needed rest, and we were *really* looking forward to being clean again.

Still, that last night, as we gazed at the sunset through the trees, Kathy said if she wasn't so tired she would love to hike on and on and on.

Kathy's foot hurt in the morning, as it often did. The wind was blowing cold and sometimes hard. I'd never been dirtier in my life. But we were both grateful we had been able to take such an incredibly beautiful hike.

Our pre-arranged ride picked us up at Horseshoe Meadows, and our timing was good getting out of the mountains. A big storm was expected the next day, with 3 to 6 inches of snow forecast for 8,000 ft. We had been living at 11,000 feet, and I didn't want to think how much snow might fall at that altitude. I hoped all the hikers would be OK, and I was glad I wouldn't be one of them as we headed to civilization with showers, restaurants, beds and a plane ride to Washington.

In spite of my problems with knees, it was a glorious 409 miles on the PCT, and I looked forward to the next year's hiking.

Chapter 12 Fall and Winter 2007-2008

"At your age any quick turn can do it."

Back home once again, I made an appointment with an orthopedist. He took x-rays and discovered three torn menisci. I remarked that it all had started with that surprise step in an unfamiliar condo, expressing amazement such a thing could result in a torn meniscus.

He said, "At your age any quick turn can do it."

Thanks, Doc. He went on to say that he thought I needed a hip replacement. He further implied I'd exercised bad judgment to have hiked in the Sierra for so long, and in general, he gave me the impression he thought if I was still walking from the bed to the table at my age I had nothing to complain about. I went looking for another Doc. (BTW, I have hiked on my original hip at least 9,000 miles since I saw him, although other joints have failed me.)

A recommendation from my hiking buddy's doc led me to another orthopedist. Pictures of mountains he'd climbed adorned his office walls. Good sign. He was considerably more sympathetic to an aging hiker, who wanted to keep hiking. We weighed the options of arthroscopic surgery to clean up the damage in my knees, medical opinion mixed about the advisability. I made the decision for surgery to clean up the damage, and--I hoped--to extend my hiking life.

It should have been a piece of cake, in and out of surgery on the same day, walking pretty normally in a week and quickly moving onward to conditioning for hiking. I had the surgery on both knees the same day, and two days later I was back in the hospital in excruciating pain with a staph infection that was eating my left knee. I was put on antibiotics and cultures identified the strain of staph. At one point when the knee was drained, I distinctly remember coming to from anesthetic hearing someone wailing in a high-pitched cry. Then I realized it was me. Not my favorite memory.

More Un-Favorite Memories

The kind-hearted doc had me on a morphine drip for pain. But morphine wasn't a good choice for me. It made me paranoid and hallucinate. Really. I saw things – Cuneiform letters written in blood on my wall. I was sure the medical staff wanted to steal fingers and hands from my visitors in some elaborate scheme to make babies. In short, morphine made me stark-raving bonkers. I was living in an alternate and very scary reality, all very real to me. Since that experience, I have great sympathy for anyone suffering from mental illness. It was no fun at all.

I called my friend, Terrie Rae, in the middle of the night, to come get me, and I tried to escape from the hospital on a walker with my IV pole while dressed in my hospital gown. Of course I didn't make it past the nurse's desk. My friend called my son, and they both showed up and waited until, in a wheelchair and utterly exhausted, I was given a sedation shot and put back in bed. I don't remember the rest of the night. Terrie Rae stayed by my side until near morning when I told her to go home and sleep. The next day I chewed her out for leaving me by myself. My drugged brain had no memory of her faithful kindness beside me through the night. I was fortunate she understood it wasn't really me who had chewed her out, but my addled brain.

Morphine was stopped, and my more normal brain function returned. I was put on IV antibiotics to kill the particular kind of infection raging in my knee and shipped off to a nursing home for three weeks. I didn't much enjoy the nursing home, but at least I was then sane.

"I won't tell you not to go on your hike. But your knee will tell you how much you can do."

By the end of January I was home and undergoing intense Physical Therapy Rehabilitation as an outpatient. My right knee became my good knee again. The left knee no longer had a staph infection, but it would never again be a good knee.

The best guess of the doc was that the posterior cruciate ligament no longer existed. I worked hard in therapy, my motivation was to get back on the trail. I had an April date with the PCT at the Mexican border. Terrie Rae thought I should be happy to be alive at that point instead of being obsessed by the trail. I *was* happy to be alive. But the determination to get back on the trail was what spurred me to work hard in rehabilitation.

I walked, first with a walker, to the end of my driveway. Then I made it halfway down the block. Then it was one block. Then it was two. I progressed to a cane. I walked more blocks. I gave up the cane. I walked some more. I went to PT twice a week and faithfully did exercises at home three times a day. Any time I did too much for a particular stage of recovery, the knee swelled, and I had to cut back how hard I worked. It took time, not just for recovery, but also to learn what my limits were and how to stay below those limits. If I worked the knee too hard, my quads (thigh muscles) simply shut down. And no matter how much weight I could lift in therapy with my left leg in exercises, I couldn't trust my body weight, carried on the left leg, going down any step more than four inches deep.

My doc was impressed with my progress and knew what was driving me. He said, "I won't tell you not to go on your hike, but your knee will tell you how much you can do." He said I had to go more slowly. The pack weight must be lighter. I must be very careful. If decided to go, he asked for a phone call when I got back to tell him how it had gone.

I switched to a Gossamer Gear Pack and saved a pound. I got a Henry Shires single person tarp tent and saved more. I made a variety of other small changes, and my base weight was down to 12 pounds. (Base weight is the weight of all gear, everything except food, water and fuel.) Even with adding water for the desert, I thought I could keep the pack weight under 25 pounds, usually under 20. (I was a bit more optimistic than conditions eventually warranted.) My cousin, Liz, from San Diego, would provide me with trail support on the southern part of the PCT, so I wouldn't be carrying any more than three day's food at a time for the first hundred miles.

In March I planted peas in my garden. I wouldn't have to be home for them to grow. I was then up to being on my feet six hours a day and was lifting 10 pounds with my left leg and 20 pounds with my right leg. A lot could happen in a month. In January I left the nursing home on a walker. In February I was just getting off a cane. In March I could walk 2.8 miles in an hour on level ground. I couldn't do more without my knee swelling in protest. I continued to plan and prepare as if I were going hiking. I would do so unless it was proved to me that I could not. I bought food and organized food drop boxes. I registered for the PCT Kickoff at Lake Morena.

Toward the end of March, I took the first official *hike* of my recovery. I drove out to the Nisqually Delta and walked the 5.5 miles of the Delta. I set no speed records and carried only lunch and water on level ground. The day was beautiful, a rare spring day with blue skies and no rain, frosty to start, but not too cold. The view of the Olympics over the water filled my heart with joy. I saw a raccoon, a few dozen ducks, and hundreds of geese, five of which decided to get up close and personal. Small birds flitted and sang. It was a great day. The knee was tired by the end of the hike and pruning in the yard for an hour or more afterwards contributed to it screaming at me by evening. But the good news was that it only took overnight to recover instead of one or two days. That was very encouraging, as I would need to recover overnight when on the trail.

I added pack weight and went up Mount Pete for my first uphill hike. It took me twice as long as before the knee problems. But I did it. With my blue Gossamer Gear pack I was like the little blue engine. I think I can. I think I can. I think I can.

I planted the rest of the spring veggies in my garden. On April 3rd I made it around the Nisqually Delta twice, with pack, 11 miles. April 8 I made it up and down Mt. Pete again and had my last PT appointment. Time to go. I flew to California to meet my cousin in San Diego. I was going on a hike. It might be 10 miles or it might be 360 miles. The knee would tell me which it would be.

Chapter 13 April 12, 2008 PCT

"Are you the Medicare Pastor? How is your knee?"

On April 12, very early in the morning, I stood at the Mexican Border and signed the register at the Pacific Crest Trail monument. I'd then been to both the northern and the southern termini; I just had to finish the parts in between. HA!

My cuz and I had sleuthed out the owner of Star Ranch, the land around the trail. We obtained permission for me to get support about ten miles north of the border. So the first day on the trail I took only my lunch, water, first aid kit, down jacket and my camera. I walked slowly, looking at all the flowers and taking pictures of each different kind. Gene, from the Star Ranch, met me at the jeep road with my gear, food and water.

The kindness of Doug and Gene made that first day into a very do-able day for an old lady with a fragile knee. I was grateful. Twelve hikers passed me that first day. I would meet many hikers in Southern California. Ninety-nine-percent of them passed me as I walked my slow and careful pace.

That night, I snuggled into my tent in a small spot in the chaparral out of view of the trail. At 5:30 the next morning I heard many footsteps. It was too early for hikers from the border and too many footsteps for small hiking groups. I couldn't see them, but they couldn't see me either. I suspected they were illegals using the PCT. After they were gone, the trail was mine. I concentrated on proper knee function at each step and reached Lake Morena by 2:30.

The next day was a zero. My *cuz* brought me a food drop and also left food for me at Mt. Laguna. It was strange to take a zero day after only two days and it was strange to take short hikes and stop, the sun still high in the sky. It was strange to have every hiker pass me with so much relative difference in speed that I likely would never see them again.

I reminded myself that I was on a walker only three months ago, hoping to graduate to a cane. I was so very lucky to be hiking at all at any speed. I was so fortunate to be on the trail.

I reached Mt. Laguna two days later. There were times the knee was painful. Critically important, I was recovering overnight. I had a bed and shower, as well as food at Mt. Laguna. In two more days I reached Sunrise Road Trailhead, where Liz met me with another food drop and tasty treats including a piece of apple pie, immediately devoured.

The weather in the desert ranged from freezing nights to very hot days. You might wonder how I was able to hike without being able to manage more than a four-inch high step with my left knee. Well-graded trails generally do not go up more than four inches in elevation in a single step. The right leg took the occasional higher step.

I saw three quail as I started out the second day from Laguna. I think I saw my first rattlesnake that day, too, but it slithered off the trail before I could be sure. Walking along the trail I heard rustling in the leaves beneath the bushes, but didn't stop to see if the rustles were snakes, lizards, a horny toad, or a bird.

Sunrise Road Trailhead was extremely windy. Dust blew into the tent, hitting the walls and falling down, coating everything inside and out. I breathed dust and ate it, too, glad to pack up in the morning and leave.

Two days later I was at Scissors Crossing. Along the way I walked past bright yellow Bush Poppies in Chariot Canyon. And I met Jellybean, who would become a friend on this trail and whom I would see in later years on other sections of the Triple Crown.

Just before Scissors Crossing, I met a day hiker, and we compared notes about flowers.

Giving me her name and phone number, she offered to bring me back to the trail from Julian the next afternoon. Perfect. Liz took me into Julian, famous for apple pie, but more importantly for me was a bed and a shower. That night I met Splash, a hiker from Seattle, whom Kathy knew and whose journal I'd read.

She said, "Are you the Medicare Pastor? How is your knee?"

When you read each other's trail journals, you feel like you know someone before you ever meet in person.

After getting gear, food, and water organized, I spent the next morning with my feet up and my head down on a pillow. My day hiker friend picked me up in the afternoon, so I could go part way up San Felipe Hills in the cool of late afternoon.

It felt good to be back on the trail even if the pack was heavy with five liters of water, my first real test with water weight. The San Felipe Hills were more like true desert in terrain and vegetation than the trail walked from the border, rocks, sand and four or five varieties of cactus, as well as agave.

The stalks that would carry agave blooms looked like giant asparagus stalks. Cholla and barrel cactus, some quite large, were blooming with yellowish green blooms. Beavertail cactus flowers were a florescent pink; flowers of hedgehog cactus had a silver shine to their pink. All were very pretty.

That evening I met two young women *cowboy camped (*sleeping on top of your tent or a ground cloth) at a bend in the trail with just room enough for one more. I loved it. Most of the rest of Southern California I cowboy camped. With a bum knee, it was much easier to simply sit down on the sleeping bag, everything within reach and no tent door to crawl through. The water cache at Third Gate contained more than 160 gallon jugs of water, all lugged up a one mile trail, 4-8 gallons each trip, by dedicated trail angels as a work of love for the trail and hikers. I took two as I was stopping for the night.

Among the many hikers camped at Barrel Springs, I met RockStar, who was to become my trail companion for much of the Continental Divide Trail years later. After my dust-filled tent at Sunrise Trailhead, my theory for the very windy night at Barrel Springs was to cowboy camp on the sheltered side of a bush and hope wind would blow dust over me instead of hitting the tent wall and falling on me.

The following day I was at Warner Springs and had walked 113.2 miles. Yes, I did it very slowly, taking extra good care of the knee. Yes, I stopped often and never carried much food. But I did get there, very encouraged. I *might* complete the hike I'd planned.

RockStar and I shared a room at Warner Springs and enjoyed the hot springs swimming pools that night. I also met Ursa Minor, hiking with huge blisters on her feet. The next morning my cuz, Liz, picked me up along with RockStar, and we went back to Lake Morena for the PCT Kickoff.

Kickoff

The Annual PCT Kickoff is an amazing gathering. Lake Morena Park was reserved for hikers and was very full, at least 5-6 people in every site, a veritable forest of tents. There were presentations on bears and water as well as vendors with lightweight gear. I had many conversations with people of differing backgrounds, personalities and ages. People who'd previously thru-hiked the PCT supported aspiring thru hikers in one grand gathering with an exciting atmosphere.

Each year the group of hikers heading up the trail had their picture taken and even section hikers were allowed. I was in that picture. Amazing. The Kickoff was like a two-day camping slumber party complete with interesting entertainment, useful information and a few hundred of your closest friends you had never met.

Eric Ryback showed his slides, the first to hike the PCT before it was a whole trail, walking from Canada to Mexico as an 18-year-old with only USGS maps and 5 food drops. Incredible. I also met Teddy, the first woman to thru-hike the PCT, SOBO (southbound) and solo in 1976, three years after the current guidebook was published.

I met Billy Goat, Tailwinds, Blue Butterfly, the Pearl Girls, Wheeew, Squatch, Free and EZgoing, Mendo Rider and a few hundred more people whose names I can no longer remember.

I also rested the knee for two whole days.

Fire and Angels

Following the Kickoff, Liz took me back to Warner Springs for a very small hike around the town and one more night in a bed. Three more days on the trail, and I was in Idlewild, diverted there by a fire with other NOBO (northbound) hikers. Fire had changed everyone's plans, and there was a scramble for lodging, but the confusion and delay was a benefit for me, allowing me to catch up with hikers I now knew as we all tried to figure out our next steps.

Papa Bear, whom I'd met in 2007 in the Sierra, was there with a car. He shuttled hikers to trailheads, and I re-planned my trip with his guidebook. Thru hikers like Jellybean were road walking around the fire so as to keep continuous footsteps from Mexico to Canada. As a section hiker, that wasn't important for me to do. The skipped section could be another year's hike. I now planned to continue farther north but still come out at a trailhead to catch my plane home at the right time. Even though I like to plan things in advance, the fire required flexibility. No one plans forest fires. Papa Bear took Sly and me to Cabezon and Interstate 10 to continue north.

I left Cabezon carrying six day's food, but detoured on the first night at a sign that promised free eats for hikers. Long distance hikers very rarely turn down free food. Four more days and I came to Big Bear. They were long days with considerable elevation gains and losses and I fell in a shallow part of the White River. I also *passed* another hiker.

My problem knee did amazingly well, but I decided to take the first exit to Big Bear as I painfully limped to the road. A zero day was in order. That night I shared a room with Jelly Bean, who had walked around the burn and caught up with me.

The weather varied after Kickoff, from extremely hot days when I felt like a dead daisy—to sometimes freezing nights. The PCT's meandering route through Southern California went over mountain ranges and drops down into desert valleys, then up another mountain range and down to another desert valley. Repeat and repeat.

Partly because of the recurring significant changes in elevation, California has at least 16 *plant communities* described in the guidebooks. The multiplicity of flowers was astonishing. Canterbury Bells became my new favorite. I took pictures of each new flower I saw, and I probably saw a dozen that were new to me each day.

I loved the profusion of flowers, spending hours the next winter looking up their names.

Sadly, many are still labeled by color in my photos as I couldn't find them in books or online. It has always surprised me how few hikers wanted to know the names of the flowers they passed along the trail. I always wanted to meet them by name, though not necessarily a scientific name. Their common nicknames were easier to remember.

When I reached Big Bear, I called Nitro. Yes, that Nitro. The one I'd met on my first hike on the AT. It is a continual joy to meet people from trails walked in preceding years. Nitro lived nearby and loved to play trail angel to hikers. She'd also been at the Kickoff and had given me her number.

Because of Nitro, I also now knew there was such a thing at the Continental Divide Trail and the Triple Crown. Ever since the AT, I'd followed her trail journal online, and Nitro had walked all three trails in the years I'd read her posts. I still had no idea *I* would walk all three trails. In 2008 I was just hoping to walk on the PCT until the time for my airline ticket home. I was fortunate to be able to walk anywhere. Nitro, at least 40-50 years my junior, was a super trail angel. She said to call if my knee got worse.

The trail community spans age ranges of people drawn together by the trail. Other hikers I met around Big Bear included Forager, Irish, Tahoe Mike, Brit, Moonshine and Rosemary, Captain Teacup, Dogwood and Grins, to whom I gave his trail name for his wide, happy grin every time I saw him. The trail community was one grand happy, somewhat sore and blistered, parade of hikers of all ages and backgrounds.

After my slackpack from Van Duzen Road south to Highway 18, I needed to hitch back to Big Bear. I hailed a very quick hitch from the first car to pass, driven by a Hispanic man with his daughter. They knew nothing about the trail. But they stopped and rearranged many boxes in their small VW to make room for me.

As I thanked him profusely, he told me the Bible said he should help strangers as they may be angels. ("Do not neglect to show hospitality to strangers, for thereby some have entertained angels unawares" Hebrews 13:2.) He didn't know I was a pastor or a Christian or would actually know that Biblical reference. I explained that hikers called people like him angels. He was a trail angel.

My knee gave me a lot of trouble on that slack pack, and I wondered if I'd gone as far as I could for the year. Should I get off trail? Should I go home even if it meant buying another airline ticket? But by the end of the day, the knee felt better again. Go figure. I, ever the eternal optimist, could envision quitting if I was hurting.

I couldn't envision quitting if the knee didn't hurt. Since it felt better by the end of the day, I went on, although I readjusted my plan once again to give myself more time. I'd been pushing too hard for the knee; I planned seven days to reach Cajon Pass.

The following day I walked through a burn area. Mandatory walking through burn areas might make all people be more careful with fire in the woods. Yes, there were flowers and grasses coming and some new growth at the base of bushes, but it would take many years to grow trees.

I followed my resolve to take better care of the knee and stopped early.

Naked Hikers

The next day was exceedingly warm, 89-degrees in the shade, and there was precious little shade. I pushed a bit and made it to a lovely stop at Deep Creek Bridge. Wonderful water underneath big trees. Hikers frolicked on the banks of the river, some even diving into a deep pool. I settled for a little wading, rinsed out my socks, and gave myself a wet bandana bath to parts acceptable to show in mixed company. Many hikers I already knew were there: Ursa Minor and Southern Gentleman, Headnout and Tagnalong, Tailwinds, Black Snake, Backtrack and Ipod. I sang Holden Evening Prayer that night for five.

The following day I was carried away with enjoyment of hiking, though my knee said I should have abided by my plan for a shorter day. We were in Deep Creek Canyon all day. The trail cut high above the creek, and we looked down on the river with its many pools and rapids.

An experienced PCT hiker had fallen to his death in that canyon a few years previously and sadness shook the PCT community. But hikers still hike the trail. Even experienced hikers can make a miss-step or be blown off balance by the wind. But then, one can as easily step off a curb in traffic by accident. A father of one of my friends tripped on a curb outside a motel on a road trip and received lasting damage. There are dangers everywhere. The trail is not unique in that respect.

Deep Creek Hot Springs are natural hot-spring pools at the edge of a delightful river with deep water. Beside the river were cliffs and rocks from which to dive or on which to sunbathe, as well as generous portions of sand. Almost everyone frolicked in the water, including me. A couple ducks came right up close and little fishies swam by my legs.

Hot spring water blended into cool creek water, making anyone's desired water temperature available. Clothing was optional. There were some naked hikers, but most the folks I knew kept their clothes on this particular day. I thought the young hiker dudes wandering around without clothes except for hiker hats and sunglasses were quite funny. I hoped they wouldn't suffer sunburn on parts normally unexposed to sun.

Camping wasn't allowed at the Hot Springs. Since I did so well getting there, and the knee felt so good, I decided to go to the dam (five miles) instead of stopping at the lovely arched bridge. (two miles). Silly me.

We had a bit of excitement leaving the Hot Springs: Tailwinds startled a rattlesnake on the trail, which startled her, too. I took a picture of the snake slithering across the trail and then gingerly passed while it was still buzzing its rattles.

Tailwinds and Ursa Minor also made their way around the snake, who seemed to have no desire to go farther than one foot off trail. We warned Backtrack and Moon Pie coming behind us, and Backtrack stayed to warn a couple other hikers. The orange-colored rattler wasn't happy to have been disturbed.

A sand bar by the river was home for the night. Loudly chirping crickets and gently flowing water lulled hikers to sleep as hiker midnight approached. (Hiker midnight is whenever the sun goes down.)

I really did plan to take care of my knee by not going very far the next day. Really. That was my plan. I even intentionally packed up very slowly so my friends, Tailwinds, Ursa Minor, Southern Gentleman, Black Snake, Crosscut, Headnout and Tagnalong, would all be gone ahead of me, and I wouldn't be tempted to try and catch up.

But I reached Grass Valley early for lunch, and the weather changed from hot to a nice cool overcast. Well, phooey. I really liked hiking when it was cold. How could I justify sticking around somewhere all afternoon when it was too cold to bathe or wash clothes? Hiking in cold weather was to be treasured in Southern California.

Contouring around hills and gullies in a strong wind, other hikers caught and passed me after a short chat. Gypsy Lulu caught up with me and slowed her pace so we could talk. I told her when she went on that I would be stopping soon. I really meant to do so. But no good place appeared, and soon I was walking the trail around Silver Lake. I didn't find the hikers' spot in the campground, though Grins later came by my tent and told me where it was. I just picked the first spot I saw. Too tired to move, I inserted my bag into my collapsed tent as if the tent was a bivi bag, and snuggled in; dry and warm, I was quickly asleep.

Cajon Pass

The plan had been to hike to Cajon Pass in seven days from Big Bear. I just kept getting places too fast. I liked being near people, who had become friends, and I made it in five.

All went well until the final downhill, a killer for me, a thousand feet down, in direct sun and no shade. Some of the trail was fairly steep, on hard packed dirt. It was difficult for someone, who must always lead with the left leg going down such a steep trail. Remember, I couldn't hold my weight with the left knee for any more than a four-inch drop in elevation. This steep trail required a deeper drop within a normal step length. I also couldn't step with the left foot in high-impact heel strike without pain.

Steps deeper than a four-inches drop give high impact. It wasn't a quick descent for me.

Stiff wind gusts threatened my balance near a severe drop off over eroded dirt cliffs. It seemed a long way down.

Across the hills and valleys past Interstate 15, I could see the San Gabriels and Mt. San Antonio's snow, smoke billowing up on the far side of the San Gabriels from another fire. Fire season seemed very early.

Finally reaching the Interstate, I was happy to stagger into McDonalds, wash my hands and face and comb my hair for a modicum of presentability. I ordered a big meal with added fruit and a large shake. Even more importantly, I sat down off my sore feet and aching knee.

As I was finishing my meal, another hiker came in, nodded to me in recognition I was a hiker, and sat in the next booth. Even off trail, hikers can pick each other out, and it isn't just the pack that gives it away. It's like having a large extended family, many members of whom you have not yet met. Seeing each other, there is an instant, even if brief, connection.

Catching a hitch to the Best Western on the kitty corner cloverleaf, I soon rejoiced to be showered, fed, and horizontal, not intending to move for a long time on a zero day. After all, I'd arrived two days early. I needed that rest day. I was quite tired, but I didn't sleep well because too many body parts were aching and calling my name. In the morning, I enjoyed bagels and cream cheese in the free continental breakfast and talked to hikers including Sly, Grandpa Kilt, and Ursa Minor.

Zero-day chores included laundry, catching up with my Pocketmail journals, making phone calls, and checking my email on the computer in the lobby. After dozing a bit, Ursa Minor and I had lunch at Taco Del Mar. She was hoping to get a ride to Wrightwood to see a doc about her ankle, which seemed to be getting worse. In the afternoon, I slept for three hours, making myself get up so I would sleep that night. I was still tired.

I walked out to the lobby just as Nitro was unloading hikers from her car, including RockStar. Nitro quickly agreed to take Ursa Minor to Wrightwood, where she was headed next after putting out water in Swarthout Canyon. In a quick juggle of motel rooms, RockStar ended up in Ursa Minor's room, as it was too late in the day for Ursa Minor to get her money back.

That night I walked across a highway to get a sub for dinner, and I'd then sampled all the fast food places on the cloverleaf and had half the sub left for lunch the next day.

Wrightwood

The following day: Oh my, was it hot. Seeing no one who appeared to be a likely ride at the gas station, I walked to McDonalds, about half a mile around the cloverleaf, and I was sweating freely by the time I got there. I'd brought my half sub sandwich from last night's dinner and ordered a large chocolate shake to go with it. They had a special of a free chicken sandwich with any drink, so I ate that too, a very nice early lunch in air-conditioned comfort.

After slathering myself with sunblock in the ladies' room, I started out to hike about 10:30. It was HOT. The only thing that made it bearable was the wind. Then my right foot decided to hurt. Hey, what was up with that? It was supposed to be my left knee that hurt, not my right foot. How can I limp on both legs at once?

On top of a ridge looking down on Swarthout Valley, I searched for a place to sit and scrunched myself into a tiny bit of shade from a small bush. After a few minutes in that uncomfortable position, I limped on down the trail another mile or two to find a more comfortable opportunity under a sycamore tree and just lay there for 20 minutes, cooling down.

I finally started hiking decently the rest of the way to Swarthout Road where my trail angel, White Buffalo, was chatting with Gordon, another trail angel supporting Nimble Will. She brought me a cold pop and some orange juice, too, which I inhaled.

I'd drunk over a liter in the short distance I'd traveled in the heat.

Loading up with seven liters of water, (15.4 lbs.) I only hiked a half-mile more before stopping. Although it was only 4:30, I stretched out in the shade and didn't go further that day. My knee liked my decision.

The next morning I was on the trail at 5:45 trying to beat the heat. I started at 3,700 feet and camped at nearly 8,000 feet. The ridge I thought so high and hard coming down to Cajon Pass looked like a mole hill from my campsite, and the hills I'd sweated over in the heat the day before seemed rather tiny below me.

I met Hard Core, Latecomer, and Whiz in the late afternoon, and Whiz took my picture to show his mother, an old lady with a bad knee. They went on, and I camped under Pine trees on a little saddle below the trail, wind in the trees singing me a lullaby as I drifted to sleep.

Before reaching Guffy Campground in the morning, Glow Worm caught up with me. He saw my gimpy-legged descent as I started down the steep trail to the spring and offered to get my water. I was very grateful. It saved a lot of work down and back up with my overworked right leg doing most of the effort. He even went back to a trail-magic cooler and brought me a lemon lime soda. What a nice young man.

When I reached Wrightwood, I found the place full up with hikers. No room at the inn. But when I walked past the already full cabins at The Pines, RockStar called out to me from inside her cabin. She had an empty bed in her room. Hallelujah. Having a shower, I became human again, clean except for the dirt streak on the back of my right leg that had become part of me. I scrubbed it twice with soap and wash cloth, but the dark streak remained.

Ursa Minor got off trail with a broken 5th metatarsal on one foot and a very sprained ankle.

Backtrack also got off trail after developing gallbladder problems. These were not planned departures like mine, but the trail, like life, throws unexpected curves to demolish carefully laid plans.

After Wrightwood came the climb up Baden Powell. I trudged up 22 switchbacks before the snow banks made counting difficult around 8,000 feet. The rest of the way over steep snow or bare hills, I could usually tell where the trail was supposed to be. It was hard to go up steep snow without a left leg able to kick proper steps in the snow, but

I made it to the top for a great view and a good lunch, watching 20-something hikers, Good Times and Squarl, build a little snowman and throw snowballs down the trail.

Next came my longest and most strenuous day, more than 16 miles. RockStar, who had started from Wrightwood three hours after me, caught and passed me just before Little Jimmy, where I cowboy camped next to a snowbank.

My last night for the year was at Buckhorn Campground, where I holed up in my tent for protection from a multitude of flies and mosquitoes, the only time I'd put the tent up since the San Felipe Hills. Late in the night, other hikers, including Circle, a woman close to my age from Portland, set up their tents nearby.

I had to have cold food my last night. The store at Wrightwood had such an influx of hikers that there had been no fuel. Mountain House spaghetti rehydrated pretty well with cold water and even cold oatmeal the next morning wasn't too bad, discovering I tasted the milk on instant oats more if the whole mess was cold.

My last day's walking and the end of my California PCT hike for the year was at Three Points. I needed a ride out. Thinking I should get more presentable, I was cleaning my fingernails with my knife when the second car went by. Perhaps he was put off by the fact that my hand with the thumb out was also holding an open knife. Oops. There just hadn't been time to close it.

After the knife was stowed, a woman and her daughter drove by from a church camp and picked me up. She was convinced it was God's doing that they were later than planned so they could give me a ride. Not only did they pick me up, they drove me below LA to Norco where my cousin, Liz, found me. The next day I was on an airplane flying over the PCT back to Washington.

I called my doc, who had said he wanted to know how far I would be able to hike when I'd last seen him in March. He asked how far I went, and I said, "346 miles." There was dead silence on the line for a minute or more. I suppose it *was* amazing. Get out of a nursing home in January. Hike 346 miles on the PCT in April and May on a leg that couldn't support weight on a step higher than four inches. It was possible though, and I'd done it.

Chapter 14 Summer 2008 PCT

Finishing Washington

My PCT hiking for the year wasn't quite finished. There were still two little pieces of trail to be completed to call Washington complete: from the Bridge of the Gods to Panther Creek Campground and from Chinook Pass to White Pass.

I drove down to Stevenson in July and a pastoral colleague drove me over the Bridge of The Gods to Cascade Locks to walk back into Washington. The bridge has no dedicated space for walkers, but since workmen were on the bridge, the cars really did drive 15 miles an hour as they were supposed to. I took pictures each side of the bridge and a picture straight down through the metal lattice floor of the bridge to the river many feet below, being very careful to hang onto my camera. Anything dropped into the river would be gone forever.

The hike past the bridge was a lovely stroll. Most thru-hikers probably see this stretch as a wandering impediment on the way to Canada, many taking the short cut on the road. But I enjoyed that little section. The trail wasn't in a hurry to get anywhere as it wandered and meandered. But then, I also wasn't in a hurry to get anywhere and just enjoyed being on the trail again.

Stopping at Greenleaf Creek, I appreciated the differences from Southern California, mossy rocks to sit on and the forest canopy impenetrable by hot sun. It would have been perfect were it not for pesky small flies and at least one mosquito. That night I stayed inside my tent behind mosquito netting.

Testing my knee, the day's climb also yielded flowers and views of glaciated peaks, Mt.

Hood, Mt. Adams, Mt. St Helens and Mt. Rainier, three I'd climbed in my younger days. Sparse but interesting flowers bloomed at lower elevations, more thickly at higher elevations: lupine, paintbrush, columbine, lilies, mariposa lilies, larkspur, bear grass, yellow violets, wild onion, wild hyacinth, avalanche lilies, daisies, yarrow, and bunch berry.

On the third day, failing to restrain myself, I walked 16 miles, reaching Panther Creek Campground a day earlier than planned. I had no intention of waiting a day for my arranged ride.

Two nice women drove me to Stevenson to get my car. I gave them money for ice cream in Stevenson, and everyone was happy with the arrangement.

Picking up a fast food dinner, I drove home. However, getting out of my car to get gas halfway home, I found I could barely stand. I had to *practice* standing for several minutes before I could pump my gas. When I pulled into my driveway at midnight, my knees, especially the left one, had so stiffened up that I could barely make it into the house without crawling. Hmm, I guess 16 miles was too much. It took three or four days for the knee to recover to what was now my *normal*.

"It's Medicare Pastor."

In September my friend Kathy and I set out from Chinook Pass SOBO for my last PCT hike for the year to complete Washington. We'd head to the AT the next week. Kathy, my Washington hiking buddy, and I were prepared to have a good time on the trail.

Unfortunately, a forest fire in Oregon made the sky hazy, and the normally clear and beautiful views of Mount Rainier were absent. The blessing when long views are obscured is that short views and flowers become more striking, not having to compete for attention with the more overpowering long vistas.

Shortly after starting on the trail from Chinook Pass, three hikers came toward us NOBO. "It's Medicare Pastor," said Forager, from Big Bear. He'd made his way north on his last state. Circle also passed us heading NOBO. How fun to meet hikers I'd met in the spring.

An elk bugled outside our tent several times during the night, waking Kathy. She said she'd contemplated getting up and stabbing it with a hiking pole so she could get some sleep. Actually, we both slept well regardless of the love-sick elk.

"What a beautiful morning."

At Kathy's suggestion the next day, we ticked off more miles than planned and camped in the only spot we could find not covered in bushes or bogs. The trees were beautiful. The night was still and oh, so peaceful. A beautiful lake, beautiful trees, a cozy sleeping bag, good company, full bellies and a great day on the PCT. What more could one want?

It rained softly all night. Stirring at 6:15, the rain conveniently let up for breakfast and packing. That wet and drippy morning, fog gave an ethereal look to the trees, stream, and lake. Kathy sat on a damp log eating breakfast and said, "What a beautiful morning." She wasn't being sarcastic. She meant it. One of the reasons I always like hiking with Kathy is she honestly enjoys the outdoors in all of its aspects. And it *was* beautiful, even in the damp.

Meandering through alpine trees and around lakes, ponds and bogs, there were no grand vistas, but trees, meadows and lakes were no less beautiful, freshly washed by the rain and viewed through mist. Our rain gear worked perfectly, ticking off our miles with stops for snacks and a brief rest, we were at White Pass. Washington was complete as was a nice chunk of Southern California, all on a pitiful knee.

My PCT hiking for 2008 came to a close, and my AT hiking for 2008 began.

Chapter 15 September 24, 2008 AT

The Body I Currently Possessed

My plan was to start hiking north on September 25 from Bland, Virginia where I'd stopped in 2007. At my new, slower pace, if the knee and other failing body parts held up, I would make it to Duncannon, PA by November 18. I wished I had the body I'd had the year before, but I only had the body I currently possessed, so I would see what it could do. My PCT hike in the spring had taught me to be thankful for *any* hiking I was able to accomplish. Each step would be a blessing in spite of failing body parts, and I would be happy.

I had a new brace for the left knee, a heavy-duty brace with metal uprights and various bars and straps. The good news was the knee felt better in the brace. I still couldn't quite do six-inch stairs independently, but I was much closer to doing so with the brace. The metal uprights prevented little sideways instabilities causing pains—minor and sometimes major. Its main function was to prevent the tibia (main lower leg bone) from sliding back when the knee bent since my doc thought those little staph buggies had eaten my posterior cruciate ligament, which was supposed to hold the tibia in place

After two days, four airplanes and two rides from angels Bobbie and Linda, my feet were once again on the Appalachian Trail taking me to a shelter that night with four other hikers.

Wind blew softly through the trees, Cicadas were noisy in the woods, and I slept for ten hours.

Sleep does a body good. So does hiking. The trail had large sections of level-ridge walking amid very short ups and downs over mountains often named Brushy. Views were hidden by trees, and there wasn't much fall color. But every now and then, brilliant red or orange shone vividly against the green of the rest of the trees, bringing a smile to my face.

My chances to get to know people would be limited by my slowness of gait and the opposite flow of the main hiker traffic heading southbound in the fall. A few were headed northbound like me. I ate dinner with Gary and Jeff, on their first backpack trip ever, inspired by Bill Bryson's *Walk in the Woods*. They, Mama Llama, and Erin were on the trail with me until Pearisburg. It was a wet stretch. The 10-day forecast was for 70-degree days, 50s in the evening, and no rain. Yeah. Right. It sprinkled, poured, and was very rarely dry all the way to Pearisburg.

Oh well, they needed the rain. Before the rain began, hikers were worried about water. Rocky AT drenched in rain meant an old lady with a bum knee walked very, very carefully.

The AT can have a sameness about it much of the time. After I stopped for a break, I had to think hard to remember which way I'd come *from* and which way I was going *to* as the rhododendron tunnel to the left looked exactly like the rhododendron tunnel to the right. Finally deciding the log was on my right as I came up the trail, I was soon on top of the ridge. Note to self: when stepping off the trail in such terrain, make a note of the desired direction to continue before leaving the trail. There are quite a number of hikers on the AT with the trail name Wrongway. I could see why.

My pack was heavy with food and water, but the weather was better as I climbed out of Pearisburg up Peters Mountain. Somehow, moisture had gotten to my camera even in its case under my raincoat, and it stopped working. Reaching the hill near Rice Field Shelter I set the camera in the sun, after which it briefly cooperated for two pictures of the lovely view before deciding to conk out again.

A younger hiker, Canyon Voice, caught up to me that day; we camped together and enjoyed conversation. It was nice to have congenial company and, as Canyon Voice said, we had a *room with a view* from Symms Meadow. I remarked about a beautiful, very large black snake I'd seen, and Canyon Voice allowed he had friends and relatives who would never put beautiful and snake in the same sentence. We would.

Starting a long section hike, Canyon Voice was trying to let his legs become *trail legs* at a gradual pace. As we walked together through the day, Canyon Voice twice got water for me.

What a sweetie. I also learned about Aqua Mira drops for water treatment. Those drops in little bottles looked much lighter than my filter.

The AT through Georgia, North Carolina and Tennessee ticks off those states fairly quickly. Virginia is another story. Many hikers tire of hiking Virginia long before they run out of Virginia. The trail tread went over rocks, down a few country roads, (mostly for detours) uphill, downhill and over few areas of flat trail. I walked Virginia in the fall.

Sun, foggy days with rain and the changing color of the leaves were all mine, as were lovely views out over valleys and forests, farms and small towns carved out of the forest. Farmlands, pastures, forests and rocky, mountainous terrain meant both cows and deer were common.

Many southbound thru hikers passed me, also day hikers and a few northbounders, their names peppering my journals. I usually stayed in AT shelters, usually simple three-sided affairs, occasionally with multiple levels. Some even had picnic tables nearby or under the cover of an extended roof. Privies were built near most shelters, and it was a wonderful luxury to sit for my morning constitutional compared with squatting over a cat hole I dug for myself on the majority of trails in the western parts of the USA.

Do not be deceived, however, into thinking the AT was always an easy walk in Virginia. The trail went uphill and downhill, over rocks small and large. I was often on ridgelines, which led me to clamber over and around rock after rock, after rock, the size of cars and trucks. It was challenging terrain for a gimpy old lady with a bad knee and what had become an infected toe.

Before Laurel Creek Shelter the trail became more like a trail and less like a rock scramble as I pushed to reach the shelter before dark. Yet on the way down the trail, I was treated to one last beautiful view of valley and mountains with evening shadows highlighting the hills. I stopped to admire the sight even though I was fighting coming darkness. Gradually losing daylight, in October, each day was shorter than the day before.

In another snippet of history, I passed the Audie Murphy

Memorial, made for the most decorated soldier in WWII who'd died in a plane crash nearby, the monument erected by people from Christiansburg.

"Isn't it nice that at our age we can be proud of our age."

The trail was rough, with many large rocks to scramble over or scoot down passing the Dragon's Tooth. If the Dragon's Tooth was an incisor, then I was scrambling over the molars. After baking my camera in the sun, it decided to work once again, giving me the opportunity for a picture of the Dragon's Tooth, a narrow rock sticking straight up into the sky.

North of Dragon's Tooth was even more challenging terrain going down fixed rebar in vertical rock to use as stairs. A younger me would have loved it. Even myself as a gimpy old lady found it interesting. While climbing backwards down rebar steps, I met a man a year younger than me, Teabags from Great Britain, who said. "Isn't it nice that at our age we can be proud of our age." I vowed from then on to consider "old lady" to be a crowning achievement, not a pejorative term.

Bobbie, who had picked me up at the airport, met me four miles in from the trailhead, and we chattered as we walked to the parking lot. Then she drove me to the little country store, so I could purchase a few items before going to The Home Place, a very popular restaurant in the woods for hikers and all sorts of other people, too. We had to wait over an hour to get a table.

Once seated, they brought us fried chicken, choice of roast beef or country ham, cole slaw, corn, green beans, red beans, mashed potatoes, gravy, biscuits and apple butter—all you can eat for $13.00.

After walking on the trail for a week or two, *hiker hunger* is common. A hiker can eat anything not bolted to a table. Hikers love The Home Place. The food was quite good, and we had peach cobbler with ice cream for desert. Yum.

After dinner it was pitch dark, and I had a mile to go to the next shelter. Bobbie took me back to the trailhead, and I started up the trail in the dark with a headlamp containing an almost dead battery. It took an odd size, 6 volts, and the country store didn't have one. Nevertheless, I put the headlamp on low setting to coax as much life out of it as possible and started up the trail. I was to discover the next day that I went *past* the shelter I was aiming for, missing the turnoff in the dark. Eventually the headlamp ran completely out of battery, and there I was on the AT with a pile of rocks on the trail behind me and a pile of rocks on the trail in front of me at last lighted sight. There was no light left from my headlamp, and the moon wasn't bright.

On one side of the trail the hill sloped steeply down and on the other side of the trail it went steeply up. So, being an old lady who didn't want to further damage any more body parts, I stopped. Right there.

I spread the tent on the flat part of the trail and cowboy camped on top of it, taking care that all roll-able objects were on my uphill side. I was safe; my tummy was full; and I ended the day sleeping in the middle of the trail. When it began to get light, two hikers came up the trail as I was sitting in my sleeping bag. I apologized for taking up the trail, and they went around me on the hillside. I hurriedly packed up before more hikers came by.

I continued up the good trail to McAfee Knob, a large shelf of rock sticking out over a drop of several hundred feet, with a breathtaking view. McAfee Knob is the most photographed spot on the AT. I chatted there with Teresa, a Chinese American born in Hong Kong, who took the traditional picture of me sitting on the overhang. It was such a pleasant morning, I could have stayed there for hours with beautiful views and good company.

However, I hike with a hiker plan, and my goal was to go past Tinker Cliffs, another interesting hunk of rocky cliffs with a steep drop on the way to Lambert's shelter. I met Rocky and another Swamp Fox by Tinker Cliffs, and they have stayed in touch on my guest book over the years since then. At Lambert's Shelter, I melted my jacket sleeve reaching over my lit stove and had to patch it with duct tape to keep the down from disappearing into the countryside. Note to self: Don't reach for anything over a lit stove.

The next day I saw two bears. There are more bears on the AT than the Pacific Crest or Continental Divide Trails. Receiving more rainfall, vegetation is thicker on the AT, making wildlife habitat compatible with higher numbers. Also, they didn't seem to be hunted.

The bears I saw were yearlings, not cubs. They didn't see me at first. I stood still, watching them until one turned away from the other and headed straight toward me, still not seeing me. I could have had a smashing picture, but I was a little alarmed at the speed with which the bear was approaching me. Instead of snapping a photo, I waved my hiking poles at him and told him to go somewhere else. Standing on his back legs, he gave me a really good look, perhaps wondering what I was doing on his mountain, before scampering off up the hill along with the other bear. It was a great bear sighting.

When I reached Highway 22, I was met by Michael, the same Michael I'd met the year before on Mather Pass in the Sierra. Michael's trail name was Sugar Daddy because he ate so much candy. So I had a welcome zero day with a young, handsome dude named Sugar Daddy, who was a perfect gentleman to an old lady the age of his grandmother.

"Hello, Dear Friend."

Two nights in a bed. Lovely. Then it took a mile or two on trail to convince my legs they wanted to walk again. Once they were sufficiently warmed up, I headed uphill on a gently graded trail with switchbacks and no large rocks. I was lured .1 mile off trail to Fullhart Knob Shelter by the promise of a privy and an early lunch. As I was eating, Canyon Voice walked up saying, "Hello, dear friend." That's how it is on the trail. When you run into someone again after a few days you are meeting a dear friend.

We hiked most of the afternoon together, chatting. The leaves of the forest understory were turning a bright orange, and we took each other's pictures, the orange leaves matching the orange bandana Canyon Voice wore on his head.

That night there were four in the shelter and good conversation.

The following afternoon, Canyon Voice and I again had lunch together before he went on ahead. His younger legs, deciding to become trail legs, could now outdistance mine. I kept track of him by reading the shelter registers, the gossip line on the AT. News passed up and down the trail by hikers signing the registers, leaving notes for those coming later.

Fall was a good time to hike through Virginia. It was rather warm in the middle of October, with daytime temperatures up to 78. Going uphill with a pack I was always warm, and I frequently shed my shirt to hike in sports bra. I washed sweat from my body each night with water in a quart-size Ziploc bag, enough to get reasonably clean. If I knew water would be scarce, I put soggy wet bandanas in the Ziploc at the last water source to use to clean up when I reached camp.

Many colored leaves fallen to the trail created brightly colored mosaic carpets. Leaves, ridgeline views and striking rock formations made all the up and down worth traveling. Walking under the Guillotine, a narrow path between two sheer trailside vertical rocks with a massive boulder stuck between them, I wasn't decapitated or mangled.

Non-hikers are certain the most dangerous animals on the trail are bears. I respect bears, but the critter who does the most damage is the mouse. Places where hikers congregate draw mice.

Shelters are notorious for them. Even likely camping spots near water have their share. Unprotected food, bandanas and hiking pole grips are all possible bedding, meals or salt mines for mice or other small critters, as well as larger ones like deer.

On this trip I took a small bear can to hold my food. It added weight to my pack, but it was convenient to stop late for the night without having to throw a rope to suspend my food. It was a silly decision weight wise, and eastern oak forests have wonderful horizontal limbs perfect for hanging a food bag. Some areas even have secure metal boxes for food, but mice remain a problem even if food is properly out of reach. Mice startle you awake in the night by running over the top of you. And *quiet as a mouse* is not too quiet. Their scurrying around as you drift toward sleep announces they are around to bother you.

I went up 2,000-foot climbs playing mind games. Carrying an altimeter on my chest strap, I could tell how many vertical feet I walked from the start of the uphill trail. The first hundred feet went by quickly. Then I began to tire and was tempted to look at the altimeter every five or ten steps. Have I only gone fifty-feet up since the last time I looked?

I tried not to look again until I was certain I'd walked another hundred feet in elevation, so I could be encouraged at the sight of changing numbers on the dial. After finally reaching the top for a few brief yards of level trail, I then headed down the other side and the whole process began again. Many days I had 3,000-feet of elevation gain and loss when adding up two or three climbs. The Appalachians may be much lower than the Sierra, Cascades, or Rockies of the West, but up and down works the same way: up and down.

God's Cathedral

I suppose playing mind games to get up two-thousand-foot climbs may not sound like fun to non-hikers, yet the beauty made up for the pain. I had trouble making forward progress because I wanted to stop and take pictures of every tree. The colors were fantastic! The ambient light changed color when filtered through colored leaves. Under bright red leaved trees the light came with a rosy hue, much the same effect as walking in a church with sunlight streaming through stained-glass windows.

I was in God's cathedral with sunlight shining through beautifully colored windows crafted of leaves. In other parts of the forest the sunlight sparkled through green and gold leaves waving in the breeze, the effect like prisms or chandeliers. Only that particular chandelier was 50-feet tall and about as wide.

The 625 feet of the longest pedestrian-only bridge on the AT stretched over the James River. Near the bridge, I met hikers from Roanoke, who knew my trail angels, Linda and Bobbie. Not only did I meet people I'd met before on other trails, I met people who knew people I knew in a growing network of trail connections.

On my zero day in Buena Vista, I ate a foot-long sandwich and wished for a milk shake.

None was to be found, so I consoled myself with milk and Oreo cookies. A funny thing: I couldn't find my pocketknife when I assembled my pack after getting off the airplane. Eighteen days later, while inspecting a rip inside my pack on my zero day in Buena Vista, I found the knife in its traveling plastic bag at the bottom of my hydration pocket in the back of the pack.

For 18 days I'd cut my cheese with my nail file and spread my peanut butter with my sturdy plastic spoon handle. Funny thing is, ever since that emergency replacement of knife with spoon handle, I continue to spread my peanut butter that way. It works more efficiently than the knife ever did. Necessity teaches hikers tricks.

Stopping for a break at Punchbowl Shelter on a hot and sweaty day, Woodman, another hot and sweaty hiker, caught up with me. We leap frogged each other on the trail for days after that. Another snippet of history was Brown Mountain Creek, an area settled by freed slaves who worked as sharecroppers, leaving remnants of their stone walls along the trail. Interpretive signs told me they'd raised corn, oats, tobacco and wheat. I didn't see how they could have grown anything in those narrow valleys full of rocks.

Since the only water source for the evening was a tiny stream half a mile off trail, I detoured, meeting Claw Hammer at the shelter. Woodman arrived before dark to get water, and we all had a lovely evening with congenial company. I slept in the shelter, and Claw Hammer had a hammock between trees. Woodman decided to hike by headlamp up Cold Mountain before stopping, and I didn't know if I would see him again.

Traveling companions popped up for a while and then went on at their own pace as I stuck to my knee-limited speed. Listening to coyotes and owls, I drifted to sleep, only to be startled awake. A large nut tree arched above the shelter and when the wind blew, a nut or two would fall and hit the roof with a sound like a gunshot. No lie.

The accent color in the forest changed from patches of red against green when I started at Bland to patches of green against yellow and brown, one small tree turning white for a pretty contrast. Sumac and other shrubs provided red as the leaf drop thickened on the trail.

Some people think white blazes (six-inch vertical rectangles painted white on trees or rocks, the trail signs for the AT) are ridiculously close together. But if you are hiking in the fall during heavy leaf drop, it is very nice to have all those blazes.

Thick leaves on the trail often looked very much like thick leaves on the rest of the hillside.

Occasionally, I had difficulty finding the next white blaze while wading around in leaves half way to my knees, wondering if I was on the trail before spotting the familiar white rectangle.

Passing an apple tree dropping apples, a green variety with a nice red blush, I picked one up for a taste. It was delicious. Crisp, sweet and juicy. As I took another bite, I was stung by a wasp, who also wanted the apple. I surrendered it to the wasp. I considered the Epi-pen my doc had given me, but just rubbed Cortisone cream on it, which was enough to take care of the problem.

Dutch Haus

I saw Woodman one more time and dropped down Fish Hatchery Road for a zero day at Dutch Haus, a marvelous Bed and Breakfast. Lois and Earl's Dutch descent was reflected in Dutch memorabilia throughout their home, which they shared with hikers. Personal touches abounded in knickknacks, tapestry, quilts and tiffany-style lamps in an atmosphere of comfort and coziness. Thru-hikers frequently don't want to leave, but unless a hiker is physically ill in some very definable way, the stay limit is three nights.

Entering Dutch Haus, smelly hikers are immediately sent to the showers, dirty clothes to the laundry and trash to proper receptacles. Lounging in the provided warm and snuggly bathrobe, pampered the hiker and their bathroom towels had 10 times the fluff of those at the Budget Inn. And food. I ate enormous meals of delicious home-cooked food. If I'd lost any weight hiking I put it all back on. The $15 dinner was well spent and the one-mile walk off trail to get there was totally worth the effort.

After the luxury of Dutch Haus, I started back up Fish Hatchery Road on a 38-degree morning, immediately meeting Daphna and Sara with dog Toby headed down, whom I would see again in the days ahead. Climbing over The Priest, I met Yoyo, a sick hiker spending the day in his sleeping bag in the cold shelter. I recommended Dutch Haus for encouragement, comfort, and care before descending 4.5 quite cold miles bundled up in shirts and down jacket, gloves, and even mitts over the gloves to protect against the cold of my trekking pole handles, quite different weather from three days earlier.

Reaching the bottom of The Priest, I speed climbed the final 2.5 miles, as fast as I could go, fighting gathering darkness. Although only in the 50s, I stripped to sports bra. Going uphill makes me hot even in cold weather and, I don't exactly know why, I hike faster in sports bra.

As I raced up the trail to get to the shelter and my water before dark, I could hear the Boy Scouts before I reached the stream. I stopped to filter water and put on my shirt, but not before a couple of young scouts approached to get water too. They looked a little funny at the strange old lady in her sports bra. Whether that was because I was a strange old lady in a sports bra or because I was in a sports bra when they were in warm sweatshirts, I do not know.

Rockett and John

Loaded up with water, I went looking for the shelter past a sea of Boy Scouts and miscellaneous weekend campers. Pegleg, a mature woman also going for water, said there were only four people in the shelter, and all were *our* age. They were Be Mom, Rockett, and John.

John was nearly 80, someone older than me. The women didn't give their ages. They were super nice folks who had a cheery fire going in the fire pit and tried to be helpful to me as I scurried to get my dinner in the dark.

But in the morning I left my new friends to go up a mountain nearly as high as the Priest, passing more Boy Scouts.

The AT used to go where the Blue Ridge Parkway now runs. In the game of politics, the trail was displaced by the Parkway and now runs through some less smooth and scenic areas, like the mountains of rocks that were mine to climb over that day. Crossing the Parkway again, I camped where some day hikers were leaving a cozy fire.

Starting up Humpback Mountain on a cold morning with blue sky and bright sun, my hands needed gloves, but hiking warmed the rest of me. The trail included lots of built-in rock steps not constructed with women's legs in mind, definitely not in consideration of an aging Grandma with only one leg that could take tall uphill steps. I confused light blue blazes for my AT white ones, a copacetic mistake taking me to Humpback Rocks with an awesome view. An Ohio day-hiking couple took my picture, and I took theirs.

I couldn't get to Rockfish Gap until 5:30, and the Visitor Center closed at 5:00. How could I call my ride? Who was at the top of the trail on the road? Woodman. After some time jabbering together, I used his cell phone to call my ride. Wonderful trail magic awaited me at my B&B in Waynesboro, too. Rockett and John would like to see me on my zero day and provide transportation for whatever I needed.

That VERY busy zero day included a visit to a medical clinic added to all the usual tasks of laundry, stores, and eating as much as possible. All of that running around was facilitated by the owner of the B&B and my new trail friends, Rockett and John.

The doc at the clinic gave me a choice: pulling half my toenail out by the roots or getting antibiotics. Tough choice, huh? I chose antibiotics. Rockett, John, and I thoroughly enjoyed ourselves, talking about lightweight equipment, older-person adventures, and all the possibilities in life.

Bill, a trail angel recruited by Canyon Voice, took me back to the trail. I think Canyon Voice told everyone he met about me. Thanks to Canyon Voice, southbound hikers sometimes greeted me by name, though I'd never met them before. Back on the trail, I watched a beautiful sunset as I put up the tent and saw the lights come on in Waynesboro as darkness descended.

Shenandoah

I awoke to a freezing morning of 30 degrees, though I slept warmly in my down bag. I wore multiple layers to start hiking, but soon shed them. Backpacking is the great warmer-upper in any weather. Well-graded Shenandoah trails were a joy to walk for an old lady with a gimpy knee.

Then came near disaster. I started to sit on a log to rest, but when I reached my left hand to the log, my left knee started to bend, and my right foot skidded out from under me, ambushed by small rolling acorns in the trail under my shoe. They acted like ball bearings. Since my left knee couldn't carry my weight when bent, it folded like an accordion.

Forced maximum flexion is not a recommended way to increase your range of motion. It hurt. A lot. I sat there in the trail for a while hoping the pain would diminish. I did need a break, just not like that. When the pain became bearable, I got up, limped a mile to the shelter and ate my lunch with my leg up on the bench of the picnic table.

My fall could have resulted in much worse damage if I'd not been wearing the brace. The metal rods of the brace prevented much lateral movement or twisting. I was thankful.

With the help of some pain meds, I made it to Loft Campground, where two bucks with very nice points were grooming themselves in my tent site. I asked them to leave, so I could erect my home, and they complied with my request.

Dressed up like Nanook of the North to begin the next cold morning, 15 minutes down the trail I started shedding layers. I was still warm going uphill, but parts open to the icy wind were another matter.

Walking through the woods I watched the seasons change from day to day. Going from Roanoke to the James River, red leaves were an understory of Dogwood. When the wind knocked those leaves off the trees to turn to brown on the forest floor, Sumac gave the red accent color. In the higher Shenandoah the Sumac was leafless, but the maple trees provided red. I learned to identify the distinctive leaves of

Sassafras and Tulip Poplar and already knew the shaggy trunks of Shagbark Hickory.

Most days I met several hikers, SOBOs and NOBOs. No Pliers, Dafnah, Sarah and their dog Toby were NOBO section hikers like me. Our shelter was full that night as we tucked in, a fire in the shelter firepit, a welcome addition on a cold and rainy night.

The next morning no one moved but me as the wind howled and rain fell in torrents. My goal was to reach Swift Run Gap and a ride to a small motel with heat and shower whose owner helped me do laundry and gave me a ride to slack pack from Big Meadows Campground the next day. Win. Win. Win.

The 17.5 miles from the campground to the Gap wouldn't be a long day for most thru- hikers. An old lady with a bum knee and a very early start could handle the distance only as a slack pack. It took me 10 hours without a pack but with an hour stop at Lewis Mountain Camp Store for lunch and visiting with Sarah and Dafnah. The wind had whipped most of the leaves from the trees over 3,500 feet, leaving winter-like views between tree trunks. An older couple gave me a ride back to my motel, so they could ask me about light-weight gear on the way.

Cold

A massive cold front moved through the nation, and that day traveling to Skyland the temperature never even hit 40. I still sweated going uphill but didn't take off many layers during the day. In spite of inclement weather, there were still a few day hikers on the trail.

On the way to a cabin at Skyland, I walked very carefully through the fallen leaves trying to disguise rolling rocks, holes, and other pitfalls. Two nights at Swift Run Gap and a night at Skyland, I'd managed to be inside for three nights and had showers three days in a row. How positively civilized was that? I also ate lots of pricey, but good food.

In the morning, a dusting of snow and very cold wind made it difficult to find the right combination of layers to wear. On a cold day, sweating is not a good thing, as wet clothing chills you when you stop for a break. Yet the cold seeps into your bones on breaks, if you dress to avoid sweating. I settled on fleece plus rain jacket to keep me warm and cut the wind. For most of the morning I kept the hood up over my white hat and adjusted the heat escape by the front zipper, unzipped when walking, closed when stopped.

The snow was pretty, but the wind fiercely howled many decibels high all day, like hiking beside a jet continuously taking off. With a temperature in the thirties plus wind chill, the effective temperature was exceedingly cold. It was windy. It was a nice day. Really. The views were glorious. I even took the .1-mile side trail to see St Mary's Rock. It seemed like a Mary should. Little Stony Man and The Pinnacle added more vistas.

The temperature in the shelter was 37 the next morning, and on the trail it dropped to 32. Even three-sided shelters were warmer than trail without those three sides. The sun tried hard to fight the powerful cold front, once getting up to 49, a veritable heat wave.

Another cold morning dawned, and I ate breakfast in bed, savoring the warmth of my sleeping bag until the last minute before packing up. I left the shelter while watching the sky turn red before the sun cleared the horizon. Then the sky was blue, and sun in the sky promised warmth.

Oak leaves were the last to fall. Some were quite pretty, a brown, green, yellow and reddish mix, sometimes all four colors on the same leaf. In the sunshine and the breeze they sparkled with a bronze tinge. On top of the Marshalls, the wind made drifts of leaves, and I waded through knee-high piles of swishing brown.

Throughout the Shenandoah I saw no bears. Perhaps they were already holed up for winter. But there were many, many deer, often heard bounding up in the rustling leaves before I saw them.

Bathed in Yellow and Orange Leaves and the Light Shining Through Them

As I descended from the Shenandoah the trails changed from

relatively smooth National Park trails to steeply pitched piles and piles of rocks. I changed from the confident hiker, though aged, to a tottering old lady, picking her way down the rocks. The last few miles into Front Royal changed to nice trail, and for one last 300-400 foot climb it was so warm I stripped to sports bra, a nice change from snow and freezing cold.

The hitchhiking grandma did well coming to Front Royal. I stuck out my thumb, and the third car stopped. A nice grandfatherly man gave me a ride and found the Scottish Inn for me. Long-distance hikers have no cars, at least with them. They are quite dependent on the good will of perfect strangers. I have met hundreds of such wonderful people over years of long-distance hiking. Hiker grapevines also help identify trail angels willing to provide transportation.

November 1 was a lovely day. It was sports-bra weather all day long through trees still clothed in colorful leaves at lower elevations. I had a positively decadent late start at 9:00. The next day, daylight savings time would change to standard time. I would need to get to my stopping point for the day by 4:30-5:30, and hiker midnight would be before 7:00.

That sounded so different. Yet it was, in reality, not very different from the day before. Changing time seemed an artificial construct while hiking. The only thing important was how many hours of daylight there were to walk. Calling it Daylight Savings Time or Standard Time was irrelevant. Still, it would seem strange to stop as early as the clock would say it was in November.

Reaching the shelter by 5:30 I had plenty of time to get my water, bathe the sweaty parts of me, and get dinner before dark. How nice to still be warm enough to bathe. I always felt like a new woman, sweat removed. If it was cold, I could live with the sweat and dirt. As I fell asleep that night, I listened to crickets again singing in the warmth.

Sunrise was especially striking, a brilliant red-orange ball before it rose and hid behind a cloud. The forest was beautiful. I felt positively bathed in yellow and orange leaves and the light shining through them, baptized in the light of God's love in yellow and orange, a nice Sunday image.

The next day was even better. The *roller coaster* (a section of continuous up and down hills) was everything it was cracked up to be, but then a whole lot more. It was a glorious day. Oh yeah, it went steeply uphill and downhill repeatedly, and there were lots and lots of rocks under foot. But the forest. Oh my, the forest was gorgeous, a riot of color, the most color I'd seen on the whole trip. After the wind had blown away most of the leaves on the high peaks of the Shenandoah, this lower area bloomed with a riot of yellows, oranges, and reds. Magnificent.

All the beauty took my mind off the struggle up and down the roller coaster of hills, and I marveled that I was the only one seeing it on that particular day. So much beauty and so fleeting a time before all those leaves would fall, brought me to tears. So many beautiful things in life are fleeting. I rejoiced that I could behold that particular forest at that particular time.

I recommend the *roller coaster* in the fall, late fall. A big advantage of section hiking is to choose the time of year best for a particular section of trail. Why go through the roller coaster in sweltering June or July? Pick early November. I was so glad I did. I finally saw two other hikers on the last hill before Bears Den, a hostel in a beautiful old stone building and another iconic AT stop. Bears Den used to be the private residence of a wealthy physician and his opera-singer wife. It looked like a stone castle, or at least the manor house. Red Wing and Hopeful, two former thru-hikers, and their very sweet, almost two-year-old daughter, were the caretakers.

I ate dinner with Red Wing and Hopeful, and in the morning I fixed myself pancakes, using pancake mix and syrup left in the community food section of the hostel. I fixed and ate two batches of pancakes, 12 pancakes, all by myself. And it wasn't even hard to do. Oink, Oink.

West Virginia

I said *good-bye* to Virginia as I passed the sign welcoming me to West Virginia. I'd made it through more than 600 miles of trail winding through Virginia. The forest wasn't as glorious as the day before, but still pretty, just a little farther along in the season, the leaves not so brilliant and darkening to browns. The reds were more burgundy, but burgundy is a nice color, too.

I stayed at Blackburn Trail Center that night, another big old beautiful house that was a private residence, yet also a free hostel for hikers. Hikers could sleep in a bunkhouse or on the covered, screened-in porch that went around three sides of the house. I chose the porch for the view and the daylight in the morning to wake me up.

No one was in residence but me. However, after a couple people passed by, I felt nervous to be there alone. So I latched all the doors to the screened in porch. Just a screen for protection.

Silly, perhaps, but latching the screen doors made me feel safer.

As I ate my dinner I noticed an unusually tall light in the distance. My guidebook told me the Washington Monument in Washington DC could be seen from Blackburn Trail Center. I drank my cocoa listening to an owl while watching the lights on the Washington Monument in the distance. Amazing.

The Washington Monument was still lit as I ate breakfast in bed in the pre-dawn hours, and I saw nine deer within two hours of leaving on a nice, warm day. Fortunately I still had my shirts on when I passed a class of 5th and 6th graders on a hiking field trip. I enjoyed being show and tell for the day as they and their leaders asked me many questions about the AT.

Before descending to Harpers Ferry, I met Boone and Follower, two SOBO thru hiking brothers, who had started from Katahdin on September 17. Wow. They'd passed many other thru-hikers and were more than half done with the trail in just a bit more time than it had taken me to do 400 miles. Ah, youth.

Arriving at Harper's Ferry, I went to the AT Conservancy Headquarters to pick up my food drop and add my picture to their records. A very nice previous thru-hiker gave me a ride to my hostel, a building built in 1840. I slept in a brass bed in a house reeking of history in the Old Town of Harper's Ferry.

People must have been smaller in 1840, judging from the headroom on the doorways and staircase. The shower had a wall of the local shale. I couldn't remember seeing a rock wall in a shower other than the house our family built in the side of a hill in Colorado when I was a kid. I played tourist on my zero day in Harpers Ferry, far more than a snippet of history to see.

If there was a museum or exhibit I missed, it wasn't for lack of trying. I toured the buildings and exhibits in the lower town telling the story of John Brown and the role of Harpers Ferry in the Civil War.

The natural setting was also quite striking as the Potomac and Shenandoah Rivers joined from each side before plunging through the gap in the Blue Ridge Mountains to the sea. The river was the reason for the town's existence, providing water power for industry. The river was also the reason the town almost died, because of floods.

Thomas Jefferson said the view from what is now called Jefferson Rock was worth a trip across the Atlantic. He may have been a bit of a romantic, but I agreed the view was lovely and took a photo of river, the old church spire and bright red sumac. George Washington did surveying in the area as a youth and was responsible for the establishment of the armory.

My health was holding good. My toe had finally healed. The ups and downs of the roller coaster seemed to have made my bad knee a little stronger. I still couldn't independently do stairs, but perhaps I could do them more easily with poles or a railing than I could before the hike.

That night I listened to the echo off the cliffs in the gorge when the train whistles blew.

"I had a choice?"

Leaving Harpers Ferry, I crossed the Potomac into Maryland for three level and enjoyable miles on the towpath, canal and railroad on one side and Potomac River on the other, a treat to have level miles. A 1,500-foot climb followed but wasn't terribly challenging. The only bad thing was a tummy upset from the burger I'd had the night before. That night on standard time it was dark at 6:00, and not long after 6:30, I was asleep.

On a Saturday with beautiful, clear fall weather so near to Washington DC, I must have seen 100 people on the trail. I also passed the Washington Monument, not the one in Washington DC, the *original* Washington monument, built by the people of Boonesboro in 1827, constructed of stone in the shape of an old-fashioned milk bottle and used as a lookout tower by Federal troops in the Civil War. I might never have known that charming bit of history without walking trails.

In spite of nearness to civilization, I saw bear scat on the trail. By nightfall I was reminded of nature's biggest critter problem. A knowledgeable hiker who passed me recommended against staying at Devil's Racecourse shelter, as it was very near a road, and some locals liked to party there. So I left my pack on the AT and went down .3 mile to get water to haul back up to my camp on the ridge above the shelter.

There are advantages to tents. They are usually warmer than shelters as the tent is not open on a whole side. The forest floor is much softer to sleep on than a shelter's board floors and my belongings were more confined and easier to reach in my tent. But I had a hard time convincing myself of all that when the shelters were so handy and required no set up or take down. They'd come to feel like my own private bedroom. What? I can't sleep in my bedroom because carousing strangers might be using it? It seemed a violation of my private space. Of course, it wasn't solely my private space, but each shelter had come to feel like home, at least my home for the night.

Another cold front coincided with crossing from Maryland into Pennsylvania. Penmar Park was all closed down for the winter under steely gray skies. Earlier in the day, I'd met one day hiker and then a whole bunch of Outward Bound hikers from a Baltimore High School. It was fun to talk with them, and they gave me Oreo cookies. Yum.

My tummy upset after leaving Harpers Ferry was only a memory, and all systems were working in the privy at Deer Lick Shelter. It was a very cold 31 degrees as I settled into my sleeping bag wearing everything I had with me, I woke up at 1:30 AM with severe abdominal pain. Sitting up seemed to ease the pain. But sitting up soon made me cold and I snuggled back down into my sleeping bag to get warm again. Then pain would return, forcing me to sit up again. I slept off and on for a few more hours, but kept waking in pain.

Finally, just before dawn, I got up, collected my things and started slowly walking to the road. My belly was so bloated that my pants were at least four inches from closure. Those same pants had seemed an inch or two too big for me the day before due to weight loss from hiking. There was no cell phone service to call for help. There were no other hikers on the trail. It was a very long two miles to the road. I walked slowly as any jolting step increased the pain in my gut. I was very glad it was only two miles as I focused on reaching the road.

The second car to pass by stopped. Was I getting good at hitch-hiking or what? It might have been due to pain lines etched across my face. The lady who stopped told me she knew I was in pain.

She took me to the Bible Church in South Mountain where she was a pre-school teacher, and I used their phone to call the Rev John Spangler from Gettysburg Lutheran Seminary where I'd been planning to stay for the next two nights. It was a long wait with increasing bouts of excruciating pain until he arrived to play ambulance driver, taking me to Gettysburg Hospital where I was x-rayed, CT scanned, and had my heart, my blood, and my urine checked. I had an intestinal blockage and was admitted to the hospital.

The nurses expressed amazement that I'd been able to walk out two miles with an intestinal blockage. I looked at them and asked, "I had a choice?" Of course I walked out. There was no choice.

They were kind and let me get a quick shower before hooking up the IV. It was probably kind to everyone else, too, since it had been five days since my last shower in Harper's Ferry. I was given painkillers, antibiotics, and a nasogastric tube. The hiker was tethered to the bed by tubes. I guessed hiking was done for the year. Ya think?

I responded very quickly to conservative treatment and was glad when the docs stopped using phrases about possible surgery. An American Methodist Episcopal seminary student chaplain's assistant (That's a mouthful for a title.) at the hospital agreed to pick up my last resupply box from Boiling Springs, which I would now not reach. The kind folks at Holly Springs B&B took my reservation cancellation, quite concerned that I find needed transportation to my daughter in New York.

John Spangler took my gear and washed all my filthy hiking clothes while I was clothed in a hospital gown. The staff at the hospital was very caring and efficient. Another chaplain visited with me the next day as well as two more local clergy alerted by the Washington Synod prayer chain's contacts across the country. An extraordinary amount of pastors gave pastoral care to one hiking pastor.

John Spangler and his wife just *happened* to be going on a quick trip to New Hampshire to visit their daughter and they drove me straight to Troy, delivering me to mine. All of that care went way beyond trail magic. Thanks be to God!

I had so very much for which to be thankful. I was thankful to be able to hike long distance hikes in spite of advancing age and injuries. I was thankful I was able to get to a hospital when I needed to. I was thankful for all the trail angels, who had helped me along the way. I was thankful for my family, grandchildren in Washington State and New York State.

Crowning the list was the birth of my fifth grandchild, 13 days after I left the trail. You can hardly beat that for an ending to a hike. You can hardly beat that even if you are not hiking.

Chapter 16 Winter 2008-2009

Decrepitude and a Dog

Another year. Another two or three hikes to look forward to. I spent the winter planning hikes.

My doctors had no idea why I'd had a hike-ending bowel blockage in 2008, nor did they have any idea if I would ever have another. It didn't seem to be connected to the trail except that I happened to be on the trail when it happened.

My friend Kathy and I often joked about our ages and states of decrepitude and rejoiced that we still hiked anyway. There is not just one way, one age, one time in life to hike. I still found it quite difficult to go up and down 6-inch stairs. But hiking with poles was just walking with two canes. HA.

Not only were Kathy and I still hiking, even though we had failing body parts, so was her dog. Tasha was then 15 years old, pretty darn old for a dog. In the fall she seemed to have a couple of strokes, losing the ability to walk, only able to drag herself around the house with her front legs. Kathy tenderly cared for her furry friend. After a few months, Tasha suddenly started to walk again. She limped and sometimes fell. She was pretty deaf. But she still loved to go out with us on day hikes. She was fitted with a bootie for the foot that dragged to protect it from abrasions, and we *three old ladies* still hiked. Tasha inspired us.

On a cold, wet spring in the northwest, 6th snowiest year ever, I managed to get my spring garden in, though I'd had to till some frozen chunks of ground to do it. The seeds were promptly covered in snow but survived to grow while I hiked on the PCT.

On one rare sunny day, Kathy and I hiked up Mt. Si with nearly full packs. It was a milestone for me, the first time I could make that climb since knee surgery and infection. I was certain I should have hiked more before heading to Southern California. But I was in whatever shape I was in, ready and eager to go. I planned what I thought were pretty reasonable days to start. I would find out if I'd have the same opinion when I got there.

Chapter 17 March 31, 2009 PCT

Greeting Flowers Like Old Friends

Liz drove me up to Three Points, and off I went. Oops. I almost had a major disaster, leaving my maps, book pages, and permits in the car. Liz saw them and beeped her horn hoping I would hear, even though I'd already gone up the trail and quickly out of sight. Fortunately, I did hear the horn and her calling me.

Returning to the car, I put the maps in my pocket where they belonged and started off again.

After leaving Liz, I saw no people all day. It was still, quiet, peaceful hiking. I loved the pine forests on the shoulders of Pacifico Mountain and kept trying to think of excuses to stop, sit in the sun, and enjoy the peace. Finding a log to sit on, I listened to the silence.

I'd discovered great joy in hiking solo. I liked hiking with other people. I liked having company. But starting out on a morning solo, having the whole world in front of me waiting for my steps to take me wherever the trail would lead was a marvelous feeling. The world before me was mine, just waiting for me to come and see it. My footprints were the only ones in the patches of snow over 6,000 feet. That is, they were the only ones except for the very clear, fresh-looking bear tracks with distinct toes.

However, I saw no bears on the way to the campground, campsites set in pine trees near granite boulders. The amenities included picnic tables, a privy, and bear-proof trash cans with a door on the back that could be lifted to show a space for food bags. After dinner, washing up, and brushing my teeth, I snuggled into my bag and tent at 7,124 feet, hoping for a nice morning sunrise.

Instead, the wind blew ferociously all night, ripping the tent loose from its moorings in the early morning. I was surprised the tent had lasted that long. In high winds at 34 degrees, I packed up and got the heck out of there. It wasn't the most auspicious start.

The day warmed up for a pleasant walk on nicely graded trail. I had views to the valley or out to the Mojave, depending on the direction I looked. Low hills in the distance were covered in orange poppies, and I saw quail, ravens, chipmunks, squirrels and a few lizards. That night I slept peacefully with no wind.

A runner and a dog came up behind me on the trail. Correction, a lot of runners, all wearing bright-orange pants with PRISONER printed on them. I must have camped near a correctional institution. Thirty or more prisoners out for their PT run panted a polite *hello* as they passed.

Well, that was interesting.

Reacquainting myself with flowers I'd seen last year, I walked three days to Soledad Canyon. The lower I dropped in elevation, the more flowers abounded: popcorn phacelia, chia, fiddlenecks, miners lettuce, baby blue eyes, bush poppy, gilia, whispering bells, wall flower, and witches hats. I loved the desert flowers, greeting them by name seemed like I was greeting old friends, bringing gladness to my heart.

Later in the day there were blue dicks, yerba santa, paintbrush, comet, lupine, more poppies, Canterbury bells, globe gilia, gold fields, coreopsis and rattlesnake weed. Ah, it was so good to be hiking again.

Having dinner at the trailer park saved having to carry water uphill to my cowboy camp in the middle of the trail below the top of a gap, the only spot out of the wind I could find. I'd seen only one day-hiker in four days, the trail my personal possession. At dusk, the moon shone brightly over my head.

In the pink rock formations of Vasquez Rocks, the next day I could see Captain Kirk and Spock in my mind's eye on the same trail where a few episodes of Star Trek had been filmed. A horse trailer drove up as I was finishing lunch. The guy with the horses looked just like Mendo Rider (PCT equestrian from last year). No, wait, it WAS Mendo Rider. Great surprise meeting.

"Hello, Medicare Pastor."

In the grocery store in Aqua Dulce, I turned around when someone said, "Hello, Medicare Pastor." Jeff Saufley, just dropping in to get something at the store, gave me a ride the extra mile to the Saufleys, trail angels I'd met in 2007. I'd informed them of my schedule, so they knew when I was coming. Instead of having a hundred hikers in their yard at Hiker Heaven, as they would have in early April, it was just me. I had the whole spare trailer to myself and luxuriated in the shower while my clothes were washing.

The trailer was filled with thoughtful hiker amenities: multiple plug-ins to charge electronics, two computers, a TV, DVD player, libraries of movies and books, a piano, a guitar, a Navajo flute, music CDs, etc. There was even a Bible and the AA Big Book. Saufleys are nothing if not accommodating. It was a great place to spend a zero day.

That Palm Sunday rest day I attended the little community church with Mendo Rider and his wife. I had a mild panic attack in the afternoon when my hike plan went missing. I sent out a "Help. Help." to my friend Kathy by email, and the next morning Donna came over with a new printout of my hike plan. Saved again.

The climb out of Agua Dulce and up the Sierra Pelona Ridge was very hard. It was hot, no shade to speak of as I went up 2,100 feet. I stopped a few times to rest and give body parts a break. But I had to stop for lunch a half mile or so before the top as I just couldn't go any farther without fuel. Fortunately for me, I found a bit of shade on some nice grass and Miners Lettuce and made myself eat, even though the heat had taken away my appetite. A hiker without an appetite was rare, especially this hiker. I stretched out on the grass and dozed for half an hour after eating and felt better.

Oaks shaded the trail on the north side of the ridge. After cleaning the box surrounding the spring at Bear Spring, I filled my water bottle, my knee liking my messing around at the spring more than hiking. Descending to Bouquet Canyon and seeing a bee swarm, I remembered an old saw, "A swarm in May is worth a load of hay. A swarm in June is worth a silver spoon. A swarm in July isn't worth a fly." (Bees need to gather nectar for a summer to survive a winter.)

Reaching Bouquet Canyon, I found no water at the cache, but the stream still ran with pools deep enough to filter. I set up camp tucked in the undergrowth so as not to be seen from the road, and as it started to get dark I looked for my headlamp and found it missing. I'd left it hanging on the bedpost at Hiker Heaven. Silly me. That was the third thing I'd misplaced. I needed a keeper.

Ah, the desert. First it fries you by day, and then it freezes you by night. There was a heavy dew in the early part of the night, but by the time I woke, everything not in the sleeping bag or pack was covered with frost.

In the afternoon I came to the Oasis water cache created and maintained by the Andersons, the next set of iconic trail angels. Besides having several camping chairs, REAL CHAIRS, a treat for a hiker, they'd decorated the little cove in the scrub oak with skeletons of various kinds, a blow-up monkey hanging from the branches, a palm tree, flamingos, and other odd surprises. Oh yeah, there was water, too, and a cooler full of ice, tangerines, and other goodies. Not wanting to leave a chair un-sat-in, I sat in one and ate a tangerine.

Donna and Jeff were hiking behind me that day. They liked to be on the trail as well as to care for scruffy hikers. The early part of the season, before the big influx of hikers, was their time for hiking. That night at the Andersons there was a mini trail angel convention with the Saufleys, Andersons, Roger and me, I the lone non-angel hiker. Terrie served her famous Taco Salad, and everyone sat around talking until midnight, real midnight, not hiker midnight.

Joe and Terrie gave me the bed in the spare bedroom, perhaps because they knew I was a pastor. But Terrie wasn't too intimidated about my being a pastor to give me her traditional *mooning* as I left the Casa de Luna, though Joe was a little aghast. I was honored just to be considered a hiker.

Joe drove me back to the trailhead, and I started out up the hill, up definitely the direction for the first couple miles, up into clouds that hid the mountain tops and blew back and forth across the valley, playing peek-a-boo with views and casting shadows playfully over hills and desert below me. The clouds eventually produced some showers as Donna walked up behind me with a cheerful *hello*. She said the Andersons would be there shortly with fresh water for the cache and for us. So we stood there chatting in the rain and taking pictures of each other in raingear in *sunny* Southern California.

I loaded up another two liters of water when the Andersons arrived. Jeff, who had not been feeling well in the morning, decided to hike on with Donna—but first, they all went for lunch someplace. Strong hikers can take their time and do such things. Me, I just had to keep going. I trudged up the hill on another long climb, this time with four more pounds of water, which meant I didn't do nearly as well as in the morning. My campsite in a lovely glade of Black Oaks on a grassy hillside came with a picnic table, a pleasant surprise after walking through miles of desert chaparral separated by patches of scrub oak. Jeff and Donna came by while I was fixing dinner; they were aiming for another three miles.

Hiking strongly and early the next day, I passed the turn off to the campsite where the Saufleys were staying. Their footprints didn't continue, so I knew they were still in camp. While stopping to filter a liter of water from a trickling stream across the trail, Donna and Jeff caught up to me. We hiked together, chatting, before they again outdistanced me, playing leapfrog until after lunch when they passed me for the last time. What fun to hike with such gracious and interesting people. I made nine miles before lunch, though I stopped a little late to do it, pleased at such good time for a decrepit old lady.

On Good Friday I sang some of Holden Evening Prayer and hymns from the Tenebrae Service as I walked beside bright-green miner's lettuce on the forest floor beneath large oaks. Although the knee complained, I walked quickly down long switchbacks with views of lower hills, Antelope Valley, and the Tehachapi Mountains.

Solid banks of flowers covered hillsides with yellow, white, blue, or purple. Bright yellow daisies and chia lined the trail; later, clumps of lupine filled the air with fragrance. I walked between two different weather systems. Behind me over the mountains big black thunderclouds were building with menacing rumbles; on the desert side the sun shone.

Hiker Town was across the highway and on the corner, a touristy hiker place, done up like an Old West town complete with dummies dressed in period costumes. Slim, a hiker who hung around the trail working odd jobs for folks, suggested I sleep in the jail, but there was already a dummy on the bed, so I took up residence for the night in a trailer bunkhouse instead. It was a good night to be inside, the trailer shaking in the fierce wind of another storm. I hoped Donna and Jeff were OK up ahead at Cottonwood Creek Canyon.

Crossing the Mojave from Hiker Town on a cold, extremely windy day the Tehachapi Mountains sported a fresh blanket of snow ahead of me. Walking on a flat desert over aqueducts taking water to LA, water was important to me as well as city folks far away. But that water wasn't accessible to a hiker. When I spilled a liter by accident, I rationed water the rest of the day.

In a serious mishap, the wind blew my maps and guidebook pages right out of my pocket. I reached for them and felt nothing there. No sign of paper anywhere in sight; they were probably miles away over the desert by the time I noticed them missing.

Reaching Cottonwood Creek I found the water cache, and I found Heinz, an older German day hiker in an RV van. He had a copy of the guidebook, and I quickly and furiously scribbled notes and drew maps to hold me until my next resupply box holding maps and pages for further up the trail. Saved again and again. If I didn't lose so many things I wouldn't have to be saved so many times.

Easter Parade

Easter morning was gloriously memorable. The morning went smoothly with one glitch: I became temporarily disoriented. (Mountaineer euphemism for being lost.) Well, I wasn't exactly lost. I knew where I'd last seen a trail sign, and I knew I was on the ridge above Tyler Horse Canyon. I also knew I was no longer on the trail. I'd followed one of the many trails made by bikers, and it put me on a jeep road on the ridge.

I could hear water running in Tyler Horse Canyon below me, but my altimeter said I was nowhere near the elevation I needed to be when I would descend to it. So, I just went up the road. Eventually I saw a PCT sign on the westward ridge running parallel to me and saw it would meet my jeep road. I didn't lose the trail again.

Gold Fields put on a flower show as did a really nice stand of Globe Gilia. The rest of the afternoon the flower show became a breathtaking Easter Parade. Whole hillsides were covered with yellow daisies and desert dandelions, alternating their yellows with gorgeous carpets of blue and white of low growing flowers, whose name I didn't know. Hillsides burst with a profusion of colors: white, pink, orange yellow, blue, purple, maroon, and lemon yellow.

These hills had burned sometime in the past, leaving Joshua Trees and Oaks as just a few charred-and-weathered stumps and branches. The foothills of the Tehachapi Mountains were mostly piles of decomposed granite sand, and between the burn and the bike riders, much of the footing was very unstable, like walking on tall, steep sand dunes.

But ah, the flowers! The flowers were trying mightily to stabilize the hillside. I felt I was committing a grave sin any time I stepped on a tenacious flower trying to bring stability and beauty to that sandy hillside. I developed a great antipathy for the bike riders, who had scoured paths of uprooted flowers wherever they'd gone joy riding.

The PCT takes a deep curve west from San Jacinto to Agua Dulce around the Mojave Desert before gradually going east again. The views were wondrous across the Mojave to the San Gabriel Mountains and all the way down to San Jacinto, many days' walk south of me trail-wise.

Twisted and contorted skeletons of Joshua Trees reigned over the views as I followed the Saufley's footsteps over sand-covered hills through more fields of flowers down to Gambol Canyon. In June, when the main body of hikers would come through Tyler Horse and Gambol, the flower displays would be gone, and they would see only sand. How truly blessed I was to have seen those flowers as an Easter Sunday gift. Section hiking has its rewards.

Many more flowers lined the trail on the way out to Willow Springs Road, also going over more old burn areas, weathered and whitened remains of Joshua Trees on the ridge looked like ghost dancers on the skyline.

For 40 minutes on a quite cold and windy afternoon, I had my thumb out to hitch at Willow Springs Road. My luck wasn't good as the cars were speeding by too fast for drivers to register my need before they disappeared past me. I would have had better luck at a turn in the highway just a bit further if I'd read Yogi's Town Guide.

Cars slow down on a turn, hikers can be seen better in that sloweddown space, and a ride might have materialized more quickly. Ken, a retired State Patrolman, did stop, asking me what I was doing out there in the middle of nowhere. He took me in to the town of Mojave, even though it was twelve miles out of his way.

In Mojave, I took a heavenly shower. I didn't think I was *that* dirty, but the black on the washcloth said differently. Mojave turned into a two- day zero, although only one had been planned. In the first attempt to get back to the trail, I found the storm had left an ice-covered road blocked off with orange cones.

Returning to Mojave, I ate meals at Denny's and had the best hot-fudge sundae ever, gifted with a bowl of extra hot fudge when I told the waitress, who now knew me after my four previous meals, how much I loved hot fudge. Yum. I also arranged a needed transportation piece by asking the server if she knew any *regulars* who might help me. Roberta, a wonderful little red-haired lady of 80 volunteered.

After I slack packed over some quickly melting snow and ice to Cameron Pass, Roberta met me with my gear. She also brought me dinner and cookies, which I ate even though it was only mid-afternoon. She refused to let me give her money for dinner or gas. Saying she was having fun, she proceeded to regale me with many tales from her 50+ years of living in Mojave and being a nurse. She was a delight.

After that lovely bit of trail magic, it was up the hill to find a tent spot among the Joshua trees, searching for shelter from the strong wind. I finally made my choice of spot tucked behind Junipers and Joshua trees without too many sharp desert pointy things. And then the wind shifted so that my tent was no longer sheltered.

I built a rock wall toting rocks from the ravine. The Incas built better walls with no mortar, but mine wasn't too bad. However, the wind blew even stronger, and the inside of the tent was catching windblown dirt. In disgust, I collapsed the tent and cowboyed on top of it. My rock wall and the juniper had a better chance of protecting me from the wind and the dirt, and I didn't have to listen to the tent noisily flapping all night.

Watching the sunrise the next morning, I listened to some sort of hen clucking in the ravine. Hiking uphill, I shortly took off coat, gloves, and both shirts to hike in sports bra. Two and a half hours later, I was 2,000 feet higher, and the weather changed from the icestorm, which had closed roads four days earlier to a sports-bra day. Flowers cheered me, and at 6,000 feet there were again pines and oaks.

Two far-away snowy mountains peeked over the farthest range of mountains to the north. I cowboy camped that night near enough to Golden Oak Spring to hear frogs singing.

"Yer head's leakin'."

I carried five liters of water uphill north of Golden Oak Spring on a nice warm day in the 80s. On some long, exposed stretches I passed windmills turning noisily to make electricity.

Green Miners Lettuce abounded on the hillsides, and there were enough flowers to entertain me. I loved to hike with just my sports bra, but my right arm was rather sunburned from the walk between Tyler Horse and Gambol Spring Canyon.

The last two days I'd been popping perspiration blisters under dead skin and was beginning to peel. I would look like I had an exotic skin disease when I saw people at the annual Kickoff at Lake Morena.

Reaching a lovely broad meadow under oak trees by 2:45, it was too early to stop for the night, so I decided to stop for a long break and have my dinner, which would rid my pack of another liter of water weight before going up the next hill. Stretching out in the shade on my foam sit pad with my legs up over my pack, I used a little of the water I'd lugged to wash face, hands, legs and feet. I even gave myself a manicure, at least I cut and cleaned my nails, and put some much needed lotion on my hands.

This scene of complete contentment was rudely interrupted by a tick that decided to bite my leg. I pulled the bugger out with a steady hand on my nail clippers, working them like tweezers, hoping he hadn't been carrying anything nasty. I remembered taking a tick off another hiker's back from under her bra strap when I was a Girl Scout. I hoped none would bite me somewhere I couldn't see or reach to remove.

Non-hikers always think bears are the most dangerous animal on the trail. Mice cause the most damage to gear. But the most dangerous animal is the tiny tick. I have known several hikers forced to leave the trail with Lyme or other diseases carried by ticks, some of which can have lasting systemic effects causing lifelong problems. I have not known anyone attacked by a bear.

After my two-hour rest with ticks and dinner, I finally packed up and went onward at 5:00. I enjoyed hiking in the late afternoon and evening when the sun wasn't so hot and I was rewarded with beautiful meadows filled with baby blue eyes.

As I was puffing up a hill, glad I wasn't in the direct sun, along came Billy Goat. Really. Billy Goat was then a 70-year-old PCT hiker. He is now a friend and quite famous, having been on the cover of the PCT Communicator, on the front page of the Los Angeles Times in 2008, and the subject of an article in Backpacker Magazine in 2017. He still hikes long trails, though pushing into his 80s. I'd met him at Kickoff in 2008, but meeting him on the trail made us friends.

Billy Goat was ambling down the trail SOBO as I was puffing uphill NOBO. He said we should chat a bit. Panting, with sweat pouring down my face, I was only too glad to do so. While chatting, Billy Goat looked at the sweat running into my eyes and said in a completely deadpan voice and a twinkle in his eyes, "Yer head's leakin'."

I laughed and laughed. It really struck my funny bone. I remember the line every time sweat pours into my eyes on an uphill trail, and I have another good chuckle.

Billy Goat said he was impressed that I, a woman over 65, (then 67) was hiking the trail. He said he didn't meet many of that age and gender who did. He said I was an inspiration. Me? An inspiration to a trail icon like Billy Goat? Amazing. I was just another hiker, although older and slower than most. It made my day.

When the forest changed from tall trees to shorter ones, I found a barely, sort of flat spot in the middle of a large, open clearing and cowboy camped under millions of stars in the night sky. Life was good.

In the night though, I had one of those *what's out there?* nervous feelings. Nothing came into the large cleared area in which I'd placed my sleeping bag. But in the morning back on the trail, there were cougar footprints in the soft granite sand, disappearing after about a mile and a half in the middle of nowhere. The prints looked fresh as they were sometimes on top of Billy Goat's footprints, the only hiker I'd seen the evening before. I wondered if the cougar might have been the source of my *sixth-sense of danger* in the night.

Seeing critter prints is fun as long as nothing is threatening, and rarely do any animals stay close to humans or threaten them. Mostly, I saw lizards. Still, I was glad I'd camped in a very large open area, which may have deterred the cougar.

An unmarked trail left a dirt road, and I couldn't decide if it was *my* trail. I walked down both directions, while rereading the guidebook pages and staring at maps before I decided the trail I'd walked down first was the correct one. My dithering around being stupid took more than an hour and a half and an awful lot of energy, physical and mental, as well as two extra miles.

Tiredly reaching Robin Bird Spring, I sat down for a late lunch.

The top pipe to the trough at Robin Bird Spring had no water, but there was a nice stream from the low pipe below the trough. I was dirty and disgusted with myself for having walked a one-mile stretch of trail three times in confusion, so I took a bath. I could fill my pot with water for bathing while standing naked in the sunshine and dispose of used water well away from the spring. Bathing helped my mental attitude, and I also washed my socks, undies, shirts, and bandanas and hung them to dry on the fence around the spring. Reasonably clean, I felt much better.

The trail led me through a burn area with a very few struggling purple flowers and white daisies poking up through fire-blackened ground next to fire-blackened boulders. Once out of the burn, the terrain down 2,000 feet to Kelso Road had non-burned boulders, pinion pines, and a few short oaks. The boulders would have been great to play on, in, and around as a kid. In my day, (How's that for an old-lady phrase?) we called it cowboys and Indians, or cowboys and outlaws or even hide and seek. I liked the boulders.

Mary Barcik, a delightful 74-year-old trail angel, who loved to hike, walked up the trail to meet me with my resupply box and water. She didn't normally serve as a resupply angel, but had agreed to meet me with my box and get a bit of hiking in herself. We sat in the shade of some bushes and talked all the time I was loading my water, making my dinner and repacking.

Somehow, probably because we were talking so much, that all took a couple hours. I went on to a saddle Mary recommended for camping and enjoyed a lovely sunset beside Joshua Trees and an equally lovely sunrise in the morning.

Mary met me the next day for a few miles of hiking. She was absolutely delightful. We enjoyed sharing hiking tales and other life tales, too. Now there was someone who was inspiring. She cheerfully kept the water caches full for hikers on a dry stretch of trail on her motorcycle, taking many gallon jugs at a time and a hundred empties back tied on her or the motorcycle for the return trip, her trail name, Motor Mary. Motorcycle worn out doing water runs, she was using a pickup when I met her.

After lunch, Mary returned to her truck, and I continued up the hill in the hot, sun, pausing in the meager shade of Joshua Trees whenever possible. They were few and small and then none at all. Less than a week earlier snow and ice had blocked my way to the trail, but snow and ice were distant memories trudging up that hill in 90-degree weather

Walking off the trail toward one lone pinion pine, I crawled under its branches, other footprints telling me I wasn't the only one who had craved shade. Later on, I stopped in deep shade cast by a cliff. My water supply was running out. I took a mouthful of water and held it in my mouth as long as possible before swallowing. Keeping my mouth closed with water inside, I imagined I was in a swimming pool feeling the water swish in my mouth. Mind games for the PCT.

Reaching Bird Spring Pass, I sat in the shade waiting until the sun went down to camp. Sitting under a somewhat scraggly tree, I watched a billion flies land on my sweat-soaked pack leaning on a rock in the sun.

Chukkars (desert hens) were clucking merrily across the road in the morning. Just as I was ready to go, Motor Mary drove up in her pickup, and we started up the hill together. She loved to hike and liked to have company, sometimes hiking with thru hikers.

We climbed up Skinner Peak, fortunate for morning shade on our side of the canyon, we passed yellow snake heads, paintbrush, maroon bells, lupine, fiddlenecks, desert daisies, desert dandelions, comets, gilia and other flowers for which neither of us knew the names. At the saddle a thousand feet up from her car, I gave her a hug, and she went back down the switchbacks. I hoped I would be that energetic when 74.

Inspired, after lunch, I hiked seven miles in three and a half hours. While not fast for a thru hiker on such nice trail, it was amazing for me. The next morning I walked the final miles to Walker Pass on bear-track-imprinted dusty trail.

Kickoff Again

When planning my hike, I'd contacted the nearest Lutheran Church for assistance. As a pastor, it seemed a logical place to search for help. I was connected with Steve, who met me at Walker Pass and drove me to Ridgecrest, where I could take a shower at the city hall/community center for $5.00, using a towel and washcloth he brought for me. I probably smelled a good deal better as Steve drove me to Loma Linda to meet my cousin, Liz, who drove me further south, arriving at Lake Morena about 9:00 that night to experience my second PCT Kickoff, even more enjoyable in 2009 because I knew so many more people. Mssnglnk, Ceanothus, Beeman, Papa Bear, Jelly Bean, RockStar, Asabat, Billy Goat, Meadow Mary, Meadow Ed, Casey, Splash, Nitro,

Teddy, Slojo, Indiana Red, Half Mile, Sparky, Warner Springs Monte, Captain Teacup, Backtrack and Cog were some of those whose trail names I wrote down. Cog had been Mr Clean on the AT in 2004. What a delightful mix of people, personalities, backgrounds, and energy.

I made out like a bandit with a playful complaint to the vendor from Gossamer Gear about changing the color of their pack from my favorite blue and was given, free of charge, a last years' model someone else had turned in. I had a new pack for *next* year in my favorite color.

How lucky was that?

Snow on Fuller Ridge

After two days of merriment, I said *good-bye* to Kickoff friends and my cousin Liz, and my hiking friends from Washington, Kathy and Roz, (now with trail names Grapevine and Lipstick) whisked me to the trail to complete the section over Fuller Ridge missed due to fire in 2008. We were all excited to be on the trail. Lipstick found us a perfect cowboy-camping spot behind a large rock just off the trail out of the wind, and we snuggled into our bags under the bright stars. One of us slept. The other two listened to high-decibel log sawing. I wasn't the log sawer in the night.

The next day was interesting uphill trail, mostly on a nice grade. We made it to Fobes Saddle, and I walked down to get water from the spring on the other side of the pass while the other two set up camp. The third day after Kickoff, we had more uphill, probably around 2,600 feet, through magnificently rugged scenery.

Grapevine struggled with her usual foot problems. We also had to use our ice axes. When I was 20, I'd been part of Mountaineer climbs up Mt. Rainier, Mt. St Helens, Mt. Baker and Mt. Hood, so I knew something about snow travel and ice axes in my ancient past, although I'd not touched an ice axe for years. Kathy had similar past experiences. We taught Lipstick how to self- belay (A self-belay involves jamming the long spike into snow at each step on the uphill side of the trail, giving you a solid anchor to hold if your feet slip.).

Lipstick had never done anything like that before. In fact, this was the first backpack trip she'd taken in her adult life. She was a real trooper, following directions from Grapevine and me, she came through with flying colors amid mastery of a large component of fear. The higher we went, the more snow we encountered, though the trail leveled out. Snow slowed our pace. We followed footsteps before us, hoping they knew where they were going.

We plugged on in the late afternoon light as the sun went below the horizon, very definitely still on deep snow, not knowing if the trail was under our feet, when suddenly, there was Taquitz Creek, and thru hikers directed us to a snow-free patch of ground, where we could camp. Putting the tent up, we crawled inside. It was too cold to cowboy camp with snow all around us at 7,600 feet.

Grapevine and Lipstick bailed out at Saddle Pass and went to Idlewild. They said they'd been having a good time, but Lipstick didn't want to face more snow and possible dangerous conditions on Fuller Ridge as a neophyte. Grapevine's feet hurt, and she feared she was holding me back. Determined to complete my planned hike, this section already skipped once, I didn't want to skip it again. I went on.

Not all of the day was on snow. I caught up with some thru hikers having lunch, who said I could descend Fuller Ridge with them. Unfortunately, I had to stop for lunch, too, and couldn't catch them before they started out on Fuller Ridge.

Getting my water at the crossing of the second branch of the San Jacinto River, by snowbanks, huge rocks and sparkling water plunging down the creek, I found the trail snow-free for the first two miles. Great. This wasn't bad. What was all the fuss about Fuller Ridge? Maybe I lucked out, and the snow would be melted all the way. Wishful thinking.

A very steep snowbank covered the trail, but it had good footprints to follow. I took the ice axe off the pack and put on my Yaktracks (tire chains for your feet). Holding the ice axe with one hand, I stowed one hiking pole and started out. Except for very brief glimpses of ground, and more rarely, trail, it was snow all the rest of the day. I tried to be VERY careful.

I slipped a number of times, but my self-belay functioned just as it should. Once, I found myself suspended by one arm from the ice axe on a steep hillside above a tree well. Younger, more able thru hikers were going through without ice axes or crampons. I was very glad to have the ice axe, and my old skills from my 20s came back to me. I had a scrape on one elbow from an intimate acquaintance with some granite but overall, I was coming through pretty well.

However, the trail was elusively hidden under the snow. I couldn't find footprints. It looked like footprints ahead and below me. But when I reached what I thought were footprints, I found only dappled shade. I climbed up and down Fuller Ridge more times than I could count, chasing non-existent footprints.

Following footprints to stay found is never a sure thing. If snow is frozen hard there are not many footprints that actually show. If sun is melting snow, footprints blend in with the snow around them. And footprints do not guarantee the one making them knows where they are either. Anyone following mine, no doubt also went up and down on fruitless wild goose chases. Such travel requires lots of energy, and I was rapidly losing all vestiges of mine. And I was losing daylight.

A sheltered valley showing real trail and a few bare spots of ground appeared just at 7:15. It would be foolish to pass up the possible camp spot under those conditions. I camped. I had no idea how far I yet had to go to get off Fuller Ridge. I wasn't exactly lost. The trail had miraculously appeared with bare ground right beside me.

But I had no idea how far I'd come or how far I was from Black Mountain Road. I slept inside the three-person tent collapsed like a bivy as the warmest option for one person. Quickly getting out of wet shoes and socks and into warm night clothes, I cooked my dinner from inside my sleeping bag.

In the morning, I wandered around Fuller Ridge for another three hours of hard labor before reaching Black Mountain Road. Being *misplaced* takes an enormous amount of time and effort. Finally at Black Mountain Road, I was ready to start my *planned* day, 16 miles of downhill dropping 6,000 feet, and it was already nearly 10:00 in the morning. I could bail out down the road, but I didn't want to have to come back and finish this trail some other year. After a snack, removing my Yaktracks and stowing them and the ice ax, I headed down the trail.

Starting a 16-mile hike at 10:00 in the morning after three hours of wrestling with steep snow was a lot to ask of an old, slow lady. Fuller Ridge is notorious among thru hikers for long switchbacks that accomplish very little elevation loss for many miles under foot. My feet hurt. They screamed. I had to take a short break every half hour. Darkness descended, and I was far from the end of the descent.

The good news was cell-phone reception was great. I could communicate with Grapevine and Lipstick. My friends decided to walk in from the bottom of the trail to meet me. Two headlamps came up the trail to meet one headlamp coming down. I drank my fill of the water they brought and gobbled energy candy they provided. They even took my pack, which Grapevine carried after giving some of the contents to Lipstick.

Wow! Did I have wonderful friends? They must have walked in four miles. I hobbled behind my two friends down the road from the water fountain. We reached my cousin, Liz, at 9:30. (Meeting Liz was pre-planned.) Not planned, my feet hurt so bad I couldn't let them touch the floor of the car and held them in mid-air while sharp pains shot through them on the drive to Palm Springs.

I needed a zero.

Luxuriating in a motel pool in Palm Springs on our zero day, my cousin laughed uproariously at white lines from my knee brace next to sunburned skin as I traipsed around in my swimsuit. Lipstick decided to get off the trail and go home. She concluded Grapevine and I were a little nuts to hike when we had such problems with aging body parts, amazed that we liked to hike anyway. Probably an accurate assessment.

After a day of rest I walked through sand from the spot Liz had picked us up to Highway 10 where I'd commenced hiking after the fire in 2008, making my missed section complete, a nice short stroll ending under the overpass talking to thru hikers including Billy Goat, Socks, and Ice Axe.

Back to Walker Pass

Time to return to Walker Pass using a reverse of the travel arrangements I'd taken to the Kickoff. Liz drove us back to Loma Linda, where we met Steve, who took us to Walker Pass. Section hikers sometimes have complicated logistics.

Having reversed the wheeled trek south, we jumped on the trail and headed north. I had a slow start trying to settle in again with my pack. Though I had a hard time moving, something had lit a fire under Grapevine, and she fairly zoomed up the trail. There was no way I could keep up with her. We made our campsite, four miles, in less than 2.5 hours, well before dark, good time for old ladies with bad knees and feet.

Grapevine led most of the next day until we began to leapfrog occasionally. Descending to Spanish Needle Creek, we found water; a little farther on we had dinner, and then we walked some more, not having the good sense to stop when planned as we wanted to get a little jump on the next day. Near dark, we made a little nest right on the trail in the bend of a gully as there were no other even faintly flat spots on the steep hillside. I thought I was going to be squashed and smothered by Grapevine's weight pressing me against some rocks, and I kicked back. Then she was afraid to sleep for fear she would roll on me again and receive another thunk. It wasn't our best campsite.

Both of us had hurting feet as we walked over decomposed granite trail. Stopping at Chimney Creek for a rest, Grapevine said she could stay there forever if a helicopter would just drop off food and books to read.

I bathed and did some laundry, hanging things to dry on a bush. An hour later we collected our drying laundry, packed up and hiked uphill to get a jump on the next day's elevation gain.

Without water weight, we went up a thousand feet in 2.2 miles to Fox Mill Spring, making the next day's hike much easier. The last mile or so we saw bear tracks.

After a frosty morning and another 1,500 feet of climb, we came out to a large burn area with no shade and very hot sun. We improvised a precariously constructed shade with our tent for a break and scrunched into a thin sliver of shade from a ledge of rocks beside the trail for lunch. As we leapfrogged down the trail, Grapevine met an angry rattlesnake, probably a diamondback. It scared her half to death, and she climbed a steep hill to get around him. I'd not seen him when I went by before her.

After dinner, we did a little night hiking. Feeling like she was in Dante's Inferno, Grapevine wanted to get out of the burn area. The moon was bright and the trail relatively level, although very sandy. I managed to not get us lost, and we hiked another three miles under the night sky.

Our last day on the trail was another hot one, making us glad we had hiked three miles in the cool of darkness. Grapevine's feet hurt before we even started out, and they just got worse all the way to Kennedy Meadows, necessitating many stops applying moleskin, second skin, and padding.

We walked beside the Kern River through a rocky gorge, thinking the river absolutely lovely after wandering through such dry and burned-over land before reaching it. I daydreamed about floating down that water on an air mattress or in a canoe. Instead, we kept walking onward over sand. I told Grapevine, "If I'd wanted to climb sand dunes, I would have gone to the beach."

At Kennedy Meadows, we enjoyed cool shade on the store porch. Grapevine's feet looked terrible. Her hiking was done. She was toast. I found out the road to Horseshoe Meadows was open, but the snow line on the trail was 9500 feet, and I was supposed to be above 10,000 feet for two of the last four days. I would be solo on snow if I went on. I'd had enough of that on Fuller Ridge. It was very hard for me to exercise good judgment and get off the trail. But I did.

We hitched a ride to Ridgecrest, rented a car, and killed a couple days in Panamint Valley, Death Valley National Park—being tourists. After church in Ridgecrest, we got a ride with Steve to Bishop where we happened upon Moonshine and Rosemary, hikers from 2008. Taking the bus to Reno, we boarded our airplane back to Washington.

I am sometimes questioned about the wisdom of solo hiking. I have two rather warped and somewhat flip answers as to why I sometimes hike solo. The first is that having planned and led a fair number of group hikes in years past, for which I was responsible for others, taking into account their capabilities and striving for their enjoyment of the hike as well as my own, I find it quite refreshing to just be responsible for myself.

The second answer is that I am too old to wait around to find the right hiking companion. It is difficult to find compatible hikers, who wish to walk long miles as slowly as I do. My friends and hiking companions who hike my speed don't want to spend that many days and weeks on the trail. Thru hikers generally walk much faster and cover more miles in a day than I am able to do.

Getting another year older each year, I have limits to the time left in my life to walk long trails. If I were younger, I might think it reasonable to wait a few years to find a suitable hiking companion. In 2018, I do not have the time to wait. Ten years ago I didn't think waiting reasonable either. I plan long hikes in some detail and send the plans to my hiking friends. If any wish to come, they are welcome. If no one can come with me, I'm going anyway.

In solo walking as well as walking with others, I have had glorious adventures, seen wondrous scenery, met interesting people, and become comfortable with myself in the wilderness. Solo hiking is not for everyone. But an amazing number of people of both genders and various ages, some of whom I have had the good fortune to meet, walk long trails, often solo. I'd become one of them.

Chapter 18 July 11, 2009 Oregon

"I feel good."

I'd walked about 1,212 miles of the PCT. At age 67, closing fast on 68, I wasn't on pace to complete the PCT by age 70 or 71 unless I picked up more miles. I decided to pick up some sections in Oregon each summer. My friend Linda, aka Gray Squirrel, wanted to come, too, for a ten-day trip. Deal. We would start in the south and walk north. But you can't walk from a highway at the border of California and Oregon. For ease of transportation, we started at Seiad Valley in California, deciding to have breakfast at the Seiad Valley Café before heading up the hill.

Walking into the café, I was excited to see thru hiker Chuck Norris sitting there. He said we had just missed Billy Goat, Tigger, Piper, Unbreakable and No Trace, who had already headed up the trail. Chuck Norris invited us to add our signatures to those of other hikers painted on the white support van he was driving. Great start. We took obligatory start pictures and headed up the trail, and I do mean up.

We climbed over 4,600 feet that day. We also met Billy Goat shuttling two packs on the trail, essentially walking each foot of trail three times to fill in miles from previous hikes in which he'd not done this section. A multiple time hiker of the PCT, he made sure to get every mile of the PCT walked to count each of those multiple times as complete.

Gray Squirrel and I had a different way of hiking together. Gray Squirrel hiked at a faster pace. Walking ahead, she stopped every hour or 45 minutes and waited for me to catch up. We hiked together, separately, both happy with our paces.

Two days later, as we finished breakfast in the morning, Billy Goat walked up with my orange PCT bandana that had fallen out of my pocket. Crossing into Oregon we took a break at Observation Gap with Boone and Musa. I'd met Boone above Harpers Ferry on the AT in 2008. I loved how hikers I knew kept popping up.

Billy Goat fixed us *Billy Beans*, his standard trail dinner, and the following day we three all hiked together separately, Gray Squirrel in the lead, Billy Goat next, and I would come along 10 minutes later when we all sat down to chat. We continued to have beautiful views of Mount Shasta to the south and Pilot Rock ahead of us. I tried to take a picture of each different flower I saw, another reason I was always behind. After a leisurely dinner, Gray Squirrel and I sang Holden Evening Prayer for Billy Goat (and just because we liked it.)

The next day we bade adieu to Billy Goat, who was going to speed along the trail to get to Callahan's for lunch and his food drop.

But coming out to the highway, I was overjoyed to see Chuck Norris and Tigger's van, Tigger, and Billy Goat, too. Callahan's had been closed, so Billy Goat didn't get his town meal for lunch, although he did pick up his resupply box. Unbreakable, No Trace, and Chuck Norris joined us, and we all shared their Pepsis and chips sitting in the shade resting and talking. Chuck drove us to our motel, and I was grateful not to have to worry about hitching.

A lovely zero day in Ashland was spent doing our laundry, a little shopping, lazing around the pool, resting on the bed and eating. I had rootbeer floats for lunch, and we ate a quarter of a watermelon for afternoon snack by the pool. Tony, the head waitress at the Wild Goose Restaurant, encouraged a local, Phil, to give us a ride back to the trail the next day.

Phil was a flake, and didn't show up. So Tony, in true trail-angel fashion, asked Felix, another regular at the Wild Goose, to use her (Tony's) car to take us to the trailhead. Tony would take no money for her efforts or the loan of her car, a gift of trail magic.

My thermometer said it was 89.6, hot for a Washingtonian. I struggled with the heat, insisting we stop for dinner and to rest before going on. That wasn't Gray Squirrel's choice; she didn't like to stop until done for the day. However, I was exhausted by heat, collapsed on my sleeping pad and hardly moved for at least an hour. As we moved up the trail after dinner, Gray Squirrel led as I trudged along behind.

I looked up when I heard Billy Goat's high-pitched voice: "I feel good." He was heading down the trail. We were headed up the trail. No one wanted to backtrack, but we liked each other's company, so we made camp right there on an old overgrown jeep road. Since I'd liked the picture of Lake of the Woods in the Guide Book, Sunset Campground was our last stop, and we were rewarded with a beautiful setting sun over the water.

The next morning at the Resort I ate two breakfasts, one after the other. Eggs and bacon were for breakfast and Belgian Waffles with strawberries for dessert. After a walk to the highway, one little piece of Oregon was done, making a total of 473.5 PCT miles for the year.

Chapter 19 August 24, 2009 AT

"A stroke of pure genius"

After family adventures with visiting grandchildren and misadventures on very delayed airline flights, I was dropped off at Delaware Water Gap at 1:00 am. Not too disappointed that my shuttle driver didn't show up in the morning, I went back to bed and slept until noon. In the afternoon I walked around the tiny town of Delaware Water Gap, mended my hat, and took a short conditioning hike recommend by the outfitter, (an outfitter is a store that sells hiker equipment.) walking south on the AT up Mount Minsie and back.

Happy to be on the trail again, enjoying the warm day, I stripped to sports bra. Twenty day hikers or weekend backpackers were also enjoying the warm day on the trail. A large family of Hassidic Jews might have been a little aghast at the old lady in the sports bra. Eastern US dress standards are different than the west, even for hikers on the trail.

I thought planning to hike all of New Jersey by slack pack was a stroke of pure genius. I may have been old and slow, with bad feet and a herkin' huge leg brace on my left knee, but I wasn't dumb. Planning my hike I saw there were roads that crossed the trail, B&Bs, or motels at appropriate distances I could manage. I didn't have to carry everything, no tent, no sleeping bag, and no food other than the lunch I would purchase at each stay for the next day's walk.

My shuttle driver took me to a road crossing of the AT 13.6 miles into New Jersey and I walked back SOBO (southbound) to Delaware Water Gap. Slackpacking seemed hard enough on my feet, though it was a lovely day. Many day hikers were out and about, including naked sun worshippers and illegal swimmers at Sunfish Pond, the southern-most glacial lake on the AT. As usual, everyone passed me.

The next day my shuttle took me back to the same road, and I walked NOBO, seeing bear prints in the mud as I began. Westerners are surprised to know that the section of the AT through New Jersey is notorious for the prevalence of black bears, not that I saw any of the furry critters. I did see a beautiful, but camera shy, black snake, an eagle and eight Turkey Vultures perched on a snag. I listened to songbirds and the buzzing and chirping of insects. Other than that, I listened to the quiet.

Since hitchhiking is illegal in New Jersey, I had to walk two miles down the road from Culver Gap. I was rewarded with meeting RV, half of a couple of mature age, while having lunch at a little café. They noted my pack, started talking trail talk, and took me home with them. I cancelled my motel reservation.

RV took me back to the AT in the morning, and I continued on, stopping for lunch at a big, shady rock across from the Mashipacong, where I called on my cell phone to check in with my next ride for the evening. Good thing I called. He'd forgotten and had a dinner engagement with his mother, begging me to get to the road by 4:30. It was 2:00, and I still had 5 ½ miles to go. I said I would do my best.

Fortuitously, the night before, RV had told me about an older route of the AT on an easier woods road on which I could move more quickly than the newer trail. I'd been pondering which route to take, but upon hearing the need for haste, the decision was made. I took off as fast as I could go down what is now called the Iris Trail, formerly part of the AT. I made my meeting with 12 minutes to spare, and Mike took me to his motel.

Oops. I made a miscalculation in my plan and realized the next day was going to be longer than I'd thought. Fortunately much of the trail was pretty easy. I walked around a wildlife sanctuary and saw herons. Going up Pochuck Mountain, I had to laugh. In the West, trail builders carefully route trails around or through large areas of rock fall. In the East trail builders say, "Oh, good, a rock fall, less trail maintenance." They just paint white rectangles on the rocks and that *is* the trail, straight up the rock fall.

Bob, the proprietor of the Cider Mill B&B, called to see if I was OK, as it was getting close to 6:00, and he hadn't heard from me. Very considerate. I told him when I expected to be at the road, and he drove up just as I stepped off the muddy trail.

A B&B is not in every hiker's budget, but this was a unique and beautiful stop for me.

Picking me up from the trail, he offered to add $10 to the bill and make me a steak dinner. I, of course, was ravenous. Deal.

He served me a scrumptious breakfast at 5:15 the next morning, and he made me a sandwich for lunch, too, as well as delivering me back to the trail at 6:00 am. The food was excellent, but my room was even more remarkable, beautifully decorated and *all white*. I was afraid to walk in the door covered with trail mud. But Bob just said, "That's what vacuum cleaners are for." I took two giant steps in my muddy socks on white carpet to reach the bathroom and immediately stripped for my shower.

Walking on a boardwalk over a swamp on my last day in New Jersey and then up Wawayonda Mountain, it started to sprinkle. Rats. That was the day I needed *dry* weather to cross very rocky trail into New York. I didn't get it.

I did get to try out my free umbrella I'd received at the PCT Kickoff. I REALLY liked the umbrella. It was very lightweight, and I tucked the handle under my chest strap and into my sports bra for stability leaving both hands free for hiking poles.

So, why did I like an umbrella? I could hike in my sports bra, using poles in both hands and not be stewing in my own juice with sweat under a raincoat. The umbrella also covered the top of my pack, keeping that pesky area next to my back from getting wet with runoff from the raincoat, soaking into the pack. I really liked the dryness and freedom of movement. It might not be useful in high winds, but on rainy days without winds I decided it would be worth the weight to carry as standard equipment.

The rain continued all day. Hailing from Washington, I was used to hiking in rain. The slug on the trail made it seem just like home. I climbed from New Jersey into New York in a raincloud, with fog or active showers all the way. Now, when I was a teenager, I'd loved to clamber over rocks. But an old lady with a bad knee and an acute sense of her limitations found the wet and slippery rocks of New York very, very challenging.

Puddingstone Rock, the book called it, large slabs and huge boulders of glacier-polished rock. They were wet, slippery and not level. Sometimes there were climbs that required both hands and a few prayers. It would have been easier on a dry day with two good legs. But I didn't have two good legs. I couldn't trust my weight on a bent knee, nor could I take big steps to land on that leg or jump, and it wasn't a dry day.

I wondered if I would make it to the road before dark. On a particularly difficult stretch it took me nearly an hour and a half to go one mile. I slipped and fell twice, once catching my neck and my umbrella on a sapling. The umbrella became toast. My neck survived, but felt like I'd been *clotheslined*. Rats. I'd really liked that umbrella. I seemed to have no broken parts, picked myself up, and resumed my trek down the mountain.

Darkness descended just as I made it to the road, and then another adventure began. It was very dark, very wet, and I was on a busy highway. By the way, hitchhiking is illegal in New York, too. I was supposed to meet my daughter at the Belvalle Creamery. Walking the highway in the dark and the rain, blazing headlights passed me at high speed. I was very glad to reach the Creamery, take off my wet raincoat, find my jacket, and have a hot fudge sundae.

Unfortunately, the Creamery was in a cell phone dead zone. I couldn't reach my daughter.

Where was she? The Creamery closed at 10:00, and I had to leave. So I walked out into the darkness and into the rain once again, down the road toward town. I wondered how the day would end.

A car stopped in front of me. Blinded by the blazing headlights and the rain, I couldn't see who it was, but I would have gotten into a car with anyone to get out of the rain and find someplace dry. Sara jumped out of the car and gave me a big hug in the middle of the road. Was I glad to see her! And also get the hug.

After an uncooperative GPS, a road closure for an hour, getting lost, making a call to Andrew, and a GPS that finally gave us correct directions, we arrived at West Point at 1:30 am. I had one day of rest and fun with my East Coast family before I flew to Maine for a date with Katahdin.

Katahdin, Maine

An airline flight, two bus rides, and a shuttle took me to the campground at Katahdin Stream. On the bus from Portland to Bangor I'd had the good fortune to sit next to Gail, a woman of mature age, a sea kayaker, who had observed harbor seals and whales for 30 years. Cool. We enjoyed conversing about our respective pursuits. She also pointed out the osprey nests on high-tension lines over the road. Unfortunately, I came down with a cold on the way to Maine, possibly caught from my grandchildren.

After setting up camp, I took a short walk to Grass and Elbow Lakes through moss-covered forest skirting bogs, and I ran into a couple day hikers. Hearing my hacking, they gave me cough drops for which I was very grateful. Mount Katahdin was on my schedule the following day.

Katahdin is of near mythical image for those thru hiking northbound on the AT. After walking for months on the trail north from Georgia, it is an emotional moment to stand at the summit sign on Katahdin realizing the end of the goal. For those who hike southbound, Katahdin marks the beginning of the AT adventure, although you have to hike up a mountain in order to begin. For me, it was neither of those, but it was the beginning of my Maine hike and a big challenge for a 68-year-old lady with a bad knee. I'd read other hiker's journals and was quite aware how hard the climb was going to be. I needed a good night's sleep.

It took me nearly 11 hours of lying down to accomplish it, but, thanks to the cough drops, I got at least 8 hours of pretty good sleep. I signed the trail register in the dark at 6:08 am, September 1st.

The trail started off nicely enough. After Katahdin Stream Falls, it became gradually rougher, and I climbed over more and more large boulders. An older couple caught up with me, and our paces seemed to be similar, although they'd caught up to me, proving they were faster. David, Ann, and I hiked together most of the day. Ann was my age, but she looked and hiked like she was on the high side of 50, maybe.

I couldn't have asked for a better day to climb Katahdin. There was no fog, no clouds, only a little wind, and the sky was blue. We were blessed.

The higher we climbed, the more difficult the trail over rock slabs and boulders grew. I had to use hands as well as feet much of the time and wished for a tail to help. Sometimes rebar was affixed to rocks to help. Most of the trail, including the placement of the rebar, seemed designed for 6' plus men, not 5'4" grandmas. Much of the middle two miles, climbing 3,000 feet up, were rock scrambles with exposure to steep drops.

I was very glad to be with David and Ann. I was possibly a bit better at the rock scrambles than Ann, and I don't have much fear of heights though I did notice the drop offs. Ann was better at everything else. We helped each other over the roughest spots. There were at least four or five places I don't think I could have negotiated without a hand pulling me up a boulder or someone to guide my feet where I couldn't see on the other side of one.

We finally came to *The Gateway*, the beginning of less steeply graded tableland. At the other end of that plateau, about a mile away, another 500 feet to the top. It wasn't too hard but it all took time. We reached the summit at 1:30 on a gloriously beautiful day—feeling we could see forever. Amazing.

We took the customary pictures by the freshly painted sign and gazed at the mountains in the distance to the west and north. The most striking aspect of the view was all the lakes. One quarter of Maine appeared to consist of water, all sizes and shapes of water. Much as I would have liked to stay there for the whole afternoon, I hurriedly ate my lunch and asked David and Ann if they would wait for me at the top of the Gateway. We were all aware that the way down would be at least as difficult as the way up.

It was every bit as challenging going down, sometimes more so. It had taken seven hours to go up. We were on the summit about a half hour and going down took nearly as long as going up. My coughing was worse in the afternoon. It was hard to make good time with both poles planted in one place while leaning over them, hacking my insides out. David, with his long legs and easy-going personality, was a great help going down as well as up. Helping me down boulders, he joked that he was catching a *flying pastor* instead of a *flying nun*.

Past the worst of the descent, I told them to go on, as I needed to stop and eat something. I should have said a better *goodbye* and *thank you*.

They were gracious, kind and sweet people, the perfect companions for me on that climb. I ate, put fresh batteries into my headlamp and walked the last mile in the gathering darkness at my own slow, limping pace. The light of campfires at the campground was a longed-for sight in the dark night as I signed in at the register at 8:01, 20 minutes after Ann and David.

It had been a 14-hour day, and I think I set a record for slowness. But I'd climbed Katahdin on a beautiful day with gracious and simpatico people. Who could ask for more? Life was good. I ate some almonds and dried pears and fell into bed.

Waking up around 6:00, I told myself to roll over and stay in bed. Taking stock of my body that morning, I was pleased. My sorest muscles were my abdominals and rib muscles from coughing so much. Next in line were my pectorals (chest muscles) from so much hauling myself around boulders or doing push-up butt hitches on those rocks.

My right quad (thigh) was only a little sore. I had scratches on my knee and my ankle from biting rocks and a blister on my calf from my brace. That wasn't a bad total for an old lady on Katahdin. Since I wasn't more significantly sore, I guessed I was in fair physical condition. I was just slow.

I'd planned a zero day after Katahdin for recovery. I talked to thru hikers, who summited that day and other hikers in the campground. Just before I ate my diner I met Bookworm, a younger hiker, who was interviewing hikers and collecting stories. Bookworm was an artist who hoped to turn his hike into visual art. He'd been in the Peace Corps in South Africa and had taught English in Korea. We had a good time talking and comparing notes about hiking and life histories, having some things in common in spite of a rather large age difference.

He would be headed SOBO as would I, but after my slow record on Katahdin I was certain he would be much faster than me.

100 Mile Wilderness

I was awake coughing most of the night, but my hike plan called for me to start walking. That I did, after soliciting the help of a pickup truck to retrieve my food-bag rope, which was stuck in a tree. How embarrassing.

I enjoyed Maine: trees, lakes, and streams, moss-covered logs and rocks. It wasn't too dissimilar to the Olympic Peninsula rainforest in Washington, although it was flatter and even more filled with beautiful lakes and moss. The trail description said to cross the Nesowadnehunk Stream on a bridge. I laughed. What passed for a bridge were three small saplings about 6-8 inches in diameter stuck over the rushing water. Frijole came by at just that minute and helped me cross.

Yellow Jacket, Tripod, Slojo, Feedbag, and Snarky were thru hikers starting their trek to Georgia. I loved trail names. Some names are repeatedly chosen, like Achilles, Rocket, and Papa Bear. Other names reveal endless creativity in choosing colorful trail monikers.

I stopped at Abol Bridge Campground because they had showers. The setting sun turned the entire sky an incredible orange that reflected back from the perfectly still lake to bathe the trees in an orange glow. Orange on orange. The very air seemed orange. I'd never before seen a sunset quite like that.

After coughing all night long, I overheard an RV camper talking to another in the restroom wondering, "…how that poor woman can hike." I probably kept a lot of people awake, but I could hike. My strong point was stamina, or maybe just determined stubbornness. I'm not sure there is a difference.

From Abol Bridge, the AT entered the 100 Mile Wilderness. It wasn't really a hundred miles, nor did it seem a wilderness in western terms, as logging roads crossed the trail. It was, however, quite remote, and town services wouldn't be available until I reached Monson. It wasn't true that there were no services at all. A determined researcher could find ways to receive food drops in that 100 miles.

Book Worm and I played leapfrog during the day as he stopped often to interview hikers. Some hikers complained endlessly about the trail. Two white-haired ladies said they were not going to do anything outside ever again once they climbed Katahdin, yet they'd walked the whole trail. I honestly do not understand that attitude and had little sympathy for those not having a good time. If you are not enjoying yourself at all, stay home and do something else you do enjoy.

The trail is not for everyone. It is work. It is sometimes annoying, frustrating, and hard, with challenges you may not have anticipated or for which you were not prepared. But there is so much to enjoy. Yes, there are roots and rocks. It's the AT. What else would you expect? There was also bear and moose poop to marvel at, frogs and toads, trees, a few flowers, berries on bushes, streams and waterfalls, other hikers to talk to, occasionally a few feet of level, smooth trail and lakes and more lakes.

At Rainbow Springs Campsite I met some women in their 70s; one had completed all of the AT including its extensions in Florida and Canada. She was lamenting that her husband was tired of hiking, though she really wanted to go west and hike the John Muir Trail. She was my kind of woman, what a delightful contrast to the complainers earlier in the day.

The trail through the rain forest required me to weave an intricate dance over rocks and roots trying to stay out of the mud. I got pretty good at zigzagging from tiny branch to tiny branch. Trail runners passed me on a very well-graded gravel crossroad before heading up a hill. It seemed strange to me to see gravel roads and trail runners in a fabled *wilderness.* But I reminded myself I'd also seen trail runners on the Wonderland Trail. Pennywhistle, a younger hiker did 30-mile days. I was in awe.

Numerous hikers with colorful names passed me the next day going both directions.

Scotsman called to me after passing and asked if I would climb Katahdin with him after he met his fiancée and marry them on top. Sorry, Scotsman, I was headed in the other direction.

Earlier hikers had complained about the rocks and roots, but what gave me trouble was the mud. Crossing a black mud bog a hundred-feet long, a hiking pole went into the mud past the basket on the bottom of the pole and was hard to pull out of the sucking goo.

Taking the side trail to the Pemadumcook Lake dock, I found the air horn and blew it, the signal for the folks at White House Landing to come across the lake in their boat to get hikers. For $40 I would get the boat shuttle, a bunk-house bed, a shower and an AYCE (all you can eat) breakfast at a rather beautiful location on the lake, a hill of lawn surrounded by woods, pocket gardens, and several cabins.

Linda, the proprietress, heard me cough and gave me sweetened hot water with lemon.

One-pound hamburgers for hungry hikers were advertised, but I settled for a half-pound burger with trimmings. Linda found some Alka-Seltzer Plus packets and gave them to me. She also fed me ripe cherry tomatoes and fresh blackberries on my zero day, hoping they would help me fight off the cough.

She told me I'd missed their resident moose, Baxter, who came every year for a few weeks, eating berries and their lawn and napping on the grounds. He'd swum away across the end of the lake about two weeks before I arrived.

Ameoba, Memere, Gray Feather, Ouch, Sky King and Pipe Smoke stopped at White House Landing while I was there. Two of the ladies were in their 70s. Long trails are not just for the young. They and their ages encouraged me.

The rest day did me good. I had my lunch on the trail the following day at a beautiful little pocket sandy beach on JoMary Lake. Since my knee had its bout with the staph infection, I couldn't really swim, as kicking hurt, and the knee felt *loose*. I surely didn't want to get in serious trouble with the knee in the wilderness, so I contented myself with wading in my underwear and splashing in the water. It was lovely, a marvelous experience all alone in a beautiful wilderness gem on a perfect day, wading on my private beach as if I owned the world. Amazing. How lucky I was to be there.

My first food drop was hidden in the bushes for me by Kathy, a local angel. The 100-mile wilderness does not *have* to be done on one food carry. I couldn't do what the young bucks do but I could plan alternatives that fit my needs. Farther up the trail, I stayed in the shelter at Cooper Brook Falls by a lovely cascading waterfall.

White Cap was the first real climb south of Katahdin. From White Cap, NOBO (northbound) thru hikers get really pumped at the view of Katahdin dramatically sticking up from surrounding lowlands and lakes. After 2,000 miles, their hike is almost over. I liked the view, but it didn't have the same emotional impact for me or other SOBOs as our hikes had many miles to go. Scads of NOBO thru hikers passed me, determinedly headed to Katahdin that day in September.

I met a hiker named Lisa, who was completing her Triple Crown. She'd walked the Pacific Crest Trail, the Continental Divide Trail, and was close to her finish of the AT. As we chatted, I wondered if I could consider doing the CDT when I finished the AT and PCT, at least the prettiest parts. I didn't know if my body would last that long as a backpacker, but it was fun to dream.

Near Screw Auger Falls, I met Gail, a woman from Gold Bar, Washington whom I would see again when I did hike the CDT. I forded the West Branch of the wide -but-shallow Pleasant River and met Kathy, my local angel with my second food drop.

Chairback was the next climb. On all fours I followed the little white rectangles that mark the AT straight up talus boulders to the top of the mountain. When nearly there, after crossing a small bog and a gap looking for the shelter, I found a sign announcing the shelter 150 feet ahead. It should have just said *up*. *Ahead* was straight up a hill just short in steepness from being called a cliff. Peering up the steep hill, I could just see the shelter roof and wafting smoke from a campfire. After I climbed the steep hill I met Bullet and West, who told me tales of their AT hike as rain fell on the shelter roof.

The following day rain added to the mud on the trail, and I fell in a bog.

The 4th Mountain bog lay in the gap between 4th Mountain and Barren Mountain. Bogs in Maine lay between rocky walls in gaps that do not drain, even on the tops of mountains. Bogs often have split-log puncheons to walk on, keeping you out of the mud. I started out on a split log, a sign commanding me to stay on the trail, so the rare plants could live.

I tooled along confidently on split logs until there wasn't one. There was only a 6-inch diameter sapling. My foot missed the branch and hit the mud. Now, looking at the mud, you have no idea how deep it might be. It wasn't just an inch of mud. I went in all the way up to my hip. If the other leg had not straddled the sapling I might have just kept on going deeper. A thru hiker named Porter came along just then and helped pull me out.

I was afraid the sucking mud would claim my shoe. What would I do in the middle of the 100-Mile Wilderness with only one shoe? My Dirty Girl Gaiters worked perfectly, keeping the mud from getting in my shoe. Under the gaiter my shoe and sock stayed clean, although there was plenty of mud on the outside of the shoe, gaiter, brace, shorts and all available skin up to my crotch.

Laughing, I remembered the sign commanding me to stay on the trail and save rare plants. I don't think I harmed any plants; I'd stayed on the trail. Well, technically, I stayed *inside* the trail, three-feet deep inside the trail. I found the whole episode hysterically funny.

Later that day I met Fox Trot. He'd just completed the PCT and decided to do the AT SOBO to Harper's Ferry for dessert. Ah, youth. He flitted over the boulders, roots, and rocks like a butterfly. Watching him I thought enviously how nice it would be to have knees, ones that really functioned. Stopping at Cloud Pond that night I cleaned off the mud.

Two more days and I was at Monson, the first town south of Katahdin. Hiking into Monson I found myself thinking somewhat longingly of New Jersey's flat spots of trail without the plethora of roots and rocks. But I enjoyed the 100-mile wilderness, its lakes and waterfalls, its green hillsides, loons on the lakes and many hikers. But I was ready for a break and the marvelous dinner served that night in the hostel. They only served dinner on Mondays. Lucky me. It was a Monday. Pretty pink and blue quilts on the beds were very cheery, the color scheme reminiscent of preschooler's bedrooms provided for burly hikers and a grandma. The beds were heavenly, with real sheets.

"So, you're still active then?"

Leaving Monson, I met NOBOs Tagless, Tagalong, and Mountain Man. I'd met Tagless and Tagalong in Virginia in 2008 as they were doing a shakedown/trial hike before attempting a thru hike. I reminded Tagalong of her hesitancy the year before. Now, their thru hike was almost complete. Congrats!. I wished I could walk as well as they now did.

Moxie Bald had an absolutely magnificent view. The best yet. Worries about a glove I'd lost that day or a sore heel foretelling plantar fasciitis or my crummy knees were only minor annoyances in comparison to the landscape stretched out before me.

Rugged ranges to the west gave promise (or threat, depending on your attitude) of the grandeur to come. Lakes with their irregular outlines and treed islands stretched out on either side. Beautiful. Beautiful. Even if I was an old lady who moved at roughly the speed of molasses, standing there I was just another hiker drinking in the view and being so glad to experience the beauty.

Two days later I reached Caratunk with its post office and few houses. There was no store, not even a gas station, and no cell service. A phone hung outside the post office to make local calls. The number for the Sterling Inn wouldn't go through. I hitched a ride with some other hikers to the Outdoor Center, finding the Inn had failed a water test and was closed.

But where was my food box that I'd sent to the Inn? A woman in the Outdoor Center made a few phone calls, gave me a cabin for the price of a large room and by the time I'd moved in and come back to the lodge for lunch, she found my box. Hooray!

On a very short nero, (A nero day is a short day, not a zero day of no walking, but not a full day of walking.) I crossed the Kennebeck River by canoe, a service provided for hikers after a hiker had drowned in 1980 when water was suddenly released from a dam upstream. My canoe ferryman was enjoying the sun while waiting for hikers.

After signing a waiver saying I wouldn't sue if I drowned and putting on a life vest, I climbed in and helped paddle across. It was a fun way to cross the river, and I'd been looking forward to it, no fording and getting wet.

Walking by Pierce Stream, multiple waterfalls of all sizes abounded, color spots of red and yellow glowed by the river in the woods and sunlight made the water sparkle. I strolled to the shelter beside the lake. Looking out at the water, my feet and knees appreciating the shortness of travel and my senses enjoying shade, sun, the lapping of water on the shore and the view. What a peaceful place to stop on a day of short miles.

I took a bath and washed my socks and sweat band bandana. My baths on the trail were quick. Standing naked in the forest bathing with cold water encourages quickness. The breeze blew me dry almost instantly, and I wasn't surprised by another hiker while naked. When in a compromising condition, I listened closely though, for the click of hiking poles or voices.

Trees were amazingly close together in Maine forests, like hedges of seedlings, then saplings, then mature trees. Sometimes it was difficult to leave the trail to attend to nature's needs, and I could see how one could be quickly lost behind impenetrable curtains of trees. I stuck to the trail and only left it to make solid deposits in my cat holes when the curtains of trees parted.

Blue against the green of forests, the lakes of Maine were nearly constant features. I could begin the day at a lake, end at a lake, and stop for lunch at a lake, all lovely. Beauty surrounded me.

There was a problem though. My right heel. I didn't recall ever having much trouble with my right heel before that trip. Perhaps once or twice, I'd had a painful heel, which would clear up and go away without much problem. This time, the pain wasn't going away. Hiking was harder when each step hurt, pain contributing to my slowness. Between left knee and right heel, I was often limping on both legs, no good leg to stand on.

A couple months earlier, a friend whom I'd not seen for 50 years had contacted me about a High School Reunion. With surprise in her voice, she'd asked, "So you're still active then?"

"Well yes, I am still active." I still hoist pack to back and do long trails. Each year something new hurts. But I am still active, very thankful to still be active, able to walk by lovely lakes, climb grand mountains and enjoy the sun on a beautiful day, even though my heel hurt.

The farther south I went in Maine, the more difficult the trail became. The 100 Mile Wilderness was relatively easy, reasonable hiking. Farther south there were bigger mountains, the Bigelows, Little and Big. Thru hikers passed me headed north. By this time in their trip thru hikers were a bit superhuman. I wasn't.

A general rule I followed: If a thru hiker told me a certain stream, trail junction, or shelter was X distance away in time, I just doubled the number given for the estimation of when I might get there.

Reaching Stafford Notch as darkness descended, I could barely make out my feet on the trail with my rather pitiful headlamp low on batteries, but there was a very bright headlamp in the campsite. Ja El, a four-time thru hiker on the AT, was kind to the old lady with the useless light and loaned me his bright one to get my water and make camp. I returned the light and settled in my tent, vowing not to go more than three steps from its enfolding walls until it was daylight.

At daylight, I headed up Avery Peak. Some of the trail was rough rock requiring use of hands as well as feet and poles. The descent from the Bigelows to the road was a fight against time, going down what was sometimes very demanding, steep trail requiring hands and feet again. I was well aware that it would only take one miss-step to come crashing down, banging soft body parts and bones on unyielding rock. I moved slowly and carefully.

A mile an hour was a great accomplishment for me on some of Maine's trails. I did enjoy the challenge of the more difficult parts; when young, I'd always liked climbing around on rocks. Each difficult rocky section was like a puzzle. Which way would be the best and safest for an old lady with a bad leg? I like puzzles.

I laughed at myself as I turned around like a cat getting ready to lie down while I tried to decide which possible route to take over rocks or cliff-like trail. Straight down? Back down? Go sideways? Right side? Left side or in the middle? Which hand holds or footholds would be best? Which route wouldn't require me to trust the left knee in a bent position? It all took time. I could do it all. I could do it safely. But I was dreadfully slow.

Yet those difficult places, too, were pretty. The lower I went, the more fall color was apparent, the trail lined with orange and gold as well as green. I came close to getting to the road before dark but had to travel the last half-mile by headlamp.

My zero day in Stafford was much needed. Both lower legs ached for hours that night in spite of Vitamin T (Tylenol) and in spite of the fact I wasn't moving any more, lying down on a good bed. By morning my body parts recovered, though my brace had tried to rub another section of skin off the side of my leg.

Billy Goat, a trail icon on the PCT, is a Maine boy. He told me, when I was planning this trip, not to overestimate my abilities in the southern section of Maine. He told me of a young woman who bailed out crying hysterically that she just couldn't stand the roots and rocks any more. I wasn't planning on bailing, but I could understand what she'd felt. It was a very difficult trail.

Looking at what lay ahead the next few days, I saw one section would require going up 1,000 feet in half a mile. That's steep. I was sure I would be using hands as well as feet to climb, with a full pack. It would be challenging.

At every town stop with cell reception I checked my email and my trail journal. I was collecting fans. Some of them I knew, like Ursa Minor, and some I'd not yet met, like Winkle. Short notes left on my guest book page encouraged me, and I needed it. A sentence or two could turn me from the edge of discouragement to an optimistic hiker.

Leaving Stafford I took a break and set the pack down on my water bladder mouthpiece, inadvertently draining most of my water onto the ground. Oops. It was a good thing it was a cold day. I wouldn't be as thirsty. The weather had changed to the 40s in the day, forecast to be 28 that night.

My campsite by the Carrabasset River was cheery with the

company of hikers, who had a nice campfire to ward off the cold as darkness settled. Lovely fall color contrasted with evergreens on the riverbanks.

In the morning it was freezing, but I was off early. I needed all the head start I could get as I climbed another mountain, enjoying the beauty of thick frost on groundcover beside the trail, glistening in the early morning sunlight. I started out with two shirts, a fleece top, and my down jacket. Before lunch I was down to one shirt.

I SAW A MOOSE. Many hikers make their way through Maine without seeing one. Some hikers see many. I was glad I saw one. He wasn't in the lowlands but up on the ridge. I heard a crackle of a branch broken and turned to see him through the trees. He moved amazingly quietly for a large animal moving through thickly placed Maine tree trunks. I had one good view through the trees, and he was gone, no time for a picture. Nice bull moose with rack.

Reaching my campsite with enough time to set up the tent and move in before dark, I also pumped my water in the daylight, camping alone by a pretty stream on an old railroad bed.

Waking before 5:00, it was still dry, but I knew the rain was coming. I ate, packed up, and was on the trail at 6:15, by headlamp for 10 minutes before the day dawned. I picked my way backwards down the steep trail to the stream crossing in dawning light and was glad I wasn't doing it in thick darkness. As I crossed the stream and it started to rain, I stopped, making sure everything was thoroughly rain proofed. Everything important to keep dry was behind about four layers, plastic plus rain covers.

Rain poured down in buckets. I decided to only go three miles to the next shelter because of the horrid weather. The first thing I did when I unpacked? Yep, I took a bath. Don't laugh, at least not too hard. After two days and no bathing, I reeked, and I was going to have to live with myself in the shelter all day.

I had extra fuel so I heated water and washed in warm water, which felt really good as the temperature was 47. I filtered the three liters of water I needed, climbed into my trail jammies and all my extra clothes too and snuggled in my sleeping bag to stay warm. Oh, by the way, the sleeping shelf in that shelter wasn't made of flat boards but of baseball bat sized logs. I was glad I had a Thermarest air mattress, even if it was a short one.

I spent the rest of the day horizontal. When not hiking, it is hard to stay warm any other way than inside a sleeping bag. Besides, the rest felt good. Night Train, a SOBO section hiker from Bainbridge Island near Seattle, sloshed in about 7:00. He was an older gentleman, who hiked twice as fast as I could. (Doesn't everybody?) He'd also section hiked the PCT and CDT. The rain was a gully washer all night long, and I was very glad to be in the shelter.

Wanting to be on the trail as soon as there was light, I was up at 5:00. I told Night Train I wished I hiked as fast as he did, so we could come down Saddleback together. The map description and other hikers had us worried about slick rocks in wet weather.

Wet weather was what we had. Streams were running everywhere, including in the trail. I laughed. I'd been saying I enjoyed the streams and cheerful waterfalls. Now I had the opportunity to walk in streams and step through the waterfalls on what was supposed to be trail. Nice stepping stones to keep feet dry in a little bog between large rocks were 2-3 inches under water. Pretty funny. Yes, my feet were more than just wet; they sloshed.

Night Train and I did walk down Saddleback together as he considerately started late. Thick rainclouds tried to lift, giving us cloud-framed views as we descended. The slopes were generally not too steep, and the rock was nice bumpy granite that grabbed the soles of our shoes.

Reaching the road, we tried hitching without much luck. I decided sticking out a thumb wasn't conveying the urgency I felt and vigorously waved my white bandana at cars. That worked. Two young women turned around to see what the emergency was and took us into Rangely. Remembering that method for all future hitches, I rationalized it *would have been an emergency* if I couldn't have reached town and my food box.

On the next day's slack pack, the sun came out, making it a lovely day. After a couple hours, my right heel started to hurt, a lot. Even when slackpacking, pain cut down my speed. Roots and rocks and lots of bogs slowed me down even more. It took a long time to cover the miles.

Closer to the highway, on really steep, rocky, rooty trail, it started to rain, at first lightly and then hard. I finally hit the highway at 6:20, in the dark. That day was supposed to be the easy 13 miles and the next day the more difficult 13 miles. I was really concerned. If I couldn't manage a day slack packing in daylight, I surely couldn't do it with full pack. I vowed to start a half hour earlier.

"I don't think a 68-year-old woman should be doing this alone in the dark in the rain."

That next day was rainy and every bit as difficult as I'd feared. It took me almost four hours to walk the 4.4 miles to Bemis Mountain Shelter, where I stopped to eat and evaluate. This was the last chance to eat under shelter for the day. I looked at the hiker log in the shelter and saw that Night Train had gotten in at 8:30 the night before. I told myself that if he could hike a little in the dark, so could I. I was from Washington, too; I could hike in the rain.

Bad Camper exchanged greetings with me, saying, "Oh, you mean the weather stinks, and you're all wet, but it is so good to be outside?"

I laughed at the hiker humor and agreed. His comment helped me chuckle through the day.

I needed the good attitude. It was a very hard day. I walked on slick boards over bogs and up and down rocky trail. I only stopped once to water a bush. I reached the top of Old Blue at 5:00 and called David, the shuttle driver/hostel owner in Andover. David said he would be at the road waiting for me. I estimated I would be another 2 ½ hours, more than half in the dark.

Leaving the top of Old Blue as the rain turned to sleet, it took me three hours to make the descent.

There were six pitches where rebar had been embedded in the steep rock to make stairs.

The first steep section the trail lost 650 feet in less than a quarter mile, the last 750 feet in half a mile. Walking the last section in the dark with only my headlamp, I was grateful for the rebar and fresh white blazes on trees and rocks that caught my light. I kept telling myself over and over, at nearly every step, "Just be careful; go as slowly as you need to. Just be careful. Don't fall." I alternated with, "I don't think a 68-year-old woman should be doing this alone in the dark in the rain."

Seeing lights on a road in the far distance, there didn't appear to be anything between me and the lights. The book said I was on a cliff. I couldn't spare the energy to be scared. All my concentration was on carefully and safely taking each individual step.

When I neared the bottom, David turned on the car lights below me, and I cheered. I was almost there. I was going to survive intact. But I was still extra careful for the last few steps.

I decided I should get off the trail in Maine and head to New York to see my family.

Perhaps the weather would be better there. I was thankful for getting down that last mountain alive and didn't want to push my luck. I didn't want to hike in truly unsafe conditions. Night Train, already at the hostel, said he felt the same way. David drove us to Grafton Notch to pick up my last food drop and then to Gorham, New Hampshire to catch a bus to Boston. Baldpate, which I'd been scheduled to climb over in another day, had a snow line considerably below the cloud-shrouded top, confirming I'd made a good decision.

Arriving in Gorham, we found Bookworm at the hostel after having had a rather terrifying experience on Baldpate. He'd fallen on black ice and slid 50 feet, very lucky not to have been injured, doubly confirming our decisions to stop. Night Train and I bought our bus tickets and went to the Chinese Buffet, enjoying our leisure and consuming three plates of food each—while dry, warm, and safe. What a contrast with hiking the day before, not taking time to stop for food.

On the bus to Boston we saw the White Mountains, white indeed, peeking out with fresh snow under layers of gray clouds. From Boston another bus took me to New York. But in New York City, the Short Line Bus to my destination was closed for the day. I needed to take a train, but this was the bus station. Where was the train? I could find my way solo in the woods, but public transportation by myself terrified me. I was definitely out of my element standing there with people streaming by me at a New York City pace while I wore a bewildered, scared look, dressed in hiker duds and carrying a backpack. The lady in the information booth looked at me like I was a country bumpkin, not far from the truth. She disdainfully gave me bad directions to the subway, not the train I needed.

Starting to have a meltdown, I tearfully called my daughter and her husband on my cell phone. They told me to go outside and get in a taxi. "It won't cost too much, Mom. Let the taxi driver take you to the train station." With great relief, I did as I was told. A very nice man in a yellow vest personally escorted me to the correct train in Grand Central Station, and a nice guy on the train helped heave my pack into the overhead bin. I liked the train station a whole lot better than the bus station. My old age showed in civilization more obviously than on the trail.

Chapter 20 New York and Tramper

Not fully recovered from my Maine adventures, I still had the urge to be on the trail. Sara had three little boys under four, who got up very early most of the time anyway. So three little boys and I were bundled into the van, and Sara drove me to Seven Lakes Drive on Bear Mountain, where we found the AT crossing. After they left me, they saw four deer and a flock of turkeys, which made their trip exciting.

Later in the day, I saw two eastern coyotes and three black bears in the zoo. Yes, the AT goes through the Bear Mountain Zoo.

Glad to be on the trail, my first steps were accompanied by inner and outer grins. After the zoo I took the side trail to Anthony's Nose, a hunk of rock 300 feet above the Bear Mountain Bridge over the Hudson River. There I met Tramper, a fellow section hiker, and we chatted a bit. Wonder of wonders, he said he could possibly help me with transportation in New York and gave me his phone number.

I had lunch with a large contingent of Koreans on a field trip on the Nose. As I ate lunch, I watched two eagles and three turkey vultures soar above and below me.

At the end of the day Sara met me at the little convenience store, The Appalachian Market, and we drove home. My knee ached, my heel hurt, and I was tired, but my psyche was restored. I loved the trail.

After three days' rest with my daughter's family at West Point, I started off again from the Appalachian Market. The forest smelled of decaying wet leaves, while fresh ones wafted down with each gust of wind. I ate lunch sitting on a Revolutionary War house foundation. Amazing. I walked on the road Washington had traveled to visit his troops. I am partial to the West, but there is a lot to be said for the woods and history lessons in the East.

That night a great number of Cub Scouts, their parents, and other campers camped nearby, and one of the adults offered me a hot meal, which I declined, as I had already eaten my own dinner, though I appreciated their thoughtfulness.

The following night, I came to a unique shelter, an old cement-block clubhouse with one wall removed. Inside were bunks for six, a table and chairs. Outside was a covered patio with two picnic tables, lawn chairs, benches, and a clothesline. Sweet, except it was within sight of the nearby road, which made me nervous.

After I moved in a hiker came by for a rest, said he lived nearby and was going for a four- mile hike. Whether it was the nearness of the road or something about his manner, I had a disturbed feeling about him. That impression was deepened when he came back about half an hour later saying that his feet hurt, and he had the wrong shoes. I wondered if he'd seen me bathing before he'd stopped the first time and had come back to see if I was still there. He knew I was in the shelter. What if he came back again with bad intentions?

What to do? There was no nearby approved shelter or camp spot going north, and I didn't want to hike in the dark. So I locked the door that was in one wall and built a barricade across the open wall space made of benches, table, upside down and precariously balanced lawn chairs, brooms, my pot, poles, etc. It was a *Fibber McGee's closet* sort of barrier. (That phrase references a very old radio show from my mother's era that had the trademark sound effects of a closet overfilled with objects of all kinds noisily crashing to the ground every time the door was opened. You have to be pretty old to understand Fibber McGee's Closet.)

At any rate, that was what I tried to build, something no one could enter without crashing something down to make a lot of noise. I put my tiny opened pocketknife on the bunk near my head. At least I would wake up if someone was after me, and I could try to defend myself instead of being a defenseless sleeper. All that was pretty silly, as there were no problems during the night. I'd just scared myself into thinking there might be a problem. But I felt better with my barricade, which no one breached.

Waking to a crisp fall morning at 38 degrees, I walked through crunchy, crackling, swishy leaves, and met day hikers, who accessed the trail from a nearby train station. (Parts of the AT in New York were quite close to civilization.)

On the trail before 7:00, under overcast skies, I walked by Nuclear Lake. (Nuclear fuels used to be processed nearby giving the lake its name.) The trail was a wonderland of pathways on fallen leaves wending through the lacy yellow of the understory of the forest. The lake itself was beautiful with bright fall leaves on the trees surrounding it, the sun playing tag with the clouds, intermittently shining on red and golden leaves. Everywhere I went, the colors were enchanting.

For unknown reasons, my heel was feeling much better, and I took out the gel inserts and needed no pain medication. I stopped for lunch at a lovely overlook above farmland and the town of Pawling, watching turkey vultures soar below and above me. At Telephone Pioneer shelter, I found an umbrella abandoned at the shelter and later in the day I tried it out in sprinkling rain.

After crossing Swamp River and the boardwalk over the swamp, I came to the hiker friendly landscaping business on Highway 22. I talked with the owner, and he had one of his employees take me to the motel.

After showering, I ate pizza 'till I was stuffed and talked to Tramper on the phone about picking me up on Hoyt Road.

The next morning, my driver from the motel was ready, and so was I, promptly at 5:45.

After scraping thick frost off his windows, he dropped me off at the trailhead at 6:00 on his way to work. The stars and the moon were still out, and at 31 degrees, it was far too cold to stand around waiting for dawn, so I shouldered pack, turned on my headlamp, and started walking.

Moving slowly down a bit of trail along the highway to a pasture, I climbed the stile (a ladder-like arrangement over a fence) and headed up the trail through the sparkling frozen grass of the meadow. The frost caught the light of my headlamp, shining like glitter poured freely on the ground, as I walked under the moon and a starlit sky. The wood of the stile was frosty and quite slippery, reminding me to be careful. A water tower constructed in 1920 could barely be made out on the skyline of the pasture, along with something else that moved in a pocket of dark fog. The moving critter turned out to be a cow trotting to the side of the pasture when I'd entered its domain. I crossed three stiles and as many pastures on my way up the ridge as daylight slowly emerged. There was only me, my footsteps crunching on frozen ground, and an occasional rustle in the grass as small birds were startled by my passing.

Reaching Leather Hill Road, I called Tramper and told him when to expect me at Hoyt Road. I was there no more than a minute when Tramper drove up. What a great trail angel! Tramper drove me back to the Appalachian Market, where my daughter had dropped me off five days before. Tramper really went out of his way to help a fellow hiker, and I deeply appreciated his help.

Three days were left for the hiking year, all slack packs. For the first one, Sara and I bundled the boys into the car at 6:30. They dropped Grandma on the trail heading southbound from Seven Lakes Drive. Looking back toward Bear Mountain from West Mountain, the sun glared off the Hudson River. Before going up Black Mountain, I crossed the Palisades Parkway, New York City only 34 miles away according to the highway sign. From the top of Black

Mountain I could see the NYC skyline. How amazing to be so close to so many people, yet feel light years away on a mountain trail.

After a lovely view down to Silver Mine Lake's bright blue surrounded by colorful fall leaves, the rest of the day was just a nice walk in the woods over a carpet of those bright leaves.

Sara picked me up at Tiorati Circle, and we drove to Silver Mine Lake for an open rest room. The facilities looked a little shabby, a lady coming out shaking her head and turning up her nose in disapproval. I thought it palatial and rather nice inside. It was clean. There were flush toilets, running water, and soap. It was even heated. It surely beat squatting over a hole in the ground.

My last two days were slack packs with a motel in the middle. Rock scrambles up Eastern Pinnacles and Cat Rocks were short and fun since the weather and the rocks were dry. And I was grateful.

As I ate lunch, Foxtrot, whom I'd met in the Chairback Range in Maine, came by going south and stopped to chat with me. It was fun to hang out with a hiker who could really hike. He'd finished Maine and walked through New Hampshire, Vermont, Massachusetts, Connecticut and most of New York in the time I'd done part of Maine and most of New York. The two of us a demonstrated the wide variety in age, ability and background of those who walk long trails. He too, as well as Lisa in Maine, encouraged me to think about the CDT after completing the AT and the PCT.

The fall color was glorious. In many places green was only an accent color against a forest aflame with yellow, orange, and red. I was especially amazed by red oak leaves. I'd never thought of oaks as being other than green or brown.

A brown, white, and black patterned snake gave me a bit of excitement in the late afternoon. I didn't know what kind it was as it lay stretched out lengthwise, so motionless he almost looked dead. I stood back a ways and took his picture before reaching far forward to tap his tail with my pole. He immediately half coiled ready to strike in half a second of time. I gave him a *very* wide berth going by, thinking he looked deadly. When I later looked him up I found he was indeed deadly, a copperhead.

Agony Grind was the official name of the last section of the day's trail. I was glad to be going down and not up, and equally glad it was still light and not raining as I picked my way down the steep rocks. I arrived at the road and started walking toward town, two miles away.

About half way there, Steve, a fellow hiker, pulled over and offered me a ride, which I gladly accepted. Although hitchhiking is illegal in New York, I do not think it was illegal to offer a ride or accept one.

Early the next morning I was out the door of my motel room and walking in the dark with my headlamp to a gas station. I didn't wish to risk being a statistic by walking in the dark on the edge of the highway with cars zipping by. I bought some orange juice at the food mart and drank it while eyeing the other customers. I hoped asking for rides while in a store wouldn't be considered hitching. The third person I asked, consented to give me a ride up the hill for the two miles back to the trail.

Walking once again, the dark lightened into day, revealing a golden yellow forest. I'd thought my hike in Virginia, West Virginia, and Maryland was beautiful the previous fall, but the leaves were even more gorgeous in New York. That week, that very day, must have been the absolute peak of color.

New York had nearly as many lakes as Maine, and I passed six my last two days. I also went through the *Lemon Squeezer*, a narrow cleft in slanted rocks, which usually requires hikers to take off their backpacks to squeeze through. I could walk through with a daypack though awkwardly. Walking over Fingerboard Mountain, Mother Nature outdid herself with glorious color.

Sara met me again at Tiorati Circle with the boys for a picnic. Four-year-old William delighted in climbing the rocks by our picnic table. Two-and-a-half-year-old Matthew found sticks in the forest to play with, and baby Nathan raised his teething cookie in a baby power salute to the day and the end to the year's hiking.

Chapter 21 Fall and Winter 2010

My Gym

I used to brag about being a reasonably fast hiker for an old lady. That changed to bragging about being one of the oldest hikers. I met four women in Maine in 2009, who were in their 70s. Way to go! But there were not a whole lot of women hikers over 65. I have no trouble calling myself old. In fact, I flaunt it. In the spring of 2010, I was blessed to be 68 and still able to hike. I celebrated my age and hiking on the trail.

However, as each year went by I had to be more and more intentional about staying in hiking shape and conditioning before I hit a trail. My friend Kathy had a gym membership and spent time and money working out getting ready to hike. From the time she was young, her parents told her, she should get a good education, so she could get a good job and never have to work hard at physical labor. So she wouldn't *work* physically unless it was in a gym or hiking. I didn't have that particular parent tape running in my head, although going to college and getting an education had always been expected. When I retired, I spent hours working in my yard. My yard was my gym.

Weeding, shoveling compost, pruning, and even splitting wood are hard work. But those activities help keep me in good physical condition. I saved lots of money not paying gym fees, as well as enjoying the fruits of my labors in good food all year long. For an old lady with a bad knee, I stayed in pretty good shape. That, however, didn't mean conditioning hikes could be skipped. El Nino weather that winter meant Washington had some of the best weather in the nation, so Kathy and I had many good hiking days.

After mild months from December to February, winter arrived all at once in March, with large dumps of snow in the mountains. My last conditioning hike was solo up Mt. Si. On the way down, about a mile from the top, I took a most spectacular fall.

As I started to slide in the slushy slippery snow, I didn't want to hurt my bad knee and just let myself fall over like a dead tree. That protected the knee but resulted in landing on my back, head down, sliding down a very steep part of the mountainside. Yikes! I managed to get turned sideways and stop about 30 feet below the trail. No body parts were hurt, the pack wasn't damaged, and I didn't even break my glasses, which were in my pocket. I climbed back up to the trail and walked three miles down to the car. That was enough conditioning. HA!

Flying east to Harrisburg, PA, a young seminarian picked me up and drove me to Gettysburg, where I was a guest of the seminary, staying in the cottage for visiting Bishops, quite posh for a hiker—and I wasn't a Bishop.

This accommodation came by way of my trail angel, John Spangler, who had driven me to the hospital at the end of my Virginia section in 2008. I walked around the battlefields in the afternoon, sobered to consider all the blood shed on those beautiful hills and valleys. If you remember your history lessons, much of the Battle of Gettysburg took place on Seminary Ridge, which was and is a Lutheran Seminary.

Chapter 22 April 6, 2010 AT

Winkle

John drove me out to Old Forge Road in Pennsylvania to meet Winkle, an AT thru hiker, who had followed my journal for a couple years. Her husband, Greg dropped her off. I was excited to meet and hike with my email hiker friend.

After obligatory *before* pictures, Winkle and I walked up the trail. It was 84 degrees when we got to the shelter after our short walk, a far cry from the snow on Mount Si in Washington a few days earlier.

The next day was also hot, 83 in the shade. Hiking with a friend was a pleasure. Our night was at twin shelters at Quarry Gap, the nicest I'd ever seen with a spring routed to a merry stream in front of the shelters and clumps of daffodils blooming nearby. The shelters, absolutely clean, had a covered picnic table and even a Bear Box for food storage.

The next day was hotter yet. My thermometer registered 89, making early April feel like July. We drank lots of water and sprawled in shade when we could find some. Late in the afternoon, Steve hiked by our shelter, the same Steve who had given me a ride to my motel on the last night of my hike in New York. It's a small world on the trail.

Much nicer hiking weather arrived that night, a cold front dropping the temperature to 44 degrees. We hiked 11 miles before lunch, not something I could have done in Maine last year or in Pennsylvania in hot weather. A bright spot in the day was passing a little evergreen tree on the trail, an Easter tree hung with many colored plastic Easter eggs.

Although I was doing better in the cooler weather, Winkle was having trouble with her knee, knee pain and a history of knee injury giving her concern. So Greg, her husband, met her at Highway 94, and they said good-bye to me. I missed Winkle. I'd enjoyed her company.

The woman at the Holly Inn gave me coffee and poppy-seed bread and drove me back to the trail. Winkle told me someone had broken her arm on rocks at Rocky Ridge, but I had no falls. Finding the *recommended* campsite completely overrun with fishermen, I had to find something else. The Regional AT Building in Boiling Springs had a bulletin board ad for a resort at $25 a night, which caught my eye. Deal. The resort had a restaurant, another bonus.

Early spring flowers including May Apples unfurling were a delight in the Cumberland Valley. I loved the way May Apples pop open like little umbrellas, but I wasn't as happy to see poison ivy. I had to look carefully before putting my body, pack, or poles on the ground.

At Darlington Shelter I met Rev, a hiking Methodist Pastor. I sang Holden Evening Prayer for him since it was Sunday.

The Duncannon, in Doyle, had been a fine hotel in its heyday, one of the original Anheuser Busch Hotels, although that heyday was long past. The sheets were clean, and the water was hot (even if it was down the hall). The bed was quite comfortable, and I took a zero day in that bit of yesteryear.

Thru hikers, or even long section hikers, are not the only ones on the trail. At the Doyle I met a woman with much more severe arthritis than mine. Her goal was to walk one mile on the AT in every state through which it passed. You do not have to be a thru hiker or carry a backpack for even a single night to find enjoyment and worthwhile goals on long trails.

"Hey, it's going to be rocky after a while."

With the help of a shuttle I made an 18-mile slack pack back to Duncannon SOBO. I set no speed records on the rocky trail trying to be overtaken with poison ivy. I moved like an old lady with or without a pack, and 18 miles was a long way for me. I reminded myself three years ago it had looked doubtful that I would walk on any trail with a staph infection in my knee. Any step I took, at whatever speed, was a blessing.

Some days on the trail were gentle climbs or level stretches in which to recover from more strenuous challenges. I enjoyed the challenges, but I also enjoyed pleasant days walking in the woods with no grand views, few flowers, and not much excitement. Peace and quiet, rhythmic, repetitive strides and the uneventful trail allowed the mind to wander or even empty of thought entirely, another blessing.

Gentle stretches didn't last all that long. Pennsylvania is famous for its rocky trail, but what I found even more challenging was the poison ivy. I react strongly to the oil in this leafy plant at any touch to bare skin. I also react if my hand touches a hiking pole, which has previously brushed poison ivy. There were times I chose not to use my hiking poles, not because I didn't need them, but because they were just one more item needing to avoid the ever-present poison ivy. Finding a poison-ivy-free place for my feet was challenge enough, not always successfully met.

The skies opened up with an incredible deluge as I approached 501 Shelter, and I ran the last 100 feet in an old-lady, bad-knee run. 501 was a *super shelter*, fully enclosed with a door and windows, 12 bunks. It was leaking rain on a long picnic table under a skylight. I was VERY glad to have made it to the shelter before the downpour. Unfortunately, I found the shelter was infested with mice, brazenly coming up through wide gaps between floorboards, running all over the place.

Not wanting to go out into the rain, then falling by the bucketfull, maybe even the wheelbarrow-full, I devised a mouse proof place for my food by putting my comestibles and smelly stuff in the shelter's empty five-gallon bucket for recyclables, turning the bucket upside down on a solid plywood bunk and putting a chair on top to weight it down.

That took care of food storage. I pushed my pot from the doorway out in the rain to get enough water to hold me for the night and went to sleep listening to pounding rain on the skylight drowning out the sounds of mice scurrying across the floor.

Weather in the eastern USA was quite variable that spring, a heat wave to very cold. On a brisk morning I almost walked in a circle on a rocky ridge, following the trail from one viewpoint to another. At lunch on a lovely lookout, I watched turkey vultures play, soaring and gliding between me and the forest canopy below my lookout perch.

Then I had a disaster when picking up my resupply box at the Post

Office. My driver's license was missing. OH NO. Nothing else was missing, only the driver's license. The postman accepted my Costco credit card with my picture as an ID and gave me my two boxes. Wondering where the driver's license was, I also wondered how I would be able to board an airplane at the end of my hike without it.

Near Pocahontas Springs, sitting in a rock armchair someone had constructed in a grassy clearing, I made cellphone calls to every place in Duncannon or Port Clinton I'd stayed or purchased anything, but had no luck finding my missing driver's license. Oh well, walk on.

My cousin emailed me, asking if the Pennsylvania rocks were as bad as the Maine rocks. No, everything is easier than Maine, at least until New Hampshire. There are plenty of rocks on the AT in every state, just more of them in Pennsylvania—big ones, little ones, rocks sometimes scattered, sometimes very, very thickly covering the trail and sometimes big piles of boulders.

Pennsylvania also has lovely woodsy trail on old dirt roads decorated with violets and bluets. The views from Pulpit Rock (a must for a preacher) and Pinnacle Lookout overlooked the patchwork quilt landscape of farms, pastures, and woods. Eckville Hiker Center Shelter even had an outlet to charge my phone. Pennsylvania wasn't all bad.

The rocks became much worse from Dan's Pulpit past Balanced Rocks. The guidebook claimed a spot I was to pass later in the day would be rocky. I kept telling myself, while carefully walking through heaps of rocks thickly scattered on the trail, "Hey, it's going to be rocky after a while." I was only mildly amused at the incongruity of the time element in the statement. Now I knew why Fox Trot, whom I'd met in Maine and then New York, had flitted like a butterfly over the rocks. Besides being young, male, and having knees, he was from Pennsylvania and must have had lots of practice with rocky trail. I didn't flit like a butterfly. I lumbered and labored like a behemoth hippo with a broken leg. But I did safely get through the rocks.

While resting at Blue Summit B&B that night, I looked for my guidebook and found it missing. Not something else lost! I'd already discovered I had no maps for that section, evidently having put them in a different resupply box. I was disgusted. I liked to think of myself as a reasonably competent trail person, not a ninny who kept losing things.

Past Blue Summit, a knife-edge pile of boulders called the Cliffs required careful navigation with a bum knee. The gentleman, a hiker from England, passed me, saying he'd seen my guidebook lying on the trail, but he hadn't picked it up. After the Cliffs came Bear Rocks, which I decided to climb for the view, meeting three SOBO hikers who climbed with me. One of them, Patty, heard I'd lost my guidebook, and they would see it along the trail. She immediately gave me hers, saying they had three and didn't need it.

Wow. Thanks. I could always just follow white blazes, but it was very nice to be able to tell how far I'd come and how far I had to go. A blaze didn't carry that information. Getting a new guidebook mid-trail was a wonderful gift.

I took a zero day at Slatington Fine Lodging— (Fine was the owner's last name.)—an old rooming house with shared bathrooms and men, old and young, the tenants. The door had a double dead-bolt lock, and I had no trouble and found the owner quite helpful as he arranged a ride for me back to the trail.

From Lehigh Gap, the trail went straight up the rocky face of Blue Mountain, 1,000 feet in less than half a mile. My bad leg was challenged, but the sky was blue, the sun was out, and the views were terrific. I sang, "Oh, What a Beautiful Morning." At least I did when I wasn't catching my breath or figuring out how to navigate over rocks.

A reroute went around the superfund site, a barren mountain needing reclamation from a century of unregulated zinc mining and smelting emissions. Still, there were blooming bleeding hearts on my trail, symbols of sorrow for the rape of the land and promise of better from Mother Nature's healing.

Mechanical Man and his wife, Crayola Lady, took me to their home and showed me to the shower, also feeding me a wonderful roast pork dinner topped off with an ice cream sandwich, all a hiker could want. They told stories of hosting trail legend Earl Schafer and showed me pictures of their son, the BMX bike racer.

Mechanical Man and Crayola Lady offered to bring my gear to me at Wolf Rocks, the farthest south evidence of glaciers on the AT, making the majority of the day a slack pack through the rainy forest under my umbrella. The rocks were large chunks, smoothly polished by ancient moving ice and slippery in the rain, requiring I move with caution to avoid a crash.

Reaching Kirkridge Shelter, I found Yoyo, whom I'd met on The Priest in Virginia. He'd walked the entire AT in 2008, but was back on the trail now because he missed it. It was nice to have company. We were in our bags by 9:00, listening to thunder and watching lightning flash over hills around us while rain pounded the roof, very glad to be dry under that roof.

On my last day in Pennsylvania, I traveled along as fast as I could go, which wasn't very fast, but it was as fast as I could go. Heading down from Mt. Minsie, I saw the smiling face of Tramper coming up to meet me. Tramper provided a ride for me half way across New York in 2009, and now he'd agreed to help this year with another very essential, and rather large, chunk of transportation.

Together, we hiked down to Deer Head Inn, where I'd stayed the previous year, and Tramper had spent the night. I used his shower before he checked out. Yay. It was wonderful and unexpected to be clean and was probably good for him, too, as I sat in the same car with him for a few hours. Driving across New Jersey and New York, we yakked trail talk all the way. What a great trail angel.

An Iguana In His Shirt

Tramper dropped me at Hoyt Road at 4:30, and I walked to the nearest shelter. I was soon drenched in sweat, and all my nice cleanliness was gone in Connecticut's heat. And, oh yes, it was raining there, too. Connecticut had trail that wasn't a pile of rocks, but I found the shelter trashed. Food was dumped in a puddle in front of the shelter, trash strewn around and the privy tipped over. Shelters are the bedrooms of hikers and it was horrible to see them damaged by vandals.

Volunteers maintain trails and shelters on the AT, and it would take a lot of work to clean up the mess, especially to restore the privy. It made me very angry. These jerks were a dreadful contrast to the wonderful, gracious trail angels, who cared for hikers and trails. I scraped up the ruined food from the mud puddle and buried it. I gathered up some of the trash. I couldn't do anything about the privy.

Leaving the vandalized shelter, I walked along the Housatonic River and hiked up Shagitoke Mountain on trail sometimes smooth, sometimes resembling Pennsylvania rocks or Maine rocks. Pennsylvania rocks were like a trail strewn with Tonka Truck size rocks, all kinds of Tonka Trucks.

Maine rocks were more often polished slabs of rock. Neither were pleasant for me in the rain. I was glad to reach Kent, buy my dinner from the IGA and go to Cooper's Creek B&B on a tip from the Outfitter. The B&B was lovely and my hosts, Cooper and Mary, were delightful.

Connecticut has uphill and I moved rather slowly, out of practice with uphill as much of Pennsylvania had been relatively flat. That conditioning hike on Mt. Si was a distant memory, and all those miles Winkle and I did so well at the start of this year's hike seemed like unobtainable aberrations. Connecticut had uphill. Yet Connecticut also had the easiest, flattest five miles on the whole AT.

Toward the end of the day, headed to Cornwall, I met Cyron, a young hiker with a very large pack and an iguana carried in his shirt. His pet iguana suffered from the cold unless warmed from his skin. I'd never seen an iguana on the trail before and haven't seen another since. Cornwall had a motel, a Post Office, a grocery store, and a package store, enough for me to get my resupply box, eat, shower and sleep. I didn't need the package store.

The next day I took a slight detour on Sharon Road as Cyron had told me a stream on the trail was impassable. As I walked, I listened to singing birds accompanied by woodpeckers adding staccato rim shots. At one point in the day two different woodpeckers did a duet in snare and tom tom, at least it sounded like that to me. I had lunch on Easter Mountain, a good place for a pastor. At the Iron Bridge I caught a ride to the Toymaker's Café. There was no bed or shower, but the Toymaker let me camp in his yard.

The Toymaker also let me dry out my sleeping bag inside in the morning and fed me hot, fresh cinnamon rolls for breakfast. Yum. Red columbine, violets and white hobble bush added to my pleasure as I walked. Three young guys in the shelter that night fed me caramelized apples for desert. Sweet. Double entendre intended. I sang Holden Evening Prayer for these Presbyterian young men, who even said prayers before eating. They appreciated Holden.

The book said the day would be strenuous, and it didn't disappoint. I was on the trail at 6:30 on a hot day, up to 84 degrees and went over three mountains for a total of about 2,400 feet elevation gain, some of it quite steep. The prettiest part was a lovely woodsy walk among hemlock and pine trees by a stream with many small waterfalls, Sages Ravine. It reminded me of the Cascades; I loved the white hobblebush against the dark water and the dark greens and browns of the forest. That night in Massachusetts other campers gave me a spoonful of chocolate cheesecake for dessert. Desserts two nights in a row.

"Now why did you go and do that?"

When it was warm enough at 5:30 AM that you could envision going without clothes, it was a sure sign the day was going to be a hot one. Hiking in heat just saps me, turning me into a dead daisy, greased pig, stewing me in my own juice or any other cliché describing heat. Even easy miles seemed hard in very humid heat.

Two bands of mushroom gatherers met me in the flat area I walked that day, one of them even interviewed me for their newsletter. Another mushroom gatherer gave me a cookie when we reached a parking lot. At the road, I could see a store close by and I needed more water due to the extreme heat of the day. I guzzled a Sprite from a vending machine at an antique store but the proprietor said he didn't have any potable water, and he looked like he wanted me out of the store. He seemed somewhat lacking in the milk of human kindness as well as water. A smaller shop had an accommodating woman, who pulled out a gallon of water and told me to take all I wanted.

The last five miles uphill in the heat took an eternity. Black flies and mosquitoes swarmed in the heat and bit hard, leaving scars. Trail builders seemed sadistic, routing the trail through avoidable rocks. Bugs tried to devour me when I bathed at the shelter and pumped my water. The shelter had a scroungy look, and something had been chewing on the wood of the bunks. The gentleman, the hiker from England, had signed the shelter register earlier in the day, saying he was evaporating in the heat. And this was spring, not summer, only May 2nd.

I woke up to banging on my bunk, looking down at my feet with my headlamp to see the mangiest looking porcupine ever, trying to get up in my bunk with me. I told him I didn't need a bedfellow, shining the light of my headlamp in his eyes. He gave me a squinty-eyed look of pain as if to say, "Now why did you go and do that?" as he clambered back down to the floor, waddled over to the edge of the shelter, down the side and out into the still fairly dark morning.

Heaven and Goin' Home

While hiking through more woods and by a lovely lake with a beaver lodge in the middle, the title of a Hemingway novel, *The Sun Also Rises* bounced around in my brain as a trail descriptor. Each day dawned on the trail. Even if the sun were hidden behind clouds, dawn came with its light every day. Each dawn, each moment, and each step on the trail had sameness, yet particularity *and* potential for something new to happen. My job as a hiker was to keep walking and see what would turn up.

Sights ran the gamut from mangy porcupines searching for salt from sleeping hikers and their gear to lovely woods, lakes, and beaver lodges seen though raindrops under overcast skies. Experiences varied from pain and exhaustion to great joy, walking by myself or making multitudes of connections with people on trails or in towns. The sun rose every day on trails rich with potential adventures.

Two days after the porcupine tried to crawl into my bunk, I had an opportunity for a very long slack pack. Who was it who told me it would be easy? The Cookie Lady? She was told by thru-hikers? Didn't

I know that I could never do what a thru-hiker does in less than twice the time they do it?

Eight miles into the 19-mile day, I realized I'd lost my belt pouch that held lots of handy little things, including on this particular day, my headlamp. I was once again disgusted with myself. Something else lost. This trip was the trip of lost stuff. Drat and double darn, darn, darn. The missing pack pouch also had my candy, my knife, my pole tips, my hat toggle, tissues, my comb, nail file, toothbrush and importantly, the extra pain medications I'd been saving up for this very long day. There was no way I could go back eight miles to get it. There wasn't a thing to do but go onward. Later in the day I met two day-hikers and expounded my plight to them. They listened to my rantings and promised to look for the pack pouch. I told them their trail name should be Sweet Couple, but they said they were not always sweet. Listening to my tale of woe, they were sweet to me.

Other than losing the pack pouch, the day went pretty well. Trout Lilies, painted and red trillium were in bloom. blue chiming bells graced the meadow and marsh marigolds made yellow splashes of color by streams. Walking by beaver ponds, I saw moose turds, so I knew there were moose in Massachusetts.

Getting tired at the end of the day, I worried as I had no sleeping bag with me and had lost my headlamp. I HAD to get to my destination before dark. The knee was stressed, and I had no extra meds. As thunderstorms hit in the afternoon, I hoped I and my trusty umbrella wouldn't get hit by lightning while we descended from high places in the rain.

I took a break at a shelter just off the trail to eat and replenish my energy, a most fortunate stop. Steve, a SOBO section-hiker (trail-named Goin' Home) said he would look for my pack pouch. Not only would he bring my pack pouch to me if he found it, he would be renting a car in Great Barrington and driving to North Adams, where he would pick up his own car to drive home past West Point to New Jersey. And when would he be doing all this? Friday. Wow.

Would he consider a rider to West Point?

Yes. Yes, he would. And for only the cost of some gas. All this conversation happened in the few moments it took to quickly chew up a dozen almonds and some jerky and pack up to fly down the trail again. He had my name, address, and cellphone number, and said he would call if (or if not) he found my pouch. I might lose things, but I was blessed again with very remarkable trail magic.

The find of a potential ride lifted my spirits, but I was still very tired and pushing my limits by the time I reached the road and the Cookie Lady's house. The weather had turned very cold, the wind blew extra hard, and storms were ready to unloose torrents of rain as the Cookie Man met me with my gear.

I now know what heaven looks like: like an old farmhouse turned into a garage, old stained carpet on the floor and a John Deer tractor pushed out of the way to make room for my sleeping bag. It was warm and out of the wind. Electric lights meant I didn't need a headlamp, and the toilet was flushable with pails of water. I was so grateful.

The wizened elderly gentleman, eager to help me, brought me a half-gallon of warm water for washing. He was indeed, what an angel looks like. My knee hurt like crazy, and I twisted my back getting ready for bed, but I was so happy to have found this warm and lighted place. And life was good.

On the way to Dalton I met Tattu Jo, a very fast, ultra-light PCT hiker out to experience the AT, the trail where long-distance hiking began. In Dalton, a wonderful manager at the Shamrock Village Inn went out of her way to drive me to the Pharmacy for a toothbrush and a comb and to a little store in the opposite direction, where I searched unsuccessfully for some sort of flashlight.

Concerned about not having a headlamp, I set my alarm for an extra early hour and left the motel at 5:30. Passing through the little town of Cheshire I found a $2.00 keychain squeeze flashlight. It would suffice to get me through the last night. The sweet woman in the store even paid part of my tax since hikers don't generally carry change. You meet a lot of very nice people when you take a long distance hike. Before leaving Cheshire while eating two hot dogs from the convenience store, I sat on a patch of grass behind some mailboxes and watched the traffic go by.

My knee started hurting on the last five miles of the day. Not taking a zero day after a 19- mile slack pack didn't allow the knee time to recover. It became more and more difficult to find a pain-free position, even when resting. I finally, gratefully, reached the shelter. Come on knee, hang in there for just one more day.

On my last day, it was a cold 37 degrees in the morning, and I was glad for the evergreens that grew beside the trail protecting me from the wind. I knew the tourist attraction on top of Greylock Mountain wouldn't be open, but I fantasized on the way up about stopping in for a second breakfast of waffles swimming in butter and syrup. As expected, no one was there. Oh well.

Taking pictures of trout lilies, trillium, and spring beauties, shedding clothes, eating, and resting the knee, I took my time that morning. An older day-hiker, who passed me going up as I was going down, asked me to look for his water bottle. Hey, I'm not the only one who loses things.

I stopped at Prospect Point to enjoy the view, the loveliest of the trip. My body was tired, and the knee felt fragile, but as I reveled in the view of North Adams and the unfolding mountains of Vermont behind the town, I wanted to just keep going. I felt like Kathy and I'd felt on our last night in the Sierra. If it weren't for exhaustion and bodies wearing out, we would keep going forever. I guess only another hiker could understand that state of mind.

After descending the steep trail on slippery leaves, I approached the highway. A man got out of his car and said, "Hey, AT hiker, can I take you somewhere in town while you're here? Where do you want to go?" Wow. I hadn't even gotten to the corner, and I had my own driver. I rode to Subway for a footlong and called Steve.

Within an hour he was there, bearing my lost pack pouch. Someone had riffled it. The headlamp, knife, and nail clippers were gone. The candy and Chapstick had been chewed. Whoever had taken the headlamp should have taken the whole thing. To pick up something someone lost and may not be returning for is understandable, but to riffle through it and leave items that would attract wildlife scavengers showed a lack of couth and kindness for the trail. How nice it was of

Steve to have looked for it, found it, and returned it to me.

So I lost some stuff but made a new trail friend. We drove to New York with a stop for pizza; I paid him a donation for gas, bought his pizza, and we chattered trail talk the whole way.

That night I lay on a soft bed, clean and with my family. I could be an old fuddy duddy grandma and lose things, having them returned to me kindly. My son sent me my passport to get me on the plane back to Washington.

It was good to go hiking, and it was even better to have family. Two days after I was home and had my new driver's license, I received a call from The Doyle back in Pennsylvania. They found my driver's license in piles of paper work. It was too late to help me get on the plane, but I was glad my identity `hadn't been stolen. And another 363 miles of AT was completed.

Chapter 23   Summer 2010

GPS

After traipsing up and down Fuller Ridge in the snow in 2009, stressing my knee and covering two or three times the mileage I would have done had I known where the trail was, I didn't want to repeat such a thing ever again. I'd talked to hikers who had no problems as one of their party had a GPS. Following the GPS kept them roughly on the trail, though they couldn't see tread under snow. I splurged and bought one.

Then I had to learn how to use it. 2010 was a heavy-snow year in the Sierra and Cascades, so I had snow on which to practice. I hiked from Longmire, up to Rampart Ridge and then over on the connector trail to Van Trump Park and down the Comet Falls trail.

Going up the trail I discovered inaccuracies. The GPS would say I was 100 feet to one side of the trail or the other, all the while I was walking on the trail. Hmmm. When I was on snow, I sometimes misplaced the trail but learned how to follow the GPS and the logical routes of trail on the hillside. My conclusion was that it was a help, even if not always spot-on accurate.

Walking on steep hillsides of snow that day was a LOT of work.

Although I was never irreparably lost, I was very tired, and thought how embarrassing it would be to have to be rescued by a ranger. I connected with the Comet Falls trail, so a ranger wasn't necessary, and I learned some of the capabilities and limitations of my GPS.

Two PCT hikes were planned for the year, a short one in Oregon and a longer one encompassing Northern California.

Chapter 24 July 18, 2010 PCT—Oregon - Yellowstone

Kathy (Grapevine) and Linda (Gray Squirrel) chose to hike some of Oregon with me, and Kathy's husband David would provide trail support, including being a great cook.

Immediately appreciating smooth western trails, I started up the Rye Spur Trail. Later in the day, Kathy and her 10-year-old Godson joined me, but they only lasted one night as her Godson asked to bail the next morning. Sky Lakes were very pretty, but the mosquitoes liked them, too, congregated in clouds and followed me up the trail.

On the third day, I climbed up to Devil's Peak saddle and passed some nice displays of alpine phlox, pink heather, white kinnikinnick, Indian paintbrush, lupine, and wallflower. White Pasque flowers bloomed among rocks emerging from snow banks. I stopped to rest on the saddle and Yellowstone, a naturalist/guide in Yellowstone National Park, came up behind me. A thru- hiker now in Oregon, she was headed for Canada after a break in her journey.

A passing hiker had told her I was ahead, and she wanted to catch up with me for company on the descent through deep snow on the north side of the saddle. Not knowing there was plenty of time to catch the slowest hiker on the trail, she rushed to catch up and fell on the rocks and hurt her knee. I have always been so sorry catching up with slow old me was the start of her knee problems. But both pleased to meet each other, we headed down from the pass.

Using my ice axe self-belay style, I went straight down as Yellowstone traversed the switchbacks in the snow. Going straight down was easier, keeping the bad leg straight on the downhill side, while I side-stepped down the snowy, steep descent. Far more able and agile than I was, once below the snow, Yellowstone went ahead, but we both camped at the same spot that night. It was nice to have company.

We tented in a barren, burned area near Lone Wolf Peak. With no shade from trees to preserve the white cold stuff, the ground was snow free except for a little three-foot patch, which I used to wash my hands, feet, and legs in a snow bath, rubbing clean snow on dirty legs.

In the morning, I followed Yellowstone, who had zoomed ahead, and reached the highway to meet Kathy, who took me to the campground, where she and David had parked their trailer. After bumping into Yellowstone in the campground, she ended up staying in our campsite, too. In the morning Yellowstone and I hiked to Rim Village at Crater Lake, furiously waving my bandana at thick clouds of mosquitoes surrounding us. The rest of the day we were tourists.

The big news for me, was hearing I had become a Grandma for the sixth time. I even had cell service to talk to my daughter and see pictures of my newest granddaughter. That's real trail magic.

The following day, Yellowstone went on ahead at her fast pace and I at my slow one, walking around the lake. Crater Lake is the seventh deepest lake on this planet, a hole in the earth left when Mount Mazama blew up about 7,700 years ago. The most intensely blue water I'd ever seen asked me to record its beauty with a picture every 100 feet, although the view didn't drastically differ in that short distance.

After passing Crater Lake I walked through a lodge-pole-pine woods that some might consider boring after the spectacular blue beauty of the lake. I reveled in the peaceful stillness of the forest and was grateful for pleasant walking on a supremely easy trail in the shade of trees.

Hatching a Dragonfly and Feeding Mosquitoes to Ants

Gray Squirrel and Grapevine joined me at Highway 138, and the next day we journeyed north, the first time we had all been together since the Sierra in 2007. We got our water from beautiful Thielsen Creek, flowing from snow banks below Mt. Thielsen's striated rocks. Making a dry camp at Pumice Flat, rocky cliffs of the Sawtooth range on one side and Thielsen behind us, I washed in a snow bank and filled the pot with clean snow for breakfast water. Hanging our food bags and singing Holden Evening Prayer, we retired for the night. Birds called through the stillness of the evening as we watched the white and golden streaks of the setting sun in the blue sky, taking pictures through mosquito netting.

Although none of us particularly liked getting up early, we liked hiking early. A 5:00 rise time was a good pattern for us since it took us nearly two hours to pack up. We were old and slow, at least I was. We stopped at Maidu Lake for a leisurely lunch, and dried out from the shower that had hit us on the way there. A dragonfly attached itself to Gray Squirrel's drying shirt, and we waited and watched for two hours as the dragonfly hatched, since Gray Squirrel had not been willing to interrupt the process. We took pictures at each stage of hatching.

Then Gray Squirrel, walking faster than Grapevine and me, went down the wrong trail. She left an arrow in the dirt telling us where she'd gone but my map and the GPS didn't agree with her choice. We yelled and bellowed down the trail and hoped she would hear us because we could never have caught her on foot. Fortunately, she did hear and walked back up the trail. Yes, it is possible to take a wrong turn on the PCT.

Except for that trail division, my new GPS wasn't something we had to depend on, but it was comforting to see the little arrow verifying we were on the trail and taking all the correct turns, GPS and paper map displaying widening contour lines to alert us to coming possible campsites.

Getting up with the alarm to do my business outside the tent, I was attacked by mosquitoes, who bit my behind three times. I quickly slapped on clothes and my headnet to deter them.

I put on pack covers and raingear just before the afternoon thunderstorm hit. It started with ice bombs, hailstones as big around as a nickel, and we moved with the hailstorm for nearly three hours, most of the way to Windigo Pass.

When the ice bombs became smaller hail, I really enjoyed it, taking pictures of the white trail and my friends. One lightning strike scared us half to death as wc didn't even count "1" between lightning and the huge crack of thunder. Still, it was an interesting diversion to be hiking through piles of hail, some six-inches deep. Evergreens bruised by falling ice smelled like Christmas, and Gray Squirrel looked like a druid striding through the woods under her poncho.

David picked us up at Windigo Pass, and we had a lovely dinner in civilization, courtesy of Gray Squirrel. It was so nice to hike with friends. David fixed us eggs and toast, and I had chocolate milk and orange juice for breakfast. It was nice to be supported by friends.

We slack packed mostly downhill in a race to stay ahead of the mosquitoes, using DEET and a lot of bandana flapping. Matt, a SOBO from Cascade Locks passed us covered up with his raingear to deter the mosquitoes. He looked very hot. That solution would have given me heat stroke. Conductor, a thru hiker, ate lunch and chatted with us. He told us you could hand feed mosquitoes to the big black ants, and they would even sit up and beg for one. Hikers entertain themselves with whatever is at hand.

Conductor made 23-mile days and considered himself slower than the guys, who had already passed us who were 30-to-40-mile-a-day hikers. We were doing 8 to 12. There is no set speed for long-distance hiking.

At Summit Lake I needed to walk the last mile to the trailhead while everyone else went by truck. I was hiking the PCT by long sections. My friends were hiking with me on the PCT. Hiking the PCT and hiking on the PCT are two different things, but there is no set way to enjoy hiking. I was hiking the whole thing, and they were along to enjoy parts as they wished with no compulsion to get every piece.

Because of the snow at higher elevations that year, many hikers chose the Crescent Lake route, but we had heard enough positive reports from passing hikers that we chose the Diamond Peak route, a most copacetic choice on a lovely day. A view south from a ridge displayed all the mountains we had passed since Crater Lake, and Diamond Peak ahead of us became more expansive with every step and turn in the trail.

In a beautiful glacial bowl with Pasque Flowers blooming at the edges of snow, we were really glad we had chosen the high route.

Although our pace was slow, we all managed fine with the snow. Walking slowly gave more time to enjoy the view. Other hikers' footprints helped us find the trail in the snow as we passed a series of lovely tarns that seemed hung in the sky between the side of the mountain and the valley below.

Our lovely campsite by Lil's Lake was well below the snow line. Rocks entered into deep water from the shore like stairs, enticing Gray Squirrel and Grapevine to skinny dip in the lake, while I had a nice wash but didn't trust my knee enough to swim. Just before we ate, Gray Squirrel went to the lake to wash her hands, and a bootlace hooked on her opposite shoe causing her to tumble into the lake with all her clothes on. Skinny dipping was better. Falling was very out of character for Gray Squirrel, as she was by far the most coordinated of the three of us. We shared dry things for her to wear, but her cell phone was toast.

Soon, dry and dressed, she tried out Conductor's game of feeding mosquitoes to black ants.

She, too, said the ants could be hand-fed.

Eventually dinner was eaten, water was pumped for the next day, and we sang Holden Evening Prayer for our last night, all squished together in the two-man tent to hide from the mosquitoes. Our last full day in Oregon had been the best. And life was good.

I sang old Girl Scout songs on the way down to Willamette Pass, and there was David, our faithful trail support. We took some *after* pictures and drove home, chalking up another 136 miles of the PCT.

Pocketmail had gone out of business. Without Pocketmail, I spent way too much time on a zero day typing on a computer to send an email to my transcriber to put entries into my journal. It was very time consuming to write by hand and then type it up again. In the guest book of my journal, Storm told me about a new device named PEEK, and I bought one to replace the defunct Pocketmail. It was lighter, too.

Chapter 25 August 29, 2010 PCT

Northern California - Grapevine

For a year on the PCT, 136 was way too few miles. Northern California was calling. The northern sections interested Grapevine, so that was where I would begin.

I supposed other people might have thought me crazy. At 69, most of my compatriots in age took trips in RVs or rocking chairs. Yet, I looked forward to hoisting backpack and living in the woods. The trail gave me great joy. I couldn't hike very fast, and I tired more quickly than a younger hiker, but I still loved being on the trail. I wasn't the only one my age or older on the trail, but I was in a rather select group.

Grapevine's faithful husband and trail support dropped us off at Etna Summit on a cool late-August morning in the 60s. Views accompanied us as we walked north, Mount Thompson in the Trinity Alps, Mount Shasta and other craggy ranges to the south and east. Peak flower season was over, but still blooming flowers graced our way, and there were no bugs.

I could tell I'd done no hiking for a month, as I couldn't keep Grapevine in sight much before lunch. However, we were both dragging in the afternoon in spite of the beautiful views inspiring us. Rocky trail hurt our feet, and we were happy to reach Shelley Lake outlet creek to find a nice campsite out of sight of the trail.

The next day was a rainy one obscuring views, although we passed two nice lakes. Even in the rain the flowers were lovely: red columbine, monkey flower, monkshood, gentian, wooly daisies, tiger lilies, asters, penstemon, pussy paws, and buckwheat. Thru hikers passed us in the rain, moving quickly as thru hikers always did.

A patch of blue sky broke through the clouds as we reached Shadow Lake at the edge of burned woods. The rain stopped, though late rays of the sun were not enough to dry anything. From our ledge by the lake, we had incredible views across the green, high mountain meadows of a very large valley to Marble Mountain and Black Marble Mountain. Everything was wet, and there was immediate condensation inside the tent from damp air, but we had reached our goal, and life was good.

I did battle with a mouse in the night. Grapevine and I both knew better, but we were tired, cold, and wet when we reached the lake and took short cuts. I didn't empty my pockets of trail bar wrappers or check for leftover food. Grapevine left her dinner cup out without cleaning it, and we didn't hang our food bags, not seeing any likely branches high enough to be beyond bear reach.

Grapevine went to sleep instantly and could sleep through anything. Not so for me. No sooner had I laid my head down than I heard rustling near the food bags near the head of the tent. I turned on my headlamp and said, "Go away," which stopped the rustling for all of 30 seconds. After a few rounds of the same, I got up and hung the bags from the only available branch protruding from a burned stump, raising the bags a whole two feet off the ground. We tossed our trail bar wrappers out of the tent hoping to keep the mouse busy. Later in the night I heard rustling in the tent and chased the mouse out again.

In the morning Grapevine found mouse droppings and muddy paw prints in her cup and the tiny outside pocket on my pants had been chewed through to reach the lifesavers left there. But the food bags were untouched at their two foot high perch. Final score: mouse: 2, hikers: 1.

The mouse battle over, the sun was shining, the sky was blue, and the views were superlative. We hung all our stuff to dry on the bushes and had a late, but dryer, start.

In spite of the lateness, we took a side trip on the Marble Rim Trail. The whole area was incredibly striking, Black Marble Mountain dominating, plus huge bands of white rock, gray marble, and some red rock mountains and cliffs, all set in lush green meadows filled with wildflowers surrounded by range after range of mountain wilderness. Everywhere we went, there were flowers. Glorious.

In the late afternoon, we were grateful that Walrus, a passing thru hiker, recommended a lovely campsite on a side trail with a view eastward from the edge of a small cliff, where we enjoyed the warm evening and sunset.

Past King's Crown and Paradise Lake, the rocks changed to boulders with fewer high crags, meadows, and flowers. Before the descent into Seaid Valley, the trail was perched on the edge of the mountain, sulfur yellow Buckwheat in banks all around us and blue mountain ranges beyond. We felt on top on top of the world.

The descent was a long way down. David met us on a road, and Grapevine got a ride. It took me two days to reach the little café 10 minutes before it closed, the motivation to arrive before closing was a delicious blackberry milkshake.

The Seaid Valley Café is famous for the *pancake challenge*. If you can eat five enormous pancakes, they are free. I saw one thru hiker try and fail. I didn't try the challenge, but their regular breakfast fare was delicious.

For the next section, David took us back to Etna Summit, and this time we walked south, Mount Shasta dominating the view for many days. Passing hikers recommended Payne's Lake for camping, but we found several parties camped there already, complete with a crying baby and very loud dogs. I didn't begrudge their presence. It was, after all, Labor Day weekend, a good time to get out. But we chose to water up and find solitude elsewhere. Then my platypus (water carrier) sprang a leak near the bottom. I turned it upside down and carried it on the outside of my pack. You learn to be resourceful in problem solving on the trail. We found our own campsite on a nice ridge with a view.

A cold front moved in during the night. Thru hikers passed us wearing very thin windbreakers, while we were wearing multiple layers of fleece, down, and raingear to block the wind. That year, terrific spring snow in the Sierra put many hikers behind optimal thru-hike schedule. They still had more than a thousand miles to Canada and wouldn't be there until mid- October. Yet they'd sent their winter gear home after the Sierra. We tried to encourage them but also cautioned them about safety and survival. We were from Washington and knew what winter storms could be like. It had already snowed at Crater Lake, and Yellowstone texted me as she left the Dinsmore's

(Rainy Pass) reporting dismal weather. Better to regret not finishing than not live to regret it. We wished them good luck. Their success would depend on the weather and their decisions.

The Pacific Crest Trail lived up to the *Crest* part as we walked between 6,000 and 7,000 feet with vast views of ranges around us. Granite cliffs, slabs, and spires were impressive.

Flowers were fewer as we moved south.

Grapevine and I were a good team, helping each other the next couple of days. She put up with me getting slightly lost for a bit and then misplacing my hat. I helped her by carrying some of her gear when she wasn't feeling up to snuff.

Hitting a crossroad, Grapevine decided to ride a day with David, and I was on my own. I scurried down to Bull Lake ahead of clouds and raindrops, quickly threw up the tent and dove in just as the rain got serious. That night I wore everything to bed including rain gear.

The 39-degree morning warmed to 80 in sheltered sun, but was 50 on the trail, making it challenging to dress correctly for the weather. A partial view of Shasta in the morning showed fresh snow. During lunch at a cross road with David and Grapevine, I spread out the tent and sleeping bag to dry, and Grapevine joined me again to climb to Upper Deadfall Lake and another cold night over 7,000 feet.

We awoke to frosty grass and my partially dried socks and bandana were frozen stiff as cardboard. The day was a long one, 15 miles. In the morning we clicked off three-miles an hour, quite fast for two old ladies. We camped on a ridge past Trinity Divide, rocky and a little slanted, but the only reasonably flat spot we could find. We were compensated with a lovely view of Shasta turning pink in the Alpine glow from the setting sun. A tiny sliver of moon shone over the ridge with one bright star, followed by increasing darkness and a sky filled with all the constellations.

Stopping for a morning snack on a knoll with a view of Castle Crags, we saw our trail for the next several miles contouring around a large, beautifully green bowl to switchback down in front of the Crags. Pitcher Plants—curiously shaped plants that looked like something Spock might have found on another planet—grew beside the tiny trickle of a stream where we filled our water bladders.

Flowers were sparse as we descended from high country, and in the hot afternoon, the tread was rocky and somewhat treacherous for old knees. The heat and the steadily descending trail wore me out. We descended more than 2,000 feet, and when the trail ducked around a fold in the mountain taking us out of the sun, I was quite relieved. Cowboy camping on a warm night near the Dog Trail was a big change from our cold nights at higher elevation. When I was only getting ready to sleep, I'd been feeling like the toddler so bundled up to play in the snow that he couldn't move. It was much different to prepare for sleep without extra layers.

Descending from Castle Crags, I discovered gnats live in the *Oak zone*, and they wanted to fly in eyes, mouths, and noses. Grapevine took the short way out to meet David, and I took the long way down to get in trail miles.

In Shasta City that night, I gorged on a gigantic burger, fries, and the chocolate malt I'd been thinking about as I climbed down the trail. David cooked meals for my zero day and provided transportation to pick up odds and ends I would need further in the hike. Grapevine had hiked as far as she wanted to go, but before they left, they gifted me with one last day of slack packing, and I climbed all the way from I-5 to Cabin Creek with just a day pack.

I Know Just How You Feel

After they drove away, I spent a day moving through the crenelated folds of green forested mountains that almost made me think I was on the AT wending my way through a green tunnel of trees. Wildlife liked the forest. I saw two bears, a mother and cub, five deer, one a buck, multiple lizards and little snakes, one with a blue tail, and was serenaded by chattering squirrels and lilting bird song. I rarely see bear on the trail, so the bears were exciting.

I came over a rise and a little ways ahead and downhill, I saw the bear cub. Baby Bear saw me and immediately scampered up one of the tallest trees I'd ever seen. Mama Bear was obscured by a bush. I started talking out loud as I didn't want a startled Mama Bear and figured she must be near.

Mama Bear moved under the tree holding her cub, squalling at it. I had to go by that tree. There was no way to walk around it. I talked to Mama Bear as she crossed the trail and scooted down the ravine into the bushes, all the while bawling for her cub, who refused to come down out of the tree and follow her.

I kept talking: "Hey, Mama Bear, I know just how you feel. I have kids, too. It's just the pits when they don't listen to what you say and stay with you. But your baby will be fine and will probably come down after I go by." I kept up mommy-to-mommy chatter in a calm voice, walking slowly by the tree with the cub far out of sight in high branches. Upset Mama Bear stayed in the ravine and kept calling her cub in agonized bellows. I made my way safely down the trail, away from distressed Mama Bear, hearing her calls until I rounded a bend in the mountain and could hear her no longer. Now that was exciting.

The last half of the day the gnats were bothersome. I had to carry both hiking poles in one hand, so the other could constantly wave a bandana to keep the little buggers from flying into my mouth, eyes, nose, or ears. Pesky critters, they were.

At Ash Camp, while setting up my campsite, two older gentlemen walked over to say *hello* and helped me hang my way too heavy food bag while I pulled on the rope over a tree branch. I needed to eat some to make it lighter. They invited me to their campfire and offered to take out my trash in the morning. I wasn't always alone even when hiking solo.

The pack was still too heavy the next day after breakfast, and I needed another day's worth devoured before the pack began to feel better. I stopped at Deer Creek for a bath and to wash some socks and undies. Getting clean always felt good, even if I knew clean would be fleeting.

I had a Garden-of-Eden feeling standing there naked and alone by large umbrella plants.

After leaving the fishermen in the morning, I saw no human, but a deer followed me up the trail and stood staring at my tent that night. I told her not to eat my laundry hanging on a bush and to keep the bears away.

Grizzly Peak was .3 miles and a few hundred feet elevation gain extra off the PCT, but it had a 360-degree view. The old fire tower on top was now a derelict, a victim of more efficient satellite imagery for finding fires. It seemed sad and lonely, falling apart but still standing sentinel over the wonderful view. Shasta had a skirt of clouds half way up the mountain, and I saw a vast amount of real estate all around me.

"Just wait 'till we tell Ma."

Five miles of trail that day had more bear scat than I'd ever seen before or since. There must have been 75 or more piles in the trail in a mile, some warm piles every 100 feet or less. Berries of all colors and shapes lined the trail: green, yellow, red, black, blue, orange, and white—round ones, flat ones, triangular ones, and spikey ones. The only edible one I was sure of identifying was Thimbleberry.

I left them all for the bears; judging by the bear scat they really enjoyed them. When I heard a bear in the bushes, I yelled as loudly as I could, and the bears crashed about in the underbrush that obscured them as they ran from my squalling.

Shasta's *skirt* of clouds moved up to be a blanket snuggled under her chin, and then it covered all but the very top of her head. I relished the cold breeze, which felt good on the hot and sweaty hiker.

That night at Moosehead Springs I heard something outside the tent. Again, I yelled loudly. Again, there was a loud crashing noise like the bears earlier in the day. I hoped a bear wouldn't get my food bag or think 69-year-old ladies were good to eat. Really, I was sure I wouldn't be as tasty as berries. My food bag was hung, and I'd yelled at the critter, which might have been a bear. I'd done all I could do. Hopefully my food would be there in the morning, and so would I. I was tired and went to sleep.

Waking up the next day, all was well.

On the first day of deer-hunting season, I stopped and broke off a long sapling branch, tied my orange bandana to the end, and stuck the branch in the long side pocket of my pack. It looked sort of like a bicycle flag, and I hoped it would convince hunters I wasn't a deer. Seeing numerous hunters on foot and in trucks on dirt roads, I heard no shots. Smart deer were far away.

I saw another bear, a scary bear. The only really scary bear I have ever seen. And it was my own fault. Coming around a corner of the trail, I surprised two extremely cute little bear cubs ahead of me. They looked at me and scurried away around the bend. I waited a minute or two and proceeded around the bend myself and found them again, and again they scurried away.

They were adorable. Their actions and the looks on their faces seemed to say: "Just wait 'till we tell Ma."

After they left, I proceeded very cautiously into an ominously quiet forest, and I made a big error. I didn't make noise. I should have. Bears behave better if they know where you are.

Suddenly, a very, very big bear erupted out of the bushes above the trail, dashed across the trail, and crashed into the bushes below. I wouldn't have wanted to meet that barreling hunk of fur, flesh, claws, and teeth face-to-face. I wouldn't have had a chance of surviving. Fortunately, she was more intent on getting away than making an introduction. Lesson to self: after seeing cubs, make noise.

By the middle of September, daylight hours were diminishing, and I'd had a 15-mile day, a real push for me, and I was beat. Although my left foot decided to hurt with each step, I made it. At Peavine Creek, I'd had to wade into the creek to pump water upstream of the dead bat resting in the more easily accessible spot. By yelling, I chased critters—either bears or cows—away from the tent. Both bears and cows snort, whuff, and crash through bushes when yelled at.

Hearing hoofs and having seen cow patties in the last quarter mile before the creek, I concluded the crashing critters were cows.

When Grapevine and I hike together, we say at least a few times every day how blessed and lucky we are to walk these trails and see these sights. In spite of a tired body, hurting feet, and a deep longing for a shower and clean clothes, I felt very blessed as I walked solo in the rain toward Burney Falls. I'd walked through beautiful country. It was Sunday, so I sang church songs softly in my head so as not to disturb any hunters, and I thanked God for the opportunity to hike these trails.

Unfortunately, I reached Burney Falls half an hour after the store had closed with my resupply box inside. There was no host at the campground. I was on foot, very tired, and frustrated. Finding a retired couple camping and explaining my plight, the woman kindly agreed to take me into town, for which I was very grateful.

The skies unleashed torrents of rain as she drove me to town, making me even *more* grateful to be headed for a motel with shower, laundromat, and a nearby restaurant. Soon I was *supremely* grateful to be on a soft bed and not planning to walk the next day.

Problems were solved on my zero day in Burney. The college-age waitress agreed to take me back to Burney Falls the next morning. And a call to the store at the park resulted in an arrangement to meet me at 8:30 to give me my food box.

Firefly, the trail angel at Old Station, had trouble explaining water caches to me over the phone, since my maps were still in the box I would pick up the following day. (Water caches are gallons of water left for hikers in dry stretches by trail angels.) However, she just happened to be coming to Burney to pick up Alice, an equestrian on the trail, who had left a vehicle at Old Station. She met me at the McDonalds to explain things. Problems solved.

Firefly drove to Burney in half an hour. It would take me three days to walk to Old Station.

Amazing. An old lady on foot does not move very fast, nor does the trail go in a straight line.

Tiring of walking, I found it lovely to sit and listen to the wind whistle through the pines and look at the views. Mount Shasta, with fresh snow, receded; bare-sloped Lassen became noticeably closer. The predominant flower was cheery yellow Rabbit Brush.

Most of the walk to Old Station was along the Hat Creek Rim, a long, dry, fault line of lava bed. That fault line made life very difficult for wagon train travel going east to west. For me, it made for grand views from Shasta to Lassen and everything in between.

On this notoriously long, dry stretch of trail, I did see the small reservoir described as a questionable water source. It was very low and scummy, the banks cow-trampled mud. My filter would have had to work very hard to get that water. Thank goodness for trail angels and water caches.

Instead of retiring and sitting in a lawn chair under an umbrella, sipping Mai Tais, I was under an umbrella, but I wasn't sitting, and I was sipping tea, Cytomax®, and water, glad I was walking Hat Creek Rim late in fall instead of July or August.

I reached the highway and campground with just enough time to get everything set up before dark. It was too dark to find the caretaker, but the sign said I only had to pay $5 since I was old. Ha. I love my Golden Age Passport. (The National Park entrance pass for older adults) While the night before, I'd listened to crickets, that night I listened to traffic. A thru hiker would have gone on to Old Station. But an old section hiker with sore feet and an aching knee was happy to stop.

Before walking four short miles to Old Station, I inspected Subway Cave, a big lava tube left centuries ago when lava flowed from cracks in the ground near Lassen. There was a .3-mile walk underground, but my headlamp was dim again, so I only went in a short way for a quick look. Lunch at Old Station included a chocolate shake, and hot Hat Creek Rim was only a memory as I slurped soft ice cream though my straw.

The Heitmans were the trail angels at Old Station, and their yard and a delightful tree house was available for hikers. I and two NOBOs, Marmite and Sherpa, gobbled a delicious dinner and breakfast, had showers, and washed our clothes while wearing loaner clothes.

I'd been fortunate to stay with four of six major trail angels on the PCT. Hiking purists debate whether trail angels are a good thing, or if they take away from the ruggedness of the trip. Sadly, some hikers have abused their generosity and help. I was grateful for each one. Firefly and I talked into the evening sharing Girl Scout stories from our pasts and Holden Evening Prayer.

A Beautiful Studly Woman

On the two days to Drakesbad, the weather was hot and cold. The day was up to the 90s. I drank more than usual due to the heat, but the last mile to Hat Creek, I was dry. I washed my feet in the numbingly cold water, washed my socks, and filtered nearly four liters of water, half a liter of which I immediately chugged. I also wet down my shirt, hat, and bandanas for the afternoon walk.

That night the temperature dropped to 26. The water bottle was still liquid until I poured the water into the pot, whereupon it instantly became frozen slush. My stove turned it into boiling water. Nice stove.

The cold encouraged fast walking, and within an hour it was 30 degrees warmer. It stayed below 80 at 6,000 feet elevation. 55-degree temperature swings during a day are not unusual on the PCT. If you live in a house, you are not as aware of temperature changes as when you live in a tent or on top of one.

Arriving at the Drakesbad Campground, some ladies insisted on calling me a *beautiful studly woman*. I insisted they insert *old*. Funny. The incident reminded me of the guy in the Sierra, who'd called the three of us *animals* as a complement. I first saw the term *studly* applied to a woman in a trail journal complementarily describing a young woman hiker. I wasn't sure how a 69-year-old woman could be called studly, but to be complemented was always nice.

A dude ranch, Drakesbad Guest Ranch, is well known in the hiker community for their hospitality to hikers with free showers, a soak in a natural warm spring swimming pool, special- rate meals and general helpfulness. I didn't try the pool, but the shower was wonderful and so was dinner. They gave me my resupply package and, insisting on paying the postage, they mailed a package home for me.

But walking out of Drakesbad was hard. The pack was again heavy with six days of food. The older you are, the slower you are. The slower you are, the more food you must carry. The more food you must carry, the slower you are. I was approaching the point of diminishing returns.

Yellowstone doesn't have all the geysers. Boiling Springs and Terminal Geyser are geothermal hot spots near Lassen. I passed them as another hot afternoon turned me into a wilted daisy. I saw a carload of hunters as I passed the first road, a gun sticking out the back window. It made me nervous. Is it sport to drive down a road and shoot from a car? I was glad they didn't mistake me for a deer.

I also was glad for a short day. I reached the river about 4:30, which gave me time for a bath and to wash out socks and underwear. The very dry-and-dusty trail had covered me with trail dust. The North Fork of the Feather River was the last sure and abundant water source for a while, and I was glad for the time and opportunity to be clean and to rest.

It was hard to complain about such good weather. I was grateful for good weather and cowboy camping, but it was hot. At Stover Spring, I found an unexpectedly running brook and some nice hunters in an RV, who offered me a soda and a camp chair. Wonderful. Trail magic comes in many forms, even hunters. The dusty trail showed me clear bear and cat prints, but I saw nothing about which to be alarmed, only prints.

A hiker commented that I must be tough. Interestingly, I have never thought of myself as tough. Persistent, maybe. Stubborn, certainly. Grapevine also said I was tough. When on the trail, I do not feel tough.

Some days the trail makes me feel young (usually in the mornings.) Other days I feel old (like 102.) Usually I just feel like any other hiker, albeit a progressively slower one. It is all in the eye of the beholder. I was concerned that I seemed to be very tired in the afternoons and knew there were still hard days left. I would have to search for that toughness others saw in me.

A falcon flew above me, circling a couple times, as if to say good morning. I saw a new flower, a fairy trumpet with fringes. Three days of hiking later I was at Beldon.

There were climbs up and down, flowers along the way, spires and crags and eventually a bubbling stream with delightful waterfalls. The descent was helped by handfuls of ripe blackberries from the bushes lining the trail, but my knee was very glad to make it down. My knee was having a hard time getting started in the mornings, and the day I walked into Beldon, it wasn't happy for the whole day. I hoped it would last a couple more weeks.

Beldon itself was a resort, not a town, but the shower and laundry were welcome, and my resupply box refilled my pack with food. After shower and dinner, I retreated to the camp spot at the end of the road.

Going south out of Beldon requires a 4,000-foot climb in five miles. Going north is not a picnic either, but I was concerned about the southbound climb. I didn't get a good night's sleep. The air was hot and noisy trains kept chugging by. It was 67 degrees at 7:00 in the morning. I didn't even bother to put on my shirts. Climbing uphill would produce more heat.

Surprisingly, everything went very well. I kept steadily moving upward past trees and bushes turning yellow and red along the trail, and the weather slowly got colder. Colder meant I moved better. At about 3,000 feet up, I came out into a clear area of low bushes to see low clouds hiding tops of the highest mountains nearby. Views of the rugged, steep canyons were magnificent. I could see rain squalls around me, and the temperature had dropped to the 50s, still not really cold when carrying a pack uphill.

I saw a small plane flying *below* me in the canyon. Those shifting clouds of fog and rain looked very unpredictable, and I hoped the pilot didn't have far to fly. Appropriately garbed now in rain gear, I hoisted the umbrella and marched into wet clouds and the smell of wet forest.

The rest of the day was wet, either rain or fog, but I covered a bunch of miles, stopping to camp somewhere in a cloudbank going downhill. In the morning I woke to find the cloudbank partly lifted and my campsite in a very pretty place on the rim of glacially carved granite overlooking a lovely little tarn. There was open space between me and other mountains, some partially obscured by banks of fog or low-hanging clouds. It wasn't raining, but most everything was damp. Well, when you sleep in a cloud, things get damp.

Lovely walking, the first few miles were especially beautiful granite valleys and lakes. I looked down on Silver Lake and Gold

Lakes, nestled in granite, as were a number of tarns (little unnamed lakes). The forest was mostly mature Red Firs that smelled just-washed.

Descending to the road I met Rob and Michelle, a delightful young local couple. I learned they were from Meadow Valley, and Rob led 6th-grade camp on trails nearby. They offered to be of assistance while I was at Buck's Lake, but I failed to get a contact number, not thinking I would need assistance.

"Where you been?"

Walking the road to Buck's Lake, I sang old camp songs, stopping briefly at the Lakeshore Restaurant and store for directions to the motel. Vague directions and a strange look raised undefined suspicions. Taking a wrong turn, I talked to a woman cleaning a Marina cabin and was given better directions along with a comment that people rarely stayed in that motel. I eventually found the motel up a side road all by itself, very deserted looking.

A car sat in front, but I found no sign of life though I tried all the doors, some of which were open. I looked into rooms that had been recently occupied, but not cleaned. Staying in an isolated motel by myself in the woods was a creepy prospect. Not only was the possibility of lodging disappearing, my resupply box had been mailed to the motel. Without the food drop, I couldn't hike further. I was tired. It was probably a mile back to the store. What was I going to do?

While writing a note to leave on the car, two guys in another car drove up. One of the guys called me by the wrong name, but said he'd gotten my box. "Where you been?" he said.

That was the wrong thing to say to a tired hiker, who had been looking for someone for an hour, wandering around on tired feet. I got testy. I was exactly where I was supposed to be at the time I'd told him I would be there. Where had *he* been?

In response, he got rude, but roared off to get my box, although I wasn't sure he was coming back.

He did return with my resupply box, but I refused to stay alone in a deserted motel. I might be comfortable alone in the wilderness, but not in a creepy, vacant motel down a dirt road in the woods. Besides, the restaurant was a mile away.

Before mailing my resupply boxes, I'd called ahead, preferring real addresses instead of post offices, precisely so I could talk to a real person. Planning a zero day, I'd asked if there was a store or a restaurant nearby. Nearby in a car is not the same thing as nearby on foot. Walking back and forth from the motel to restaurant for food three times a day would have added up to six miles, not a rest day.

Food now in my pack, I found my way to the B&B farther down the road. It was more expensive, but it wasn't creepy, and it had food for sale, too. There was no TV and no cell reception, but the room had a Jacuzzi, and I was inside when it rained outside. Breakfast was a huge garden scramble (who knows how many eggs) with sausages and lots of veggies in it, fresh fruit, juice, a large blueberry muffin, a sweet roll, and three cups of tea. B&Bs are nice.

Discovering a place on the map for an additional food drop to augment my carefully made hike plan, I wondered if someone could bring food to me. A young teacher named Rob who led 6th-grade camp was enough clue for the woman at the B&B and her sister to find the full name and phone number of the couple I'd met on the trail. Rob and Michelle agreed to meet me Friday afternoon at the Quincy-La Port Road on the PCT and bring me food, which I would leave for them to pick up at the B&B. Yay. I didn't have to carry more than three day's food at a time for the rest of my hike, making the next six days before my last food drop a much more enjoyable prospect. That done, I dried my tent, cleaned my filter, soaked in the Jacuzzi in my room and read *National Geographic*. And I ate. Nice zero day.

Distance is a relative thing. Walking on pavement to the restaurant when wanting the knee to rest for a day, was too far. So I gave the knee a break and bought sandwiches from the store downstairs. On the other hand, I was excited to have only 100 miles more to hike. A hundred miles seemed quite short compared to 500, 400, 300, or 200 miles.

The third day from the B&B, the weather changed to sun. I walked ridgelines with peek-a- boo views through the trees and crisscrossed a paved road. Eating lunch and drying out my gear in the sun, I waved at passing logging trucks.

I was hungrily wishing for a country breakfast and a Belgium waffle before my newfound friends and trail angels, Rob and Michelle, brought my food for the last three days. They also brought water, a muffin, treats, and a roast beef sandwich. I ate the roast beef sandwich on the spot. The muffin would supplement my breakfast. Yum. Thank you. Extra food was much appreciated, and talking with Rob and Michelle was a delight.

Three more days. I could see the smog over the Sacramento Valley and the line of coast range mountains. The pointy and jagged Sierra Buttes to the southeast were getting closer.

I passed two hunters on the trail, who were amazed that I was alone and had come so far.

Silly men. They should meet some thru-hikers. In comparison my hike was short, though it was a long ways for me.

Rabbit Brush and Paintbrush still bloomed, amazing to see in nearly mid-October. Long past blooming, Mule Ears' dry leaves covered wide areas of hillside, rustling as I walked through them. They sounded like crumpled paper or discarded Christmas wrapping paper on Christmas morning.

Topping MacRae Ridge on a blue-sky, sunny day, I could still see Pilot Peak, and even Shasta's white, peeking over mountains in the north. I ate lunch viewing Spencer Lakes nestled in a glacial valley sculpted out of rock. Beautiful. After lunch and more climbing, the lakes in Lakes Basin came into sight. Over 7,000 feet, picture-worthy vistas abounded, and I began to meet more hikers.

The wind blew hard the day I passed the Sierra Buttes; its whistle and roar was my usual accompaniment throughout the day, and the noise wore on my nerves, though the striking and rugged Sierra Buttes entertained my eyes.

Past the Buttes, the trail stretched out over the Manzanita-covered mountainside, high above the steep and rugged valley below. It was a long walk, exposed to the sun and over talus (large rocks), scree (gravel- size rock) and any size rock in between. I wouldn't have liked it on a hot day, and found it hard on the feet even on a relatively cool fall day. An old lady with a bad leg had to move slowly all the way down. Reaching the highway I had marvelous good fortune: the first car stopped for my upraised thumb and a nice elderly gentleman delivered me to the Sierra City Hotel.

The lovely old hotel was a one-man operation. Bob checked me in, ran the bar and was also the cook, bottle washer, maid, and server. He was very helpful and promised a ride back to the trail after my rest day. Why was I taking a rest day this close to the end of my hike? Because I was tired. I'd walked nearly 500 miles, and I still had three days to go.

Bicycles

It was an uphill day. Coming out of towns are like that. My rest day helped, as did mental preparation. I do better if I know what is coming. Unexpected uphill on days I thought should be easy discouraged me more than facing a known climb.

Despite being illegal on the PCT, five bicycles passed me. The biggest **no bicycle** signs I have ever seen were at those trailheads. Yet every bicycle rider I saw innocently claimed not to know they were illegal. In a pig's eye.

Other than bicycle riders, the day was a good one. I found a nice flat area near the trail and spread out my cowboy camp and ate my dinner while watching the orange glow of the sunset followed by moon-and-star-decked sky.

The next beautiful day I went over 8,000 feet headed toward Donner Pass, the Sierra Buttes to the north and the snowy mountains above Lake Tahoe to the south. Illegal or not, the PCT was a popular bike route from Donner Pass to Sierra City. Each biker I met claimed their bikes didn't harm the trail. It must be other bikers, who caused damage. But on foot, I could see ruts cut by tires into soft forest duff. The next rain would carry the loosened duff down the trail, leaving larger and larger ruts, exposing rocks as time went on. Especially on switchback turns, there were deep grooves, loose dirt, and duff.

Bikers left a bad taste in my mouth for the end of the trip. I met an organized group, a biking club, not just one or two by themselves. I told them this was the Pacific Crest Trail, created by an act of Congress for hikers and that bikes were illegal.

They laughed and said, "So what? Was I trying to make a citizen's arrest?" More laughter.

I lost my cool and yelled at them, but they cared not a bit for what the old harridan had to say. It was most unsatisfactory yelling at the backs of bike riders going up the trail. I was just an impotent old lady. I wept for the conflict and how poorly I'd handled it, and I wept for the trail.

Not long after the bikers, I was very glad to meet an older, enthusiastic day hiker and later, a dad with two 12-year-olds eagerly out on their first backpack trip. As I left the Peter Grub Hut, a mom and her 20-something daughter questioned me about backpacking and the trail. Those hikers were antidotes to my distress about bikers. I needed to see people who truly cared about the trail and didn't just ride through digging up dirt.

Thankfully, the rest of the day was more uneventful and always beautiful. The willows by the streams in the meadows were turning a nice bright yellow in contrast to the browning grasses. Castle Peak looked majestic against the sky, and some die-hard asters still bloomed.

After going under I-80, Bill Persons popped me into his little convertible and took me to their home. God bless trail angels.

Bill was sympathetic to the bikers and calmed my ire. Bill, now passed away, headed many volunteer maintenance crews on the PCT, and he and Molly had been incredibly gracious trail angels and friends of the trail. In 2010, they fed me a delicious dinner and breakfast and drove me to the airport in Reno.

With the completion of Northern California, I walked 635 PCT miles in 2010, truly blessed to still be able to travel through such beautiful country.

Chapter 26 Fall and Winter, 2010-2011

Knee Replacement

While I was still walking in California, Yellowstone emailed me that she needed a knee replacement. Her knee problems had begun with her fall trying to catch up with me in Oregon. I was so very sorry she'd hurried that day. Her knee replacement was three weeks before mine.

Replacing my knee on Nov 30, 2010, my doc discovered my Posterior Collateral Ligament, but could find no trace of the anterior cruciate ligament. For three years, I'd been wearing a brace for the wrong problem. The brace *had* helped prevent lateral or twisting motions, though it might have helped more if it had been an ACL brace. The knee replacement meant I could ditch the brace altogether.

Yellowstone and I compared notes on recovery. My recovery was fast initially, but I hit a snag after 3 to 4 months, possibly due to old scar tissue on the lateral side of the knee. I did achieve better function. I could go up and down stairs independently. But residual pain persisted. I was able to hike up Mt. Si in March (8-mile round trip and 3,000-feet elevation gain and loss), but the knee took more than one night to recover.

The middle of May I started very seriously walking nearly every day, starting slowly at 1 mile and methodically adding a mile each week. I was trying to convince the knee it could recover overnight and hike every day. I road walked. I trail walked. I walked to doc and dentist appointments. I walked to the grocery store. I got up to nine miles.

The knee still hurt, but not badly. I thought it could be controlled with rests, Tylenol, and an occasional pain pill. I didn't want to damage it further, but my physical therapist said repetitive movement would be key in recovery. So I planned to repetitively move it along a trail.

My doc said I needed to keep my pack light. I spent more money getting an eight-ounce Hexamid tent, a pocket filter from Aquamira®, and a few Cuban-fiber stuff sacks. I decided to go stoveless, saving the weight of stove, fuel, and pot. I figured I could be loaded with food for four days, carry an extra fleece and some water, and my pack would weigh 23 pounds. My Doc suggested the knee pain might eventually go away. That would be nice, but I was prepared to hike anyway.

Chapter 27 July 24, 2011 PCT

Oregon Snow

On the PCTL chat line, I met a 75-year-old hiker, who was proud of being a Tough Old Broad, TOB for short. She was indeed tough. A fall had resulted in a broken hip. Not much deterred, two months later she went to Alaska to work on trail maintenance on the Iditarod, Alaska's famous route for a sled-dog race.

Leaving my car with Gray Squirrel in Vancouver, Washington, I took the train to Eugene, meeting TOB at the train station. She had a glass of wine, and we chatted, had dinner out and then went back to her house, where I slept on her deck, as I was allergic to the cats in her house. It was a pleasant night with a lovely new friend.

While enjoying our chatter about various adventures, TOB drove me to the trailhead.

Although she'd done many amazing things with her recently pinned hip, hiking with me into Rosary Lakes was her first post-surgery hike. When we came to the lake outlet, she turned around as she didn't want to risk a wrong step crossing slippery rocks.

I headed on with an exhilarating sense of freedom. I liked hiking with people, but I liked hiking solo, too. Each had its own lovely flavor.

The mosquitoes were doing their *Oregon-in-July bad thing,* and I did a lot of bandana waving as well as putting on generous applications of repellant.

Arriving at Bobby Lake, I met Marmite and Sherpa, whom I'd met at Old Station in California in the fall. When hike-planning now, I always wonder who will be the previously met hiker I will see again on a new trail.

If 2010 had been a high-snow year on the PCT, this one was an *exceedingly* high-snow year. On my second day, four miles of trail were on snow. At first it was just small patches, then bigger ones, and then visual sign of the trail disappeared, along with the footprints of Marmite and Sherpa. I kept making forward progress, but walking on snow while looking for trail is more strenuous and time consuming than simple trail.

I was glad to have my GPS and also glad someone had walked the trail before me, leaving footprints. Still, I was misplaced several times. It wasn't that I didn't know where I was. My GPS clearly indicated my position with a tiny triangle. It also theoretically indicated the trail painstakingly drawn in by myself on Garmin Base Camp on my computer before transferring to my hand-held GPS.

How did I find trail in the snow? Like a trail planner, I used my eyes looking for gradual inclines. I looked for the occasional trail marker, although there are not as many on the PCT as the AT. I looked for downed logs cut in two, making way for a trail. I checked map and compass as well as GPS. I angled forward and crisscrossed the supposed trail showing on the GPS while searching for footprints or any two-foot or more section of melted out bare ground I could identify as trail. And I guessed.

At the trailhead to Elk Lake, Mt. Bachelor, Broken Top, and Southern Sister, stunningly promised good hiking ahead. But first, my dear friends Grapevine and David met me at the trailhead, and we headed to their trailer for a night with shower, laundry, and a bed.

Dead Woman Walking

In the morning, Grapevine and I hiked together. Oregon was my first real test of the knee replacement, and Grapevine had undergone back surgery in the early spring, so we were both exploring how *repaired* bodies moved on trail.

We made it up to the top of Koosah Mt, with just a few snow patches on the trail. We gazed south to Diamond Peak and Thielsen, fading in the distance. Closer at hand, Mt. Bachelor, Broken Top and South Sister commanded our view.

Starting down toward Mirror Lakes we ran into snow, a lot of snow. Under the snow, the trail was relatively straight to Mirror Lakes, though we couldn't see it. Following the GPS, we came to Camelot Lake, had a *first lunch* while resting after our snow slog, and then passed Sisters Lake, both beautiful in the snow.

It wasn't so beautiful slogging *through* the snow, finding occasional bits of trail following the GPS. Arriving at a snow-free spot on the Wickiup Plains Trail, we had *second lunch*.

Descending a rather steep slope with no sign of the switchbacking trail, I was delighted when we found our destination snow-free between two forks of Mesa Creek. Monkey flower, marigolds, and shooting stars grew beside a crystal-clear stream. I was ecstatic that we had successfully followed the GPS. Grapevine was too exhausted to care about the flowers, the GPS, or anything else as she crawled into the tent.

The following day the trail was 95% snow, and therefore, very difficult, especially for Grapevine. A dead woman walking (her words), she was worn out before noon. It *was* difficult to walk on snow, sometimes hard, sometimes soft and sometimes very steep. Her foot with the ankle fusion didn't adjust well to slippery snow and I was an old lady too, with a knee replacement. Although my knee performed stellarly, it would never be a normal knee. We made fewer than seven miles, hiking all day, falling behind schedule, and we knew we had to bail. I didn't do so with very good grace, and I'm lucky Grapevine is still my friend. She made the right decision.

In the morning we slogged through snow-filled mountain meadows and over snow-covered mountain streams. We stayed pretty *found*, although we rarely saw trail tread. Once, I was sure I saw the trail on a dry patch of ground at a lower elevation, but when we came closer it turned out to be the remains of an old rotten, reddish log.

We planned to bail on Glacier Way Trail, but while having our mid-morning trail bars by a lovely stream coming directly out of a snow-bank near a patch of blooming Pasque flowers, we saw a hiker who had come up from the Obsidian Trailhead. Grapevine was no longer interested in going one step farther on the PCT. She was focused only on getting off trail **ASAP**. She had no interest in anything whatsoever other than following that hiker's footprints **out**. The hike had become a mission to get Grapevine out of the mountains.

There was no way we could split up under those conditions. In all that snow, someone could have been irretrievably misplaced without the GPS. We walked out together, I stalking ahead and Grapevine limping behind.

We *were* able to contact David by cell phone, and he and Gray Squirrel met us at the trailhead. Grapevine left with David to recover at their trailer, while Gray Squirrel and I camped at McKenzie Pass, ready to continue hiking the next day, a section of trail skipped.

What a Difference a Day Made

What a difference a day made. There was no more than five inches of snow in a few patches. Trail over lava fields made sore feet, but there were no problems with snow. Lupine perfumed the warm air and bear grass gloriously waved standards guiding our way, honoring our journey with large white heads of multi-bracketed blooms.

By late afternoon we were at Big Lake Youth Camp, a Seventh Day Adventist Camp and popular trail stop for PCT hikers. In short order we were welcomed, told of a place to camp, given ice cream, sold dinner tickets, and promised showers when the campers went to campfire.

Marcus, a German thru hiker who had learned his English in Australia, stopped at Big Lake Youth Camp, too. He was a charming companion and congenial soul. He'd hiked the AT the previous year and become hooked on long trails, a strong hiker regularly making 30-mile days.

After Linda and I had a zero day and Grapevine had had three, Grapevine had recovered her energy and some optimism, bought her own GPS so she wasn't dependent on mine, and was ready to go on with us. Yay. We went to Safeway where I bought earplugs, but not for their usual purpose. My pinched toes had made a blister, my big toe rubbing on the one next to it. I stuck an earplug between the toes. It was soft, but just substantial enough to hold my toes apart, giving the blister time to heal. It felt much better, almost instantly, my favorite blister trick.

We all celebrated my birthday one day early at a Mexican

Restaurant. I was happy to be able to hike at age 70 and to have friends. For a birthday present, the three of us hiked together once again. We had snow with patches of trail for four miles, but we almost always saw trail or footprints. Walking high on the slopes of Three Fingered Jack, we had lunch looking at its red rock striations, and there were many flowers.

Walking through burned areas, no shade meant no snow. Appreciating recent trail maintenance, we reached Wasco Lake for our campsite as planned. Grapevine's feet were in pain the last two miles, and she decided to bail to meet David guided by her new GPS. I was glad she'd enjoyed the day in spite of her foot pain and would have a good hiking memory and not just the miserable walk out the Obsidian Trail. We ended the evening with Holden Evening Prayer.

"A Hell of a Day" – or Three

Gray Squirrel and I started out in the morning by saying *good-bye* to Grapevine as she left for her two-mile walk to Jake Lake to meet David. She'd made a wise choice. The day would be taxing for Gray Squirrel and me, and we weren't recovering from back surgery.

At Rock Pile Lake, we had mid-morning snack and topped off our water, afraid we might find the lake at our destination full of snow. We had far more snow-free trail than we had a right to expect, but when we walked on snow, it was treacherous. We had to bushwhack (off-trail walking) down and up steep slopes to avoid possible death on even more severely steep snow slopes. It was VERY HARD WORK. Yet the views were glorious. We watched Sisters, Washington, and Three Fingered Jack recede behind us and Mt. Jefferson, South, and North Cinder Peaks come near, as well as looking over lower mountains both east and west.

Gray Squirrel said, "It was a hell of a day."

At one point my knees both felt like overstretched rubber. We thought what we were doing on steep snow was nuts. But then we took turns being Tom fool leading and Jack fool following after and went on. Yes, the lake at our destination was full of snow. We found barely enough bare and level ground for the tent in front of large melting snowbanks.

In the morning, almost immediately, we hit more snow. Two things made this hike possible for me even in all the snow. My GPS and my new knee. I absolutely couldn't have survived those strenuous snow days without the new knee, and the GPS kept us *found*.

Halfway through the morning we hit real trail all the way to Milk Creek. Halleluiah! Other hikers had warned us about an avalanche at Milk Creek. But after what we had already gone over, it was very anti-climactic. We camped before Russel Creek, hoping the creek level would be lower in the morning.

A moderately dangerous crossing, Russel Creek's rapids descended a rock-walled canyon below the crossing. We took everything out of our pockets, plastic bagged our electronics, unbuckled our pack straps and held on to each other in recommended safe fording fashion. The water was mid-thigh deep with splashes up to the butt and ice cold.

It felt like wading through dry ice, colder than cold. It was a short crossing of a few steps, but by the time we reached the other side our legs and feet had passed from numb to burning, and I was worried because toes on my right foot turned dead white. After drying off and a little time, color came back.

Dry and slightly warmer, we headed up through snow to Jefferson Park, one of the jewels of the PCT. The lakes were emerging from snow, and flowers grew in the meadows, pink and white Heather, Shooting Stars and Paintbrush. From Jefferson Park, we went straight up snowfields aiming for the GPS waypoint at the top of Park Ridge. Going straight up was hard work, but less dangerous than dealing with steep snow on side hills in the woods, where the trail was supposed to be.

From Park Ridge, we had a stunning view back to Mt. Jefferson and Jefferson Park. And to the north, Mt. Hood stood out in all her glory. I was glad to see nothing but low mountains between Park Ridge and Mt. Hood and NO SNOW. At least, no snow after we plunge-stepped (walking straight down in big steps through snow) descending from Park Ridge.

After four rugged days, we were very tired. On the way down, Gray Squirrel decided to bail out with Grapevine and David when they met us at Breitenbush with our food drop. So Grapevine and David met us with sandwiches and my food drop, and all my friends left after putting up my tent for me. The trail that year wore out my two hiking friends. Although I was pretty worn out, too, I was too stubborn to stop, though I was really wishing for some snowless trail.

My wish was granted. The trail was so good I went past my planned stop and walked 16 miles, amazing for me. The highlights of the day were privies at both Breitenbush and Ollalie. It doesn't take much to make my day, just a chance to sit down to do my business twice a day.

Maybe you don't appreciate how wonderful that is until you are 70.

An added bonus for the day was meeting three young, strong thru-hiker dudes who talked to an old lady on the trail. I caught up to them in the evening to camp, and we sat around and talked trail around a nice little fire until after hiker midnight.

That night, I started hatching a plan to finish the area Grapevine and I'd skipped. If I could hike this well the next couple of days, gaining a day on my schedule and giving up a planned zero day at Timberline Lodge, I might have time to finish Oregon. And I really wanted to finish Oregon.

The trail has both physical and mental requirements. Non-hikers, and some hikers, often think hiking long trails just takes a lot of strong brawn. Well, it does take a reasonable amount of physical strength, conditioning, and outdoor skills. I do not want to make light of the difficulties and challenges of long-distance hiking or the skill sets needed to safely traverse wilderness. But not just physical strength is needed.

Gray Squirrel was a much stronger hiker than I could be. But she was just out for a hike of a few days. It wasn't important to *her* to finish what *I'd* planned. *I* wanted to finish Oregon. I wanted to hike the PCT and the AT. And I was stubborn enough to keep going through snow, fatigue, and sometimes, pain.

Sometimes my plans had to change to fit my physical limitations. I had to know what those limitations were, and I had to learn how to work with them. But more than brute strength, physical prowess, or gear, the deciding factor of success for me on multiple section hikes was mental strength and wanting to finish what I'd started. I wanted to hike the PCT. I wanted to hike the AT. So I did.

The next day I walked 21 miles. Thru hikers will tell you that Oregon is easy trail. Yes, it was very nice. I couldn't remember going 20 miles in one day since I was *in* my 20s. If anyone wanted to shoot for long-distance miles, that was the trail for it.

Leaving the campsite with its carpet of bunchberries, I took a lovely walk in the woods, two climbs, and lots of gradual downhill. Early and late-season flowers bloomed together on that hot day. If you are a flower you need to bloom sometime snow-free, and that year the late-melting snow pack didn't leave much time snow-free before winter would set in, early and late seasons compressed to one.

The following day I hiked 19 miles, nothing short of blazing speed for an old lady. I set up camp twice that night. All settled in my tent, listening to the wind, I was concerned I'd not checked for *widow makers* (trees likely to fall). Sure enough, there was a big tree leaning right toward my tent. I packed everything back up and headed up the trail again in the fading daylight. I may not be terribly afraid of bear, but I could envision dying under a falling tree.

Making excellent time, I arrived at Timberline Lodge on the side of Mt. Hood by 9:00 in the morning, in plenty of time to check in and make the breakfast buffet. I had to pay a cancellation fee plus my room fee since I arrived a day early. But at least they had a room available. The breakfast buffet at Timberline was legendary for hikers. I ate my fill, four extra fat slices of bacon along with eggs, potatoes, sausage, and then a Belgian waffle heaped with strawberries and blueberries, followed by watermelon and pineapple. Yum. After that I had more bacon. The remainder of the day, I rested, washed, and ate more high-priced tourist food in ample quantities.

Leaving Timberline, the trail took me around the side of Mt. Hood. At one point in the morning I missed a turn in the trail while following footprints ahead of me. They led me out on an extremely steep ridge of loose, sandy ash left from Mt. St Helen's volcanic eruption.

I stood on shifting ash, looking precipitously down on the impressively rugged power of Big Sandy River, one wrong step or the bank giving way, and I would have been old-lady toast. I and the footsteps I was following worked our way back to the trail through thick brush, accumulating more scratches to add to the collection on my legs. That sheer drop to the river was more terrifying to me than any of the snow on the whole trip.

Ramona Falls was lovely, water splashing over rocks like white pillows in a pile. A couple friendly day-hikers promised to call Gray Squirrel to tell her I would be at Cascade Locks on Saturday. I loaded up with heavy water at Muddy River, not muddy at all, and headed up a 1,500-foot climb to end the day.

That night I slept like the dead for about five hours before hurting shoulders woke me. The pain wasn't from carrying a pack, just arthritis combined with not moving even a hair after I fell asleep. Little sleep meant I felt tired all the next day. Stopping for lunch, I plopped down using a log for a pillow and slept for 20 minutes before I could even eat.

The last mile into Indian Springs was a traverse over an open area allowing views of steep mountains deepening into the Gorge of the Columbia. Sticking up over all the lower mountains to the north were Mt. St Helens, Mt. Adams, and Mt. Rainier—three snowcapped volcanic peaks. I felt like I was standing on the edge of the world with bright red Paintbrush as an extra garnish.

Getting my water from the spring, I fixed dinner before heading down the Indian Springs trail—steep and not very maintained, to the Eagle Creek Trail, a PCT alternate and one of the most popular trails along the Columbia Gorge.

About a mile down the trail, as I passed campsites, a man came up to the trail to bury food left by previous campers. I knew the voice. "Paul?"

"Pastor Mary?"

Paul and his daughter, Ruthie were from the church I served as pastor for 16 years, They and two of their friends were packing up to leave. What great fun to meet them.

Next was Tunnel Falls, plunging straight down 150 feet, trail cut through the rock behind the falls, green moss and lush growth everywhere. A cable was attached to the rock wall if needed for balance, but the trail was three-feet wide and not slippery. Below Tunnel Falls, Paul, Ruthie and their friends caught up with me, and we walked together.

The Eagle Creek Trail is filled with beautiful waterfalls. Doffing packs, we walked in to Lower Punch Bowl Falls, where we could see people jumping into both Upper and Lower Punch Bowls. I probably saw 75 hikers that last day on Eagle Creek.

Leaving Paul, Ruthie, and their friends at the trailhead, I took the side trail to Cascade Locks where I immediately had a burger, fries, and milkshake.

Gazing at the Columbia, and later, resting my eyes, I waited for Gray Squirrel and her partner to arrive. They drove me to their home in Vancouver, fed me a gourmet dinner, and provided shower and washing machine to make me presentable. I was three days earlier than planned and had time to hike the skipped section.

We all went to church on Sunday morning before I hopped in my car and drove south to McKenzie Pass. Parking the car, I walked into Lava Camp to spend the night. Trail angel, Lost and Found, was sitting in a large bug tent waiting to host hikers. After I set up my tent, she and I and one long-distance hiker from Ashland sat and talked trail.

On the trail at 7:00 the next morning, I made good time on mostly snow-free trail. The highlight of the day was coming into the Obsidian area, hillsides around me and trail under my feet made of obsidian sparkling in the sun as I walked on a mountain of black glass. Shining black glass, snow, and rushing water beside high tarns. Absolutely stunning. The beauty of any flowers was eclipsed by obsidian. Obsidian Falls was nice, but it, too, took second place to the sheer beauty of those shining hills of obsidian.

If Grapevine and I'd continued on that earlier day instead of bailing down the Obsidian trail, we would have been on deep snow, and I would never have seen the obsidian. I was sorry for my bad attitude walking her out to the road that day and thankful we had skipped. The day I came back was far more beautiful than the one I would have had on earlier snow.

I didn't plan to go all the way back to the highway on the Obsidian Trail and had all my camping gear with me. But I just kept walking. Reaching the highway, all I wanted to do was get to my car. It wasn't a well-traveled highway, but I hoped for a hitch before dark. I kept walking on very tired feet and waved my white hiking hat at a car going the wrong way. When they stopped, I offered to pay them to turn around and take me the six miles up to my car, which they did, refusing my money. I was very grateful to have arrived at my car after a long day.

I ended up driving all the way home, all night long, a 7-to-8-hour drive after an 18-hour day. I don't recommend it.

I didn't plan it. But I just couldn't sleep until I reached my own bed. I guess if the snow doesn't kill you, it makes you stronger. I finished Oregon.

Chapter 28 September 1, 2011 AT

Southern Maine Mahoosuc Notch

The same David, who had brought me to Gorham in 2009, picked me up there after a night
and a day of travel from Washington State. From the trailhead, I started an immediate river fording on wet trail. Hurricane Irene had passed through New England the week before. I knew I was on the AT. The trail had rocks and many hikers.

Still adjusting to East Coast time zone, I went over Bald Pate Mountain, the mountain Bookworm had told me had been covered in black ice in 2009. In the beginning of September 2011, it was a granite-topped mountain with lovely views. Among at least 21 hikers I saw that day, were Knitty and Gritty, a young couple from central California, whom I would continually meet on most of the year's AT hike.

Southern Maine was the most difficult part of the AT, followed closely by New Hampshire. After picking up a food drop at a road, my pack was very heavy going up Old Spec. Thirty-four hikers passed me. I chatted up Knitty and Gritty and Gardener, hoping for company through the Mahoosuc Notch the next day. Although the company was agreeable, I almost didn't make it to the campsite that night. My last day in Oregon on the PCT I'd walked 18 miles. But in Southern Maine I could barely make it nine, and part of that was in the dark.

After topping the Mahoosuc Arm, I had a long, very steep descent, much of it steep rock slabs down which I went very slowly. I felt akin to an orangutan, using tree branches to lower myself down rock slabs. I slipped once down two feet and scraped my shin on unyielding rock.

Mostly I climbed down backwards, a safer option than forwards. Then I ran out of daylight.

Putting fresh batteries in the headlamp, I resigned myself to being even more slow and careful. When I filled my water bladder at the stream, I was surrounded in the dark by a huge cloud of white moths attracted to my headlamp. I strung the bladder on my belt instead of trying to stuff it in the already overfull pack and walked forward into the darkness guided by my headlamp and left almost magical, white fluttering moth wings behind.

Where was the campsite? The trail was hard to follow, on overgrown rock slabs alternating with puddles.

Finally I saw lights. Halleluiah!

Gardener was looking up the trail to see if I was coming. I would never have found them in the dark, off the trail at the campsite, without her headlamp shining at me.

Up with the tent, down with dinner, and into bed.

The Mahoosuc Notch is known as the most difficult mile on the AT. I surely hope never to do anything more difficult. It started to rain as Gardener, Frank, and I left the campsite. Oh good, rain-slicked rocks. Fortunately, it only rained enough to slicken the rocks; it could have been much worse. The Mahoosuc Notch is a mile's worth of huge blocks of rock peeling over the eons from the steep cliffs that tower over both sides of the Notch. Into the jumble we went.

It wasn't too bad at first, but without Gardener and Frank, I am not at all sure I could have made it all the way. Frank led, and Gardener came from behind. A few times she gave me a butt boost or let me stand on her thigh, so I could get up the side of cliff-like rocks. At least twice, we took off packs to crawl through holes or caves. At one cave-like passage, seven hikers, including Knitty, Gritty, and my group of three, had to pass packs person-to-person, which is difficult while sitting at an awkward angle under the rock roof of the cave.

When Frank found himself going headfirst down the side of a bunch of rock, I was sure he was going to come to a bad end and couldn't even watch. Although he fell, he survived with a scraped elbow. I found a different route. The Mahoosuc Notch does not exactly have trails, and hikers simply find their way through the piles of boulder blocks with an occasional white blaze.

Some people make it through in two hours. It took us more than four. I should have done push-ups for a year to strengthen my arms for hauling myself up and down those rocks. Coming out the other side of the Notch, Gardener and I stopped for lunch while Frank pushed on.

Knowing I was through the Notch, Gardener left before me. So tired from all the clambering over rock, I found it hard to walk the next mile and a half—even on easy trail. As I approached the shelter, Gardener played her penny whistle to cheer me up the hill. What a friendly gesture. Expending all my energy for the day, I'd gone a total of 2.9 miles.

I left camp early the next morning, trying to make up for my limitations with more hours on the trail. Going up East Goose Eye, I could see Gardener, Knitty, and Gritty coming behind and below me. I sang *Oh What a Beautiful Morning* for them, and Gardener played it back on her whistle.

After they caught up with me, Gardener helped me on some hairy ladders going straight down sizeable cliffs, and then they were off ahead of me. Uphill was hard because it was uphill. Downhill was difficult as I was afraid of falling down steep, wet, rock slabs. I did a lot of tree rappelling, hanging onto the trunks or limbs of trees backing down rock slabs of various steepness.

And then it rained. And hailed. I plugged on.

Coming to two rather horrid, short jumbles of rocks, I negotiated the first one by myself and met a couple of trail maintainers, who gave me water. By myself, the second jumble would have stymied me. I simply wasn't tall enough to reach handholds on the rock.

After having taken a break at a side shelter, Gardener was again my rescuer. Coming up behind me, she carried a huge, monster-class pack, but she was tall and strong. She climbed ahead of me and sat on a rock ledge dangling her legs over the edge. I reached as far up as I could to grab her ankles and pulled myself up. This trail is not for the faint of heart. Or short people.

Following Gardener, I trudged onward. About 8:30 I spied a rare flat spot beside the trail with a big rock beside it. I sat and considered my situation, while eating the dinner I'd hydrated an hour before. It would take me at least another hour to reach the next shelter, and I could hear thunder.

The next storm approached rapidly. There had already been one shower from a passing thunderstorm, and I didn't want to be walking in another in the dark. So I set up my tent in that little flat spot, took off my filthy clothes, put on my jammies, and crawled in. I hadn't gone to bed so dirty since the Sierra. But I was dry and safe as the rain pelted down. I'd only come 6.8 miles.

I got up early thinking discouragingly that I couldn't possibly make it 13 miles to Gorham in one day. But as I started down the trail, three NOBO hikers from the shelter said they'd heard about me. One said I was an amazing woman, which struck me as incredibly funny since I was the amazing woman, who couldn't make it to the shelter the night before.

Onward I trudged. After a couple miles, here came Gardener behind me. Wow. I thought everyone would have been ahead of me. Gardener told me of a short cut on a blue-blazed trail that she, Knitty, and Gritty had decided to take. The only *blue-blaze trail* (not the white rectangular blazes of the AT) I'd taken was in New Jersey, and it was the AT in previous years. (Blue blazed trails are not the official AT.) But when Gardener said, "It cuts off 5 miles," and I realized I could get to town for my zero day AND BE CLEAN, the decision was made.

For a while Gardener was content to hike with me, and we had a nice time chatting. We took the Peabody Brook trail, a pleasant trail, although it was like walking on ice over some very slippery board puncheons. We nicknamed the board puncheons *death boards*, but they did keep us out of the bogs as we went by a lovely brook with little waterfalls.

Knitty, Gritty, and Gardener chose to camp outside of town. But I went on, walking down the North Road to the AT and then to the highway. I caught a hitch into town to The Barn, a hiker hostel, and picked up my food drop. A hot shower followed. Yay. And clean clothes.

Double Yay. I ate a footlong at a Subway because it was close. Hearing the rain outside The Barn, I thought of my trail friends tenting in the rain. I was glad to be warm, clean, dry, and horizontal. Maine was done.

Chapter 29 New Hampshire

Sending my gravity-feed filter home from Gorham, I switched to iodine tablets. They were lighter, and I'd been having trouble with the filter. Meeting Gardener, Knitty, and Gritty at the White Mountain Lodge and Hostel, we made mountains of tacos for everyone that night at a hiker party.

The next day was a wet one; rain continued all day. I walked through many puddles, and my feet were soaked. Descending became a challenge with lots of Bald-Pate-type rock, mostly grippy, some slick, and all very wet.

In fact, the trail was usually a stream. I slipped and fell once—just on my behind so no damage done. That night the shelter had a nice group of hikers traveling together, glad to be under shelter as the rain poured outside.

Work for Stay

The climb up North Carter took me a lot longer than anticipated because I moved pathetically slowly over rough trail. That night at White Mountain Lodge, Geriatric—an older NOBO hiker—had suggested a strategy for the Wildcats, a series of peaks in the White Mountains creatively named A,B,C, and D: I could climb to the top and take the gondola down. Then I could climb up the other side and take the gondola down a second time, avoiding the treacherous downhill climb. It sounded like a good idea to consider.

Mt. Washington stuck its head above the clouds, and Bunch Berries along the trail were a cheery bright red, reminding me of Christmas Holly. Blue Bead Lilly added blue ornaments to the Christmas theme. The day went well until the last half mile down to Carter Hut, when I had to back down most of the trail. My knees were not good enough to go forward on deep steps and uncertain rock.

Reaching the bottom and discovering the lake had flooded the trail,

I waded through water up to my knees, not in the lake, but on the trail, which had become an extension of the lake.

Traveling through the White Mountains, there were no shelters; there were nice huts for paying customers, posh touristy lodging. Thru and section hikers didn't usually have the kind of cash to be paying customers. The hiker method for crossing the Whites was to show up at the huts and hope you could get a *work for stay*. After paying customers ate and had a program, thru hikers could eat the leftovers and wash dishes, clean something, or do some other chore for the privilege of sleeping on the tables or the floor.

I didn't know if this would be a good idea for me as I needed the hours on the trail, not washing dishes, but it was a trail tradition, and I needed a place to stay. Most thru hikers bypassed the flooded trail to Carter Hut, so I had no competition for a *work for stay*.

I didn't have an entirely positive experience, partly because I was old and the Cru were young. (Staff at the huts are called Cru, a unique spelling of crew.) I also didn't like waiting outside like a second-class citizen. The Cru almost forgot I was there before calling me in to eat and wash dishes, pots, and pans and scrub a filthy drain rack with a toothbrush.

Although the only other hiker had finished his work and was lounging around, the Cru head was about to invent more jobs for me to do. Finally I said, "I have done enough." I set up my stuff in a corner, but the partying of Cru went on well after 10. The other hiker knew one of the Cru, and they made love for about an hour and a half outside the open window.

Evidently he made her very happy as her moans were quite audible through my earplugs, as was their bouncing. Finally the Cru chief went out about 11:00 and told them to be quiet. I didn't get a lot of sleep.

Before leaving the hut, I enjoyed chatting with one of the women— a paying guest. The rest of the day was spent getting over all the Wildcats. I did well until the descent between C and D. And the descent from D was known as the really bad one, so I didn't descend it.

I followed Geriatric's advice and took the gondola down, walked the half mile to the Visitor's Center, left most of my gear there, and slack packed back up the mountain from the other side. It *was* very steep, one section a 1000-foot elevation gain in a third of a mile, straight up some really nasty pieces of rock. I was very glad I'd gone up instead of down, and I made my gondola-ride connection, the last ride down to Pinkham Notch that night.

Dinner and breakfast came with the room at the Joe Dodge Lodge. The early 6:30 breakfast gave me a 7:00 start on the trail which I needed.

Presidentials

Climbing up Mt. Madison, the first of the Presidentials, wasn't all that bad. I actually felt like a hiker instead of a decrepit old lady. I even *passed* a group of four young people. A miracle.

The last mile and a half was all above tree line and absolutely beautiful. Negotiating the tread over large talus chunks, I summited Madison, and while I perched on a rock on the mountaintop, another hiker took my picture. Mt. Washington and the other Presidentials were beautiful against blue sky. The hard part was my pathetically slow descent down the last half- mile to Madison Spring Hut.

After my experience at Carter Hut, I chose to be a semi-paying customer, eating my own food, but getting a third-tier bunk for $35. Perfect. The rules and feelings for hikers were entirely different in this hut. They didn't make the *work for stay* hikers wait outside. They waited in the dining room, freely moving around.

In the morning I arose as quietly as I could, using the red setting on the headlamp so as not to disturb other sleepers. Gathering up my breakfast, I ate in the dining room, and I was the only one up that early. As everyone else was awakened, I packed up, folded my blankets from the bed as instructed by hut personnel, and was ready for the day.

Outside the hut a very confused young lady moose had been hanging out each morning for several weeks, looking sort of lost standing there while everyone took her picture. The Cru were hoping she would be claimed by a studly male moose as rutting season began. Standing around looking lost wasn't normal moose behavior.

A cairn-marked trail took me on a side trip up Mount Jefferson, though I saw no view from the inside of a cloud. However, I did see the team carrying up the Flag of Remembrance for 9/11. Every peak over 5,000 feet in New Hampshire had a flag flying on it that afternoon.

The slow old lady—which was me—finally reached the top of Mt. Washington and the Visitor Center. I was very tired and had a bowl of clam chowder and some hot chocolate from the snack bar, giving me enough energy to reach Lake Of The Clouds Hut.

It was closed for the season, and the Cru was doing end-of-year cleaning. I begged for the emergency shelter nicknamed *The Dungeon*. Hikers were only supposed to use it in an emergency, but I figured a 70-year-old lady with a knee replacement at the close of a long day *was* an emergency, or would be one, if I had to walk after dark.

Actually, I wanted to be there, though they said I could sleep above. I was looking forward to silence. That basement room was nicknamed *the dungeon* because it looked like one: a room about 9x9 feet with stone walls, one high window, a heavy steel door and two triple tier bunk shelves crammed on two walls. But it suited me perfectly. I was the only one there, sleeping in silence. Knitty and Gritty came later and slept upstairs.

The next day, 13.6 miles of trail took me over more mountains named for Presidents and eventually to Webster Cliff, a steep descent with some scary rock climbing near the top beside a drop off of a couple thousand feet.

I stowed my poles and back climbed down very carefully. The total descent was three miles and three-thousand feet, some parts of which were very steep. I didn't finish in daylight.

Darkness was coming earlier every night, and by 7:10 I had to use the headlamp.

Coming out at the road at 8:00, there was no traffic. The road had washed out to the east by the earlier hurricane. There was no cell reception, and Highland Center with my food drop and a bed were four miles to the west.

Although my knee was really hurting, I walked on, singing songs and talking to the moon to try to keep my mind off the pain. About half way to my westward destination, a car came by going east, but they were kind enough to turn around and take me west for the remaining two miles to Highland Center.

The girl at the front desk was Turkish, and I surprised her, using a little of my old Peace Corps Turkish. She took pity on an exhausted old lady, who happened to speak a little of her own language and checked me in and found me dinner. She told me not to tell anyone or she might get in trouble, but she gave me a very good impression of the Highland Center. I thought she deserved a bonus.

At 11:00 at night, after a long, hard day, I almost fell asleep while eating the huge and delicious plateful of leftover pork chops, potatoes, stuffed peppers and broccoli. I was exhausted. Ever since I'd stepped on the AT in 2011, the trail had been tough. The saying on the AT for NOBOs was that three-quarters of the miles of the AT are completed before reaching New Hampshire, but only one-quarter of the work.

Southern Maine was the most difficult, but the days in New Hampshire were hard, too, for an old lady with a knee replacement. The knee was better with a replacement than without one, but as a friend and colleague told me after her replacements, "It's just not as good as the original equipment." In addition, a 70-year-old does not hike like a 20-year-old.

Fortunately for me, the next day provided miles that were almost easy, and I really needed *easy*. I couldn't have added four non-trail miles to my day after the grueling night before. Paul, with whom I'd breakfasted, had a car and gave me a ride back to the trail. From the road, the AT had a few rocky, rooty and boggy places but then, miraculously, miles of level trail. I'd not known New Hampshire *had* level trail.

I also saw my first real displays of fall color for the year, red maple trees. I found a soggy piece of real estate near the trail to Zee Pond, just big enough to put up my tent. My Cuban-fiber tent floor kept me dry, on soggy moss in a bog in a thunderstorm, and I was glad to be alone and horizontal.

Reboot

Feeling old, tired, and discouraged, I was so looking forward to my next zero day. The level trail long gone, I was really tired of crappy trail in the north woods. My idea of a reasonably good trail became simply one on which I could descend without having to turn around and go backwards or hang onto trees to keep from killing myself.

At Gale Hut, I learned the weather forecast was: cold and rainy. I was further discouraged by stern written warnings to avoid Franconia Ridge in bad weather, though there were no good bypass trails on the map. The day after the rain, I would be on Franconia Ridge with miles of open and exposed trail above tree line. The forecast meant cold and frost, possibly ice, on all those rocks. My mood became even gloomier. What should I do?

While eating my lunch in a hut, in walked Reboot, a very nice, optimistic 26-year-old SOBO. He heard my woeful tale and said he was willing to do Franconia Notch with slow old me, though he normally hiked three times as fast.

What a boost. Just knowing someone would be hiking with me made all the difference. The moral support from a cheerful person brought back my own natural optimism, and I hiked on while Reboot ate. After he caught up, we hiked together to the tent-and-shelter site.

The next morning I left the campsite before 7:00, headed up and over Garfield, a 4,500-foot mountain, followed by Lafayette Peak, 5,200 feet. Knowing Reboot was going to come behind me later gave me encouragement as well as incentive to see how far along the trail I could be by the time he caught up.

Below me, a group descended into the foggy clouds to Greenleaf Hut, and a NOBO day hiker passed me and commented on the "totally nasty" day. Perversely, I liked seeing the wind-swirled clouds, valleys appearing and disappearing through the moving banks of gray. I sang into the teeth of the wind, and I reached the top of Lafayette with Reboot right behind me.

Briefly and barely seeing the next ridge, the clouds seriously descended, and the rain became more earnest. After that it was just a long, six-mile slog downhill. Reboot was pleasant company, and as we chatted, the miles went by. There were only a few tricky spots on smooth, slippery rocks, and most of the trail could be descended forwards, not backwards.

Once down, we crossed under the bridge and stepped up to the highway. After watching the traffic zip by for fewer than five minutes, we caught a hitch from a woman hiker who drove us right to Chet's Place, the hiker hostel in town.

Reboot and I bundled up our laundry and headed to the laundromat and ate dinner in loaner clothes. We demolished a tasty pizza and came back to the hostel with clean, dry clothes.

I was shortly tucked in a bunk, cozy and warm, fed and clean, ready for a lovely zero day of rest, though Reboot headed on the next morning. I was very grateful that this athletic young man took time in his thru hike to walk with me over Franconia Ridge. Graciousness comes in all ages of hiker.

My rest day was wonderfully filled with REST. Finishing all my little chores, I sat on a chair in the driveway giving my toes a manicure when Knitty and Gritty walked into town. (Retrieving their resupply box on an even longer road walk than mine, they'd dropped behind me.) It was very good to see old friends. I loved the camaraderie of hikers at hostels and shelters.

But, honestly, I couldn't get good sleep with the young crowd. They had energy and stamina for a party into the night. I gladly absorbed their exuberant energy, but the peaceful nights I slept alone on the trail brought me better rest in the still quiet of the forest. One was good for my psyche. The other was needed for my aging body.

Knitty, Gritty, and I paid for a shuttle farther south, as that part of the trail would be easier NOBO than SOBO. They would get back to the road in a one-day slackpack; it would take me two. They sped ahead, and I trudged behind. The weather turned cold, no hiking in sports bra. The trail had its share of rocks, roots, and mud, but it was still a pleasant hiking day.

I met Frank, who had helped me through the Mahoosuc Notch, as he came down from Eliza Brook Shelter. He was a day ahead of me SOBO but going NOBO two days meant I ran into him again.

Needing to turn into a hermit for a good night's sleep, I walked past the shelter and found a tiny stealth site not far from the crossing of pretty Eliza Brook, just big enough for my one- person tent among bare branches of bushes and small trees. I slept like a tired log.

The next day was up and over Kinsman and back to the hostel, descending a few tricky spots before the last few miles of level trail. I reached the highway before 4:00. A quick hitch within five minutes gave me the bonus of a local, who listened to Vermont radio. He told me The Green Mountains in Vermont were open. That had been a real question, as the trail had been closed for a month from hurricane damage. Now I could get through the Greens and complete the AT. Yay.

The hikers at the hostel saved me a lower bunk, looking out for the old lady. Sweet. The Hostel was full that night: The Lazy Bastards, Tonka, Panda, Super Bubba, Fish Hook, Knitty, Gritty, and Rook were my friends. I liked and appreciated them all—even if they were all young and stayed up late.

I used my headband over my eyes to block out the light and tried to sleep. They all eventually went to sleep, leaving the light on. I got up sometime in the night and turned it off to the sound of gentle snoring emanating from every bunk.

Catching my shuttle back to Kinsman Notch once again, I started up Brook trail, a steep trail with lovely waterfalls. Rebar in steep rock and wooden steps bolted to the rock aided on the steepest rock slabs. It took me three hours to the shelter and two more to reach the summit, but the reward was great.

The views from Moosilauke in a bright-blue sky were superb. I also saw Reboot again, who had taken the weekend off to visit friends. Among the many day hikers on Moosilauke were a couple from England on number 24 of their quest to complete the 48 4,000-foot peaks in the area. There are many ways to meet challenges in the wilderness, not all involve backpacking or speed of hiking.

Moosilauke was my last 4,000-foot mountain. On the descent to

Glencliff, I was able to descend forwards, not backwards, though it had a few steep parts. I almost had to ford a river at the bottom, but found a way to rock and tree hop across. I looked pretty funny in the middle of the river, an old lady with a backpack leaning on hiking poles while stepping up to precariously balance on a six-inch-diameter tree and stepping off the narrow trunk to rocks in the middle of the river. There was no one to take my picture, but the mental image remained in my mind.

The Welcome Hiker Hostel was less than a half-mile down the road, a unique lodge run by Uncle Walt. The shower and bathroom facilities were semi-outdoors behind and under tarps, the loft indoors for sleeping. Other hikers came in that night with wet feet from the river crossing, and I was very proud of my dry feet.

But my feet didn't stay dry the next day.

It rained steadily most of the day, and my umbrella earned its keep. After a number of clothing adjustments, I settled on one shirt. On downhills I wore the raincoat for warmth more than rain, but my rain pants were on the whole day, and my feet were wet and muddy. However, I was cruising at much lower altitude, warm with no wind.

I walked *real* trail all day, though it was somewhat muddy with occasional rocky patches and, of course, roots. This was still the Appalachian Trail, not a western trail, but there was a noticeable improvement and no rock scrambling was needed. I wanted to reach the shelter, but I just didn't have it in me and stopped at Bracket Brook. I could only do what I could do, not necessarily what I'd planned.

A 15-mile day started in the dark and ended in the dark, over rock changing from grippy granite to glacially polished quartz and quartzite. Quartz was prettier but more treacherous than granite when wet. I mentally sang old Girl Scout songs to keep myself moving steadily over Smarts Mountain, hearing the songs in my head but having no breath on an uphill to sing.

I met four section day hikers: Goat Boy, Old Geezer, Wildflower, and Tomcat, one my age; none were young. They'd hiked all of the trail from Georgia by day hiking and remarked on the tough trail coming up Smarts Mountain. I had to tell them that was the easy side of New Hampshire. They didn't seem to know weather was a problem in the Presidentials and Franconia Notch or that the trail would become rougher, so I was the bearer of bad news. They looked like they were thoroughly enjoying themselves, though, and I wished them luck, betting they would eventually get to Katahdin.

When I reached the shelter I was pleased to find another *mature* hiker, Phoenix, age 75. *She* was an inspiration, still hiking after a lung had been removed. I was very impressed. Let's hear a huzzah for older hikers, who keep going though body parts fail.

Wow. I'm still alive.

The next day was a 16-mile-long, mostly easy walk in very wet woods, which ended long after dark. Daylight disappeared just before Velvet Rocks. Anything with rocks in the name tells you what's to come, and in the dark with headlamp it was no picnic.

While clutching a knotted fixed rope descending backwards down rocks, I marveled at the sudden change in my long but fairly easy day, which had degenerated into one of those *wow, I'm still alive and not dead* moments. Making it down the rocks, I appreciated the AT white blazes except for one very swampy area, which took me three tries stomping in soggy moss and mud to find the trail in the dark.

Reaching the highway after 9:30, I'd been trying to call my motel by cellphone for an hour, with no success. The motel was almost three miles away. Who would pick up a hitchhiker, a very bedraggled elderly woman with a backpack and an umbrella in the dark pouring rain at almost 10:00 at night?

Glaring headlights zoomed by and fast tires sprayed puddles at me, leaving me even more wet and desperate for a ride. Fortunately for me, a young woman (who had hiked the Long Trail in Vermont with her 70-year-old mother) recognized I was a hiker and stopped. Salvation was sitting in an enclosed metal box on wheels that we call a car. I am certain I soaked her car seat and left puddles on the floor.

She found my motel, and I let myself into my room with the key left on the unoccupied desk, took a shower and collapsed into bed. My knee was REALLY unhappy with me. I hoped it would get happy again after a day of rest, and I rejoiced to be horizontal, dry, warm and clean.

I'd finished New Hampshire. My rest day was nearly as close to a zero as one can get and still have measureable mileage: .7 miles. Mostly I ate and rested the body, especially the knee. I put ice on it and hoped it would let me continue. I would have to go at a slower pace. I considered taking two zeros, but the motel was full for the weekend with an event at Dartmouth College. I changed my hike plan and hoped to make it to the next road to stay in a hostel there, taking another zero day if the knee so dictated.

Vermont

"The Lord Said to Noah, 'There's Gonna Be a Floody, Floody'"

In the morning the knee was better. The swelling had gone down, giving it nearly normal flexion. I liked Vermont. The trail was the easiest I would encounter. My knee calmed its anger at its owner, and the forest was lovely, green and, in some places, very golden. Unfortunately, the mosquitoes liked the weather, too, and I was their favorite meal. I'd sent my repellant home as there had been no mosquitoes in Maine. I picked up some *natural* repellant in Hanover and found it worthless. I kept my long sleeve shirt on, even though I felt like a basted turkey all day with the warm humidity and my sweat.

In a poor, flood-damaged little town, the hiker-friendly general store was gutted, and even though it still had its "Welcome Hikers" sign, no one was there. There were very few hikers in Vermont following damage from Hurricane Irene.

With my cellphone, I was in text contact with Reboot, three days ahead. He said he would tell me if he couldn't get through somewhere. Wildlife in the wetness included small creatures, cute little orange newts, squirrels, grouse, and a variety of birds, frogs, and toads. Wild raspberries and blackberries along the trail were the gift of the morning.

That year the AT was very difficult. I had scheduled too many long days for my old body, and the decreasing daylight added to the struggle to make the miles. When I didn't make miles at the speed I thought I should, my head was filled with negativity. I told myself to think about the things I enjoyed as an antidote.

First off, I enjoyed being there even at my age. That was a biggie. I enjoyed the raspberries on the trail, sunshine, gentle breezes discouraging the mosquitoes, dappled sunlight in the forest, golden leaves on the trees, views of farmland and hillsides, trees changing color, occasional bursts of color in late-blooming flowers, bright berries on bushes, apples on trees, people who encouraged me by signing my guest book with encouraging notes, and the stillness of the forest. I might be old and slow and failing to reach planned goals in a timely manner, but there was so much more to enjoy than simply reaching a goal on time.

Yes, there were more ups and downs than the profile showed in planning, and the last mile was rocky. I had to ford one river, and then I had wet feet. There was a large marshy area lasting nearly forever, a river washed my shoes clean before more marsh changed clean back to muddy grossness. But the trip up Dana Hill seemed easier than the profile had indicated, and I reached the shelter before dark, giving me time for a Ziploc bath and washing socks. Then I discovered I was missing my spare sports bra. Can't have everything.

The next morning I was on the trail at 5:30 with my headlamp on to begin a 16-mile day. It turned out to be an earlier rise than planned, but I woke up worried about the day and thought getting started was better than worrying.

The day was up and down and up and down and up and down again. There is a sameness, a sense of repetition about long-distance hiking, especially on the AT, step by step repeated all day long, day after day. To help the time and miles pass, I created a song in honor of that repetition. My poles beat out a three-tap rhythm on a four-beat measure. (I move the left pole half as often as the right.) My poles were saying methodically and rhythmically, *step by step rest, step by step rest.*

Step by step. (rest) Step by step. (rest) All along the trail. Step by step.

Step by step

Way to get 'er done.

Many long days on many long ways. That's the way it comes.

The one long line could be changed to innumerable descriptions such as: Through Rhodie Forests and Hobble Bush Hills or Some trail is easy, some beats your butt or Through snow, sleet or rain and sunshine too or Up lofty peaks and through muddy bogs or Down tree rappels and veggie belays or Up another mountain and down another vale or Through springtime flowers and autumn's falling leaves. The permutations were endless.

The tune was simple and stayed in my head, helping me get through the miles, especially uphill, while entertaining myself with supposedly clever verses, only clever to the mind-numbed trail walker.

I only had to use the headlamp for the last mile. The guy at the Mountain Meadows Lodge wasn't concerned whether I would get there or not when I called him on my cell phone. He told me if I arrived, he would give me dinner. Once there, he gave me far more than I could possibly eat, I showered and washed a few things—including my *only* bra—and fell into bed.

The next couple days were fairly uneventful walking. I met the four older hikers doing the AT by day hikes on another little section, and I saw the first real trail damage caused by Hurricane Irene as I crossed a river. I had to crawl on all fours on a ladder that had been made into a bridge. A nearby house had lost its access to the road when the bridge was swept away. I wondered where the family who lived there was. Were they in the house? Staying with relatives? Homeless?

I spent the night at Minerva Hinchy Shelter listening to hard rain falling. Throughout most of Vermont, my feet were never dry until I took shoes off at night and inserted feet, dried with a bandana, into my sleeping bag.

I started the day with dry feet before the heavens let loose with a gully washer. It rained so hard, water misted through the umbrella from the force of the rain, while I hunched under it not even moving. The umbrella earned its weight again by keeping my core mostly dry.

After the gully washer eased, it rained most of the day, with a brief letup for part of the afternoon. I might have liked this part of Vermont on a day when I didn't feel like someone was trying to drown me. Even the fallen bright red leaves looked forlorn and drowned on a trail often turned into either a river or a lake. In ankle-deep water, I slipped and slid all the way to Little Rock Pond for a late lunch.

The creeks boiled with brown water, making me very thankful for all the bridges still standing. One *bridge* was a single steel girder stretched across a ditch over brown rushing water instead of the small rivulet it was supposed to cover.

My gear, especially my sleeping bag, the long underwear, which were my jammies, my bed socks, and my down jacket, were kept dry with multiple layers of protection. As my mother might have said, "I won't shrink." As long as I was moving I would stay warm. The bigger danger was over-heating and sweating up clothes, which could chill me when stopping for a break. I *must* have dry, warm nightclothes to live to hike another day. So I had an umbrella, a Cuban-fiber pack cover, a plastic garbage bag and Cuban-fiber stuff sacks inside the garbage bag. Everything essential stayed dry.

In the midst of all this wetness, for some odd reason, I decided being soggy didn't have to dictate how I felt. I powered up to the shelter and belted out every verse I could remember of the church camp/Sunday school song, "Lord said to Noah, There's Gonna be a Floody, Floody." It seemed quite appropriate and tickled my funny bone so that I giggled up the hill even though soaking wet.

At Lost Pond Shelter, I had company. Since the hurricane damage had closed Vermont for a month, there were very few hikers on the trail and it was a real treat to have company in a shelter. Hard Candy, Pack Off, and I were glad to be together on bare boards under a roof.

In the morning, the rain had stopped, but there was standing water everywhere. Apologizing to my feet and promising they would be dry on my zero day, I walked through minor lakes of standing water to the privy. It was a disaster. The hole was filled with water, which I was sure would become part of the raging brook. *Everything* was standing water.

Later in the day, I found Griffith Lake had overflowed in two places, and all the carefully set rocks to cross a brook with dry feet were under water. I was already wet, so I just waded through.

Making it to the road before dark, I caught a hitch from two slightly scruffy good old boys. They thought it was great that I was doing the trail (at my age) and insisted on shaking my hand like I was a celebrity, which I accepted with good grace but thought very funny. I was just a soggy, bedraggled old-lady hiker. They took me to my lodging, and I splurged for dinner that night at a very nice restaurant, although I was a little ashamed going to a nice restaurant before taking a shower. The tables were very close together, and I had a definite layer of *hiker stank*.

My server graciously took my order and brought me my steak, but my closest table neighbors probably were not happy to be near me.

Sleeping late, I luxuriated in bed listening to the rain outside. Yep, more rain. The weather forecast was for nothing but rain for the foreseeable future. Five more days to go, and they would be wet ones. I was very thankful for the existence of shelters. My tent could have kept me dry, for the most part, but over the course of multiple rainy days, wetness eventually comes in with you in the small space of a tent. I wasn't looking forward to walking through five more soggy days, but I was glad there would only be five.

At the laundromat, I ran into OD Green, a past SOBO thru hiker. Seeing my duct-tape- patched raingear, which I was wearing while everything else suddsed in the washer, he recognized I was a hiker.

We talked trail, and he gave me a ride to the nearby grocery and back to Sutton's Place, where I was staying. Most wonderfully, he got all excited about the project of finding me a ride at the end of my hike. I needed to get from the Long Distance Hiker Association Gathering to West Point, NY and my daughter. We exchanged contact info, and I was buoyed up in spirit to know someone was working on the final necessary leg of my journey.

I usually had good luck hitching into towns. Going back to the trail, I usually paid for shuttle or taxi as I needed the time spent on the trail, not standing on a road with my thumb out. On OD Green's advice, I decided to try hitching. But no one wanted to pick up the old lady with pack, umbrella, hiking poles and duct-tape-patched rain pants on an early Sunday morning.

Perhaps they were all on their way to church. I felt like I was in the story of the Good Samaritan, except I hadn't been beaten by thieves and left for dead at the side of the road. Eventually I reached the trail, but it took two hitches and more than an hour.

Kathy had written to ask if the fall color was at the height of the season in Vermont as I walked through. Well, not really. Much of the forest was still green although there were a few red maples, yellow leaves, and Hobble Bushes in color. But the rain was knocking the colored leaves off the trees into the trail, making temporary color mats of glistening red, orange, and yellow, shining like somewhat bedraggled jewels. Sometimes the jewels were just sunk under water or trampled in mud.

MUD. Vermont lived up to its muddy reputation. Everything was so wet and muddy that falling was a real threat. I fell near White Rocks and wondered if I'd broken my wrist, a common fracture in the elderly. I hiked with my hand cradled in my pocket for a good long while until it felt better. Falling later, my new knee hit a book-sized rock hard enough to dislodge the rock from trail. Plastic and titanium seem to be strong stuff, and the knee replacement seemed none the worse for wear. I tried to be careful but felt like I was pushing my luck in all the wetness, four more days left to hike without damaging anything.

Mentally, I sang a lot of the day, which helped me cover the miles. On a Sunday, I switched from Girl Scout songs to hymns.

Three rain-drenched weekend hikers passed me on their way out, envious of my umbrella arrangement. I loved to have male hikers come up to me all excited, asking how I'd attached the umbrella so it could be up at the same time my hands held hiking poles. I told them, with a somewhat straight face, the first thing they needed to do was to get a sports bra, then tuck the pole of the umbrella under the pack chest strap and then into the sports bra for the second stabilization point. After laughing, a few male hikers said they thought they should consider doing just that if it worked that well.

Heading into Bennington began with a downpour. After that ended, the afternoon was devoid of raindrops. Yay. Losing the duct tape holding my shoe together, I walked back on the trail to find it, but no trace of its silver could be seen as far back as I walked. I hated the thought of leaving trash on the trail and mentally apologized to trail maintainers, or whoever would find that wad of duct tape.

On my last full day on the trail, I'd so wanted to have my feet only a little wet instead of soggy. After a morning of bounce and weave over mud pits or water streaming trail, I stayed mostly dry, that effort all for naught as some beavers dammed the next stream. The puncheon boardwalks were a good eight inches under water through an extensive swamp. There was no way through except to wade on top of the boards. On the bright side, at least temporarily, my shoes were much cleaner.

I saw no people, but heard from and saw a huge flying wedge of geese far above me. The trail ranged from pretty good to absolutely crappy with mud and rivers flowing where trail should be.

No views.

Death board puncheons over marshy areas had no cross-hatching on them, leaving them like wet glass in the rain. A few days earlier I'd seen a big, burly day-hiker crash painfully on slippery boards. So when I walked on them I slowed to the pace of a little old lady on ice.

Are you Medicare Pastor?

For my last night on the AT, the clouds disappeared, leaving a clear sky and cold temperatures. I was barely warm that night, wearing everything I had, including dry-but-mud- covered rain pants in my relatively clean sleeping bag. In the morning, the reward of finishing the trail and transportation to somewhere warm lured me out of the sleeping bag and down fairly good trail into Massachusetts.

At the green footbridge, Bag Lady, sent by my friend Amoeba, was holding a bundle of bright, colorful balloons. "Are you Medicare Pastor?" How fun to be met with balloons!

I'd not realized, when I made my hike plan for the AT that year, the ALDHA (Appalachian Trail Long Distance Hiker Association) Gathering was meeting in North Adams, Massachusetts two days before I was to finish. When Amoeba sent me news of the Gathering and also invited me to her own prior mini-gathering, I walked long days in Vermont, arriving four days earlier than scheduled.

Giving me the balloons, Bag Lady picked up another hiker, Patagonius, stopped for burgers, and drove us to the pre-gathering party in Amoeba's family farmhouse. I had my shower and borrowed clothes while mine washed, spending the rest of the day eating and talking to the group of hikers gathered there. Billy Goat was there along with Captain America, Memere, Gray Feather, Pipesmoke, Frog Caller, Queen Diva, Tiger Balm, and many more. Some I'd met along the AT or PCT. Many were in my age bracket. What a hoot. They celebrated with me, and we all talked trail long into the night.

For two more days, hikers filled an extensive meadow with a forest of tents while we attended the Gathering in North Adams. I couldn't have asked for a more perfect ending to the AT.

Oops, the Medicare *Pastor* forgot it was Sunday morning and failed to show for the hiker worship service in the dewy wet meadow. How embarrassing. At least I had no responsibility for the service. And OD Green had indeed found me a ride all the way back to West Point with JB, a thru hiker who had completed the CDT.

Once in a Lifetime?

The 2011 hike on the AT was a strenuous hike, definitely the most difficult part of the trail, although the entire AT was challenging. I am a western girl and an old lady, partial to trails one can walk without having to use hands as well as feet scrambling over rocks. Still, the AT, while having an Eastern Forest feel instead of a Western Mountain feel, was a beautiful trail.

The Rhodie forests of the south, the Hobble Bushes of the north, pastures and farmland, history and stone fences, lakes, rivers, snow in the spring, snow in the fall, fall color and not so much fall color, all were worth seeing.

And the people. People are always on the AT. Almost every day I saw at least one other person, even when hiking in November. Some of the people I met, I am fortunate to call friends.

As the years went by, knee problems made me walk more slowly, and I had less opportunity to know as many people, especially going in the opposite direction from the flow of hiker traffic.

But there were always people, no matter the time of the year. They brought companionship and joy as only hikers sharing what they love can do. I experienced plenty of trail magic, trail angels appearing when I needed them. On the AT, even the most macho, independent hiker, who'd begun their hike soured on life, came to realize kindness and help freely given by total strangers is the norm, not the exception. Many hikers, so helped, go on to give that help to others.

Completing the AT, I wondered what should come next. There were times on both the AT and the PCT when the thought of buying a travel van and doing a few day hikes now and then certainly seemed appealing, especially on long slogs uphill or when walking on snow or with wet feet. Yet I didn't think I was quite ready to hang up the backpack.

I'd become accustomed to taking long hikes every year. I was no longer taking *a* section hike. My mindset had changed. I'd become a regular long-section hiker, a different mindset than a thru hiker or a day hiker. I didn't take out five months to do an *adventure of a lifetime*. After finishing a hike, I started planning the next year's hikes. Doing 300-400 miles on each trail each year was a doable *yearly* adventure, not a *once in a lifetime* opportunity. I didn't thru hike and didn't consider hiking a complete lifestyle change followed by re-entry into the non-hiking world, but I'd developed a *lifestyle* that included hiking two long sections of some trail each year, every year.

I still had about 80 miles to finish the PCT, but I was used to planning two long hikes every year. There are a great many trails in the world I have not yet walked. God blessed this world with beauty, wilderness, and people. I hoped to see more of it. I needed a spring hike.

Chapter 30 Fall and Winter 2011-2010

CDT Planning

I planned to head to New Mexico in April of 2012. I didn't know if I would have the physical ability or the time allotted to me in life for completion of the Continental Divide Trail. At 70, I considered *living* a year-to-year, month-to-month and day-to-day opportunity. But what the heck, I might as well give it a try. If I were not to finish, at least I would see and experience *more* of the wonders of the trail. If I *were* to finish, that would be spectacular.

One can't finish without beginning, but beginning the CDT was really just a continuation. I section hiked. I wasn't ready to stop section hiking. While I could, I would.

The older I became, the more I needed to prepare the body for backpacking. Among other preparations, I found myself walking 7 ½ miles, through a bit of rain and snow, pack on my back, through the streets of Puyallup. I mailed food drop boxes. Getting a lot of strange looks, I walked through the South Hill Mall with a pack on my back to get my grandson's birthday present. I didn't see anyone else in their rain gear hefting a backpack while buying grandchildren's B-day presents. I now had six grandchildren and would soon have a 7th.

At the time I began the Continental Divide Trail, hikers chose from three places to begin.

At that time, about half of CDT hikers chose the *official* start at the Crazy Cook Monument, which had very difficult access. About half chose the Columbus route with easy access. A few diehards began at Antelope Wells, the farthest south point in New Mexico's boot heel. I chose the Columbus Route for the ease of access. I also read more journals of hikers on that route who enjoyed it, and several who did the other, not enjoying it as much.

There were not many purists on the trail then. One of the

challenges on the CDT was choosing your route. It wasn't a matter of following every white blaze as the AT, or of following one established and marked trail (except for alternates in Oregon) as the PCT. No two CDT hikers hiked exactly the same trail. Checking out at least three different maps and a guidebook I made choices. Map and compass skills were considered very important and a GPS handy. I was only mildly accomplished with a map and compass, but I carefully laid out all routes on my GPS.

My pack would be a little heavier in 2012 than in 2011 as 1) I was afraid of freezing at night in New Mexico. 2) Water would be an issue. 3) I was older and slower and had to take more days (hence more food) in remote areas between trail towns than average hikers. 4) I'd gotten all techie. Both Pocketmail and then Peek had gone out of business, so I bought an iPhone. I added the smallest size Goal Zero solar charger, which I would carry on top of my pack, to keep GPS batteries and iPhone in business.

My knee Doc might not have been too happy with the heavier pack, but I thought I could keep the weight down below 30 pounds if not below 20 pounds. It probably averaged 25 pounds through most of New Mexico.

Navigation and weight were two of the challenges on the CDT. There would also be fewer people. Thousands of hikers were then starting on the AT each year and hundreds on the PCT. Only about 50 were starting on the CDT in those years, and not all of them started on the same end of the trail. Another challenge would be hundreds of fords of the Gila River. It might only be ankle-to-thigh deep. Or it could be too deep to ford. I wouldn't know which circumstance would be mine until I got there.

I needed flexibility on the CDT. Although I always planned more extensively than most thru-hikers, planning helped me be flexible when I needed to be, and I planned possible route changes, too.

Some might consider these challenges to be dangers, but I find it healthier to consider them challenges, which I would try to meet with planning, good sense, and experience. Nothing was certain. But then, nothing is certain whether one goes hiking or stays at home. It was more fun to go hiking.

Chapter 31 March 30, 2012 CDT

Columbus Route Roads, Deserts and Blisters

First, of course, was getting there. Two planes, a city bus, and a Greyhound Bus, and I was in New Mexico. El Coyote met me at the bus stop in Deming, and in the fading light he wanted to show me the road I would be on a few days later. I appreciated his efforts, but in the fading light of dusk we almost hit a cow in open-range country. El Coyote said we must have missed it because I was a pastor. Interesting thing for a professed atheist to say.

Cowboy camping outside their trailer on my first night in New Mexico, I was ready to start.

After a lovely sunset, stars and moon looked down on me, a dog or two barked in the distance, and the sound of traffic was sparse.

After setting a water cache for me, giving me a lay of the land tour and stopping at Willy's, a ranch on the way, to let them know I would need water the next day, El Coyote drove me to the border. At the border he checked in with Border Patrol cars and customs, so they wouldn't hassle me as I was taking my *starting* pictures at the border. Then I headed back up the black top highway three and a half miles to Columbus. Yep, my CDT walk began on a blacktop highway.

I was hot before I reached Columbus, the Chihuahua Desert in New Mexico near the Mexican border, not the same climate I'd left in cold and rainy Washington State. Stopping at the first of two museums in Columbus, the Columbus Historical Museum, the hostess was kind and gracious, sitting me down to cool off, while I watched a video about the Pancho Villa raid in 1916. A relative on my mother's side had fought Pancho Villa, giving me an extra interest as I enjoyed the museum.

The spigot in the cemetery was the last water stop before trudging into desert heat, mesquite bushes, cactus, mainly prickly pear and cholla and a few yucca. Nearing South Peak of Tres Hermanas, I saw poppies, yellow daisies and palo verde beginning to leaf out.

Having been warned about staying on the good side of ranchers by not scaring the cows, I took care not to camp too close to the water tank, I spread my gear in a sandy draw a little above an obviously dry stream bed with fewer pointy things to puncture my air mattress than the rest of the desert floor. The temperature an absolutely lovely 67, New Mexico was a wonderful place to be in early spring.

Off the desert floor on the sides of hills the next day, was more obvious life: poppies, desert chicory, pincushion, five small deer, two jackrabbits and a turkey vulture. I saw a couple dozen cows throughout the day. Few natural water sources in this part of New Mexico meant I shared water with cattle. I was grateful cows would share.

Winding my way through tall mesquite bushes to the water cache, I wouldn't have found it without having marked it on my GPS. Stopping at Willy and Rose's house for more water, I needed the 2 ½ hour rest on their shaded patio more. Walking cross country for five miles following my GPS, I ran into the dirt road I was searching for just as daylight faded. I cowboy camped again in another sandy draw.

The next morning was 38 degrees, and I was glad to keep clothes on, covering the sunburn I'd already acquired. I found the water tank as El Coyote had told me. But a fierce wind blew away my foam sit pad when I turned my back to pack up. It was out of sight and half way to Mexico in a quick moment.

From the highway, the desert looks quite barren. Up close and personal while walking, I saw poppies and chicory in abundance, as well as phacelia, bright pink low-growing flowers, yellow and white daisies, rattlesnake weed, ajo lilies and purple vetch. Thanks to the flower app on my phone, I identified a flower I'd never seen before, a long-nosed rock trumpet. Several stands of ocotillo were loaded with buds not yet blooming.

Ibex have been sighted in the Florida Mountains, but I knew of only a few hikers, who had chosen to walk cross-country through those mountains due to all the thickly growing pointy things to shred your legs. I took the road around as more befitting an old lady, finding a sheltered area in Headquarters Draw behind a 10-foot road berm breaking the 40-mile-an-hour wind.

Stopping at a small lapidary shop and museum to use a restroom, I met two older gentlemen. The Geode Kid was well known in rock-hound circles and had written a couple books. His partner, the talkative one, was a tall, thin man with a long wispy white beard, who walked with the aid of a walker. I bought a little geode to mail home.

On roads all day, I found I liked roads. I could walk faster on a road, but speed came with a price. A little blister developed on the bottom of my heel. After slack packing through the town of Deming, the blister grew to half-dollar size.

Blisters come in two basic types: friction blisters and compression blisters. Friction blisters are common on heels, toes or sides of feet, friction blisters are caused by something rubbing on something else, shoes on heels, toes on each other, etc. Feet swell as the day goes on and often change sizes on long-distance hikes. Shoes that fit just right in the store when trying them on, often are no longer just right on the trail. Heat and wetness also contribute to friction blisters.

Compression blisters are something else, but no less painful. Compression blisters are caused by repeated compression of a body part, especially heels on roads. Because the surface of a road is nearly level, feet make repetitive contact with the ground the same way at each step, giving an even, ground-eating rhythm, faster than the variety of step patterns required by an uneven wilderness trail.

But the repetitive pattern, besides being fast, compresses the pad of the heel into the calcaneus (heel bone) over and over again, each step almost always repeating the identical impact as the step before, resulting in a compression blister on the bottom of your heel. Healing such a blister on the trail is difficult, if not impossible. Have you ever tried walking on your toes to keep pressure off your heel? For miles? For days?

It was a very good thing my hike itinerary included taking four days off to visit an old college friend in Las Cruces, whom I'd not seen for fifty years. I could hobble around her house on my toes while the blister healed.

I also needed to deal with a few problems. An email from Lynnae, one of my trail angels ahead, said my bear can with food and medications had not arrived. Although I could buy more food, medications were another matter. Besides the knee replacement, I have all the accouterments of old-age conditions and needed my medications. After a phone call to my doc, Walgreens came through with more meds and a phone call to REI brought a new foam pad to replace the one blown away in the wind.

My friend and I had a lovely time catching up on the last 50 years. An Ethnohistorian of Southern New Mexico and retired curator of the New Mexico State University Museum, she drove me 120 miles to see the International Center of the Camino Real Museum on the Jornado Del Muerto, a quite interesting museum in the middle of nowhere, three miles off the highway below Socorro.

Before leaving La Cruces, an email brought the news my bear can with its food drop finally *did* reach Mimbres, after being lost in the mail for more than a month. Hooray. I could leave

Deming with only five day's food instead of having to carry for seven, and I would have extra meds. I was so relieved. My blister had healed, and after Easter Sunday services in Las Cruces, I was on the bus back to Deming.

After a *girl's breakfast out* with El Coyotes' wife Mary, I headed out into rangeland and desert, passing multiple water sources, all for cattle. I stopped at Spyder windmill merrily pumping clear clean water from the ground into a tall tank, from which I dipped my water.

Pet Cows and Lightning

The *trail*, more properly called a route, was sometimes on dirt roads that came and went away. Much of the time I walked cross-country, sharing the range with cows. I moved slowly and talked to them, trying not to spook them as this route of the CDT was available to hikers at the forbearance of ranchers. Cows were used to cowpunchers usually arriving in trucks, jeeps, and cars, but not walking hikers.

They considered anything approaching them at ground level to be dangerous. In the springtime, spooked cows run in fear, losing track of their calves. I was told it takes a lot of cowboy time to help them *mother up* again. I didn't want to get on the wrong side of cows or ranchers.

Entertainment during the day, besides finding water and talking gently to cows, included flowers I was amazed to see blooming in the supposedly barren desert. The most exciting find, though, was the petroglyphs near Detention Dam. I needed sharp eyes to find them, but they were one of the reasons I'd chosen the Columbus route. The history of New Mexico encompasses the history of native people long predating those of my heritage, and I wanted to see the petroglyphs recording their existence.

Detouring up to Frying Pan Spring for my water, I loaded up and searched for level ground to camp. Resting in the middle of the day, meant I reached camp as darkness was falling. Two sloppy wet bandanas in a plastic bag made a very refreshing bandana bath as stars began to fill the sky.

Showy white desert primroses still bloomed in the morning before they wilted in the heat of the day. Passing them, I walked through the remaining stone walls of a station on the Butterfield Stage route and remaining pieces of adobe walls at Fort Cummings and pondered what life had been like with stage coaches making the trek through the desert, defended by soldiers. Human history intertwined with wilderness.

Leaving Cemetery Hill, I walked by what Wolf (author of the CDT Guide Book) calls a reliable water source and Ley (creator of Jonathon Ley Maps of the CDT) calls icky cow water. I suppose it was both, a thick cake of scum resting on top of the water. I treated all my water with a Steripen (ultraviolet light) or iodine tablets, sometimes both, but I passed that water source for the next.

Thirty head of cows milled around the stone walls of the boxed spring I wished to access. Sitting down on the hillside of yellow flowers, I ate my lunch talking to cows. They became so used to my presence that when I went down to get my water, they didn't move away. In fact, when I left, they started to follow me. Not needing 30 head of pet cows following me on the trail, I yelled and waved my poles to make them uninterested in me.

The rest of the day was open desert and cross country. One way to get an idea of the vastness of open spaces in New Mexico deserts is to walk through them. Most CDT hikers whose journals I'd read, traversed this desert with map and compass, but I was glad to have my GPS routes showing as a pink line on its map. I kept checking the pink line, coming back to it when I found I'd gone astray. My rest break was in the shade of a single yucca surrounded by lots of not much of anything else.

In that open desert, I think I saw a Mexican Grey Wolf as it loped crosswise ahead of me on my line of travel, turning to look at me a few times. I didn't think it was a coyote or a dog.

Maybe the cows had reason to be spooky.

The sunset was glorious as I camped on flat desert with mountains miles away from me in most directions. I had excellent cell reception. After laying out my cowboy camp, I checked the weather report, which forecast no rain. Taking my Ziploc bath in a little of the precious water I'd carried, I saw lightning flashes in the south and very serious lightning strikes straight to the ground near Cooke's Peak. Very soon, lightning was striking mountains on all sides of me. No matter which direction the weather moved, I was going to get hit by a thunderstorm, regardless of that weather report forecasting no rain.

Oh Lordy, I was smack in the middle of a very big level expanse of open desert, not even a yucca in sight. If I set up my tent, my tent pole would be the highest point for miles around. I didn't want to be a lightning attractant, so I quickly made the tent into a bivy, pounding in the side stakes, shoving gear inside and crawling inside my bag in the *bivy-tent* without using the center pole. When the storm hit, I held down the tent edges over my head while strong winds swept across the desert tearing at the tent. Theoretically, you shouldn't lie flat in a thunderstorm as ground current can fry more of your flat body if lightning strikes nearby. But I was more afraid of sticking up above the desert surface. I was lucky. I stayed mostly dry, didn't get hit by lightning or fried by ground current, and the storm passed.

In the morning, everything was wet and the weather cooler. Packing up, I headed out across the desert again. At least it was no longer dusty. The dry White Rock River had a steeply cut bank, but a crumble in the bank wall only required two sit-down butt slides, easily done and a parked flatbed truck with no one present provided some shade for a break.

Near the edge of the desert, a windmill pumped sparkling clean water into a tank beside an old ramshackle cabin. Drying out tent and sleeping bag, treating water, washing socks and bandanas, snacking and journal writing, I took a long, lovely break by the cabin.

Chapter 32 Mountains and Cold

"I refuse to die of hypothermia at 9,000 feet. I'm gonna go to 8,000 feet."

Heading into hills polka dotted with junipers, it was still hot as I walked by several ranch houses with "no trespassing" signs. I'd become proficient at rolling under barbed wire, where there were no gates open across the road. But I felt uncomfortable walking past so many "no trespassing" signs.

I was on a county road, though—from the signs—I wouldn't have known it was a public road. My last water for the day came from a solar well marked on the Ley map. It was close to the road and near a friendly-looking house without "no trespassing signs." I'd seen no people all day.

The last hour or two were the best hiking as the day cooled. I finally pulled off the road just as it was getting dark and kicked dry cow pies to the side to make my campsite. (Cows know all the best sites in the shade or out of the wind.) Taking my bandana bath, I sat on my air mattress under a sky filling with stars.

The next day I saw my first natural running water in New Mexico— Berenda Creek. Much of the time it was dry, but it bubbled up from underground to run for short stretches far up the canyon. Heading up the canyon, I passed a house that had at least 10 dogs, all barking furiously. Two were loose, and one looked like he wanted me for a snack. Fortunately his owner called him off. No one was ever going to sneak by that house.

Clyde Chandler of the Tierra Blanca Ranch stopped his truck and chatted with me on the way to a corral to move some cows. He was very friendly, saying he'd had no trouble with CDT hikers but thought people should have formally asked him to route the trail through his property. (When I talked to Jim Wolf later, he was surprised, as he thought that had been done. I guess communication can sometimes be misunderstood.)

A group of 27 hikers in a boys' group came down the trail, led by a couple of adults. The leader was a young, very fit woman, who looked like she knew what she was doing. She was packing heat, the first hiker I ever saw doing that. One of the boys had a bow and arrows. He'd tried for a wild turkey and missed, but the turkey ran into a tree and broke its neck so they'd had it for dinner the night before I met them.

Past McMullin Spring, the trail became intertwined cow paths, and I needed the GPS to discern the right one. Climbing steadily uphill, the desert floor long past, I saw bear scat but no bruins and found a slightly sheltered clearing at 7,000 feet. I put up my tent for the first time in New Mexico and properly hung my food bag, also for the first time.

Going up nearly 2,000 feet the next day, I managed to get off trail following other roads TWICE because I neglected to look at the GPS. Totally discouraging. A GPS only works to keep you found if you look at it.

The CDT is the only major named trail I have been on where cow paths are more prominent than the trail. I also found low cairns (piles of rocks that mark the trail) hard to see for a short person. More seriously, Donohue Spring had no water. I was thirsty all day, rationing what water I still had. After expending my energy on fruitless quests down wrong paths, the trail proceeded to kick my butt. I was tired, thirsty and out of sorts as the trail kept disappearing. I always walked only half the speed of the average thru hiker, but it felt like I was hardly moving at all.

I once gave a presentation about my travels and someone commented to me in amazement, "Distance doesn't mean anything to you at all." That is not correct. Distance does mean something to me, every labored step. And yet I like another hiker quote read somewhere, "Anywhere is walking distance, if you have the time."

I traveled through lovely, if dry, forests of pinion, oak and ponderosa, nice pocket views of Cooke's Peak to the south and desert to east and southwest. I saw Mimbres Valley once, though I failed to get pictures that day. I was just trying to make my leaden legs work.

Reaching Emory Pass a little early, I easily found my bear can with food and a gallon of water tied to a tree by my trail angel, Lynnae. Yay. Thank you. I surely needed that water. I unpacked, added bear can, food, and water to my pack and drank a liter of water on the spot. Reaching my campsite at close to 9,000 feet, the snow on the opposite hill told me it would be a cold night.

A cold day followed that cold night. Though my campsite had been sheltered, all night I could hear the wind roaring through the trees around me. The trail from Emory Pass to Hillsboro was good, well-graded trail, but the wind was rising. My face was so cold I masked it with my bright-orange bandana—bandito style.

New Mexico is not just flat desert; Hillsboro Peak is 10,016 feet. It was cold, but the biggest problem was high winds. One of the two buildings on top of Hillsboro was an unlocked cabin used by hikers, a very appreciated shelter, where hikers could eat lunch out of the wind. Leaving the top of Hillsboro in strong wind and a temperature of 31 degrees, I practically ran down the trail, going as fast as an old lady with a titanium knee can go, though I can no longer really run.

When I was 1,000 feet lower the temperature had dropped to 26 degrees. That's not the way it's supposed to work. Evidently a very cold snap had hit the area.

I wore my Dri Ducks raingear for a windbreak, tops and bottoms, and bandanas over my face. Much of that high-country vegetation was scrub oak and gooseberry bushes. Even though I stepped as carefully as I could over thorny branches, my Dri Ducks tore twice. They are known to be fragile as well as light weight, but I don't think anything could have stood up to those thorns. My Dry Ducks were soon to match the duct-tape repairs on my Marmot Precip Pants I'd worn on previous hikes.

It began to snow, a fine light powder accumulating less than 1/4 inch, but at 23 degrees it wasn't going anywhere. Those were pretty extreme conditions. I'd been expecting to spend a night or two in the 20s in New Mexico. But I didn't expect to be hiking in the *daytime* at 23 degrees. My water bladder hose froze, no surprise at that temperature. As long as I kept walking I was warm enough, and I was very glad I'd brought heavy gloves even if they weighed 6 oz.

They were worth their weight.

I must have a pretty warped sense of humor, because the thought going through my mind in those conditions was, "*I refuse to die of hypothermia at 9,000 feet. I'm gonna go to 8,000 feet.*" Note I didn't say I wouldn't *die* at 8,000 feet, just that I was going there. I laughed at my statement and kept repeating it to myself all afternoon. It was too soon to know if I would die at 8,000 feet.

The trail stayed at 9,000 feet until almost dark when I reached the spring that was my goal. The ground wasn't perfectly level, but with darkness setting in, this was it. The temperature was 26, and I was sure it would be colder in the night.

I set the tent low to try to keep in heat and climbed inside. I wore everything I had to bed, including rain gear. The exertion of getting all available clothes on warmed the tent to a comparatively balmy 30 degrees. Eating was important, but so was preserving heat. I needed calories inside me to make calories of heat, but I also needed to preserve that heat as quickly as possible. Already partly in my sleeping bag, I quickly made a very large flat wrap roll up of meat chunks and cheese, ate it as fast as I could, drank some slushy Cytomax, tossed water bottles in the foot of my bag so they wouldn't be frozen in the morning, and snuggled into my bag, pulling the drawstring tight around a tiny hole to allow fresh air for my nose.

My Western Mountaineering Versalite was rated to 10 degrees. I draped my down jacket over my hips in the bag as I always do and was comfortable after my feet warmed up. In that potentially dangerous weather, my decisions and gear seemed to be adequate. I went to sleep, hoping I would wake up in the morning, and I did.

Morning was cold, in the 20s. Packing up was the hardest part, gloves interfering with packing. I had to stuff my hands in my pockets to thaw between packing chores. But the cold front moved on, and as I lost elevation, the day warmed up, and so did I.

I chatted with a turkey hunter in the morning, and after lunch I walked a lot of miles on a dirt/gravel road on the edge of a mesa, views to mountains in the north and west. An interesting sign informed me that the lovely juniper trees encroaching on the mesas were being removed to encourage wildlife habitat. Good for the wildlife, but I liked them for shade.

My trail angels on McNight Road had been recruited by Lynnae, as I needed cat-free lodging. Jan and George were wonderful. They immediately showed me the shower and the laundry. They fed me, too, which I wasn't expecting. George was an excellent cook, and that plate of spaghetti with big chunks of tomato and mushrooms was perfect. Treated like a visiting relative in a cozy warm house, it was hard to believe I'd been in dangerous weather the night before.

My zero day with Jan and George was lovely. Among other things, they took me for a ride to show off the area, driving past the Ponderosa Ranch of TV fame. They fed me delectable barbeque ribs, I sang them Holden Evening Prayer, and we talked church as well as trail.

Saying *good-bye* to my wonderful new friends in the morning, I headed down the road to the Allie Canyon trail on a Goldilocks day. Not too cold. Not too hot. No high winds. Just right.

Allie Canyon had interesting rocks to look at and water in the creek, remarkable, as New Mexico creeks do not always have water. There were half a dozen four-inch fish in Allie Creek, either brave or foolhardy to be fish in a stream that dries up some years. I loaded up with water, as there would be none in the upper canyon. As I began my lunch, a turkey hunter came by, and later in the day I saw two turkeys. The hunter must have seen the hapless turkeys, too, as I heard a shot.

Seeing my first CDT sign, my route coincided with the *official* one for about three miles. It was 55 degrees as I camped that night at 8,800 feet elevation, quite different from the freezing cold three nights earlier.

I hiked up and over Signal Peak, down, up and along Tadpole Ridge. I still struggled slowly with uphills, especially above 8,000 ft. I didn't seem to have manufactured enough red blood cells for the altitude, or maybe I was just old. Tadpole Ridge went up and down the same 200 feet over and over again, the views spectacular, wide open spaces north and west of me showing ranges of mountains, clefts for rivers and broad mesas.

Walking down Sheep Corral Canyon, I reached my stopping place by the first pool of water in the canyon at 7:00, plenty of time to set up tent, eat and clean up. I took a bandana bath, my feet especially appreciating the removal of layers of dust. Not rinsing the dirty bandanas in the precious canyon water, I just dumped them in a Ziploc to carry out.

The Gila "A better woman than he was man"

Oh, what a difference a day made. One of the joys of New Mexico was the variety. I experienced blazing desert sun, high-mountain snow, and cold canyons and views. Now I descended to the Gila River, an entirely different and wondrous section of New Mexico.

Arriving at Sapillo Creek about 1:30, I walked right in to cool off my feet before lunch, knowing I would be fording it and the Gila after lunch. I would ford the Gila River more times than I could count over the next several days. Sycamores along the river had not yet leafed out, their white bones of bough and trunk showing brightly against blue sky and reddish rock overhangs. A duck skimmed by around the corner, a big yellow butterfly flitted by me, and Turkey Vultures soared overhead. It was a wonderful spot for lunch. After I ate, watered up, and washed my socks, I set out to see the Gila.

I forded it a dozen times that first day, knee deep or as deep as my shorts depending on the wideness of the river. Rock formations beside the river were spectacular. How lucky and blessed I was to see such sights. Once again, I was overcome with emotions previously experienced in the Sierra standing by the river at Grouse Rock Meadow with towering granite massives around me, wading in my seemingly private lake in Maine, walking through stunningly colored woods in Virginia and any number of other wondrous sights, a solo purveyor of incredible wilderness beauty. I couldn't move fast on a trail, but why should I care about speed when confronted with such splendor?

Not all was bliss. Some of the entries to river crossings were ankle-deep muddy bogs. The trail between fords was sometimes deep dust or sand, quickly coating soaked shoes and socks. I walked even more slowly, but it was all worth it just to be there. On the dusty, sandy tread I saw tracks of cat, bear, turkey, and deer, and I heard coyotes, sharing my trail with wilderness inhabitants.

Early in the morning three kayaks glided by. The kayakers were complaining about the water level being low. Bad for them, good for me. Day two on the Gila brought at least 50 more fords, though I lost count after 24. The deepest ford was nearly to my waist. Another had very swift water, though not so deep.

Entries and egresses from the river were either very sandy, (slow going) alluvial plains of river rocks, (slow going) or sticky, gooey mud, which was ankle or calf deep. (slow going and tried to suck my shoes off.) I was very, very careful, slow and deliberate on every river crossing. Then again, I didn't walk that fast anyway.

When four riders leading four mules passed me heading south, one 72-year-old gentleman rider was impressed that I'd walked from the Mexican border. He said I was a better woman than he was man. To each his own; he was a better rider.

Trees along the river were a mix of sycamore, ponderosa pine, juniper and cottonwood.

Rock formations along the banks around every bend displayed colors ranging from brown to red to orange and yellow with a little purple thrown in for good measure.

Since I didn't reach Doc Campbell's store in time to retrieve my resupply box, I took the access road to Wildwood Retreat. No one was there, and the hot spring pools were drained. I saw no information about price, but I was seduced by an empty, unlocked cabin overlooking the river. So I dumped my pack on the porch and took a shower while my dinner hydrated. When the retreat caretaker came by, I dickered for the price of three nights lodging and some transportation, staying an extra day to see the Cliff Dwellings.

The campground host agreed to three nights at a 15% discount, a ride to the Visitor Center three days later and a ride to Doc Campbell's for groceries and my food box, as well as a ride to the Cliff Dwellings.

Major score. I hadn't planned on that bed, but it surely felt good.

After snarfing down two high-priced sandwiches at Doc Campbell's, I toured the Gila Cliff Dwellings, tucked in cool caves in gorgeous rock. The caves had been used for centuries, the dwellings inside them constructed about 700 years ago. I walked in wonder through rooms where ancient people led their lives. Surprisingly, following others before them, the Tularosa Mogollon Indians probably only lived there a generation or so.

As always, I liked knowing the names of the flowers, learning the bright yellow flower that carpeted the hills was golden corydalis, also called scrambled eggs. Prolific after burns, they were especially profuse after the Miller Fire cleared other vegetation. The Cliff Dwellings, including 700-year-old wood posts, were successfully defended against the fire, though the surrounding hills showed blackened tree trunks along with bright yellow flowers.

Walking from Cliff Dwellings to the Visitor Center, I was hot, the pavement rough on my feet. After the Visitor Center, I walked at least another mile before being picked up by the sheriff, a good thing as he gave me a ride to Doc Campbell's. Three thru hikers passed me as I rode with the sheriff, the first I'd seen in 200 miles. I never learned their names or talked to them since I was in the sheriff's car, but it was always good to see hikers.

Eating dinner that night on my cabin porch, I watched ducks on the river 25 feet away. I saw the new green of leafing trees and gazed at turkey vultures soaring between me and some hoodoos (columns of weathered rock) across the river. It had been a very enjoyable tourist sort of day.

A new camper named Anna pulled into the Wildwood Retreat, and we got to know each other. She volunteered to send a package home for me when she went back home, and she gave me a ride to the Visitor Center again, so I could buy presents for my grandchildren now that I had a way to send them home.

After walking back to Doc Campbell's, I met hikers doing the Grand Enchantment Trail, Doc Campbell's a resupply point for hikers walking either the CDT or the Grand Enchantment Trail. From the stack of hiker boxes, many would be coming through that year. Buying food for dinner and some ice cream, I walked back to the Wildwood Retreat.

Anna took me to the trailhead in the morning and walked with me a short ways. Even on a cold morning the usual plethora of fords were necessary. I carried a pack heavy with *eight* days of food. Since I would always be along the river, I carried no more than one small bottle of water, helping lower the total pack weight. Since I wasn't carrying much water, I could carry more food.

The river once again cut between deep cliffs. My trips to the Visitor's Center had informed me that the dark-brownish red/purplish layer of rock was an older basaltic/andesite layer, and the sand-colored rock above the andesite was a sandstone conglomerate. A number of caves were cut into the top layer, one looking substantial enough to have been an archeological site.

Besides the interesting cliffs, the birds were singing and the sun was shining on my cool morning walk. Passing the first hot spring early in the day, I warmed my hands in the water. As I walked along, the cliffs changed from smoothly curved to blocky chunks with square spires and vertical fractures.

After lunch the trail just got better, jaw-dropping awesomely incredibly beautiful. The rock cliffs and spires took off from the river-bottom and soared at least a 200-500 feet straight up beside the river, those on the Middle Gila the most awesome.

At Jordan Hot Springs, I took a dip in perfectly clear warm water reminiscent of a Japanese outdoor spa. After dinner, I walked on between towering cliffs and spires. I could have gotten a crick in my neck, fallen on my face, or run into poison ivy while gazing upward in awe but I couldn't stop looking.

At 6:30 I suddenly felt tired. I'd traveled longer than planned, even though carrying eight days' food. The next day my pack would be a little lighter.

Fording in the morning was very cold on my feet, though fording the same river in the heat of afternoon, the cold water was something my feet enjoyed. A side pond in The Meadows had

6-to-8 four-inch catfish, almost eating size, which delighted me. After lunch the trail was rougher as it wound around the base of cliffs rising straight up. The thought of some shard deciding to fall straight down encouraged me not to tarry there.

Walking the Gila was relaxed and enjoyable as I'd planned shorter miles to accommodate the heavier food carry. Since I passed my planned miles the first two days, I consequently passed my *must make* miles early the next day, walking farther a bonus. I could put in miles but feel no pressure to make my destinations. Stopping for dinner below cone-shaped spires, I went on after eating, not feeling too tired to hike even more.

A turkey waddling up the hill on the opposite bank, a duck, turkey vultures, numerous birds, beetles, and the catfish were the wildlife I saw. As I prepared for bed that night, I listened to the river and the frogs.

On a cold (38 degree) morning, the thought of putting on wet shoes and crossing rivers wasn't appealing. Lounging in my bag, I had breakfast in bed before I could face the idea. A Father/Daughter duo of section hikers passed me as I was packing up, and we talked for half an hour as the morning warmed. Continuing up the Gila was still interesting, but the cliffs gradually reduced in size. Lacking spectacular cliffs and rock formations, the canyon became more like other pretty canyons with a rushing mountain stream.

A cold wind met me at Snow Lake as I left the Gila, preventing a leisurely stop. Ominous clouds, wind, and a splatter of raindrops spurred me to pack up as soon as I finished lunch. The scenery changed on top of T-bar Ridge to miles of rolling grasslands at an 8,000-foot elevation, seeming to go on forever. Dark clouds went away, but the wind remained on that high, windswept prairie. There was no point in stopping early in the wind, but I finally reached shelter in pines after 7:00.

Cold at 37 degrees encouraged me to stay in bed again. But since my tent faced open grasslands to the east, the rising sun quickly warmed the tent, finally motivating me to eat breakfast while listening to a pack of coyotes. The trail that day was a dirt road, eventually winding through pine forests, 2.5 miles of cross country thrown in to give the feet a change of tread. Of the few cars on the road, half stopped to ask if I was OK or needed anything. New Mexico receives pluses for the friendliness of local people.

Ten antelope ran across the open country, stopping to look at me, running more, repeat, repeat, repeat. Antelope are very curious critters, but with their bounding leaps they quickly moved across open spaces leaving equally curious me behind. I also saw three elk. I had no bandana bath that night as there was no water, just enough left over wetness to clean my grimy feet with the bandana carried for two days in a plastic bag.

Slow starts were becoming a habit. I was, after all, half a day ahead of schedule. A slow start meant getting up at 7:00. While I was still abed I heard four screeches and thought "cougar."

I left the running water in Cox Creek with clean socks and bra and a load of H_2O. At the top of the road, I discovered cell reception and saw I'd received 157 emails. It was nice to be in contact with the universe again and nice to know people wondered how things were going for me. The rest of the afternoon was spent putting one foot in front of the other, mostly descending. The trail was a little sketchy at times, steep and rocky, especially through a burn area. Even if roads were faster, it was nice to be on real trail tread.

The trail was such a very *daily* affair. Day by day, each day unfolded with new sights to see, new experiences at which to marvel, hypnotizing me into a trail zombie. It was as if I had become addicted to anticipating new adventures on a two-foot-wide path or, in New Mexico, a dirt road, revealing the world one step at a time.

Searching for water, I took the route through Govina Canyon and found the lower third running nicely with clear water. After a pleasant walk in relative green through surrounding dusty hills, I reached Lopez Tank (A *tank* is a large cow pond) and had a nice lunch break after a bandana bath. Feeling much better to be clean, I celebrated by putting on my clean bra.

While at Lopez Tank, I heard a turkey on the opposite hill. A little later, a hunter came by and walked around the tank. After the hunter departed, I heard the turkey again. I wished the wily turkey luck in staying quiet when hunters were around.

The views from Wagontongue Mountain were scant, blocked by trees, but farther down, a burn area revealed wonderful views north, west and east. I had cell reception that night to talk to TOB, (Tough Old Broad) my Oregon friend. She was happily looking forward to picking me up early the next day.

Tough Old Broad

I walked to a patch of sunlight for breakfast, searching warmth. Coming down from the high point, I passed two families of cows and four elk and found TOB at the trailhead. I'd walked 277.6 miles from the Mexican border. On the way to Albuquerque we stopped in Socorro for burgers, fries, and a milkshake to make my tummy happy.

Jan, a friend of TOB, now my friend, too, fed us a gourmet dinner and once again, I and my clothes became clean. My zero day in Albuquerque marked a new month. April had rolled away with trail miles, and now it was May.

I added a piece of gear. Regardless of having survived my night in the low 20s, many nights I felt cold. Down is an insulator, not a heat producer. I didn't produce enough heat to fill the inside of the bag so I went to REI and found a Cocoon liner. In effect, it clung to me and made the space I needed to heat smaller, allowing the down to better insulate my conserved heat.

TOB was now my trail partner. Her friend Jan drove us to the Lobo Road Trailhead north of Grants because that was where TOB wanted to hike. We had a late start, and we two old ladies didn't walk fast. Tough Old Broad was indeed tough, but I was trail hardened, and she was just starting out. I was 70, and TOB was then 76. She was a runner, a grand dame of running from Eugene, Oregon. But running is different from hiking with a backpack. She was game and determined and had long trail experience, having also completed the PCT. But she couldn't move very fast on the trail.

Hiking along the Mesa, we had great views out over Grants and ahead to Mount Taylor. White flowers and brilliant red claret cactus added to the beauty. But our late start, slow pace, and rest stops kept us from completing our scheduled mileage, though we walked until nearly dark.

I slept well, the new liner doing its job very nicely. TOB did not. Our campsite wasn't ideal. I can be reasonably happy with less-than-perfect campsites, but my trail companions are usually more particular. TOB had only a foam pad and no air mattress. Failing to get a good night's sleep didn't help her. As the day wore on it became apparent to me and also to TOB that she wasn't going to be able to keep to our hike plan.

She was very disappointed in herself as she took pride in her physical condition. In the past she'd always had been able to go backpacking without a lot of preconditioning. I didn't say anything, but about 4:30 she volunteered that she wasn't going to be able to go on as scheduled.

We checked the maps and decided the best option was to go back about a mile and a half to a good road, where she could get a hitch to the paved road. My Cibola National Forest map showed the roads needed for bailout, and she had the phone number for the trail angels in Grants. She didn't think I needed to go back with her, but I wasn't willing to leave her until she was on the road, as she'd missed trail turns a number of times as we walked. I hoped we would get cell reception at the road.

So, in the morning, we walked back to La Mosca Lookout Road. Being as independent a cuss as I, TOB was getting tired of my worrying about her, but I did worry. The road looked well-traveled, and we had seen a car there the day before. The gravel road would connect with the paved highway. But I still worried as I left her at the lookout shelter.

Ojos and Water Lessons

A few hundred feet after starting back, four elk ran across the trail, and I wished TOB had seen them. I dipped a liter of water from

George Tank, scummy with algae, but after pushing the algae aside I found clear water underneath, which, of course, I treated. Reaching Ojo Piedres, (Eye of Stones) I found good water in abundance. I washed socks and bandanas and loaded 3.5 liters of beautiful, clear water. When I left TOB, I had nine miles to make up. Stopping at 7:45, I was only 3.5 miles behind schedule.

Up at 5:30 the next morning, I still needed to make up miles. Passing two *brown water* sources, hoping for something better and not wanting to add weight, I considered getting water at Del Dado when two hunters on three wheelers drove up. I asked if they had any extra water and one pulled out a dust-covered liter bottle and gave it to me. I said, "Thank you very much." After they drove off and I tasted the *water* that I realized it was flavored with something cloyingly sweet. I had to force myself to drink it, but it kept me hydrated.

Water lessons from New Mexico: 1) Brown cow water won't kill you if you double iodine it. 2) Put your treated brown cow water in the hydration bladder. Sucking brown water through a tube so you can't see it is best. 3) Algae-covered cow water is pretty good after pushing algae to the side and you treat it. 4) Any motorist is a possible source of water and usually happy to give it to you. 5) Check the bottle. It might be flavored, but it can keep you alive even if you don't like it.

Road lessons: Road walking is faster than walking on trail tread. Dirt roads are easier on feet than pavement, but even dirt roads are harder on feet than trail tread.

If the AT is sometimes known as the long green tunnel, New Mexico must be known as the wide open spaces, separated by belts of trees and gullies. There were a few sparse flowers, a few daisies, a rare paintbrush, a yellow trumpet shaped flower, a low, ground hugging, white daisy. Little nosegays of tightly clustered short daisies reminded me of wrist corsages worn with a low- cut formal dress.

I reached Ojo de Los Indios by 5:30. (Ojo is Spanish for eye. Desert springs are often called Ojo with a descriptive word following, in this case Indios, Eye [or spring] of the Indians.) Ojo de los Indios, a wonderful cement circle overflowing with beautiful, clear water, was off trail and down a steep rocky path. It had no flat ground for camping. I had a bath, washed socks, undies, and bra, filled up containers with 3 ½ liters of water, ate dinner, and then trudged back up the steep and rocky trail to find a campsite. I'd caught up with mileage and was back on schedule.

"Go away. It's too cold to bite you today."

The trail to the edge of the Mesa was well marked with cairns, although actual trail was mostly absent. I did my small bit toward trail maintenance by rebuilding a few cairns that were falling apart. At the edge of the escarpment, the view was beyond vast. I saw no sign of humans in that wide expanse, but there was brief cellphone reception, long enough to get 43 emails before it disappeared. I was very relieved to discover TOB had made it out safe and sound, getting back to Albuquerque before lunch the same day she left the trail.

The word mesa means table in Spanish and mountains in New Mexico are often flat, tabletop sorts of mountains. At the edge of the Mesa, not only could I see out for miles and miles, I could see layers, layer after layer of mesas descending to Arroyo Chico then rising beyond to the next range of mountainous mesas, a vast uneven layer cake, out of which some giant had taken a few bites leaving canyons through the layers of mesas to the valley floor below. Cabezon Peak and the double top of Cerro Cuate rose from the desert floor. There was so much encompassed in that view over the Arroyo Chico it would have taken hours standing there to take it all in.

Descending the layers of mesa cliffs, I took pictures of the views and the flowers: tiny yellow and white daisies, paintbrush, vervain, phacelia, penstemon, and my favorite, mariposa lilies. I also watched storm clouds all around me, clouds dropping rain, but it didn't hit the desert floor. Falling sheets of rain dissipated in the dry desert air, never reaching the ground.

Stepping carefully, I went down the sometimes very steep trail. A grandmotherly shaped rubber ball bouncing through the rocks and pointy things was an image I didn't care to pursue. Hurting feet also slowed my pace. My big toe began to hurt. Favoring the big toe with a change of gait then made the outside of my foot hurt. It's hard to limp correctly when both sides of the same foot hurt.

I finally reached the road off trail to Ojo Frio. Frio means cold, and the water and the desert wind both lived up to the name. I put iodine tablets in the cloudy water instead of using my tiny Steripen, (The Steripen treats water by ultraviolet light) and stood in the cold wind washing socks, bandanas, and parts of me.

With no possible sheltered campsites near the water, I once again loaded up and moved down the trail, finding a little spot tucked between two junipers. From my sheltered roost I had a fine view of Cabezon peak and much of that grand valley. Beautiful.

The sunrise tempted me to sit still and watch, but I couldn't cover miles without walking. The day was an absolute gift of fascinating terrain. As I descended multiple mesa walls to the very dry river bottom of Arroyo Chico and climbed up the opposite side of equally tiered mesas, I passed through different vegetation zones.

Hookers evening primroses dotted one of the layered mesas; *forests* of cholla cactus filled another. I followed rock cairns as I fought the wind. In rock-less sandy areas, cairns changed to white-tipped stakes driven into the ground. On the far side of the dry riverbed, there were white sand verbena, and throughout the day I saw penstemon, phacelia, spectacle pod, short yuccas, claret cactus, and an orange mallow, much smaller in dry New Mexico than its California cousins on the PCT.

Besides the ever-present turkey vultures, I saw quail and an interesting bird with a call similar to a meadowlark. The tightly coiled rattlesnake was a little more exciting. No rattle was raised, its body tightly curled in the cold wind. He flicked his tongue at me as if to say, "Go away, it's too cold to bite you today." I took his picture and gave him a wide berth.

The main attraction was the rocks. The trail wound in, around, and steadily upward through all those wonderful walls of mesas. I was fascinated by wind-sculpted rock. An under layer of sandy rock had eroded first, leaving a harder cap on a column, as if it were a Corinthian column transplanted half way around the globe.

Pockets and holes in ledges of rock invited my imagination to see castles, lairs for wildlife, or the homes of some imaginary earlier, shorter human beings. Besides the fantasy-inspiring and ever-changing rocks, there were lovely grand views of Cabezon and other basaltic plugs in that beautiful, remote and interesting valley.

The weather wasn't as beautiful. It wasn't the day for solar power. By 10:00 big black clouds formed all over the grand valley. I could personally guarantee that *some* rain hit the valley floor in the afternoon. Hail, too. Some areas had a considerable downpour, and I was a little unnerved to hear rolling thunder directly overhead. I was walking in open areas with nothing higher than a juniper or two dotting the landscape.

My main problem was the wind. It blew quite hard, usually from the side and occasionally head on. It takes energy to walk in high winds, and I didn't make very good time. When I reached the road by 6:30, TOB and David were waiting for me.

David worked at REI and had volunteered to ride along to the trail crossing, knowing exactly where it was, though he couldn't clearly show it to us on any highway map. He was another long-distance hiker yearning for the trail, sharing tips about light-weight gear. I jumped in the car for a rest, to organize my gear from the resupply box, and to eat my dinner. My timing was good; it started to rain.

We chattered a mile a minute. I was happy to hear that TOB and Jan would be able to join me in the section past Cuba for some shorter mileage days.

Daylight wouldn't last long, so I left my angels, David and TOB, heading out again into the wind. Just short of a mile, I found a sheltered spot for my tent at the side of a juniper. Although I could have done without the high winds, the day had far exceeded my expectations for beauty and interest, my favorite day in all of New Mexico.

Queen of the Universe

The next day, too, was beautiful, but tiredness affected my enthusiasm. I mentally sang songs to keep up my pace across the flat area before Deadman Peaks. After Deadman, I walked from mesa edge to mesa edge followed by even more trail along the tops of mesas, viewing Cabezon until I crossed to a different mesa's edge, overlooking a highway running toward Cuba.

Clouds built up, and I could see areas all around me drenched with thunderstorms and ahead, a striking mesa built in terraces of rock. As I trudged along among the rocks, sometimes walking on smooth, but not slippery, slabs of sandstone, a sudden impromptu waterfall cascaded from a ledge. It was pretty, but it was also indicative of the dangers of flash floods. Too tired to make a 15-mile-day, I didn't make it to Jones Spring.

Stopping 2.5 miles short, finding a campsite wasn't easy. I finally found a mostly flat, very sandy spot sheltered by junipers. The rain had lessened to just a few sprinkles, and I managed to get the tent up and me inside, still dry, a feat on wet sand. Wet sand also made stably staking the tent a challenge, even with big rocks piled on top of tent stakes. The wind gusting past the junipers battered the tent walls, and I had to reset my stakes more than once.

In the morning dropping down to Jones Spring, I picked up water for the rest of the day.

The water looked clear, and I used the Steripen, (I ALWAYS treat my water) but it tasted vaguely soapy. I was glad I usually drank it with flavoring, tea or Cytomax.

Following a long flat section of sagebrush, the next mesa was formidable. It was only a 300-foot elevation gain up Mesa Portales, but the trail wound beside massive gray rock formations, down and up gullies of loose, sliding dirt, up very steep switchbacks, and over a few places that required hands as well as feet, handholds and footsteps carved in sandstone for a few steps.

The afternoon trail wasn't as exciting, sandy paths on mesa's edges with great views.

Imagine walking laboriously over dry sandy beaches. Finally reaching the hard-packed dirt road, my feet didn't like that much either. I was tired. I was too far behind schedule and too tired to complete five miles of road walk into Cuba. I just hoped to reach the highway and hitch a ride. I would have to pick up the skipped section another year. While 13 miles was doable, 18 wasn't.

Finding shade, I sat to give my feet a rest and have a snack before the last push to the highway. Across the open valley, I watched a dump truck go down a parallel road. After a short while the dump truck came back on the road near me.

The driver got out and politely introduced himself as David Cordoba. He'd helped hikers in the past and told me a wonderful tale about bringing hot water and a tub for a bath to an Englishman on the trail a few years ago. He keeps his eye out for hikers, giving water or rides if needed. David was a gem. I could tell he thought he might be threatening to a lone woman hiker, as he told me those tales at a polite, reserved distance. I appreciated his thoughtfulness and loved his stories.

Hearing my plan to walk to the highway and hitch a ride into Cuba, he offered to take my pack, dump his last load of dirt, (he was working for BLM on a land-reclamation project) and wait for me at the highway. So I walked the last mile free and easy with just my poles. And I got to ride in a dump truck, which was way cool. Dump trucks are very tall, and the cab in which I sat as queen of the universe towered above the cars that passed us.

For my delightful day in Cuba, I had a large room with TV, microwave, refrigerator, and a very comfortable bed. The Korean woman at the motel was especially helpful with filling any of my needs, giving me soap for laundry and driving me to the laundromat, where I met the cousin of my dump truck chauffeur.

Mostly, I ate. For lunch I had half a rotisserie chicken, half a can of green beans, half a cantaloupe and three cinnamon rolls, and I didn't feel overly full. Dinner was the same, with the substitution of a pint of ice cream for a cinnamon roll, and the addition of a bottle of chocolate milk. Hiker hunger is an amazing thing.

Company

The evening was made perfect when Gail, the Washington State hiker, whom I'd met on the AT near Screw Auger Falls in Maine, checked in. She was a couple years younger than me, a much stronger hiker, and the first hiker besides TOB I'd seen on the trail since the Gila River.

TOB and Jan drove up from Albuquerque, and we headed out of Cuba together. Gail would catch up with us in another day. After hiking alone for so long, it felt like a party. The day was beautiful, and we were happy chattering together.

Road walking was faster than trail for old ladies. (TOB and I were the old ladies, Jan considerably younger.) The last two miles went more slowly as we gained elevation, the weather clouding up with big black clouds and rumbling thunder. We donned rain gear, and the raindrops stopped, but we didn't complain. Reaching the trailhead, we found water with plenty of time to set up camp, take baths, and wash socks. It was so very nice to have company.

On a beautiful blue-sky morning, we wound our way up Rito de Los Pinos, a cheerful, bubbling stream with pools and waterfalls. New Mexico continually amazed me with its great variety of terrain and vegetation. I'd walked through the Chihuahua desert in the south, climbed a 10,000-foot mountain, forded the beautiful Gila River hundreds of times, walked high grasslands, seen mesas with wind and water-sculpted rock, and now found mountains not dissimilar from those in Colorado or Washington State.

I'd walked over paved roads, dirt roads, cross country scrub, graded trail, and trail unseen, sand and rock, sandstone and granite, high desert, and now, lush, well-watered mountains. All that, and I'd skipped part of New Mexico in its mid-section to await for me the next year.

Climbing into San Pedro Park, which got 35 inches of rain a year, flowers were blooming: lupine, white and purple violets, red columbine, white and yellow marsh marigolds, valerian and others whose names I didn't know. Passing beautiful meadows after Rito de Los Pinos, we walked along the Rio Puerco.

As skies changed to threatening clouds and the temperature dropped, I wore my fleece, and we put on pack coves and raingear, catching up with Gail, who had passed us early in the morning. Camping a mile or so before our destination, Gail had already hung her hammock. (Gail, and a number of other long-distance hikers prefer hammocks to camping on the ground in a tent.)

We were over 10,000 feet, with snow patches along the trail, when we were confronted with a very large meadow whose recently melted snow had left a sloppy marsh. TOB and I had very cold and wet feet in the ankle-deep water of the meadow though Jan managed to keep dry with high Goretex boots.

Passing Rio Vacas, we went up the hill and into the trees. It started to rain and sleet just as we were setting up our tents next to snow banks. It would be a cold night.

The weather forecast was for sunny mornings with thunderstorms in the afternoon, but we woke to the sound of thunder, 34 degrees inside the tent with ice on the outside. After we started walking, snow pellets the size of peas began to fall. I sang *Walking in a Winter Wonderland* as the ground was coated white. Thunder followed lightning within a count of two or three as we walked through high open meadows.

Then we misplaced the trail or the trail misplaced us, and we walked in a very large circle always making right-hand turns. But the GPS said we were to the left of the trail. Huh? The second time around, we took more time and found the correct trail. I felt a little better about losing the trail when I read Wolf's description admitting the area was confusing. I also figured out we had indeed made right turns, but from the wrong trail which was left from the right trail. I thought I knew my right from my left.

When the sun eventually came out, we had a long break while TOB and Jan cooked a late breakfast, and we dried out tents and sleeping bags. The day proceeded with more clouds, more thunder, more rain, and some dry times, too. Our destination was by a bubbling brook, a couple thousand feet lower than the night before, but it was still pretty cold. We hoped the next day would bring sunshine.

It was 37 degrees, and our shoes were still wet when we woke up. Leaving first in search of sun, I found some not far down the trail.

Standing in the sunshine warmed my feet, and TOB and Jan caught up and enjoyed the sun, too.

TOB left us at the road as she had planned. She would make her way to the highway, hitch back to Cuba and meet us again around a few mountains before Ghost Ranch. Jan, a strong hiker 20 years younger, hiked with me. Happy to find Fuerte Spring had water, we watered up and found a lovely meadow for our tents. Dinner over, we snuggled down listening to an owl talk to its friends.

Frost coated our tents in the morning, and it was 35 inside. By the time we dried tents and bags in the sun, we didn't start walking until after 9:00. Our trail left the road in lots of blown- down trees and proceeded to disappear. We knew where we were, on a particularly steep-sided gulley with trail on one side and road on the other. We couldn't see either.

Bushwhacking on steep slopes, we finally found the trail, which again became obscure, and finally, we found the road. All that effort would have been completely unnecessary if we had stayed on the road instead of trying to follow the trail. We were very frustrated and had wasted a lot of time and energy.

Finding *real* trail to Ojitos Canyon, I was happy to reach Skull Bridge, though on very sore feet. I seemed to be trying for a case of plantar fasciitis on my left foot and scrambling up and down steep slopes chasing illusive trail had not helped. Although it had been fun to hike with Jan, I was very glad to be horizontal in my tent. Even at low elevations, it was cold in the morning, but the sun was on us before we left our campsite, walking the road along the Chama River.

Oops. I realized I'd given TOB the wrong road directions. But just as we sat down for mid- morning break, TOB drove by, cleverly having put together clues from the hike itinerary, finding us even without good directions. Jan was happy to see her, and so was I as I could then slack pack even if I lost my trail companion to the comforts of a car.

They drove by Gail up ahead and came back to tell me directions for the walk to Ghost Ranch. The cross-country section turned out to be much more pleasant than expected, carpets of daisies on the desert floor and many mariposa lilies, when I topped a rise and had lunch looking at the multicolored mesa cliffs near Ghost Ranch.

Tough Old Broad and Jan were a joy to hike with, and I sadly said *good-bye* as they drove away in the morning, also providing transportation to civilization for Snores, a young thru hiker. And Snores provided me with jerky from his resupply box when I found mine had gone bad.

Amazing how things seemed to work out, although not always as planned.

I spent much of my zero day with Gail talking trail and sharing old Girl Scout stories. She loaned me her emergency beacon, hopefully NOT to use during my last stretch. She was also getting off trail at Ghost Ranch but would begin again in July from Rawlins, Wyoming, coming south through Colorado. Our paths could cross again in the fall. I then went into panic mode discovering my Steripen charging cord was missing, and I didn't have enough iodine left to make it all the way to Cumbres. Gail helped me out again by giving me her Aqua Mira drops. Saved again.

Chapter 33 Northern New Mexico

After walking cross-country on a steep hillside north of Ghost Ranch, two thru hikers, Greg from Prudhoe Bay and Clermont from France, passed me. Walk the trail and see the world—or at least people from all over the globe.

Flowers of the day were stands of delightful wild blue Iris. Groves of pinion pine had been replaced by groves of aspen. Unfortunately, sitting under the aspen for dinner wasn't a good plan as tent caterpillars dropped annoyingly from infested branches on and around me all the time I was eating.

I briefly saw Greg and Clermont again before they quickly outdistanced me. Seems 70- year-old ladies do not walk as fast as 20 or 30 somethings with testosterone. Following the trail on old, sometimes quite obscure, roads through beautiful, expansive high-mountain meadows punctuated with aspen and scrub oak, I was impressed with the green. More green than I'd seen in all the rest of New Mexico.

Green was accompanied by the yellow of dandelions. Yep, the same dandelions that grow in your lawn. In the wild, dandelions on the hillsides made lovely yellow carpets. Larkspur and iris added blue and purple to the palette. Pink bitterroot grew in the roadways, and the day ended with yellow glacier lilies in the old road and on the hillsides. I walked between 9,000 and 10,300 feet and camped by an open meadow.

In the cold morning, I stayed in bed and watched the sky lighten with a pink glow as the sun came up, the sun's rays hitting the tent and warming it within 20 minutes. My hands were not even cold packing up.

Soon after leaving my campsite, I saw three elk. My trail meandered up and down and around the mountains, sometimes beside snow, sometimes beside flowers. Lunch was in an emerald-green meadow with a bubbling stream.

Reaching Rio Vallecito shortly after 6:00, I had plenty of time to bathe and have a needed wash of undies, bra, shirt, and socks. Lying in the darkness of the tent, I listened to the river that would be my morning ford, the log bridge, tipped by a spring flood, lay at an unwalkable 45- degree angle.

After my ford, the trail warmed me by presenting me a thousand feet of elevation gain rather quickly, the second thousand feet more gradually but steadily up. I walked through beautiful mountains with rolling hills, green meadows, aspen, fir, ponderosa pine and spruce.

Reaching Hopewell Lake I was greeted by Sara, the camp host. She had my resupply box and graciously gave me fresh water, an avocado, and a Clementine while my dinner hydrated. Although there was no cell service, she arranged to get a message out for me. I was a day ahead of schedule and hoped my pickup driver could meet me a day early. I had accumulated extra trail bars I didn't want to carry, so I left them for Sara to enjoy.

Three elk crossed the trail as I went up Jawbone Mountain to camp at 10,100 feet, among Glacier lilies and violets. It was too cold for a bath, but I managed a quick wipe down for legs and feet. My feet received priority care, even in the cold.

No early sun shone on me, and both tent and bag were dewy wet. But *"What ya gonna do?"* I packed up anyway. The day was almost all trail, the first part technically road, but sometimes so faint no track showed. After good water above Jawbone tank, I came to large, open meadows set at right angles to each other, with snow on mountain ranges around them.

I prefer western trails to the AT for the wide-open spaces and grand views. I suppose that is why I like the desert, too. Although I wouldn't have liked the desert in summer heat. Walking the length of each meadow added pleasant miles. Walking on roads through woods was nice, too, but my aching body parts distracted me there. Walking through open country, gazing great distances, kept my eyes feasting, and my aching body parts diminished in importance.

Lunch was drying time for tent and sleeping bag. Descending to the emerald-green valley of the Rio Antonio gave me a lovely resting place to eat dinner and treat water before heading up the Mesa, climbing the edge of the escarpment on a long gradual slant overlooking the Rio Antonio drainage. Lovely.

As I neared the top, the wind picked up, buffeting me around as I walked an edge with a drop of hundreds of feet. Fortunately, the wind was blowing me *into* the mountain, not trying to pluck me off of it.

Three deer showed themselves to say hello just as I was ready to stop and watch a glorious sunset. Funny isn't it, one day I could feel tired of hiking, and the next beautiful day I felt like walking forever.

I lay in bed watching the sky change colors in the early morning light through the large door of my Hexamid tent, perfectly made for lying down and looking out. I packed up and immediately felt like I needed a nap. Good thing there was only one remaining full day on the trail. I was accumulating tiredness.

Altitude may have been a factor. Most of the day was above 10,000 feet as I progressed at a crawl, struggling up Brazos Ridge. From its top, snowcapped mountains of the San Juans showed to the north in Colorado. A thru hiker might not have been quite so excited to see the snow. But I wouldn't be heading into those mountains until late summer. I could just enjoy the view and anticipate the joys to come at a later date, snow melted and gone.

The wind tried to blow me away all day. Not able to decide on its direction, it blew a dust cloud at me from one direction and 30 seconds later blew another from the opposite side. On Osier Mesa I walked into head wind, very tiring, both physically and mentally.

In the evening, as I was getting my last bottle of water from a stream, a local couple from Chama stopped to see if I was OK. New Mexico has such nice people.

After I headed away from the road, two elk and I had a stare down for long moments. The elk won the stare down, as I moved first, and the elk bounded off into the woods. That night, tucked into a sheltered spot with no snags or severely swaying trees nearby, I listened to the wind blow hard in the trees around me. Snow banks within feet of my tent promised a cold night.

I slept warmly, though it was 37 in the morning and miraculously, my hands didn't seem too cold packing up. Then came trouble.

I knew there might be a problem when I saw so much snow near my tent. I was positive I was on the trail when I began that last morning. But before long—after one lone, obscure scrap of red surveyor tape at the start of newish looking trail from the road—I was in a pile of snow banks and a forest of blowdowns with no sign of CDT markers. The trail was in the map book, and I had the route on my GPS. I did some cross-country following the GPS. Unfortunately the trail wasn't always where the GPS said it was. Eventually I found it at the 11,000-foot-high point. Snow and downed trees made it hard to follow trail, easily disguising switchback turns under snow banks or jumbles of tree branches on the ground, and I had snow and downed trees all morning.

I was obviously the first hiker to have taken the trail instead of the road. There were no footprints in snow except for mine and the elk. What's with those young macho hiker dudes who were ahead of me? They took the road; the 70-year-old grandma *opened* the trail. I thought that was pretty funny. But they were smarter to take the road and avoid the headache I'd chosen. It made for a more difficult start to the day than planned, though I didn't get misplaced after the first wandering confusion, even walking through many more snow banks and through, around and under many more downed trees.

Tracks left in mud appeared to have lasted all winter. Several times I saw muddy tire tracks on the road leading to and away from 3-foot-high, 10-foot-long, and 20-foot-wide snow banks completely covering any drivable surface. The tracks emerged on the other side out of the snow banks. I also saw some fine bear tracks in the mud and snow. Bear tracks in the mud could have been very old, like the tire tracks. Bear tracks in the snow must have been fresh.

The afternoon went much more smoothly than the morning as I reached the Colorado border amid clusters of bright blue Chiming Bells waving good-bye to New Mexico. The view from the ridge looking down on Cumbres Pass was spectacular. The Colorado Chamber of Commerce should use that shot in early spring for their slogan. "Colorful Colorado." It was all so green. I gazed out to a beautiful green valley, a blue lake, mountains all around and the San

Juan's white snow enticing me to come back in August.

My last trial (not misspelled) was walking an open ridge leading to Cumbres Pass, a wind tunnel between two masses of mountain. The wind was so strong, I almost couldn't walk forward at all. I could barely stand up. Putting my head down and leaning into the wind, looking only at my feet, I struggled not to be blown over sideways. Fortunately, it was a short ridge.

About 15 minutes after I arrived at Cumbres Pass, Kevin, sent by Jan, arrived to drive me back to Albuquerque. I had not walked all of New Mexico. More miles awaited for the next year. But 521.6 miles of New Mexico made a very memorable spring hike on the CDT.

"It depends"

Almost any question about the CDT could be answered: "It depends." That is: there are not many cut-and-dried answers. The CDT was more free form than the AT or PCT.

There were choices of where to start and which route to take, multiple possibilities all along the trail. My speed was quite variable, too. How long would it take to hike from point A to point B? Would it be on road or trail, at what elevation gain? Would it be cross-country where you can see your destination? Or would cross-country mean dealing with steep hillsides, snow, or downed trees? Young hiker dudes can whip out 20-to-30-mile days easily, some older ones, too. I couldn't. Speed and distance depended on the trail, and it also depended on the person hiking.

Was the trail well marked? I chose the Columbus route for ease of access and small historical rewards. In that era, almost half of the CDT thru hikers chose similarly. I didn't see a CDT sign for many days. But I was never really lost—between Wolf's descriptions, Ley's maps, and my GPS.

I couldn't have walked this hike without a GPS. I can read a map, but my compass skills are barely adequate. However, I learned how to program a GPS route and follow the bright magenta line. I would argue that map and compass are limited to telling what direction you are headed, and along with the contour lines and place names on the map, your approximate location. But if you are not clearly on a named place on the map, and you can't sight on three known points for triangulation, you do not always know your exact location.

With the GPS, I always knew where I was within a hundred feet. Breakage or battery loss could render the GPS useless, but a compass could break, too. For me, GPS plus map was the best combination, and I was able to have a constant reference to the GPS with batteries fresh from my solar charger in sunny New Mexico.

There *were* times the trail seemed a figment of someone's imagination, with all sources, Wolf, Ley and CDTA map book. On the other hand, this trail wasn't too hard for a 70-year-old grandmother traveling alone, as long as she kept her wits about her and her map and GPS at hand. I didn't make every turn correctly. And I did lose the trail, but I could always find it again. I was prepared for sometimes poorly marked trail, but I didn't let that scare me unnecessarily. I had the tools to help me find my way and had practiced using them before I set foot on the CDT.

In New Mexico 3/4 of the trail was some kind of road, from sections of blacktop to a track so faint I could barely follow. Roads could be rocky and steep or flat and well-graded. Country dirt roads made me want to sing like John Denver. On others, all signs of travel had long since disappeared.

People in New Mexico were friendly. Cars on back roads often stopped to inquire if I was OK or needed anything. New Mexico might be the best state in which to hitch a ride or find assistance, even though population is low outside of a few cities.

I carried lots of maps as well as GPS. I had every day's route programmed into the GPS with my own points indicating each turn in the trail, all drawn on my home computer and transferred to the GPS with a click of a mouse and many phone conversations with Garmin's customer service. Ain't technology grand? Even for a non-techie grandmother. I also carried Ley's maps, Wolf's descriptions, and the CDTA map-book pages. In addition, I carried National Forest maps for information regarding bailout roads, two of which were used when

TOB left the trail.

I like history as well as trails and enjoyed historical points of interest in New Mexico. My old friend Terry, in Las Cruces, contributed to the accumulation of history with our trip to the museum Jornado de Los Muertos. The Columbus route went by an old fort and passed native people's petroglyphs. I walked in the Gila Cliff Dwellings imagining those who lived there.

Ghost Ranch had Museums covering history from dinosaurs to Georgia O'Keefe.

I treasure the memories of people, who helped me along the way: El Coyote and Mary in Deming, Lynnae in Mimbres, George and Jan on McNight Road, Anna at Wildwood Retreat, David Cordoba and his dump truck south of Cuba, Gail at Ghost Ranch, and TOB and Jan, who became my friends as we hiked together.

New Mexico is do-able, even for an aging hiker. Three extra food drops beyond regular thru hikers' resupply points accommodated my slow pace and need for a lighter pack. Lynnae had never before provided a food drop for a hiker at Emory Pass. David from the REI in Albuquerque was willing to drive out with a food drop on the highway two days from Cuba, and Bryce from Big Mountain Sports in Santa Fe set up the food drop at Hopewell Lake with camp host Sara. Those extra food drops were key in helping me cover the same trail as thru hikers, even though I could travel only half as fast. I wished for a food drop at Snow Lake, but it was so far in the back of beyond, it was beyond my ability to arrange.

Logistics were challenging and navigation necessary. Scenery was varied. Learning opportunities were many, and the people were wonderful. It was a great hike.

Two months' worth of weeds and gardening awaited me back home in Washington. Of much greater importance, my newest granddaughter had been born the day I left the trail, and I looked forward to seeing her.

Chapter 34 July 2012

PCT – Skipped Sections Completed

Two small sections were left in California; I'd skipped them one year due to knee problems and one year due to snow. Now I planned to do them in July with no snow and (hopefully) no new knee problems.

In the heat of July hiking out of Kennedy Meadows before the Sierra could be brutal.

Before I arrived, Mary Barcik, my friend and trail angel from Kelso whom I had met in 2009, told me I'd lucked out, and the temps should be only in the 90s. To one from the Pacific Northwest, it was hard to fathom temps *dropping* to the 90s. But I was determined to finish the PCT. RockStar, whom I'd met in 2008, would join me for the last three days. My cuz, She Who Hikes in Car, and her daughter, Sheila, would be trail angels.

Fresh off the plane arriving at Reno from Washington, my cousin and her daughter dropped me off at the bridge over the Kern River, and—with no pack, wearing town clothes, and carrying hiking poles—I walked to the campground where they met me for a bite of dinner and gave me my gear. It was warm enough to take my shirt off and let the warm breeze caress my skin as I walked. A lovely way to start a hike.

Mary Barcik, now 77, had hoped to do some of this hike with me, but a bout of shingles changed her plan. Nevertheless, Mary did come to see me off, stayed the night in the campground, and walked two miles with me. Just as in 2009, we jabbered all the way, catching up on life on a cool and pleasant walk to the next bridge. Mary said I must have *good connections* upstairs because the weather had been 20 degrees higher the week before.

After Mary turned around to walk back to her car, Rattle Dancer and Doe, section hikers in their 60s, met me returning back the way had come, daunted by the lack of water. They'd been counting on Halfmile maps and Yogi's book for water sources. But this was a hot, dry year and both Halfmile and Yogi focused on thru-hikers, who walk this section a month earlier. I was thankful for Mary and RockStar's heads-up messages about water before I left home. I could still get in trouble if the creek 12.7 miles past the Kern River was dry. But I was only counting on two water sources for the trip. Rattle Dancer and Doe had depended on more.

Walking through burn areas, some old and some from the more recent fires in 2008, I was glad to find deep shade for lunch and a nice breeze all afternoon. There were no big displays of flowers; a few were still sprinkled beside the trail. Cowboy camping in trees by the bridge over the Kern, I took a brief bath, washed my socks, and loaded up with water. As night fell, I listened to the birds singing in the trees.

In the morning it was 27 degrees. Brr. I was glad not to have hot weather, but 27 in July was colder than expected. While packing up, I heard the long howl of coyote or wolf, making me smile, glad, whatever the critter was, it was sharing the wilderness with me. I left the Kern with a full load of water.

Walking along the trail above the meadowland and hearing a cow's continuous bawling, I wondered if a predator had picked off a calf. Then I saw Mama cow standing in the middle of the meadow and baby coming from the side. The calf stopped halfway there, as if wondering how much trouble he was in. Mama cow still loudly bawling, walked toward him, whereupon baby calf galloped the rest of the way to Mama and started nursing. No more bawling Mama cow.

Domestic bliss reigned in cow land.

The day was a very long uphill climb of 2,700 feet. Between 9,500 feet and 10,500 feet was a real struggle. All those little red blood cells carrying extra oxygen that I'd had in New Mexico in the spring seemed to have left my body. It doesn't take long to lose conditioning.

The rewards for the work were many: views of Beck and Monache Meadows, Olanche Peak beside me, Mt. Langley, Kaweah Peaks Ridge, Mt. Whitney, and Kern Peak farther away, red-orange trunks and twisted roots of upturned Foxtail Pine and flowers: blue flax, ranger's buttons, cow parsley, red columbine, wild geranium, chiming bells, and corn lilies added to others seen the day before. There was more to see than I expected in that short section.

It sprinkled around midnight that night, but by morning the tent was dry. Leaving with 4 ½ liters of water, ten pounds, would be enough to get me to Horseshoe Meadows if it wasn't beastly hot. It was a lot of weight for me to carry, but water is life.

The climb out of Death Canyon wasn't as bad as its reputation. It was uphill, but I loved the nicely graded trail of the PCT, and I continued to have luck with cool temperatures in the 70s.

The day was flowerless except for one brief area, but a granite playground on all sides gave me plenty to look at. The trail was California decomposed granite, and my poles made a swishing sound at each step as they poked into the tiny pebbles of the trail, like a snare drum played with brushes. Most of the trail was firm, a few places like walking on sandy beach. Foxtail pine and junipers were prevalent. Snags left standing without their bark had long spiral bands of red, yellow, and brown. That night I took my bandana bath with just a half-cup of water. I should have drunk the water, but it made me feel better to be clean.

Hearing yippy coyotes having a party, I decided they were celebrating that I was almost done. As I came to the Trail Pass trail, I had a nice little mental click in my head for completion of that section.

Arriving at Horseshoe Meadows before 11:00, I didn't expect my cousin until mid- afternoon. So I ate my lunch and bragged about my hiking prowess to those at the campground. I do love to brag about being an old hiker on the trail. I also took other people's pictures, gave lightweight hiking advice, and prevented one group from heading down the wrong trail. I felt like a Jr Ranger.

When my cuz arrived, we went to see the *real* Ranger and picked up the hiking permit for my last section. We met my buddy RockStar, and my cuz washed my hiking clothes for me before she said good-bye. What a dear thing. I hopped into RockStar's car, and we drove to Red's Meadow to camp. We hiked the little loop hike to the Devil's Postpile and the short piece of PCT to the Resort.

RockStar and I enjoyed hiking together. We did a lot of chattering, catching up with the last four years. RockStar had thru-hiked the PCT in 2009, all the way from the Mexican Border to the Canadian Border in one hiking season. All that was after hiking from the Mexican Border to Ashland, Oregon in 2008. She started over again in 2009 because she wanted a true thru hike.

And people think *I'm* crazy. She had, however, led a more sedentary life since then and had put on a few pounds. In 2008 she'd been a faster hiker than me, but now she was content to hike at my pace. I was delighted to have a trail companion.

In the morning we saw a martin for the first time. Think a longer, sleeker version of a squirrel that scurried across the trail and up some rocks.

On a long, hot, strenuous afternoon, we climbed more than 2,000 feet. The 90-degree weather had found me. Ugh. But although the way was long and took a lot of energy, the views were terrific. Ritter and Banner Peaks and a saw-tooth ridge were classic Sierra. And Shadow Lake was almost too perfect to be real with tall peaks behind, granite all around, and outlet creek plunging into the valley.

Monkshood and larkspur joined many bright flowers as we reached Badger Lake. Our nearest camping neighbors had bear problems that night, with much yelling and banging to scare the bear away, but no bear came near our campsite or our bear cans.

A thunderstorm came through at 4:00 in the morning, drenching our tents, and we left our campsite with threatening clouds in the sky, hiking with pack covers on. After a little rain and hail, the rain stopped, although it remained cloudy all day.

The weather didn't matter much to me as we were surrounded by beautiful scenery: high mountain lakes, flowers, beautiful streams with crystal clear water and craggy mountain peaks with glaciers and granite. Glorious. What a nice section to end my quest to walk the PCT. We climbed past Thousand Island Lake, every bit as beautiful as advertised. We went over Island Pass and past Rush Creek with its many waterfalls, climbed on bare rock over Donahue Pass, and down past a lovely tarn at the base of Mt. Lyell, the highest peak in Yosemite.

After a few tricky crossings of Lyell Creek, we camped in a lovely spot above it. The sunset was a beautiful end to the day, as was my bandana bath. Perfect last night on the PCT.

Morning was all downhill or level through beautiful meadows with mountains in the distance, the Lyell Fork a bright blue reflecting the sky. I finished the PCT at Toulumne Meadows, 10 days before turning 71.

Meeting Liz and Sheila at the grill, we had hamburgers and ice cream and switched to tourist mode to see the sights in Yosemite Valley for two more days before RockStar headed home, and my cuz took me to the airport in Reno.

With the PCT and the AT completed I turned my focus to the CDT.

Chapter 35 August 2012

Continental Divide Trail—Colorado

Grapevine planned to walk about 2/3 of this hike with me, her husband David providing us both with trail support. But while in Canada with their Godsons, Grapevine's recurring plantar fasciitis flared so that she could barely hobble. They both said they'd committed to the Colorado trip and knew I'd planned it with David's support. So they drove all the way from Washington to support me even though Grapevine couldn't hike, a gift of true friendship.

Wheew (PCT 2008 trail name) in 2012, known as Chosen, was to join me right after Wolf Creek Pass for the rest of the trip, though she'd been warned I was slow and said she would walk behind me like a puppy dog because I had the GPS. I planned to leave my car in Buena Vista with Carol, the secretary at the local Episcopal Church. I would walk to the car from Cumbres Pass where I'd left the trail in the spring.

Sleeping with a Sheepherder

David drove for two hours to drop me off at Cumbres Pass at 7:00 am. The green valley I remembered from the spring, surprisingly, was still green with a few flowers remaining in the middle of August.

I was now 71. But my slow pace up the trail wasn't entirely due to age. A significant problem was the altitude.

I live at sea level. My spring hike through New Mexico helped acclimate me to altitude, but then I was home at sea level for more than a month. I finished the PCT going over 11,000-foot Donahue Pass. Then I was home for two more weeks. I started at Cumbres Pass in Colorado at 10,000 feet and soon was at 12,000. My red blood cells had whiplash.

Chugging along very slowly, taking many rest stops, I walked just below or above timberline on my entry into the San Juan's. Each step brought an unfolding of more beauty. I was nervous climbing up Summit Peak between two storm cells, but I had no rain or lightning in my immediate vicinity. Trail tread disappeared going over Summit Peak and down to Dipping Lake, but there were enough cairns to quickly find my way.

Descending to the first of the lakes, I saw a big flock of sheep surrounding it. The Sheepherder on horseback was going out with four dogs to bring the sheep closer to his large tent. He was a Mexican, originally from Chihuahua, and spoke only a few words of English. My Spanish was from high school more than 50 years ago. With a few words and a lot of arm waving, we managed a little conversation.

He didn't think the lake water good enough for me, offering to fill my water bladder from a stream, he took my water bladder and galloped off. Before riding away, he invited me to stay in his big tent. I looked at all the sheep poop around my planned site near the lakes and hoped the area by his tent would be better.

After reaching his tent, I sat on a large rock resting and eating my dinner, watching the sheepherder come over the hill with a few hundred sheep and six energetic sheep dogs. I'd planned to set up my tent, but with six large, inquisitive, unruly dogs jumping all over, I was afraid if a large dog jumped on my tent like they jumped on me, even by accident, the tent would be toast on the first night of a multiday trip.

Milling sheep covering the area meant I had not avoided the sheep poop. There were no trees for food-bag hanging, I was quite tired, and another thunderstorm was approaching.

So I slept with the sheepherder, Grigo. More precisely, I stayed with the sheepherder in his heavy canvas tent. In the square tent, his sleeping bag was stretched along one wall. There was a small wood stove vented through a hole in the tent wall, and a chest which held his belongings. There was just room enough for my sleeping bag to fit beside his.

Grigo was proud to say he'd worked in Durango for four years before sheepherding and asked the same questions of me that others ask when they meet a long-distance hiker. Where was I from? Where was I going? Why didn't I carry a gun? Between his few words of English and my few words of Spanish we had a limited conversation. I was amazed I could remember enough Spanish to tell him I was 71 years old and a grandmother. He was properly impressed I was on the trail. It rained hard in the night, with much thunder and lightning, and I was grateful for the shelter of his sturdier tent.

Yes, as he gestured to me to come into his sleeping bag, I think he would have liked more intimate female companionship. I was neither shocked nor offended. Sheepherding is a lonely occupation. But he was a gentleman when deflected with "no comprendo" or just no, although I thought I *comprendoed* accurately. The next morning I gave him a few bucks for his hospitality to encourage him to help other hikers. It had been a unique experience.

Lightning Russian Roulette

After mid-morning snack at Dipping Lake, I headed back up to 12,000 feet. The Continental Divide Trail is often right on the Divide, above timberline most places in the San Juans. The biggest danger was afternoon thunderstorms.

By the end of the morning, there was a black sky to the south, with lots of lightning and thunder. I put on rain gear and pack cover and dived into a scrubby high-altitude spruce thicket just as lightning cracked nearby, and the storm hit. Huddled in my meager shelter, I watched the ground turn white with hail for miles around.

I was lucky it hit while I had even a bit of shelter as the next three or four miles was all above timberline. Sitting for a good hour, I listened to the thunder and counted the seconds between strike and thunder to judge the distance of the lightning. I had no desire to leave my tiny sheltered spot while lightning cracked, and thunder boomed. While watching the storm slacken, a covey of ptarmigan waddled by me only a few feet away. (Ptarmigan are medium-sized chicken- like game birds.) Unfortunately, my camera was inaccessibly buried under layers of rain protection.

Eventually the storm diminished, and I sloshed up the trail through ice and water, wind and cold. My highest point of the day was 12,300 feet. I did make one wrong move in spite of warnings in the Wolf book and on Ley maps. I followed nice big cairns and obvious trail, once again finding the dominant trail wasn't the CDT. Thanks to my GPS, I didn't go far before realizing my mistake.

In the morning, the sky was blue and clear, the ground still cold from hail. My playground for the day was between 11,000 and a bit above 12,000 feet. I dried my tent and sleeping bag at mid-morning snackbreak, ready for the next night. And I enjoyed walking by Blue Lake, white pearly everlasting on its banks, a bright contrast to bright blue water. Lunch was by another lake with mountains for backdrop.

The afternoon of the next day, black clouds congregated to the south, and thunder echoed over the valleys. I was pretty nervous on the climb up to 12,150 feet, but blue sky continued over me. I stopped to get water about a mile from my destination, and just as I was finished, a thunderstorm hit. Once again I threw on the rain gear and dove under a tree, this time a bigger one in a grove. And I sat watching the rain and counted the lightning to thunder intervals - 4-5.

I had no problem with diving under cover and waiting out the storms. The problem was: there wasn't always cover to dive under. I'd been very lucky so far, but it felt like playing Russian Roulette. And I knew it could get worse as some of this year's hike would rise to 13,000 feet. I'd hoped the pattern of afternoon storms would lessen towards the end of August, but that appeared to have been wishful thinking.

When the sun came out, and the sky was blue, I walked my last mile and camped in some trees near a bubbling creek just below timberline on the Middle Fork of the Conejos River. The view from my tent was spectacular, green tundra-like high country and mountain cliffs. I was in camp in time to take a Ziploc bath and wash socks and underwear. I hoped they would dry hung on the outside of my pack before the next day's thunderstorm. As I stretched out preparing to sleep, a lovely doe stood on the stream bank staring at me as I took her picture from my tent. I drifted to sleep listening to coyotes.

Walking with a Dual Focus

An ominous start to the day was waking up to big, black clouds stretched over picturesque mountains at the head of the valley. I needed to keep my eye on the clouds as well as the scenery.

The scenery was gorgeous: three high mountain valleys that reminded me of the Napeequa in solitude grandeur, only higher in altitude, a few lakes scattered around the high country and a variety of streams and forks of the Conejos, all easy to step across. On a high traverse, meadows were filled with bright-blue gentians, and a hawk or eagle flew above me.

I didn't go uphill with any speed, and I was tired before I thought I should be. Must be getting old.

Patches of blue sky over me were encouraging. Though gray clouds hung over one pass, I kept out-walking them, aware if lightning hit me I would roll a few hundred feet on the steep hillside before I stopped. But no lightning hit me. In fact, as I walked, I only had six drops of rain all day. But when I put up my tent for the night at the Adams Fork of the Conejos, a quick hailstorm hit, and I dove into the tent to wait out the storm in comfort.

I walked long high traverses above timberline from 11,300 feet to 12,700 feet, cloudy and gray all day, with intermittent light rain, great views sometimes obscured by rain clouds, and fog.

I was too concerned about possible lightning to take more than two brief breaks to eat a trail bar and to change batteries on the GPS.

My dual focus changed from watching scenery and the weather to watching the trail threaten to disappear in the grass and gray clouds threaten lightning. I was slightly misplaced three times, but with the GPS I was always found again, or I should say, the trail was found again. I always knew where I was. My goal to reach trees before the day's thunderstorms began meant going almost all the way to Elwood Pass. It seemed almost a crime to rush in such beautiful scenery. Finally reaching the shelter of big trees, I collapsed for lunch at 2:30 and an old lady's well-deserved rest.

After lunch I discovered I was within a couple blocks of the road. So I meandered over to the road between showers and road-walked to Elwood Pass, arriving as Kathy and David drove up. What great friends to find me in the middle of nowhere with my food drop. David cooked my dinner on the tailgate. More thunderstorms were coming, so I threw up my tent, and my support team departed. Reclining in my tent, cozy and warm, I read about the next day's trail while three storm cells, one with hail, passed by.

With blue skies and only a few puffy high clouds, the next day was more pleasant. I had more time to view my surroundings, and flowers entertained my eyes: low growing yellow daisies, penstemon, yarrow, western fringed gentian, fairy trumpets, paintbrush, mountain avens, bistort and white daisies. I loved the flowers' bright colors, red, blue, yellow, white, and purple. There was wildlife, too: two elk, four deer, a martin, a pair of falcons with beautiful under feathers, numerous chipmunks, and squirrels.

The elevation was lower and the trail gentler. I had a lazy afternoon arriving ahead of schedule at my destination. Usually a pretty clean backpacker, the weather and water sources had not been cooperative, and I really needed a shower. I lose interest in being clean in proportion to decreasing temperature. Oh well. I cut and cleaned my fingernails.

Coming into Wolf Creek Pass, I traversed around the head of a valley and climbed up another ridge of mountains overlooking the ski area. I know the Continental Divide Trail should be on the Divide when possible, but it seemed a bit silly when there was a more direct way through the valley without all that climbing.

I met Kathy and David at the pass and soon had a shower, clean clothes, and a happy tummy. (David cooked delicious a dinner.)

On my zero day, in a break in the weather, Kathy went out for a bike ride as biking didn't irritate her plantar fasciitis. I mended my pants and duct taped small holes in my rain gear. We drove to a store for cheese, and David made chocolate chip cookies to top off the day. Eating is what zero days are for.

I was a little concerned I'd been having symptoms related to high altitude. I didn't have headache or nausea, more common symptoms, but I had fatigue and a cough, and I was noticing shortness of breath when resting. I hoped my body would make more little red blood cells soon to cope with the altitude.

Opinionated Hikers

Chosen, whom I'd met on the PCT in 2008, showed up to hike with me from Wolf Creek Pass. Even leaving the pass in clouds and wetness, she was impressed with the trail, saying it might be her new favorite trail. Passing a trail maintenance crew hauling rocks to improve the trail, we thanked them profusely and took their pictures. Without such people there would be no trail.

A lovely little tarn, Rock Lake, would have been a good spot for lunch but for the rain. At a short break in the wetness, we settled for sitting on a log, our break cut even shorter by more raindrops. I had a good time with someone to talk to until Chosen told me she didn't like to talk while hiking. OK, I could live with that. Since she was able to go much faster than I could, I told her to go ahead, and I would meet her at Archuleta Lake, our destination for the night.

Hikers and a group on horseback passed me, and at our campsite there were more hikers than I'd seen all the way from Cumbress Pass. After dinner and chores, Chosen and I talked for a while with two other hikers until another group said we were too loud. Geesh. It wasn't even 7:00. Oh well, we stopped socializing and went to our individual tents, which we would have done in 10 minutes or so anyway, as it was getting cold.

In the morning Chosen hiked on ahead, saying we would meet at Piedra Pass. I only saw her once from a distance, but we both liked solo hiking. The trail went up and down a thousand feet, twice, with a few more ups and downs added for good measure. I crawled like a slug at every uphill.

The inevitable thunderstorms were around, but never over me. Most of the day had some sun, and the views were incredible as we walked on the actual Divide, mountain ranges around us in all directions. Our two hiker friends from the previous night caught up with me on the last climb, and we all camped at Piedra Pass, enjoying the high country.

Chosen had been too busy prior to the hike to actually look through my hike plan and was surprised to learn it called for hiking off the CDT down Squaw Creek for our next food drop.

Since she could cover ground far more quickly than I could, she decided to go ahead and hitch back to her car, either moving it farther ahead or heading for Minnesota. She wanted to get back home, pick up her doggie, and head to Florida to be with her daughter, who was battling cancer. They were both in my prayers.

As for me, I continued hiking at the pace I could hike, glad I was still walking. The scenery continued to be fantastic. The San Juan Mountains are jewels on the CDT, tracing a horseshoe- shaped curve in southern Colorado. Some thru hikers bypass them due to snow in the early summer, but that's like missing a main event. The only mars to the scenery were the stands of dead trees, decimated by bark beetles, dry and dead reminders of how beautiful they too had once been.

Our hiker friends from Archuleta Lake passed, and I knew I wouldn't see them again before I left the trail for my resupply. While walking on a mostly open ridgeline, it started to rain and hail, and I dove under a tree and ate an early dinner. Simply hydrating food instead of having to cook it on a stove meant it was ready to eat any time at least an hour after adding water. The short storm quickly spent itself, and I reached Cherokee Lake after other hikers had left. More threatening clouds convinced me that stopping would be good, so I quickly threw up the tent and beat the rain.

In the morning, bugling elk stirred me to walk on steep hills far above timberline. I had trouble going uphill, just didn't *feel right*, tired and panting more than normal. Discouraged, I wondered if I should be hiking at high altitude.

After lunch, an older hiker passed me going the opposite direction, complaining about rocky trail. He complained about New Mexico, the water, the route, and more. I'd enjoyed New Mexico and told him my route; he'd stuck to the *official* one. I had mixed and matched *official* and Wolf routes and had a good time. He looked askance at me and said that was *a different world* than he'd experienced. Scathingly, he said his pack was heavy because the *lightweight gear* he'd started with didn't hold up for him. He didn't seem to be having a good time.

Even when I was discouraged, I was having more fun than he was. I had to laugh at how opinionated hikers are. Chosen certainly had her strong opinions about how to hike and what food to eat. So did I. So did this elderly gentleman. We just didn't hold the *same* strong opinions.

Going over the last 12,350-foot mark, I moved better. Better because it was after lunch? Better after laughing at myself and hiker opinions? Better after an attitude adjustment? Getting stronger? Who knew? But I liked moving better.

The older hiker had it right about the trail, though. It was very rocky, and my feet complained. The trail was also quite eroded, and I sometimes walked in knee-high ditches. Without maintenance, in another 20 years, they would be shoulder deep ditches. Pushing through overgrown willows added to the fun. At Squaw Pass I couldn't find the trail at first, and it started to rain. Umbrella and pack cover fended off the rain, but my shorts and feet were soaked by foliage and bogs. It almost made me think I was in Vermont. Avoiding high, thick, wet grass, I pitched the tent, had dinner, and was serenaded by lovelorn elk all night and in the morning, too.

The air, the foliage, everything, was wet and muddy. It took a long time for the sun to clear Chieftain Mountain to reach the valley as I slogged through the wet. I watched the stream grow from a trickle to a good-sized creek with crashing rapids and waterfalls. Descending, I saw a deer and happily identified yellow shrubby cinquefoil. A strange pink flower took me six years to identify from its photo; it was prairie smoke.

Reaching the campground shortly after lunch, I found Chosen had come and gone with horse riders to get her car at Wolf Creek Pass, cryptically telling Kathy and David that we were incompatible hikers. I wondered what she'd been expecting when she said she wanted to hike with me. Hikers come in many different personalities. There is no one right way to hike, and there is no one right personality. We all have our own issues and life problems, which affect who we are. The trail (the world and God) holds us all.

David and Grapevine cleared out of the trailer, so I could take my bath in the sink. I was so filthy. Getting clean felt good. It was wonderful to have friends, who had come to the end of the earth to support me. After a relaxing afternoon and evening and a good dinner, too, we were happy to be inside for the afternoon thunderstorms.

On my rest day, David heated boiling water to do my laundry in a bucket. It was nice to get hiking clothes clean, even in a primitive campground. I hung them on chairs to catch the morning sun, along with my drying tent. Shoes, clothes, and gear dry, I was ready to go again.

David fixed us elk steaks for dinner, along with broccoli and potato. Yum. After dinner we took a walk around the campground, stopping to talk to John and Marvis from Texas on a fishing trip, who were eating a nice catch of German Brown Trout along with corn and even peach cobbler done up in a Dutch oven like I used to do in Girl Scouts. We had a fun conversation, and they fed me trout and cobbler. Yum again. Hikers can eat double meals.

The "Window"

John liked to hike, too, and he walked to Squaw Pass with me in the morning. He shared plums and grapes, as I treated water for him at the pass for his way back down. During the day I passed six different hikers in groups of two. The last two looked at me like I was crazy when I told them my destination was Buena Vista. Well, I didn't expect to get there any time soon.

Struggling up the last hill, I listened to thunder and watched dark skies beyond the ridge. Eyeing a scrubby patch of very short alpine trees and deciding where to pitch my tent, it started to rain. Dashing into the patch of trees, I sat on my pack, umbrella over me. When the rain stopped for about two minutes, I hurriedly set up the tent, putting in the first basic stakes and the central hiking pole before it again began to rain and hail.

Grabbing my pack, I dove into the half-erected tent, awkwardly holding the tent's side out with one arm while half lying at an angle. Throughout the squall, I couldn't change positions, unpack, or put on my coat. It was better to be cold and dry than cold and wet.

Still in my cramped position, I heard voices. Gail, whom I'd met on the AT in Maine and in New Mexico in the spring, had arrived with her son Greg in rain and hail. I hadn't known for sure if our paths would cross. Not only did we meet, they decided to share my small clump of trees, setting up camp in the rain. Finally, the rain stopped, we settled in together, anticipating a cold night at 12,300 feet, the ground now dressed in wet hail.

That night a mouse ran up the wall of my mosquito netting. It must have been a well-used campsite to support active mice at that elevation. Waking early, my body was tired of lying down and ached in every horizontal position. High altitude had prevented good sleep, having to consciously deep breathe every several breaths. Funny, I wasn't bothered with shortness of breath until over 12,000 feet and at rest.

From our high perch below a large, distinctive opening in the rock wall of the Divide called

The Window, the sunrise was beautiful. I love to take sunrise pictures, but Gail and her son were more interested in firing up their stove for breakfast. We were all cold. After packing up we said our good-byes, they heading south and I north.

Pushing through willows and walking in ditches, I passed a number of high-mountain lakes, and the willows changed color to paint the high country shades of yellow in contrast to the dark green spruce in the valley. Lovely.

Leaving the lake in the morning, I saw fresh cat tracks, and as I approached the first pass, I saw a critter, possibly a cougar, too far away to positively identify. Hearing my movement as I pulled out my camera, it went over the ridge like a flash. Later I heard coyotes.

Huffing and puffing, again I moved like a slug on every uphill. Thinking the stress of trying to go faster, might give me a heart attack,

I didn't push myself. I just didn't feel right over 12,000 feet. But I was thrilled to be walking in awesome country on top of the world, reveling in fantastic views.

I'd seen the Rio Grande Pyramid and *The Window*, that remarkable straight gap in a rock ridge line, from both sides that day. A new range of mountains, the Grenadiers, came into view, rugged and pointy, reminding me of pictures of Peru's Machu Pichu on a smaller scale.

By beautiful Ute Lakes, I passed three large groups of backpackers at the beginning of Labor Day weekend. Glad to reach my destination, finding a lower campsite at 11,600 feet, I was happy it didn't rain.

But I woke up to clouds. Uh oh. Not a good sign. I had many climbs and spent most of the day well above 12,000 feet. Half way up my first 1,000-foot climb, it started to rain. Up went the umbrella, and I needed it frequently as rain or hail storms passed by.

My trail went over Hunchback Pass down to Bear Town, then up to a crest, then up and down a few times more, all while multiple rain squalls blew by. Breaks and rain-free times were short, but the views were outstanding. A passing bow hunter excitedly told me he'd just seen a moose, and I saw 21 hikers in groups out for the long weekend. As I walked through high open country under my umbrella, I hoped lightning would find other places to hit. I had plenty of company with other hikers (sans umbrella), who wished the same.

Stony Pass and Silverton

David and Kathy were waiting for me at Stony Pass. Kathy loved to climb summits, even with plantar fasciitis, and she almost summited the peak by the road before I arrived. Reaching the truck, I felt whipped after only a 10-mile day.

The ride down the Stony Pass Road was very steep and rocky. I don't know if David ever forgave me for abusing his nice truck on that horrible road. We were all glad to reach Silverton, for differing reasons.

My zero day coincided with Sunday, so I went to church. Afterwards, I called Punkie, or Liz, as she goes by now, an old friend from Girl Scout Camp more than 50 years ago. Amazing. The CDT put me in touch with my past, first Terry in Las Cruces and now Punkie.

Punkie drove from Durango to Silverton, and we went out to lunch, showing each other pictures of family, adventures in hiking (me), and llama trekking in the San Juans (Liz) as we caught up on the last 50 years. Past lives of old hikers can dot long trails with old friends, adding to hiking enjoyment.

I had my ice cream fix with a gigantic cone while walking around Silverton with Liz. David cooked us elk steaks with lovely fresh asparagus for dinner, and it was time to hit the trail again, so David and Kathy drove me back up to Stony Pass, though I know David hated that road.

I set out with good cheer under fluffy clouds in a blue sky and hoped my red blood cells were catching up to the altitude. In the afternoon, in dry comfort on my ridge, I watched a storm one valley over.

Wildlife included several marmots, an eagle, and a ton of mice in the meadows. I'd never noticed so many mice before. Yarrow, alpine cinquefoil, a few paintbrush, yellow daisies, marsh marigold and penstemon were still blooming, though it was the third of September. I learned a new flower, king's crown. I was amazed how fast fall was approaching. After returning to the trail following a zero day, the high meadows were browner, the willows more yellow, the king's crown more red.

That particular section of the CDT is the longest continuous section of any United States Scenic trail above timberline, more than 20 miles. I was walking on top of the world, though not a level world, numerous 500-foot climbs along the way provided ample exercise. The grand horseshoe of the San Juans enabled me to look at the north side of mountains, (I'd walked by on the south side many miles before) and I could identify Rio Grande Pyramid and the Window from a different perspective.

Feeling Funny

After lunch, I began to fade. Though the uphills were not more difficult, I became more slug-like going up them. Marcus, from Germany, whom I'd met in 2011 in Oregon on the PCT, came toward me. We were both excited to see each other and chattered quickly before going our separate ways. Marcus was the first SOBO thru hiker of the year, a strong hiker doing 30-mile days. He said he might take a bike trip across Asia for his next adventure when he finished the CDT. He was way beyond my class of *old lady hiker*, yet I was happy to count him as a friend.

Seeing Marcus gave me more energy for the last stretch. Passing a small stream, I hydrated my dinner before the last little climb to the lake where I met Sara, a young Colorado Trail section hiker, and a couple from California hiking a short section. We camped by the lake at 12,200 feet, Sara's tent close to mine. Besides having my daughter's name, she was an interesting young woman, who flew C130s for the Air Force and loved climbing, rafting, and hiking. We talked until darkness fell. The people met on the trail were as varied and interesting as the many flowers beside the trail.

I woke up a few times in the night to concentrate on breathing but still slept fairly well. I woke to a frosty world, 36 degrees inside the tent. Sara and I were packed and ready to go at the same time, so we said good-bye and left in opposite directions.

After the first 700-foot climb, I walked by broken-down cabins and mine tailings, the remains of the mining town of Carson.

The second climb of 1300-feet took me to the 13,250-foot-high point, concurrent with the Colorado Trail since the midpoint of the San Juans. Climbing slowly, stopping to catch my breath and slow my heart rate whenever I felt *funny*, I tried to listen to whatever my body told me and not to assume I could *power through*.

From the high point, the view changed entirely, going up and down increasingly lower peaks with broad, sloping east sides and rugged rocky west sides, sweeping views mainly to the east. In the canyon immediate west of me were yellow groves of Aspen, a startlingly red mountain and a rather large lake. Again the storms missed me, barely. The wind didn't. I found it hard to dress for the weather. One minute I would be cold, in the shade of clouds with howling wind, and the next minute in bright sun, too hot for whatever I was wearing.

Much of the Continental Divide Trail is a shared-use trail, different than PCT and AT, where bicycles are not allowed. Passing two bicycle riders, I thought I wouldn't have wanted to push their bikes through some of the talus slopes I'd walked. Riding through them wasn't possible, even for daredevils. Pushing and hauling, they took their bicycles over the rocks to ride again where trail was friendlier.

Bow hunters I passed were surprised to see me. I suppose it might have been surprising to be met with a pack-carrying grandmother on the trail, when they were hunting in wilderness.

Walking 14 miles on a day with only small, puffy clouds, I felt like a real hiker.

A very brazen bunny rabbit ran around my campsite that night; I hung my food bag on a poll in hopes that would discourage the bunny. I'd arrived too late to hang properly for bears, and hoped they were not around. I seemed to be getting more acclimated, or perhaps I'd just descended lower than 12,000 ft.

The rest of the way to the highway consisted of two low ascents of very gradual up hills followed by smooth, gentle down hills. Patches of golden aspen shown against the backdrop of the mountains, and I could see the red mountain in the valley to the west and the Snowy Mesa to the east. Virtually every step of the way through the San Juans had shown me a view. I didn't walk to find a view. I walked to see how views changed.

At the highway, I met Kathy and David one last time before they headed home to Washington the next day. *Thank you* was way too little to say for the trail support they'd given me. I hoped they'd enjoyed southern Colorado while waiting to give me food drops.

Without David and Kathy's support, I had a new challenge—one I'd been worrying about since I'd started the trek into the San Juans. How could I carry enough food for eight days? I'd carried eight days of food beside the Gila River, but a river in a nearly level river valley meant I did not need to carry much water. I could carry eight days of food with no water and no big climbs. I couldn't carry eight days of food and liters of water, too. Water is heavy, and my trail wouldn't be level or at low altitude.

The hosts at Raven's Rest Hostel gave me Debbie's phone number. She agreed to take me back to Spring Creek Pass in the morning and would also bring me a food drop in four days at highway 114. It cost me some cash for this arrangement, but my aging body needed to **not** carry eight days of food plus water going up and down high mountains.

Debbie was right on time. She took my food drop and told me she'd have *my back* if I ran into any trouble. She planned to bring her sleeping bag with her the day she brought my food drop, in case I'd had trouble getting there at the time planned. Neither one of us were too sure exactly where the trail would cross Highway 114.

Embrace the Brutality

I took the 1,500-foot climb up to Snowy Mesa slowly, if not as a slug, then as a turtle.

Pikas with cute round ears lived above treeline in the rocks and were industriously gathering grass for the winter. Pikas are small alpine mammals about the size of hamsters, but related to rabbits. David told a story, perhaps true, of a trail crew in Washington that struggled to remove a very large rock from a trail. When they finally succeeded, they found a Volkswagen-sized pile of grass and a very angry pika. Pikas are also sometimes called rock rabbits or conies. The ones I saw that day, mouths full of grass, were intent on winter storage in the talus field.

I also walked by a well-camouflaged ptarmigan, who was so still it looked like a rock.

When I stopped moving, it's low, soft humming coo gave away its presence.

On top of Snow Mesa, I saw a sheepherder's tent in the distance and a wall of sheep moving across my trail ahead of me. They moved amazingly quickly, disappearing over the curve of the hill by the time I reached the spot where they'd crossed my trail. I also saw an eagle and almost walked over two more rock-resembling ptarmigan before they moved.

Stopping for the night at 11,600 feet, I camped between tall, cliff-like mountains near a high mountain stream with yellow daisies all around me. Stopping early, I avoided another night of breathlessness above 12,000 feet.

Start at 11,000 feet. Climb to 12,000 feet. Descend. Repeat. Repeat. Repeat. End with a long descent of 2,000 feet. Top with wildlife. That was the next day.

Details: The second 1,000-foot climb came close to doing me in. It was very steep, and the altitude was, well, the same altitude as the others, but my body said it was much higher. I had to rest every three or four steps, steps that seemed like climbing a ladder while I was weighted by lead.

It was the day for septuagenarians. The first two gentlemen I saw were 75 and 74. Another 74-year-old gentleman, who worked in Alaska for the National Park Service, was traveling with two young people. Later, Remy, from Bellingham, a good looking young man thru hiking the Colorado Trail, passed me moving smoothly and with energy, even uphill. Marcus moved like that. But I didn't. Later still, an older gentleman with a heavy pack passed me. All were pleasant folks.

Finishing brutal climbs, I walked five miles down the Cochetopa. One of the phrases thru hikers have used to describe hiking on the CDT is "embrace the brutality." I don't really like the phrase, but on that day it really fit.

My last pass of the day was next to San Luis Peak, one of Colorado's many 14ers. (Mountains over 14,000 feet) Many thru hikers climb it as they go by, but I left that to the big boys (or younger boys and girls than me). I didn't need to go up a 14er when I'd had trouble breathing at the altitude of the trail. Although I loved the high country, I was glad to descend the Cochetopa to views of a different kind and better breathing.

"Thank you for the picture, Mr. Moose"

As I descended past flowers and beaver ponds, two deer said hello. Then there were moose—two cow moose in the willows beside the trail. As I was taking their picture, papa moose, a big bull with a huge rack, suddenly stepped out of the bushes near me. He was magnificent. His rack was so big it looked like he had to be careful with head movements to keep from being overbalanced. I already had the camera out and quickly took his picture, but I didn't stand around staring. Definitely big enough to be dangerous, he was only 15-feet away from me. Saying, "Thank you for the picture, Mr. Moose," I left before he could be upset. Finally stopping for the day near a tree appropriate for food-bag hanging, I ended without high-country vistas. But I'd seen a perfect moose.

Most of the next day was spent continuing the long descent along Cochetopa Creek with a few little up hills to remind me I was hiking, not strolling. The morning color was provided by aspen gold against spruce dark green; the creek danced downhill between beaver dams. Although I didn't see him, a beaver felled a big aspen about 20 feet below me, crashing right as I passed.

That was startling.

Kinnikinnick and juniper ground cover brought back memories of growing up in Colorado Mountains. Predominant plants in the valleys were rabbit brush and sage. Purple asters, yarrow, harebell, shrubby cinquefoil and a couple kinds of yellow daisies also still bloomed.

I must have been thinking deep thoughts, mentally singing or playing trail zombie, hypnotized by repetitive steps eating the miles, as I made a wrong turn just before Ant Creek, but I quickly found the trail again.

The meager stream by my campsite was enough to allow me to collect water for a bath. It was only in the 50s, but I felt so filthy I had to clean up and even put on my clean sports bra. I felt great afterwards, though freezing during the process itself. I washed socks, too, all in half a Ziploc bag of water, settling down in my tent after a beautiful sunset and hiker midnight.

The morning was cold, as usual, around freezing. The sun within yards of me, I only had to pack up and walk to it. Walking along the edge of Cochetopa Park for miles and miles, I looked back to see San Luis Peak sticking high above the valley. I marveled that I'd been on that ridge two days ago. Again the predominant color was provided by rabbit brush and golden aspen, the backdrop changed to lodgepole pine.

Highway 114

Passing a few hunters, cars, and a couple of hikers, I stopped at Lukan Creek for water before arriving at Highway 114 around 5:30. Debbie was supposed to meet me at 6:00. The CDT crossed the highway west and downhill from the pass.

As I waited prominently beside the blacktop highway, I hydrated my dinner and cleaned out the *scuzzies* from my bottles with the help of a few weed branches used as scrubbies. There were no highway CDT signs at the crossing of the trail, and Debbie had never helped a hiker there before. An hour later, a little concerned not to have seen Debbie, I hailed a passing car, and the driver said he would see if she was ahead at the pass. Finding her, the friendly driver told her my location. Mission accomplished and food drop delivered—thanks to Debbie and the passing driver.

Food stowed in my pack, I headed up the road until I saw a possible tent site in a grove of aspen across the creek. Four more days to go.

The easy days of Cochetopa were past. The trail wasn't terrible, but I was tired, had a sore heel, and wondered why I'd taken up this pastime instead of driving around in an RV as everyone else my age was probably doing. Grouch and grumble.

As I headed up the road beside Lukan Creek on a frosty morning, I passed a very elaborate hunter camp with a tent the size of a small circus tent and a generator humming for heat. I didn't know whether to laugh in ridicule or be green with envy.

Although sunshine was replaced by clouds, it didn't rain on my forest walk through mixed pines, firs, and spruce as two brothers passed me hiking south. One had a 22 for hunting small game. He seemed to think the CDT was an outdoor survival hike with guns needed.

Ridiculous. I feared for the very tame bunny six days back. The brother without the gun was carrying his brother's food and a heavy town coat tied on top of his pack. I thought the guy ahead should leave the gun at home and carry his own food. And that town coat would be useless as raingear if it rained very hard. I was a little concerned about them. Good raingear would be worth a whole lot more for survival than a 22. Dri Ducks, though somewhat fragile, actually shed water and are really cheap, less than $20 for a rainsuit. I reminded myself I wasn't in charge of how the rest of the world hiked.

Two Colorado Trail hikers, one from Denmark and one from Indiana, camped with me at Baldy Lake. The young man from Denmark had finished the Pacific Crest Trail and was walking the Colorado Trail as a little extra before returning to Denmark. His Danish trail name meant *Walking Animal,* and he'd met Billy Goat, so we had a friend in common. As I sat at their campfire enjoying conversation, I observed Walking Animal had the same Hexamid tent as mine. What discriminating good taste.

After a relatively warm and breezy night, we were all up and underway about the same time, they to head south and I north for another day of forest walking with red or yellow barberry groundcover beneath the trees.

After lunch, I caught a lovely view of peaks north, east, and west from Sargent's Mesa, but as I started down to Tank Seven Creek, it began to rain. On with the rain gear and up with the umbrella.

Arriving at Tank Seven Creek, I barely had the tent up before the next deluge began. It poured so hard raindrops hit the ground with enough force to bounce through the mosquito netting. After the storm passed, I took care of water, dinner, and camp chores, and I put a few stray logs in critical areas around my tent as splash guards. As I was finishing dinner, another storm came through, and later still, another—

thunderstorms with fireworks and hard rain. My splash guards helped a little.

One thing about camping under trees, when it rains that hard, even when it is not raining, it drips all night. It didn't just drip. It rained all night long and was raining hard when I woke in the morning. I had to pack up in the rain, my least favorite thing to do.

During the day I was tricked a few times, thinking the sun was coming out by the light reflected from golden leaves of aspen. Rain continued intermittently all morning and into the afternoon, my only view swirling clouds and raindrops. The sun came out enough to see my shadow three times, for about 15 seconds each.

Stopping at the pass early enough to give my tent some time to air out, the inside and everything in it was dry until I shoved the wet pack in a corner. I was warm in my bag, but getting up and packing was difficult the next morning at 36 degrees. However, the uphill trail soon warmed me except for my face and fingers. I had to walk three miles before the sun shone on me, and when it did, I was at a high elevation with wind that cancelled the sun's warmth until mid-afternoon.

Monarch Pass

My back and feet hurt all day, but I made it to Monarch Pass. In the store at the pass, I asked for sign-making materials to get a hitch to Salida. Seeing what I was doing, a guy offered me a ride to town before the sign was finished. Sweet.

At the hostel in town, I met Transient and Roaring Lion, SOBO CDT hikers. It was wonderful to again be clean, have clean clothes, be among *hiker trash* and stuffed with pizza. (*Hiker Trash* is a strange but endearing term meaning other long-distance hikers.)

Our shuttle the next day took us all back to Monarch Pass, where I headed north and the others south. First off, there was a 1,700-foot climb back up to the Divide as the trail curved back on itself before dropping to parallel the highway.

On the way up, I passed the remains of low rock walls used by native people of the ancient past to herd elk to the kill. I wouldn't have noticed them except for the description in Wolf's book. It was mind boggling to imagine hunters with bows and arrows on that same ridge 5,000 years ago. I saw no elk, but I did see spectacular views to the north, snow on the higher peaks left from the earlier storm quickly disappearing in bright sun.

The trail became *unfound* (another hiker euphemism for being lost) briefly after Boss Lake Reservoir, but I made my way to the old jeep road and started ascending Chalk Creek, finding a small, level campsite. It was below 30 degrees in the night, and my choice of campsite proved poor, with thick layers of frost covering the tent in the morning. Stuffing a frost-covered tent into a small bag with bare hands was an unfavorable experience reminding me again never to camp right next to a stream.

I went up searching for sun and eventually found some. Finally reaching the pass above Chalk Creek, I was startled to find a hunter perched on the ridge watching me strain upwards. He asked if I'd seen any sheep (big horn, not domestic.)

Nope. I'd been far too busy watching my feet and panting, and I was glad he'd not mistaken me for a sheep.

Dropping down to Hancock Lake, an especially pretty high lake tucked on a shelf below the Divide, I had brunch. As I was eating, the lake was deluged with day hikers and hunters coming from the north, the first day hiker an older lady, delighted to see me solo hiking, as her friends had been giving her a hard time for doing the same.

From Hancock Lake, I walked down a *very* rocky jeep road, encountering day hikers, hunters, and bicycles. My feet were not happy with unstable loose rocks—the only tread to walk on. It was worse than Pennsylvania. Farther down, I was blessed with better trail in the guise of an old narrow-gauge-railroad bed, the Denver, South Park, and Pacific.

Walking easily again, I talked with day hikers heading for the narrow- gauge tunnel cut through the mountain. There they would exchange car keys with hiker friends coming from the other side, each then continuing to a car parked at a trailhead, no one having to retrace their steps.

My trail left the railroad grade past Tunnel Lake, taking me over the Divide. Stopping in very pretty high country for a late lunch, I dried out my tent and sleeping bag, wet from the morning's frost, and revamped my shoe inserts for feet unhappy about the earlier rocks. Walking down to the North Fork of Chalk Creek on newly constructed switchbacks, I met three bow hunters. They seemed surprised I was hiking, perhaps not knowing some people choose to walk in the woods without trying to kill game.

After I put up my tent and ate dinner, the cold settled in fast with the setting sun. Hunters all drove home for the night, and the hunter parade back *up* the road started at 5:00 in the morning. Camped by the jeep road, their headlights pierced the darkness shining brightly into my tent.

I saw more hunters in two days on the trail than there could possibly be game to shoot at.

With all the cars and hunters around, every self-respecting deer, elk, or sheep should be far away. However, Colorado has so many little jeep roads extending into every obscure valley as the result of the search for silver in years past, maybe there *was* no deeper wilderness into which critters could escape.

The other side of Tin Cup Pass held beautiful Mirror Lake. It wasn't being a mirror that day, but it was still beautiful, Aspen on the walls of Garden Basin glowed red-tinged yellow above blue water, and I had my lunch. Friendly hunters extended offers of help, amazed I'd come more than 300 miles unharmed, long-distance hiking beyond their fathoming.

On the CDT I'd become used to sharing the trail with bicycles, motorbikes, and ATVs of all kinds. Mostly, I was OK with that, although I thought the ATVs in particular greatly added to the eroded condition of the trails.

But my last day revealed dangers in sharing the trail with vehicles.

On a trail just wide enough for a three-wheeler, I heard them coming and stood on the extreme edge. The two young dudes didn't slow down even a hair when they saw me, recklessly careening over bumps as if the trail was their private racetrack, their wheels passing inches from my feet. If I'd not been standing on the very edge, I would have died.

Later, an adult, supposedly responsible for the two ahead, came by and slowed to talk to me. He had a sheepish look on his face when I thanked him for slowing when the others had not. Somehow I thought the responsible adult should have been in front, not behind, or at least had better control of or training for his younger charges.

Push to the End

Reaching the top of the ridge, I said *good-bye* to mountains behind and *hello* to those ahead.

Step and Machine, a couple of SOBO thru hikers told me they'd seen cars on Cottonwood Pass Road, the dirt road on the west side of the pass. It was Sunday, and the hitching prospects would be much better on a Sunday afternoon, people headed home at the end of the weekend. Prospects would be better than on Monday as written on my hike plan.

I decided to go for the road that night instead of waiting until Monday morning, a 16-mile day and a big stretch for an old lady. After adjusting my shoe inserts, I zoomed down the trail with a sort of old-lady zoom. I didn't stop to eat or get more water, though I did stop to take pictures of beautifully shimmering golden aspen on the climb out of Sanford Creek.

Reaching the road just as the sun went down, I was quite worried about finding a hitch in remaining daylight. Taking two steps on the road, I heard the approaching car. No thumb out for me, I grabbed my white hat from my head, waved it wildly, and the car stopped.

A young couple and their small son on the way home from Crested Butte to Boulder happily gave me a ride 21 miles to Buena Vista. Halleluiah.

We had a lovely time talking about backpacking, and they drove me to my car, which I'd parked with Carol and Charles all those many weeks. Carol and Charles took me in, even at such a late hour, putting me up in a wonderful guest room, where I had my shower and tumbled into a real bed.

Colorado's hike added to New Mexico's equaled 833 miles for the year on the CDT. Not a bad start for a trail I didn't know if I could finish. I still didn't know if I could complete it, but I decided I would continue to act as if it would happen on the chance that might turn out to be true.

Chapter 36 Fall and Winter 2012-2013

Why do older hikers keep hiking?

I can't answer for every older hiker. But in my case, I keep hiking because I continue to enjoy being out on the trail. I learned to make allowances for the limitations that came with age. Now, if you are an older hiker, and you have no limitations, cheers to you. But I have my limitations. I slowed a little more every passing year, and I needed to be sure my medications for various ailments were with me. I needed to find more frequent food drop options than the average long distance hiker, I couldn't do what the young and super buff could do, not even what some older hikers could accomplish. But I could do what *I* could do.

In spite of my limitations, I didn't lose enjoyment of the trail. One of the people who talked to me at Many Glacier Hotel in 2017 said he thought it would be much more difficult to do a trail in sections over many years than to do a thru hike because you would have to face the pain of getting trail legs *every* year instead of just once.

I never looked at my hikes that way. I did work at home to try to be in shape before beginning a long trail section each year, with varying concentration and success, depending on the year and other activities in my life. But I always looked forward to being on the trail and anticipated joy. As the years passed, it simply was how I lived. I lived on the trail in the spring and in the fall. That had become normal, not unusual. Not a one-off sort of thing; it was a way of life.

Spring was rolling around again; where should I hike? I had one more year I could manage a spring hike on the CDT if I planned it correctly. RockStar was interested and available to hike part of the section I'd missed in New Mexico, and the Great Basin in Wyoming could be done in spring. Nothing else on the CDT would be snow free in the spring.

Prep Time

Liking my Zpack Hexamid tent so much, I decided to get a Cuban Fiber pack as well. My new pack had various attachments I liked, a *load lifter* to help adjust the load carried, a detachable lid for use slack packing, two waist-belt pack pockets and holsters on pack straps for my water bottles. Even though it was Cuban Fiber, additions to the basic pack meant a few extra ounces, but I liked having those options.

I was thrown off my training schedule when I had a basal cell carcinoma removed from my forehead, the best kind of cancer to get if you get any. But the Doc said no speed walking or strenuous activity for a week and a half after surgery. Frustrating.

However, surgery went perfectly, and so did healing. I ended up with a 6th of a facelift, and I was sorry I couldn't plan cancer to get a full facelift. I showed up Easter Sunday with a big fat bandage on my forehead and one eye half shut. Since everyone was going to look and gasp anyway, I wrote Alleluia in glitter on tape and put it over the bandage. My Doc was a good seamstress, putting in 30 very fine tiny stitches. I was fascinated to watch her handiwork progress as she showed me with a mirror. The resulting scar is difficult to see unless I have my super short haircut for hiking.

In 2013, I drove to New Mexico, making my journey a road trip as well as a hiking trip. I stopped to see Tough Old Broad in Eugene and my cousin in Oceanside, and I drove to Lake Morena for the PCT Kickoff just for fun. I helped with registration and saw Billy Goat, JB, and others I knew from past years.

Driving on, I appreciated blooming palo verde and ocotillo below Phoenix and Tucson, waved at the exit to Sierra Vista, where I once lived, the Chiricahuas where I once hiked. I couldn't go to New Mexico without saying *hello* to trail angels El Coyote, Mary, George, and Jan. When driving 12 or 13 hundred miles, what's a little hundred-mile side trip? I had time only for brief chats and hugs, but it was worth the effort.

An Old Lady

Uncle Tom, a thru hiker at George and Jan's, chided me for saying I was an old lady. I explained I didn't see being old as a putdown. I was 71-years old. That was simply a fact. I wasn't 20, 30, 50, or 60. There was nothing pejorative about being old. In fact, when *I* spoke about being an old lady, I was *bragging.* I was 71-years-old, getting close to 72, and I was still hiking. How cool was that?

I didn't want to be 20 again. I was quite happy being 71. I was quite happy being old.

Others thought being old was bad. Far more important was what I did, how I treated others, how I lived out the gifts God had given me at whatever age I found myself. I call myself an old lady. I say it realistically, with joy and laughter—bragging.

Hiking through New Mexico that year was drier than the year before. As I drove north to Grants, I left water caches, gallon jugs of water hidden in bushes or under trees at places I could later recognize where there was access by road, and I left a food drop at Pie Town on the way.

Chapter 37 April 18, 2013 CDT

New Mexico - Mumms

My first little bit of trail was the five miles from the trailhead north of town back to Grants, slack packing thanks to trail angel Hugo Mumm. Back in town after my walk, the Mumms and I had a nice visit as they told me of petroglyphs they'd found quite by accident while day hiking. I set out one more water cache and a food drop in a bear can. Trail gossip that year reported a water cache stolen, a horrible thing. Water was life. I carefully hid mine.

Other trail gossip made me wonder if hikers were doing due diligence before starting out on the CDT. It *is* a wonderful trail, but it's not at all like the AT or the PCT. Some hikers seemed not to carry maps, know alternate routes, or understand water challenges. I hoped I'd paid proper attention to my planning so as not to endanger myself or others.

The Mumms drove me to Highway 12 where TOB had picked me up the previous year, and I set out with a full pack and full load of water. After they drove away, I immediately thought I was going to die under the weight of my pack. My break in conditioning due to skin surgery was telling. I was incredibly thankful I only had five miles to walk before I could stop and (I hoped) eat dinner and breakfast. Drinking a night's water before lifting that pack again would help.

Tia Vinces Spring was dry. But friendly hunters passing in a truck graciously gave me all the water I could carry. I wasn't excited about again adding 6.6 pounds, but I was thrilled to get the water.

Mangas Mountain is one of the few still-manned lookout towers in the US. Dave, the tower guy, had water for hikers. I warned him there would be a pretty big bump in the numbers of thru hikers that year, and I'd passed a dry water source, concerned the good folks supporting hikers might be overwhelmed at the increase in hiker numbers.

I saw two elk and prairie dogs running across the road and heard several turkeys, though I didn't see them. More exciting, I saw a lynx. The critter, smaller than a cougar but with the same color coat, had a short tail and was definitely feline. Turning to look at me, it revealed the tufted, foxlike face of a lynx.

Pie Town and Toaster House

Walking nearly 23 miles on dirt roads put me a day ahead of schedule but trashed my feet. I needed the extra day to heal. Not brazen enough to camp on private fenced land beside the road, I thought the best choice was to walk to the hostel in Pie Town, squeaking in to the Toaster House by the last shreds of daylight.

The Toaster House was a unique, easily identified hostel. How often do you see toasters hanging all over a gate and fence? Toasters had been donated over the years by those who had experienced Nita's hospitality. Raising a family of five children in that house and now living three miles out of town, she'd hosted hikers for 40 years.

Now, the door was left open for hikers, and bikers, too, used the beds, kitchen, wood stove for heat or cooking and the pantry, refrigerator, and freezer stocked with food. The porch was filled with old car seats for comfy seating in the shade. We were welcome to stay, eat, and use everything for a simple donation in a can. Nita, an amazingly gracious woman, even loaned her car to a hiker to get to a store 20 miles away.

A stop on a highway a long way from most anywhere, Pie Town specialized in pies for those who stopped for gas or rest, more kinds of pie than you could imagine. Yes, I had pie—Mexican apple with green chilies and pine nuts. It was delicious. What a great place.

Later, I and other hikers piled into Nita's car as she showed us the metropolis of Pie Town, population about 65. She LOVED Pie Town. Everyone should love their town that much.

That night, hikers sat around telling hiking stories way later than hiker midnight. Hiker Bob, who should have had the trail name Hatter, as he made high-end custom hats for a living, was the source of the funniest tales in Pie Town. I was glad to know I wasn't the only hiker, who talked to body parts while hiking the trail. (As in, "It's OK, feet. You really can make it the last three miles to Pie Town. Then you'll get a reward of two days off trail to rest. You'll like two day's rest, won't you?")

There were some very funny stories of hikers being surprised by others while talking or arguing out loud with body parts, flies, the weather, or themselves, not realizing anyone else was around. Of course, people who go off on month's long hikes are considered certifiable by the rest of the world, anyway. The stories just confirmed our lunacy. Good times. I laughed so hard tears ran.

I was amazed how much food was in that house. The hiker box of free stuff was over flowing. Meat and beer were in the refrigerator, and local folks kept dropping by with more donations. Cookies, more pies, ice cream, pepperoni, and chickens appeared, adding to already bountiful supplies. Yogi's CDT book said to pack snacks for Pie Town as there were no stores. Many, many hikers couldn't possibly have eaten all that food. Also observing non-hikers coming by to get food, I concluded Toaster House was an informal food bank as well as the hiker hangout.

I ate breakfast from the hiker box and had two pieces of chocolate pie for lunch. One of the restaurants was open for dinner, so four hikers, Nita and two locals ate together. Good food and good company.

Before leaving Pie Town, I had a 16-mile slack pack. My new pack had a detachable lid, detachable pack pockets, and detachable water-bottle holsters. I strung them all on a strap around my waist and fit in snacks, lunch, first-aid kit, and three liters of water. I wore gloves, head band and Dri Ducks jacket over two shirts for warmth. As I ate the food and drank the water, I gained space to store a jacket and extra shirt. The headband went into my pants pocket when not in use, and the gloves hooked together to hang over the waist strap as the day warmed. Camera, cell phone, GPS, and altimeter/clock were all attached by carabineer or in my pockets. I felt equipped for the day's needs, and it was much lighter than carrying all my gear in my pack.

Travel that day was a fairly uninteresting road walk. But it was level, smooth, and the miles went by quickly. Reaching Thomas Ranch at 3:00, RockStar, driven by Sparky, another 2009 PCT thru hiker, picked me up, all of us driving back to Pie Town, stopping first at the Pie-O- Neer Cafe to pick up RockStar's birthday pie and sampling others. Gee. It was nice to have hiker friends.

Back at the Toaster House, we found 10 more hikers had arrived, making it a full house with people sleeping on bunks, couches, and the porch. It was always a fun time on any long trail when hikers got together, and this stop was no exception.

A Spaghetti Dinner that night benefited an animal shelter on a local ranch. People came from miles away, at least as far as south of Reserve. The Community Center was packed. After a dessert auction, entertainment was a band and dance, all of it a wonderful opportunity to observe a New Mexico community in action. Nita, owner of the Toaster House, was obviously a very important person in the community. She greeted everyone with big hugs, making sure all had a great time. Megan, from the Pie-o-neer café, another organizer of the event, played in the band.

Back at Toaster House once again, we ate RockStar's Birthday pie and ice cream and exchanged hiker stories. The *official* CDT bypasses Pie Town. If you hike or drive in that part of New Mexico, don't miss Pie Town. It was an iconic stop.

Company on El Malpais

Now I had company. Sparky drove us out to Thomas Ranch, and RockStar and I hiked north under gray and cloudy skies, not a bad thing, as there would have been no shade walking that road under a blazing sun. The miles went by companionably as we talked. Finding our water cache, we loaded up, attached the empty plastic jugs to our packs and went on, slowly. Water was heavy. Although not in any particular hurry, we covered a sufficient number of miles before 5:00. RockStar dealt with a leaking platypus (water bladder) and wet sleeping bag, but the dry air of Central New Mexico took care of wetness.

That night it rained. Walking on New Mexico mud made hiking shoes into platforms shoes, the mud very sticky as it adhered to the bottom of our shoes, more with each step, until we were elevated an inch or two. We staggered on appearing and disappearing platform shoes as mud fell off in random chunks. We liked the coolness of the day, even if we didn't like the mud.

My advance planning and preset water caches made the central section of New Mexico doable for us, even though we couldn't go the pace or cover the miles of thru hikers. We found our second water cache slightly chewed on by some critter, but more than enough water was in un-chewed jugs.

As we camped that night, people in a passing car, complete strangers to us, gave us slices of banana bread. We wondered if they'd seen us at the spaghetti dinner in Pie Town.

We decided to go for the Rim Trail before La Ventana Arch as it looked so nicely maintained at the trailhead. It *was* very nice, with views out over miles and miles of black lava fields. We walked near the edge of yellow, white, red, and tan cliffs and saw a golden eagle before the nice trail ended at a viewpoint of a big arched window of rock below us, La Ventana Arch.

Then came the descent from you-know-where on very steep, unmaintained trail of loose rock. Small cairns marked the way, and sometimes we saw them. Between my knee replacement and RockStar's extra pounds on pack and body stressing her ankles and balance, we made VERY slow going. Finally reaching the bottom, we found we were both still in one piece, although extremely tired. Then I discovered I had a three-inch-long barbed cactus needle stuck in the back of my hand. I hadn't even noticed it while I had been sliding down the crumbly hillside. After a lot of wiggling around, the cactus gift was removed, and I was none the worse for wear. I put put antibiotic cream and a Band-Aid on the puncture site.

Walking two more miles on pavement to Mumm's water cache, we retrieved our previously placed bear cans containing food and loaded up with water. Again, the preplanning and preplacing of needed food and water made the section possible for us. Totally exhausted, we set up a very late camp. It felt good to lie down.

The next day was El Malpais, the badlands, a rough walk on lava fields, both aha and pahoehoe (two different types of lava). The lava fields in Oregon had been rough on hiking pole tips, but at least there had been trail. On the Zuni Acoma Trail through El Malpais there were cairns to follow, but no real trail tread. Some of the cairns had been in place for 700 years.

The Wolf guidebook calls this section a "bothersome walk." We made slow going but found it interesting. Many 10-15 foot ups and downs added together made legs and feet tired, and uneven lava underfoot made us slow.

Thru hikers passed us flitting lightly over the lava: Dane, Jelly Bean, Bamboo Bob, Why Wait, and Sycamore. We were happy to see Jelly Bean, our friend from 2008 and 2009 on the PCT. I was amazed how many hikers I saw, twice as many on the short trail from Pie Town through Malpais as I'd seen the year before on more than 500 miles in New Mexico.

Emerging from El Malpais, we found our water cache and staggered under full water load to our camp. After taking a bandana bath in a cupful of water, I put on a clean bra, and we both enjoyed being horizontal again.

The next morning was cold, 31 degrees, as we started our walk through Bonita Canyon. We found a Horney Toad beside the trail and saw five antelope from a distance. At our last water cache, we had so much we had to dump some, not leaving it for another thirsty hiker as we had to walk the empty plastic jugs back to a trashcan. We camped very early, and my feet and knee were quite happy about the early part.

The day into Grants was a pleasant walk listening to trilling birds and enjoying rock formations along the canyon wall. I tried to teach drivers to slow down as they passed us, so we wouldn't eat dust thrown up from their tires. Some drivers were very considerate; others not so much. Hand motions didn't seem to carry much influence from someone not wearing highway- worker orange.

At the stoplight in Grants, driving by in a car, Jelly Bean and other hikers hollered "Hey Hiker Trash" in salutation. She and Problem Bear came back to McDonalds to talk with us as we ate. While RockStar stayed at McDonalds with our packs talking to Problem Bear, I walked 3.5 miles through town to Mumm's and my car.

Then we drove to five miles below Cuba for the other miles I'd skipped in 2012. RockStar dropped me off, and I had a nice five-mile walk without a pack to finish off New Mexico. One good-sized state of the Continental Divide Trail was done.

North to Wyoming

Heading north to Colorado, we played tourist, stopping at Mesa Verde. About 30 to 35,000 ancient Puebloans lived there in 1200/1300AD, far more than in the surrounding area today. Two young women of the Acoma tribe were in my tour group. I thanked them, their tribe, and their ancestors for allowing hikers to walk the lava fields on the Acoma-Zuni trail through the lava beds of El Malpais. It seemed like the right thing to do.

We stayed with my Girl Scout friend and her husband in Durango, stopped for lunch with two of RockStar's friends in Grand Junction, and pulled into Rawlins, Wyoming. The next day we placed three water caches in the Great Basin of Wyoming on the way to Pinedale to meet our friend, Tailwinds, another 2008 PCT hiker.

Tailwinds was a wonderful trail angel. She fed us far more than we could eat, and the next day drove us all the way to the south of the state past Rawlins to Smiley Meadows, with a stop at Farson for ice cream. The little store in Farson had the biggest scoops of delicious ice cream I have ever eaten. If you ever drive past Farson, Wyoming, you *have* to stop for the ice cream.

As we drove south of Rawlins, the country looked greener, and snowbanks still lingered on the ridges we passed. Black storm clouds provided dramatic photos as Tailwinds said good-bye. She had a long way to drive back home, but she had a hard time leaving us, enviously watching us walk down the road.

Chapter 38 May 15, 2013

The Great Divide Basin

Walking the dirt track leaving the road, we watched the sky to the west and north.

Lightning spit from black clouds. When our luck at avoiding the storm seemed to be running out, we quickly put up our tents and dived in as rain and wind hit. After the storm passed, snuggled in for the night on not entirely level ground, we listened to coyotes, songbirds, and an occasional frog.

In the morning as we hiked, we saw snowy tops of mountains farther away and ridges of high plateaus holding lingering snow near at hand. Antelope were our main entertainment, but there were flowers, too—blues, yellows, and whites against the browns and dusty green of ground and sagebrush.

Fording the North Fork of Savory Creek, we watered up. At our lunch stop we dried our sleeping bags and tents. In the afternoon black clouds blew north of us, and we started getting light rain around 4:00. I thought it would blow by, but RockStar was a more cautious hiker, and we stopped at a flat spot beside the dirt road and put up our tents.

The next couple days included some gravel-road walking that was hard on my feet. But we also added to our flower sightings: arrow leaf balsam root, paintbrush, very small yellow daisies, purple vetch (loco weed), white vetch, yellow pea, and tiny white forget-me-nots. Antelopes constantly entertained us, their white butts bouncing over the sagebrush hills, looking like some wild sort of Pacman game. We loved the antelope.

After passing four reservoirs with increasing alkali patches and sour smell, we were glad to find our water cache at Little Sage Reservoir. The official CDT, shortly after Little Sage, routed us cross-country paralleling the highway. There was no trail tread, but there were signs warning us to stay on a 30-foot easement. Cross-country travel didn't always have that degree of accuracy, but we did our best.

Thunderstorms hitting us, soon we were walking on platform shoes formed of the stickiest mud I'd ever seen. The highway would have been much preferable and seemed to be going the same direction. As we trudged through the sagebrush and assorted gullies over mud, large black clouds bore down on us. We still had half a mile to the next crossroad, but it was time to stop.

Hurriedly selecting a spot, we threw up tents in about three minutes, diving in just as the storm hit with rain, high winds, and one loud peal of thunder.

In the morning it showered three times while we packed up inside the tents, not leaving our shelter with alacrity. Mercifully, the rain stopped while we took the tents down, mud even stickier than the night before. Within three steps we had platform shoes that also stuck out two inches wider than our shoes. The road we soon reached was also mud, giving me, not platform shoes but three-inch high heels. I don't wear high heels. I didn't like high heels on my hiking shoes either.

Eventually that road met a slightly better road with firmer, less sticky tread. When our route went steeply up the last Mesa, we chose the gravel road instead, carrying us out to highway 71. It didn't seem wise to be lightning attractants sticking up on the rim of the Mesa into all those black clouds—even if it had a prettier view. So we road walked the last six miles into Rawlins.

Happy to be out of the wind and off our feet at our motel, in short order we were clean, had clothes laundered, and were eating delivered pizza while watching TV, as the rain poured down in the parking lot outside. We took a zero day in Rawlins.

The day out of Rawlins was a walk over what first, second, and third glances might have called a lot of nothing but sagebrush. But it turned out to be a more interesting day than we'd anticipated.

The old dirt road, which was our trail, had some very beautiful rocks underfoot, so we rock hounded our way along the road/trail picking up small red, purple, pink, and mustard-colored rocks. This made our forward progress even slower. RockStar and I both liked rocks, and I was careful to pick up only little ones, so I didn't add much weight. Later, I learned much of the rock was Chert, used by Native Americans for arrow points,

The Ferris Mountains in the distance were white with the snow dropped in the high country in the earlier storm. Antelope and flowers entertained us. But the exciting moment was coming around the corner of a hill to see wild horses. They caught our scent, or perhaps our view, and ran away. Nice day for a pile of sagebrush.

The Great Divide Basin is a rather large chunk of Wyoming with no water outlet to any ocean. What rain or snow falls, stays within the basin, disappearing in the ground or evaporating in dry desert air. This high desert may look like a barren place to humans, but critters including pronghorn (commonly, if incorrectly, called antelope), mule deer, feral horses, and occasionally elk call it their home. Technically the Great Divide Basin extends even further south than our starting point at Smiley Meadows, but it was the second day out of Rawlins when we really *felt* like we were in the Great Basin.

Traveling cross-country, we looked for cairns or Carsonite Posts— thin, six-inch-wide strips stuck in cairns or ground. Quite a few posts were missing or had been knocked over by wind or critters, so it was nice to have Bear Creek waypoints on GPS.

Passing scenic Red Hill in an area called the Red Desert, RockStar spotted a hollowed-out nest in the ground with three greyish eggs a little smaller than robin's eggs. We looked at them but didn't touch, hoping mama bird would return to care for her eggs.

Trail leaving the highway was well marked, but we immediately had to roll under a fence and confront a multiplicity of arroyos (gullies) above the flat basin. We luckily chose the correct arroyo to descend and then just followed our route, a straight line extending as far as we could see across high desert sage.

It was hot, and we were glad we had chosen to walk this section in early spring. Various animal bones along the track indicated a harsh environment. The snow on Ferris Mountains, which we'd seen the day before, was now melted and gone.

Besides many antelope even on our dry basin crossing, there were flowers: lavender fleabane and a nice stand of yellow peas a couple miles from Bull Spring, another solar well. We set up our tents partially sheltered from persistent desert wind, and it was so nice to have abundant water that I filled my Ziploc and had a bath, and we both did some wash.

Alas, wind shifting, the sage didn't protect us from the wind as we had hoped. By evening I suggested to RockStar that there was a more protected spot tucked in the taller sage that would be big enough for both tents. She wasn't interested in moving as she was eating her dinner and relaxing. I hoped the wind would die down at dark, another false hope. About 11:00, after getting no sleep and listening to the wind try to tear down our tents, she asked if I thought we could move the tents in the dark. Yep. So we did.

By headlamp, we threw heavy stuff like water in packs and zipped loose or light stuff into the tents. Carefully pulling out tent stakes, we carried each tent one at a time, quickly erecting each one in the new spot protected by high sage bushes. We did get some wind, but nothing like the gale that had been hitting us before, and we promptly went to sleep. Thank you, tall sage.

The next day was another walk through a sea of sagebrush on a very straight double track dirt road. Imagine looking as far as you can see down a double line of dirt to the far horizon, walking to that spot and seeing the same thing. Repeat endless times.

The other constant besides the double lines of dirt through the gray-green sage was the wind. Yet even in the sea of sagebrush there were flowers, bright patches of purple vetch, yellow peas, paintbrush and sulfur flower.

As we neared the road to the last BLM (Bureau of Land Management) solar well (1 mile off trail), a truck came up behind us on the desert track, and we didn't even hear it until he beeped his horn because the wind was loudly roaring in our ears.

The driver was checking on the solar pump providing water for wild ponies. We passed numerous very large piles of horse poop. Did you know wild horses poop together in massive piles all together? Funny, both meanings of the word.

So what was our reward for trudging on endless roads through the sagebrush? Lots and lots of antelope and then wild horses. We saw too many antelope to count, and, more exciting, we saw seven or eight bands of wild horses, some with foals. Sorrels, bays, blacks, whites, and pintos looked down at us from nearby ridges. Wild horses running were especially beautiful, the epitome of freedom.

Finally topping the ridge we had walked toward for miles, we started down the other side, and my left knee decided to hurt at every step. I was worried, but after two miles of limping down the road, it just as suddenly and inexplicably stopped hurting. Go figure. It was swollen when we stopped and would only bend about 90 degrees. I hoped a good night's rest would fix it.

The wind was too strong to bother with tents, so we cowboy camped at the reservoir after getting water from the outlet. I liked cowboy camping, but I'd seen one tick, and RockStar had seen several, making us nervous not to be in our mosquito-net enclosed tents. Still, the blue water in the reservoir was pretty, even with no trees in sight, and there were interesting water birds with black-and-white markings on their breasts on the water. Cows could be heard lowing in the near distance, and the moon was full and beautiful as dusk fell, and we slept.

"Did you see us? Weren't we beautiful? Weren't you impressed?"

We had a cold start when the sun rose, and the temperature was 32. The wind, which had died down in the night, picked up again to add wind chill as we trudged down more dirt track roads over more hills and valleys of sage. We watched the antelope watching us.

The fantastic parts of the day were two bands of wild horses. Instead of running away from us as others had, they ran towards us and past us. The first band made at least three passes, dominance behavior that seemed to us as if they were showing off. Panting and heaving from their run, they finally stopped near us, as if to say, "Did you see us? Weren't we beautiful?

Weren't you impressed?" Yes, yes, and yes.

The second band of 10 or so beautiful horses included many colors: white, black, grey, pintos, a white and gray pinto, sorrel, bay, and a reddish chocolate brown. Exhibiting the same behavior as the first band, though not quite as close, perhaps because foals were in this group, they passed us twice. RockStar took great video of both groups as well as still shots.

As the last band of horses galloped off, we saw Tailwinds drive up to our prearranged meeting place, and we walked to her car. Sitting inside out of the wind, Tailwinds fed us chicken, watermelon, and spinach salad till we were stuffed. Then she made the comment that if it had been stormy, she would have taken us to Lander or Riverton for the night. Since it was so windy, it was still a good idea. Would we like to go?

How could two dirty, tired hikers turn that down? So Tailwinds drove us across half of Wyoming and we found ourselves in an unplanned motel in Riverton, clean, fed, and on real beds. I iced my knee, and RockStar teased a tick off the back of my leg.

Tick City and Deafening Wind

Tailwinds drove us back to the trail in the morning, and we started hiking just a little before 8:00. Our packs were heavy with five day's food and two day's water. Four miles in, we discovered a lovely spring, so I drank extra water and filled up the load again.

As we climbed out of the Basin into Crook's Mountains, we saw many flowers, white phlox, small yellow daisies, balsam root, pretty cinquefoil, purple vetch, tiny, desert primrose, golden draba, and tiny white daisies. We also had more interesting terrain, rocks and TREES.

After days of nothing higher than sagebrush, trees were a welcome sight. RockStar said it was more interesting to follow roads with squiggles than perfectly straight roads.

Antelope and a few wild horses were too far away to be interested in us. Shooting stars looked incongruous among the sage along with bistort, a little white-fringed star, and buttercups. As we descended to Haypress we saw lupine, swelling buds of iris and budding onion.

Stopping early, both of us contentedly drifted off to sleep before it even got dark.

After our lovely campsite warmed by the rising sun, we left trees behind, and spent the day with vast views of sagebrush rippling in the wind like the waves of the sea. Looking north, we could see the white, snowcapped Wind River Range.

Taking a break looking at sheared sheep on a hill, we said *hello* to Julio, a sheepherder from Peru. I tried to converse in my fractured high school Spanish, but this time I couldn't shake the words loose from the back file in my brain.

Walking through tick city, RockStar and I each pulled one off skin having a nibble and flicked off and stomped others, who were crawling on our clothes. Where there were cows, there were ticks. And there were cows.

Though happy to reach our water cache, my replacement knee complained bitterly at the load of water. I limped down the trail another three miles before we finally found a spot to put our tents, not easy in seas of sagebrush. We hoped we didn't have any ticks in the tents with us.

Packing up in the morning, we traveled over more billowing seas of sagebrush. It was fairly uninteresting. Black and brown cows just didn't have the same *cachet* as antelope and wild horses.

An energy draining, strong wind, headwind or from the side, blew all day long. RockStar put on her tunes and her earbuds, and I sang Girl Scout songs in my head while the wind drowned out conversation, beating on our ears, bodies, and psyches.

Concrete posts told us we were now on the historic California and Oregon Trails. The Wind River Range was definitely closer, its snow-covered peaks a magnetic beacon drawing us forward. Making camp in a grassy meadow mostly out of the wind, RockStar found another tick crawling on her. I squished it with tweezers.

We saw more traffic as we neared the Sweetwater River. After the arid terrain we had traversed, the Sweetwater looked like a huge amount of water. While eating lunch at a corral with a CDT information kiosk, we watched a band of dark clouds and lightning pass north of us.

Phlox and shooting stars grew thickly by the river, perfuming the air and iris bloomed a pale lavender blue. There was moose poop at Sweetwater, too, animals changing with habitat change.

Retrieving our water cache, we saw no reason to stumble cross-country through tick- infested sage with the nearby road running parallel to our route. We could see the Wind River Range clearly now when storms or low hills didn't obscure it.

Finding a rare sheltered spot in shining sun, we stopped for the night. Shortly after 6:00 a lightning storm hit, but we were snugged in, had dinner already eaten, and were as prepared as we could be as thunder boomed over our heads.

Awakening to gray skies, the wind already blew cold, and my fingers felt frozen by the time we were packed. Warned by a hiker journal about the large numbers of ticks, we again chose the road instead of sagebrush. I walked fast, trying to get warm in the blasting cold wind; RockStar began more slowly with smaller steps. The wind hit us both, a headwind all day, no matter which direction the road turned. I wore a hat, a headband and my rain-gear hood, but the wind was still deafening. We couldn't hear cars or talk unless we were yelling face-to-face. We were sick and tired of the wind, but it didn't care about our feelings and blew even more ferociously.

The road, however, was smooth and gradual as we road walked to South Pass City. The rain showers missed us. We liked the mines outside South Pass City and the historical video we watched while eating lunch inside the old dance hall out of the wind.

Somewhat reluctantly, we prepared for our last 2.8 miles to the highway. We could see an approaching storm and knew our luck was running out. We were going to get very wet. But as we stood taking pictures of the Continental Divide Trail information board, a car drove up behind us, and we were happily stunned to see Tailwinds. Hooray.

Taking the easier option, we ended our hike at South Pass City instead of facing the battering wind and rain on the last 2.8 miles to the highway. It wasn't a tough choice. Tailwinds drove us to her home by way of Farson, and we had another ice cream cone.

Finishing New Mexico and adding the Great Divide Basin for a spring hike added 309 miles to my total for the CDT before RockStar and I headed north to the Tetons and Yellowstone to play tourists. Yellowstone (the hiker) met us for a day of personal touring, Yellowstone (The National Park) was her office. Cool beans. To fly home RockStar left me at Jackson, and I drove to mine. Our spring hike and touring was over, and it was time to plan the next hike.

Chapter 39 August 2013 CDT

Colorado - Hikers Four

Before driving to Colorado, I had a lovely visit when my daughter's family drove across the country to Washington, a whirlwind of a week with five children eight and under. There were trips to beaches and playgrounds and taking William, Sara's oldest, to the archery range with my son and his two kids. All played in Grandma's backyard and picked Grandma's veggies. We had great fun and it was a bit of a zoo. The day before leaving, everyone was all together, and there were 12 for dinner. I loved it. I loved being Grandma. Unfortunately, perhaps from my grandchildren, I came down with a nasty head cold the day before leaving for Colorado.

Happens.

It took three days of driving to set up two cars and connect assorted people, who would be hiking in Colorado: RockStar, Grapevine, Trew, and me. Grapevine's husband David would be trail support for the first week. He decided his trail moniker should be Trucker 1. Eventually we all piled into David's truck, and our group was finally assembled from the far corners of Arizona, California, and Washington.

Driving to the end of a road near the Colorado/Wyoming border a quarter-mile from the trail, four hikers walked a short way in to set up our tents as Trucker 1 drove away. Trew (a hiker from Arizona) hiked a bit farther along the trail, so the ladies would have privacy, and so would he.

On the CDT by 7:00 in the morning, we ladies were all moving slowly; Trew could have done the distance twice to our once. There were many flowers this first day, and all were lovely. We barely made out rugged peaks east of us though smoky haze.

On the last descent of the day, Grapevine fell and gashed her elbow, ambushed by loose rocks on a steeply descending road. We cleaned it up, treating with antibiotic cream and Band- Aids. Trew also fell on that descent, and due to our slow speed, we barely made our destination before dark.

Starting early the next morning, we listened to elk bugle and coyotes howl as we walked in a very lovely meadow with large swaths of white pearly everlasting. Each descent from valley to valley contained a few treacherous spots, but no one fell.

The last two miles were very hot as the trail went through old burn areas with no shade cover. Hiking in heat was never my favorite thing to do, and I was glad to see Trucker 1's white truck. Trucker 1 drove us to the campground, and soon four hikers' resupply boxes and miscellaneous gear was disgorged from truck, tents were erected, and food sorting commenced. Trucker 1 also brought tasty salads and fruit. Good trail angel.

The next day was all climbing, hot in the afternoon even in relatively shaded forest.

Grapevine said I should use the word brutal to describe the hike in my journal, but I told her I was saving the word for another day.

We passed several streams, a couple lakes, and a few ponds, though there was no water at our 10,700-foot campsite, which was tucked into a small stand of trees in a beautiful meadow. Lost Ranger Peak was a short distance away awaiting the morrow's climb.

Grapevine and I summited Lost Ranger Peak one rest step at a time. (A rest step is a hiking or mountain climbing pace in which a brief rest is taken at each step, a little like stuttering with your feet.) The altitude was combining with my cold to make breathing going uphill difficult, so I took a Diamox. It was still hard to go uphill, but I seemed to breathe more easily even when panting. While we were resting and snacking on top, we saw three bighorn ewes.

Walking through high country, we saw many lakes, ponds, and great views of mountains all around us, nearby and far away. King's crown and white gentian were flowers of the day.

Mountain bluebirds darted by, and I saw three eagles in the sky as I lagged behind the others to take flower pictures.

A group of five guys and an equal number of dogs passed us,

heading out for a week. Not long before we reached our campsite, we passed a fairly large group with llamas. The campers were smart enough to be settled into tents when we were still walking.

It was beautiful country. But the last mile and a half the regular afternoon thunderstorms on the Continental Divide brought us thunder, lightning, rain, and hail. Nothing like a thunderstorm at high altitude to get your adrenaline to speed you down the trail.

Grapevine and I huddled together under trees to avoid the hail. As we peered out at hail covering the ground in a blanket of white, she remarked how beautiful it was. The two of us tented fairly far from the others in order to find level ground without hail, perched above a lake. We saw a lovely rainbow. Sunset brought more lovely colors, and we could see over the plain to the east as lights in distant habitations turned on. It was a cold night with ice on the ground, wetness all around, and a breeze, but we were tucked into the tent, dry and warm.

The next day we walked through pretty scenery. RockStar powered up a hill ahead of us, and we didn't see her again until Fishhook Lake. Trew had lunch with Grapevine and me, and he and Grapevine walked and talked together for a few miles. We passed lovely lakes. Trew spending an hour simply sitting and looking at peaceful Lake Elmo.

Not long before we reached our campsite, I recognized the orange shirt and unique hat from Bolivia on a hiker coming up the trail. I'd met Mike north of Wolf Creek Pass the year before.

Always fun to meet a hiker seen in previous years.

Grapevine and I sang Holden Evening Prayer for her last night on the trail. She said she wanted to get up at 5:00 to hike out but RockStar and I talked her into 5:30. Very funny as the day before she'd expressed amazement at our 5:30 rise time.

Dumont Lake, blue water surrounded with fields of yellow daisies, was the scenic highlight of our day into Steamboat Springs. We met several bikers (bicycle) on the trail. All were very friendly and very excited about the big bike race the next day, the USA Pro Challenge ending a stage at Steamboat Springs.

Grapevine hiked the last mile to Highway 40 with one foot in a flip flop due to blisters. Trucker 1 met us and dropped RockStar and Trew at the motel and took me to my parked car. After showers and laundry, I visited a doc for some meds to fight my nasty cold. We all had dinner at Jalisco, a good Mexican restaurant, eating tons and taking the excess back to the motel.

A gap in the CDT required a five-mile walk on Highway 40, which RockStar and I clicked off in the morning. Trew and RockStar watched the finish of the big bike race, while I searched for needed items in stores. The bike race finish line was a couple hundred feet from our motel, and RockStar was so close she could have touched them as they went by. Trew was very excited he'd been able to watch the race. Trucker 1 cooked us all dinner, gluten free and vegetarian to suit everyone's needs and desires. What a gem!

Hearing his dad had taken a fall, Trew decided to go home. His dad was OK, but in his 90s, so Trew was concerned. The change in plans meant he would drive my car to Berthoud Pass to pick up his van and leave my car there instead. Section hiking often involves complicated logistics.

Hanging around one more day, Trew supported one more slack pack. The Belgian and Stag, two thru hikers passing us were in a different league than RockStar and me, but we were happy with ourselves for walking 12 miles in five hours without packs. It was great to have support for slack packing. The four of us all had one last dinner together at a pizza place and ate until stuffed to the gills. I sang a blessing before we parted ways.

RockStar and I would miss our little group. As RockStar said, it took a couple days for our group to get used to one another and jell. Now that we had become a real group, we were sorry to go from four to two. Hiking in a group adds complexity to a hike, each person having different needs and desires, quite different from solo hiking. Each way of hiking has its good points and its drawbacks. Now we would be hikers two.

Hikers Two

Before heading to Berthoud Pass in my car, Trew drove us to the trail. RockStar and I headed up the trail, *up* the operative word most of the day. I stopped frequently as my antibiotic was wreaking havoc on my digestive system even if killing upper respiratory infection bugs. The former wasn't a pleasant addition to the hike, though I surely did like breathing better.

In the afternoon, black clouds, lightning, and thunder hammered all around us. I prayed we would get past our high point of 11,450 feet and into thick trees before the storm hit us. Tucking things in plastic bags or Cuban fiber bags, we put on raincoats.

Over the high point and into the trees, our luck ran out. It rained, hard and for hours.

Standing under a tree while it hailed, we hoped it would blow over. Nope. Didn't.

Eventually we moved on down the old overgrown road in the rain. The trail needed some love. Many good-sized old trees lay over the trail. As Wolf's book said, they kept bicycles off, but it wasn't easy to negotiate over or under them in pouring rain at the end of the day. RockStar wasn't used to so much rain, not having encountered this kind of weather pattern on her PCT thru hike. She had real difficulty getting under some of the blowdowns and came close to a complete meltdown at one spot. I helped her regain calmness.

We were pretty well soaked by the time we found a stopping place at a creek. The rain stopped briefly for pitching tents, which we did in the middle of the trail to find a flat spot. Then it was a race with hypothermia to get wet clothes off and dry clothes on. I was certainly shivering, and RockStar had trouble with a slightly wet sleeping bag. But we did survive and looked forward to being dry again another day.

Finding something mostly dry to wear the next morning was a challenge. My pack was festooned with wet clothes hoping to dry, and my feet sloshed in wet shoes even before we walked in wet grass. A short way down the trail beside a stream, we watered up for the day and headed uphill. As the sun hit the trail I was able to get shorts and shirts dry-ish. Somewhat later, we stopped to dry out sleeping bags and tents.

That all took time. So did going uphill. I could hardly believe how long it was taking us to cover ground. Many little *extra* elevation gains and losses were quite steep, not negotiated quickly. Once I thought we could see Ethel Mountain and Lost Ranger Peak in the distance northwest of us. Sheep Mountain and Parkview rose ahead in the direction we were walking.

Shortly after noon, lightning and thunder began again. Already? It hailed as we stood under trees. Finally reaching Troublesome Pass, we camped quite short of our goal for the day.

The next day we walked around Haystack Mountain, a number of steep ups and downs hidden in contour lines on the map. Continuing to climb the high ridge past Haystack, SOBO thru hikers Chris, Charlie, and Greta zoomed past us. Sigh. Plodding upward at less than half their pace, we eventually came to the top of the ridge for a rather beautiful long walk above timberline with the world stretched around us. Bright blue harebells bloomed in clumps sprinkled among bright white yarrow. Lovely. RockStar said the walk on the ridge was spectacular.

Another 1,000 feet to the top of Parkview and our views increased to 360 degrees.

Wondrous. The small emergency hut on top had no trail register, but numerous people had signed in on the walls, door, and the beams, though we refrained from adding anything.

Then began the descent of horrors. First off, we overshot the CDT and chose one of three other more-defined trails. Coming back as the GPS told us, we saw the first three cairns leaving the nice trail straight down. Then the sorry excuse for a trail disappeared and left us with extremely unstable talus, and later, scree. (Big rocks and little rocks) We could see a couple cairns much farther down, but negotiating the steep slope of unstable rock was a nightmare and took us two hours to go .6 miles. We were not the caliber of hiker as thru hikers.

RockStar fell once. I fell twice. On the second fall I twisted back to face the hill as I fell and didn't stop but kept sliding an extra two feet on my belly, feet first down the steep incline. Then when I tried to stand, I slid another. I had no lasting damage, but since it had started raining before I fell, I was a muddy mess. As we reached a muddy road, the rain stopped, and we slogged the last five miles down to the highway, considerably later than anticipated.

Latecomer, a 2008 hiker and friend of RockStar, was our resupply person at the road and had brought treats. The best treat was that he drove us to Grandby, where we got a room, and I took a shower while he and RockStar went out to eat. I was muddier. We both were very glad to have a welcome, if unplanned, stop in civilization.

RockStar was fed up with the rain and difficult trail. A friend with a car was too much temptation not to accept the opportunity to take a few days off. My friends come along to do some hiking with me, but I was on the CDT to complete it. I went on solo the next day.

Latecomer drove me up to the pass in the morning, while RockStar went back to sleep.

Hiker 1

The trail started out on gently graded uphill through trees, mist rising from wet valleys. One stretch of trail badly degraded by motorcycle use was deeply rutted in granite sand. On another stretch, the trail edge was almost chest high, and I walked on the trail edges instead of the bottom of the V where I couldn't stand.

Making good time going down to Trout Creek, I nibbled on raspberries growing along the trail. Larkspur and monkshood cheered my route. From Trout Creek, the way was up, a gradual grade becoming steep rocky road before the ridgeline. As I strained up the road, a motorcycle roared past me, his backside disappearing up the hill, the only person I saw all day.

The approach to the pass was lovely high forest with a gazillion moose turd piles followed by many rivulets in the high meadow bowl. They combined to make a stream. After eating my dinner, I made my last push to the pass. All day I'd wondered if thunderstorms would stop me, but there was NO rain. Amazing.

Topping the pass at 7:00, the other side was a broad, green high mountain valley under craggy cliff ridges. The Ley map suggested hikers take the cliffs to the right of the pass. That route looked too risky for me, so I declined the suggestion and took the trail to timberline half a mile lower.

Two cow moose noisily munching on willows looked at me, but didn't seem to care that I was taking pictures. They owned the landscape. I was just a visitor. A minute later, I spotted a campsite under trees and stopped. RockStar would be sad she missed the moose, but she wouldn't have appreciated the long day.

In the morning as I looked out over the green valley, I saw a moose on the other side. The hiking day was just a very long downhill slog. Trails were nicely graded with few blowdowns, though occasionally a little rocky. As I neared a highway before veering further down trail, I met a few tourists, day hikers and fishermen. Jeff and 72-year-old Dave passed me headed for some fishing. Yay for septuagenarians.

Rain sprinkled briefly, just enough to wet the umbrella, and I finally dragged into town at 5:00. Not bad for an old lady, but I was completely bushed after a 16-mile day.

I checked into Shadowcliff, a resort perched on a cliff overlooking Grand Lake. Getting to the women's hostel room on the third floor up steep stairs wasn't appreciated at the end of the day. The word garret described the tiny room, which could sleep three women, but I was lucky. They were serving dinner that night, which was unusual.

After my shower I put on the cleanest clothes I had, running shorts, knee-high bed socks, and my long underwear top. I might have looked a bit odd, but the laundry was a half-mile away in town, and I wasn't going anywhere until morning.

I tried to stay awake until 9:00. Couldn't do it. Everything ached, and I welcomed the oblivion of sleep while thunderstorms raged outside. In the morning, Adam, another guest at the hostel, told me the thunderstorms had knocked out all the power to the town of Grand Lake that night. I hadn't noticed.

Though I woke up feeling much better, I needed that zero day. I walked half a mile to have breakfast and do my laundry. RockStar arrived at 4:00, and we caught up on our separate adventures, mine more strenuous than hers. After a lackluster dinner, we consoled ourselves with a stop at an ice cream shop for a cone and chocolates. Hikers have such a tough life.

The next day was very tough, though a slack pack supported by RockStar. The first seven miles were delightful, finished by 10:00. But the last 5.8 miles took until 5:45.

Jackstraws

Walking out of town, a wonderful sunrise reflected in lake water, and a bull moose crossed the road, followed by another. Their coats looked moth-eaten, though they both had nice racks and didn't mind me taking pictures. After that, I had a lovely walk beside the lake. Bright red rose hips contrasted with the greenery, and I sampled raspberries as I walked.

My trail left the lake for Ranger Meadows, and wet grass slapped my feet and legs, quickly soaking shoes, socks, legs, and the bottom of my shorts.

When I came over the ridge, the river cheerily rushed over rocks. Columbine Bay was next, the serenity of the view disturbed only by a few sightseeing boats and later, personal watercraft.

Columbine Bay became Grand Bay, and my trail took me around an inlet to a locked Ranger Cabin with an ominous sign: Caution. Knight Ridge Trail unmaintained. Expect blowdowns. Someone had scrawled *impassable* on the sign. Well, I'd heard about blowdowns on Knight Ridge, but journals I'd read said others had walked through, so off I went. Smarter hikers than I bypassed that side of the lake for a longer walk to avoid the mess I soon encountered.

First there were a few blowdowns, then a really big pile of blowdowns, and then the trail disappeared beneath piles and piles of twisted logs. With the help of my trusty GPS, I figured out the path and before long found traces of trail. I even saw another moose, two deer, two eagles and a couple ospreys.

But the trail became worse. I kept looking at the GPS to figure out where the trail went.

Finally I neared the top of the ridge and saw utter destruction everywhere I looked. Downed trees were a massive pile of jackstraws going every which way, with no sign of trail except for the red line on my GPS.

Very, very slowly, I made my way through the hideous mess, often walking on logs on top of logs on top of logs, praying I wouldn't miss a step, fall, and break something. It was utterly exhausting. Sometimes I would find ten feet of ground (not trail), and then I would get a trapped, claustrophobic feeling confined in a giant playpen. Would I ever get to the other side?

Funny, the sign on the end of the trail said the trail wouldn't be cleared until all the trees fell down, out of concern for the safety of the volunteer trail crew. I had news for them. On top of the ridge and for quite a ways on either side, there were no trees standing.

On the descent from the Ridge, I did find some trail maintenance, for which I was eternally grateful, else I might still be climbing through hideous piles of logs.

RockStar was waiting. A slightly weird campground host had objected to her waiting on the campground road instead of the trailhead, but she was visible as a beacon of hope at the end of the day. It had been a crazy day, from the sublime to the ridiculous, a lovely lakeside soliloquy followed by the truly hideous, toughest slack pack ever. The Mahoosuck Notch seemed easier.

Well, maybe not. I was glad for my bed in the hostel and that I survived to tell the story.

James Peak

The next day the trail was—trail. How refreshing. No disastrous talus and only 6-8 blowdowns in 15 miles. Just trail. Hooray.

Monarch Lake was lovely in the early-morning light, high and low peaks reflected together in the glassy stillness of the water. Continuing around the lake, I steadily chugged up the hill, chatting with a couple older equestrians three times during the day but never getting their names.

The afternoon was more level, a little downhill and a little climb before descending to Devil's Thumb Park. When it started to rain a little, I put up the umbrella and hiked along watching a deer, grateful for the good trail. Nowhere in the park leapt out at me saying, "Camp here." So I consulted the Wolf book and decided to go further, camping at the crossing of Cabin Creek, where I got my water for the next day and had dinner. Not every day on the trail was hard. This one was a lovely walk.

In the morning before I was out of the tent, two hikers went by using headlamps. On my climb to Devil's Thumb Pass, the two young hiker dudes with headlamps came back down.

They'd just gone up to see the sunrise. A little farther along, I met Ed and his dog from Buena Vista. He told me his mother was 76 and had just stopped taking overnight hikes on the trail. Yay for 76-year-old hikers.

Reaching the ridge, the views were spectacular. I could see back to Parkview, but more amazingly, all the central range of high peaks in Colorado along with the towns of Winter Park and Frasier. Amazing. I could also see clouds building in the sky from 10:00 in the morning.

On the way to Rollins Pass, three young hikers passed me, impressed with my age and efforts. Three runners also passed like racehorses in contrast to a walker, who was a slug. Many cars and hikers were at King Lake, very pretty in a rugged bowl that still had a little snow. At the pass were lots of motorbikes, bicyclists, ATVs, and cars, people were out enjoying Labor Day Weekend. Above timberline, I was worried about clouds building and had no privacy to attend to nature's needs, so I just kept going. On the south side of the pass, nicely placed cairns and posts guided the way, though trail tread disappeared. Sheer cliffs dropped to lakes east of the Divide.

A couple of backpackers and a man with two llamas passed me shortly before the rain started. I donned a rain jacket and put up my umbrella as lightning and thunder began. Yikes. Could I trust I wouldn't get hit by lightning, or should I go lower? Where? I chose to descend on a diagonal line about 300 vertical feet to a small clump of trees at the edge of timberline. Judging by the amount of elk poop, elk had liked the sheltered spot, too.

The rain stopped briefly, though my marvelous view informed me more storms were on the way. Putting up my tent and climbing inside,

I was happy to be dry and among trees with just enough water for breakfast and a bottle of Cytomax to last to a water source five miles further up the trail. It would do. Stopping was a good call as it rained for three hours.

At 4:30 am lights in the valley seemed as bright as they had during the night. Having a little trouble breathing in the night, I started myself on another three-day course of Diamox as per doc's orders. I didn't acclimatize to altitude any better at 72 than I had at 71. Wind in the night gave me a dry tent and mostly dry shoes by morning.

Taking the tent down in the dim light of early morning, I saw three bighorn ewes. They didn't stick around for better lighting, but I was happy I'd seen them. Packing up, I headed back to the ridge, my feet soon wet again in the willows and grass. The night before, I'd chosen well, my campsite the only place trees came that close to the ridge. Reaching Roger's Pass, I met Helena and Elenia, who were kind enough to give me a bottle of water to last a few more miles.

Ahead of me was James Peak. *The trail takes me over that?* Yep. So up I went. Not fast, just up. Runners came down followed by day hikers, some of whom had already passed me going up. James Peak, elevation 13,294 feet, had expansive views of mountains stretching out on all sides. Also in plain view across the valley were clouds and rapidly approaching rainstorms.

Some 15-20 hikers stood with me on top of James that Labor Day Weekend, and I quickly took pictures and prepared to descend. We all skedaddled off the mountain. Of course, they skedaddled much faster than I did. Fact—13,294 feet was a very long way above timberline and sheltering trees. I could be hit by lightning in such an exposed place and die. Even more likely, I could die by tripping over my feet running down a mountain. I was an old lady with a knee replacement. I couldn't run without killing myself. So I walked.

Watching speedier hikers disappear over the ridges below, I slowly but steadily followed, and all of us were chased by rumbles and cracks of thunder, some lightning quite close to me. It was a long time before I reached trees. By then, that storm was over as I sat down to lunch and dry out in the now-shining sun.

Descending far down a valley, I begrudged each downward step knowing I had another 1,500 feet to climb up to Bill Moore Lake. Before climbing, I needed water, and just before I reached the creek it rained again. But a passing jeep stopped, and its driver gave me the water I needed. Under my umbrella, I headed on. People in jeeps and SUVs headed home through the mud on the rough, rocky road. They smiled and pointed at the crazy lady trudging through the mud and rain with pink gaiters, a bright-red umbrella, a backpack, and hiking poles.

After another slow slog uphill at the pace of a crippled slug, the rain stopped, and I put the soggy umbrella in its little case hooked to my belt. About a mile and a half from the lake, I saw a bear on the other side of a meadow. Seeing me, he took off down the hill away from me, a nice healthy looking animal with shiny black coat.

Making the lake just after 7:00, I was soaked one final time pushing through high, overgrown drenched willows near the outlet of the creek. A rough jeep road came in from the other side of my campsite, and several parties were camping near the lake, the air heavy with smoke from campfires made with wet wood.

Why should I spend my fast receding energy fighting more wet bushes to dip water from the lake when all those people had water they'd brought in cars? I asked for water, settled into my private copse of trees, ate the dinner I'd hydrated early in the afternoon and went to sleep.

My bladder woke me up shortly after 4:00, a good thing even on a short day as I wanted to get over the next 13,000-foot peak before thunderstorms. I took my first good sunrise picture of the trip as I slogged up the trail in slow motion and climbed Flora Peak, elevation 13,132 feet. The winds were strong all morning, and I wore most of my clothes as well as raingear for a windbreaker.

Admiring the work of trail builders, I climbed through boulder fields, where the trail was easy to follow and often *paved* with large, flat boulders. Views from the top were again spectacular. Much of the central range was visible as well as the ridge I'd traversed, Devil's Thumb, even Parkview seen in the distance. Grays and Torreys peaks were near, and I remembered having climbed Grays twice, 50 years earlier, once taking a classmate nearly to the top, though she was on crutches after an ankle surgery.

Since the wind was still brisk and the downward trail was clear, I descended without taking a break. Finding it much less rocky on the south side, I watched two glorious eagles and a darker large bird. One of the eagles seemed to alternate flying with the stranger with stooping and diving behaviors, aerobatics, dives, and rolls. Glorious.

A number of day hikers ascended as I went down and found a spot in some black, lichen- covered rocks out of the wind. A fine place to eat my last trail bar. It was so lovely sitting in the sun out of the wind gazing at the mountains around me, I could have stayed all day.

As I finally got up for the remainder of the descent, Pat, a mature hiker from the local area, caught up with me, and we chatted on the way down. Reaching the pass, I found RockStar waiting with treats, and we drove down to Winter Park for lunch at McDonalds.

I was tired with the accumulated tiredness of having walked for days. It was all I could do to get my shower, wash my clothes, and lie flat on the bed looking forward to a zero day, taken up, as usual, with a few errands, a lot of lying around, and even more eating.

Alternate Routes and Bobtail Creek

After my day of rest, RockStar headed up Flora Peak for an early morning day hike, and I headed SOBO up the ridge at the pace of a slug. I was no longer the spry young thing I had been in college when I climbed these high peaks 50 years ago. Age does make a difference.

But I still enjoyed the hiking. Contouring around the high ridges and watching clouds build, I saw a half dozen ptarmigan.

As I ended lunch, a few raindrops fell. The CDT was a long ridge walk well above timberline, and I was concerned about making it in daylight under the best of conditions. Now it was already raining and thundering. What to do? I looked at the Ley maps and saw a thunderstorm avoidance route. Yep, that was the trail for me. I just had to make the correct turn.

Luckily, I ran into Walter, a 78-year-old gentleman, who knew the trail junction I needed. In fact, he was going to head down that very trail. We had a lovely time chatting as he told me about the jagged red mountain near us. The *glory hole* was formed in the 1980s when, with no warning, the mountain collapsed inwards. Later in the day from higher up, I could see how the lines of rise from red side and white side would have come together in a peak.

Walter also knew all about the Henderson Mine, a molybdenum mine. (Molybdenum is an element used in steel alloys.) Since the price of molybdenum had tanked, there wasn't a lot of activity around the mine now, but he'd taken a mine tour and told me of the underground city, complete with roads and stoplights.

Walter got in his car at the trailhead, and I headed up the dirt road leading to Jones Pass. I walked well at the lower altitude on the good mountain road with minor car traffic. There I met Giraffe, a NOBO section hiker. Too bad we were going opposite directions as he wanted to talk, and so did I. But clouds were lowering, and, even doing this route, I would be above timberline an hour or two. Giraffe had started at Cumbres Pass on August 4th and had experienced only four days it had not rained.

Just as I'd left trees on the way up, the rain came in earnest. Drat and double drat.

My raincoat and umbrella kept me reasonably dry, and eventually I made it over the pass and down the other side. The wind made my bare hands very cold, but I didn't want to get my gloves soaked and left them stowed in the pack. The hand used to hold the leading edge of the umbrella so it wouldn't blow inside out was freezing.

From Jones Pass I could see back to that arcing line of ridges hidden in clouds. Rain and thunder confirmed the lower route had been the right choice. The view in the other direction revealed the beautiful valley of Bobtail Creek. After descending to the creek, I quickly put up my tent.

I really liked Bobtail Creek. I'd seen no people all day, but about half way up the creek, I saw four wonderful bull moose, good looking animals with nice racks. Observing them before they saw me, the biggest, presumably the oldest and in charge, frisked around dominating the other three. But once distracted by the passing hiker, they all stood still, keeping eyes on me until I passed.

The upper valley had more than one trail, and missing a turn I was misplaced for about an hour. With the help of GPS and quite a lot of work on a steep hillside, I was *found* again. Trails paralleling each other with prominent cairns on both were the problem. A steep ridge between them confused me *and* my GPS before I made it over the correct pass.

It rained around me all day amid distant rumbles of thunder, but only 10 drops fell directly on me. I reached my destination at 4:00, put up the tent, got my water, and took a Ziploc bath from head to toe. In an orgy of cleanliness, I also washed shirt, bra, undies, and socks. They might never dry on a rainy hike, but I made the effort. Then I sat down and ate and ate and ate. I hadn't stopped to eat all day, worrying about thunderstorms, which had not come my way.

The morning dawned with not a cloud in the sky. Unfortunately, my trail sign didn't face my direction, and I walked right by without seeing it. A third of a mile later, sure I'd missed it, I headed back to find the correct trail.

Reaching Ptarmigan Pass, Dillon Reservoir was laid out a few thousand feet below me. By then, of course, there were clouds. Again, it didn't seem prudent to stop for lunch with so much more to walk above timberline. The high point was another couple hundred feet higher than the pass under black and threatening skies.

I descended as fast as an old lady with a replacement knee could go to get to treeline. Then it was a steady slog downhill with a little time out to gnaw some cheese and stuff almonds and chocolates in my mouth on the way down. RockStar met me at the trailhead in her car, and I walked the last mile and a half without a pack.

"Take the trail...Unless you just need a break or the weather sucks."

At the First Inn, people were very apologetic. In spite of contacting them over a month before leaving for the trail and having given the street address for mailing our boxes, mail wasn't delivered to street addresses there. No boxes. No maps. No food. No meds. RockStar had even driven by on Wednesday reminding them we needed our boxes. Arriving early in the day Friday and finding no boxes at the motel, RockStar picked up her box at the Post Office, but couldn't get mine without my ID.

I needed my box from the Post Office, and I was also worried about needing an extra day to complete the section after Twin Lakes. A bike path went to Copper Mountain, and the notes on the Ley map said to "take the trail ... Unless you just need a break or the weather sucks." This year, the weather always sucked. The solution for both problems was to take the bike path.

RockStar could pick me up part way and drive me to the Post Office when it opened at 10:00. Taking the bike path was shorter than the trail, giving us an extra day.

The bike path was lovely. Passing the bright blue water in Dillon Reservoir, there were walkers and LOTS of bikers. I called RockStar when I reached the exit for the Post Office, and she was quickly there, though the trip to the Post Office was fruitless. Either my box was lost in the Post Office, or it had been already sent back to my home address. It was a very good thing I carried extra meds in my resupply box in the car. *The missing box turned up back in Washington almost a year later. Perhaps the Post Office person didn't look hard enough in Colorado.

Back on the bike path, I hooked up Pandora and Judy Collins and other 60s artists accompanied me all day between mountain towns.

Dillon Reservoir had been built after I left Colorado 50+ years ago. I remembered there was some controversy about moving the town of Dillon for its construction. Dillon, Silverthorne, and Frisco, although of older origins, resembled YUPPIEVILLE, mostly in positive ways. Nice bike paths signed and routed me through and between towns and recreational facilities. With people and condos everywhere, it wasn't at all as I'd left it 50 years before.

On Main Street in Frisco, I saw tables and chairs in the shade of the US Bank. No one was using them, so it was a perfect place for me to sit and eat lunch. Past Frisco, Clear Creek had rapids and beaver ponds. The walk reminded me of 60 years before when I and other young children would play in creek water in our underwear. RockStar parked her car at Copper Mountain trailhead and walked 1.5 miles to meet me. After walking back together beside the creek, I dumped even my daypack arrangement in the car and walked free to the correct ski lift to finish the day's walk.

There were, of course, clouds and thunder in the afternoon. It was pouring in sheets when we left Safeway after picking up what we needed, but our hike had been dry. Driving to Breckinridge and the apartment of one of RockStar's friends, we ate a nice roasted chicken dinner, beans and cheesy garlic bread with ice cream and strawberries for dessert.

"We don't need no stinkin' raincoats. We got umbrellas."

After a zero day, Olive drove us back to Copper Mountain. The CDT was contiguous with the Colorado Trail in this section. The CT had better tread and was better marked and better graded. Nice.

We moved up the trail, if not at high speed, at a good, moderate pace for us. RockStar insisted on regular snack and lunch breaks instead of my frantic efforts to outrun thunderstorms.

It started to rain about a mile or so before Searle Pass. On with our raincoats and up with our umbrellas. I'd convinced RockStar to buy an umbrella. I like my friends to have fun on hikes, not be miserable. The short rain was a good equipment test, but we were even happier when the rain stopped. Reaching Searle Pass, we had lunch even though clouds filled the sky. On towards Kokomo Pass, we saw marmots, pikas, ptarmigans, and squirrels. The not-so-wild life included two women hikers and a dog.

We were lucky to get from Searle to Kokomo with no rain. That extremely wet summer for Colorado surely did make everything green, and there were far more flowers than I was expecting for that time of year. Relieved when we descended from Kokomo Pass, RockStar found us a good campsite, beating a big thunderstorm.

It poured at least three separate times in the night. I had trouble with backsplash, and a little water traveled down the elastic tie of the bathtub floor, nothing a couple bandanas couldn't handle. A bathtub floor refers to a clip in tent bottom of Cuban fiber with 3-5 inch lips holding gear dry.

Packing up, we headed out under cloudy skies on a wet morning for a long descent to Eagle River and the remains of Camp Hale, where the troops of the Tenth Mountain Division trained during World War II before going to Italy. We stayed on the trail and walked by old bunkers and the possibly (according to rumor) old shells in the meadow.

The rain in Colorado also seemed to delay the Aspen's color change. By the same time in 2012, I'd seen many more golden leaves than the few visible in 2013. Still, I liked facing mornings in the 40s more than the 30s.

Trudging up the hill out of Camp Hale, we paralleled Highway 24. Chinchilla and Pyrite passed us going SOBO. Later, we passed them as they dried out their tents in a bit of sunshine. We were not the only ones having difficulty with the rain. They, of course, moved twice as fast as we did and hoped the lingering warm weather would get them through the San Juan's before heavy snows.

We saw scat, chipmunks, squirrels, and a muddy worm along with flowers called *butter and eggs* and an unidentified purple starflower. Walking on a well-graded railroad bed, big yellow mushrooms covered the pine forest floor, and we passed the remains of two big coke ovens.

Reaching the highway, I waved my hat at the first car to drive by, and RockStar was embarrassed by my ride-hailing technique. It was effective, though. The car stopped in the middle of the road and the gentleman in the car, who was returning to Colorado Springs from a golf tournament, gave us a ride to the Leadville Hostel.

In the well-organized hostel, we chose the $30 room and washed our bodies and our clothes. Our trip to Safeway and dinner was in a loaner car, very helpful as Leadville was pretty spread out for tired ladies on foot. Dinner was superb at a little restaurant named Quincy's, which served only filet mignon: six-ounce steak, nice salad, baked potato, and bread, meat cooked to perfection, and all for $8.95.

Howard shuttled us to the trailhead in the morning for a slack pack day. The weather was freaky, raising and lowering clouds revealed the peaks and obscured them again. We met a tall young couple from Holland as they passed us heading the same direction on a 16-day trip.

Calling the hostel from the last high point, we said we would be an hour earlier than planned, and we almost made it on time down the steep and rocky descent. Our Netherlands friends, Ann and Peter, were camped at the trailhead, and we hoped to see them again. They walked much faster than we did, but they would take a side trip to climb Mt. Elbert (Colorado's highest mountain) and also take a rest day in Twin Lakes. Howard from the hostel picked us up at the trailhead.

That night we were clean again after only one day on the trail. What luxury.

Starting from the trailhead early the next day, an hour later we hoisted umbrellas for the first shower of many, the rain from a hurricane in Baja California pushing north. Early in our hike we had a Colorado record-breaking wet summer; now we had leftover hurricane.

With all the rain, RockStar was becoming proficient with the umbrella. As an afternoon shower began, and I regretted not putting on my raincoat, she said, "We don't need no stinkin' raincoats. We got umbrellas." I'd made an umbrella convert.

At 4:30, we reached a large campsite, got our water, ate dinner, and were ready to hang the food bag on pre-hung rope when it started raining again and the food bag didn't get hung that night. It rained all night long, and my Hexamid tent, used for 3-4 years, failed me. Everywhere it could leak, it did. We packed up lots of wet stuff. Wet stuff weighs more than dry stuff.

Descending to the Mt. Massive/Mt. Elbert trailhead at Halfmoon Creek, we hollered good morning to Ann and Peter. They later passed us at the high point on the longest climb of the day, and we arranged to have dinner together in Twin Lakes. The double lakes came in view as well as the route up to the high country I would take the next day, an especially beautiful mountain dominating the view.

Arriving at Twin Lakes we checked in, with the usual drill of showers, organizing, and setting tents and sleeping bags to dry. We hung out with Ann and Peter in the afternoon and enjoyed a tasty dinner with their delightful company. Cowboy, a hiker/employee at Twin Lakes, helped me repair my air mattress. Equipment was breaking down. It had been a long hike.

Last Push through High Country

In the morning, I ate the hiker breakfast put out by the Inn and said *good-bye* for a few days to RockStar. She was afraid of being a drowned rat two nights in a row. So was I, but I wanted to finish Colorado more than to stay dry. I walked two miles to the bridge, picked up the CDT on the other side of the lake and headed up a 3,300-foot climb, kind of tough for an old lady. As usual, other hikers passed me. The weather held clear all the way to the top of Hope Pass before a squall hit. In spite of the rain, the view of the Collegiate Peaks was glorious. It reminded me again of my 20s, and how I'd loved to climb the big peaks. After donning raincoat and taking a few pictures, I headed down the other side, a long way down.

Two young women, a couple, and a single guy all passed me going up as I descended.

When I reached the road I found quite a few cars, a lot of day hikers, and numerous campsites along the road. After getting water, I picked one. And it wasn't raining.

As I finished packing in the morning, a group of five passed me to climb Mt. Huron, one of the plentiful nearby 14ers. The sun was shining, if not on me, on the mountains around me.

Aspen made color spots on the slopes, and I moved up the mountain reasonably well.

The climbers turned left for Mt. Huron, and I turned right for Lake Ann, climbing slowly to the lake and the ridge beyond it. My body could tell this was the second hard day in a row, but it gladdened my heart to see towering peaks all around me and Lake Ann below. Less than 100 feet from the top of the ridge, it began to rain, thunder growling from the other side. NO. Raincoat and umbrella went up. Rain paying no attention to my plea, there was nothing to do but go forward toward the thunder. Trees were a long way down no matter what I did, and I didn't want to go backwards.

There were no views from the ridge that day; I was in a cloud of fog and pelted by hail. I could barely make out a huge valley, ice pellets pounding my legs turning my tan bright pink, and the wind didn't let the umbrella do a very efficient job. Oh well.

Making my way down switchbacks, I reached trees but was too cold and wet to stop for lunch. I grabbed a Snickers bar, almonds, and jerky to eat as I walked.

Every time I headed uphill I did my imitation of a crippled slug. Bad imitation. A slug would have been faster. And it rained. All afternoon it was either raining, had just stopped, or was about to begin. My umbrella did, well but my gloves were soaked.

Going by Illinois Creek I saw a cow moose peering at me over the willows. At Prospector Gulch it started raining again. Rats. I was lucky to find a spot just big enough for my tent, mostly on dry duff under a tree. I was bushed on my last night before Cottonwood Pass Road. I was running out of steam, but I was dry and warm, or would be warm when my cold hands warmed up.

I had a hard time getting up in the morning. I walked downhill to Texas Creek, walked to the bridge, had a short climb, and I was done.

Chuck met me in 10 minutes, driving me to my car, which had been parked in his yard for weeks. I drove to Olive's in Breckinridge to gather stuff left there and then to Denver for a visit with the sister of my heart. It was lovely to lie abed in the morning. Eventually I moved.

My God-sis in Denver was at least 10 years older than I was. So, at least in her 80s, maybe more. She and her neighbor, about the same vintage, were politically active and socially concerned activists. Scrappy elderly ladies. I loved my visit. I had a very good time being the youngest of three old opinionated ladies. We could all take on any issue and enthusiastically and joyfully argue our opinions.

The rain in Colorado in 2013 wasn't a problem just for *me*. There were record rains and destructive floods causing loss of life and property. Though I didn't like so much rain, I was from Washington and knew how to hike with an umbrella.

Last Stitch in Trail for 2013

I wasn't quite finished with the CDT for the year. I had now hiked all of Colorado SOBO from 1 mile below the Wyoming border. I had hiked Wyoming's Great Divide Basin from Smiley Meadows to South Pass City. I needed to stitch those two pieces together.

Leaving Denver, I drove to Steamboat Springs to meet RockStar. My friend had been touring other places while I'd been hiking and visiting. Amazed she stuck around to give me trail support even though she didn't hike much in Colorado, she was in for this last part.

Setting a car where we would finish, we drove to Rawlins. It was WONDERFUL to have a beautiful sunny day and exciting to see antelope again after all of Colorado's rain. We gave five stars to Rose's Lariat, a Mexican restaurant in Rawlins, a tiny place with excellent food and the most incredibly light and tasty strawberry sopapillas I'd ever eaten.

A bit of pre-adventure began the day. Highway 71 south of Rawlins had a sign announcing possible road closure. What? We can't get to our trail? We drove on and hoped for the best.

About 20 miles down the road, we ran into construction. The flagger let us by, cautioning us to drive slowly. The road definitely required us to go slow. It was completely torn up in preparation for more paving. Reaching our destination, we parked the car and started up the hill.

Most of the trail was on a ridge with lovely views, north, south, east and west, and the temperature was comfortably between 60 and 70. The trail had cairns built of abundant quartz in the area, some milky white, some a crystalline variety looking like fractured ice, some rose- colored and some a coral-orange.

Two cowboys looking for their cows passed us at lunch, cows and chipmunks our wildlife. An alternate road paralleling the trail sped our walk and took us by log cabin ruins, the smaller cabin, mostly intact though roofless, added interest to our walk.

Tired and ready to stop by the time we hit the creek, even without a good camping spot we plopped down on top of greenery hoping for another sunny day to dry whatever would need drying in the morning from night time condensation. It was dark by 7:30.

We heard quite a few elk, probably as close as a couple hundred yards away, but we couldn't see them through the trees and bushes. Even though we camped near the stream and on all sorts of green, we were again in the land of dry Wyoming and had no condensation problems.

The ridge we walked on felt like it would never end, the Continental Divide Trail running right along the Divide. We could again see Hahn's Peak, which we'd viewed at the beginning of our hike in August, the best view from the top of Bridger Peak. The trail bypassed the peak by 25-50 feet, but even I could make a peak that close to the trail.

The wind was ferocious at times, cold one moment and hot another, making it hard to tell what to wear as we hiked on an old jeep road. We saw three ATVs, a dune buggy from Bridger Peak, and two people leaving their summer cabin traveling by ATV. They told us it was supposed to snow the next day. We hoped they were wrong.

Someone had left water for CDT hikers near a trailhead, and we took a little as insurance.

The short half-mile on the highway was brutal with the wind; blasts tried to pick me up and throw me into a car lane! Fortunately cars were sparse. Reaching our destination by 5:30, we found water and places for our tents.

Although it rained a little in the night, the tents were almost dry when packed, the sky clear and the trail gradual in ascents and descents. Through lovely meadows edged with contrasting dark green trees, we caught views to Bridger Peak in the north and Hahn's Peak in the south, and felt gratified to see Hahn's come closer as Bridger receded.

A few flowers, a bright paintbrush, two kinds of yellow daisy, a scraggly lupine and a few pearly everlasting were making a last gasp before supposedly coming snow. The wind was cold and sometimes fierce. As we watched dark clouds approaching, accompanied by rolling thunder, our lunch was cut short. We hastened to prepare for what was coming but weren't quite fast enough. Scampering as fast as we could down an open ridge, thunder cracked above us, wind blew hard, and hail and rain pelted us as we ran.

In the shelter of trees, we made some clothing adjustments and went on. For a number of miles the CDT was mostly cross-country travel, marked with posts and cairns. In the fog that came with the rain, it took two sets of eyes to find the next post or cairn. RockStar stood by a post, and I walked out to find the next one staying in sight and hearing. That post located, we would repeat the process. We didn't wish to be lost on the second to last day of trail.

By the time we reached our water source, the rain had ceased. Watering up and feeling sprinkles, we went only a short distance to stop at the first decent campsite.

It rained off and on in the night, occasionally sounding like sleet instead of drops. The tents were wet in the morning, and it was cold, 36 inside the tents. Heading out, our shoes, damp from rain the day before, received fresh doses of cold wetness from greenery and bogs. It stayed in the 30s all morning. The fog, pushed by the ever-present and very cold wind, turned grass and trees white with thick frost of rime ice. We stopped to take pictures of rime-iced trees even though the temperature was literally freezing plus a substantial wind chill.

We were on a mission to reach the car, stopping for pictures but not for lunch. Clouds lifted briefly just enough to see the Hogg Park Reservoir, and by two o'clock the sun came out, though we still had to put up our umbrellas one more time before the border to fend off rain drops and pelletized snow.

The state border was marked with a white quartz line on the trail and a large deposit of mica on the ground. We took our state line pictures and soon found the intersection with the short trail to our dirt road and RockStar's car. Yay. The hike for 2013 was officially over, and Colorado was complete.

However, not all the adventure was done. We still had to get to my car. On the map, it looked like the shortest, most efficient route was highway 71, then Sage Creek Road from highway 70. So we took FR

550 to 70 and drove west to Sage Creek Road, there called Deep Creek Road. After driving in six miles, barricades and road-closure signs stopped us 12 miles or less from my car.

We had to drive all the way back to Encampment, then to Saratoga, inquiring at the police station if the Jack Creek Road was open all the way to 71. It took more than four more hours to reach my car, and RockStar had to drive directly into the setting sun on Jack Creek Road.

At long last, we both drove to Rawlins in the dark through construction. Adventure had piled upon adventure, but all was well, and life was good.

Chapter 40 Fall and Winter 2013-2014

Reciprocity

The winter of 2013 I had surgery. Men of a certain age can have problems with their prostate. Women of a certain age have trouble with their bladders dropping. Human animals don't seem to be built as strongly in that area as we might desire. The surgery should have been a relatively easy one. Unfortunately, a stitch or two was too tight, necessitating another surgery two days later to repair the first. Two surgeries that close together are hard on a body. Nothing *showed* but I found it more difficult to recover my strength from that particular surgery than from others. Nonetheless, I worked at it and did recover. And planned the next year's hikes.

I'd run out of trail on the CDT that could be done in spring. So my first hike in 2014 was the Camino De Santiago in Spain. That's another story only included here to say it prepared my body for hiking on the CDT.

To hike again was the motivation that kept me on track to recover following surgeries. Two long hikes a year were also paying dividends to my body. I was still getting older, of course. And we all someday completely wear out our bodies. Yet in spite of surgeries, even as my body was heavily used walking up and down mountains, I seemed to be staying healthier than other people of similar age, who didn't hike or work so hard at conditioning.

There was a beneficial reciprocity between the conditioning efforts to be ready for long- distance hiking each year and my general wellbeing. Focusing on recovery from surgeries so I could hike kept me active and fit. And the more fit I was going into a surgery, the better I could recover.

I am quite certain hiking is not a panacea to fix old age. But at least for me, long-distance hiking for 2-3 months each year contributed greatly to my general physical health and attitude toward life, even as years went inexorably by, wearing on that same health and attitude. It wasn't a draw between them. Age would win in the end. But I was far healthier as I aged than I'd expected I would be; the trail itself the reason that was so.

Chapter 41 August 5, 2014 CDT

Wyoming - Tailwinds

RockStar was again good to go and both Tailwinds and Yellowstone agreed to give us trail support in their respective areas. Detailed planning allowing for limitations in speed and the distance between resupplies, called for one complicated resupply box delivery, arranged with three people I'd never met before. I picked up RockStar at Boise airport on the drive from Washington to Pinedale, and we were good to go.

Tailwinds drove us 100 miles to South Pass City for a little three-mile walk. Kind of crazy to do 200 extra road miles to walk three miles, but the itinerary didn't work with adding *leftover miles* from the previous year. The crazy beginning also allowed us to stop again at Farson for another spectacular ice cream cone.

Back in Cora after our little walk, Tailwinds and her partner Fred fed us a wonderful dinner and assisted with final organizing. The next morning Tailwinds drove us out to highway 28, and we set off for real. Old dirt roads became sketchy before they turned to trail, and this approach to the Wind River Range was probably only frequented by CDT hikers; more popular approaches were farther north.

Our trail went up to 9,200 feet. We carried bear spray now, which had been recommended for grizzly country extending all the way to the Canadian Border. Packs were heavy with our choice of bear cans, and we were very slow going uphill through bright green meadows, flowers, and more small streams running than I'd expected for August.

Umbrellas were dual purpose. When it wasn't sprinkling, they provided shade from a hot sun. Drying off after a brief 10-minute rain squall, we pitched our tents between blowdowns by the river.

My water purification systems failed. It was a good thing I had a hiking companion. Tears in plastic bags allowed my Steripen to get wet from a leaky Aqua Mira bottle, leaving that bottle empty—which meant a failure of my back-up, system too. Even very experienced hikers can make stupid mistakes like neophytes. RockStar gave me Aqua Mira for my water.

Once I figured out my shoulders were happier with less air in the air mattress, I had a pretty good night's sleep. Even old hikers can learn new things, or perhaps old bodies require new things to be learned.

The foothills of the Wind River Range reminded me of the Southern Sierra, only the rocks were whiter, and—as RockStar reminded me—there were no aspen in the Southern Sierra. The correlation in my mind was based on the dryness of the air, the heat of the sun, and the sense that there were big mountains coming.

Contouring around the Southern Winds, we continually dropped into draws with trickling creeks and climbed up ridges, moving from hills of sagebrush to forests of aspen and pine. A lovely red tail hawk spoke to us disapprovingly from a nearby tree as we shook RockStar's Tyvek ground sheet preparing to pack it after lunch. Later, I startled two large birds, perhaps some kind of goose, although not the familiar black-and-gray Canada Goose, and RockStar was very excited to see her first moose.

Beating the rain, we arrived at our campsite by 4:00. After the storm passed, we got our water, and I took my usual bath in a Ziploc bag, washing underwear and socks in leftover water. I am one of the cleanest long distance hikers I know. I feel better clean, good for my psyche as well as my body.

The morning was uphill, sometimes steeply. NOBO Big Daddy D walked with us and chattered. He'd read my journals so to him I was the *famous* Medicare Pastor, which I thought hilarious. Talking with him helped us move along, though he eventually moved ahead of our slow pace.

Crossing the Continental Divide at 10,200 feet, we had a late lunch. The afternoon climb was in alpine fir by a lovely stream, yellow daisies and pink monkey flower on the banks. On the descent we peeked through trees at Little Sandy Lake, tucked below towering mountains.

Fording two mountain streams, my feet were wet. RockStar changed to crocs for fording, but I was used to just walking through in my hiking shoes.

It rained, sometimes with a hard shower; then it hailed. Setting up our tents in tiny flat spots, RockStar gave me a Platy Patch for a leak in my water bladder. She'd now twice rescued me from equipment failures.

Cirque of Towers

It was hard to get enthused in the morning, everything wet with condensation and cold, we didn't move very fast. The trail was rocky, with a few blowdowns to climb over or around. We were briefly misplaced, forded two rivers, and climbed up and down hills, only making four miles by lunch.

The afternoon had a better trail, and after our second ford we had a great view of the Winds and the route to Cirque of Towers, which was an alternate route famous for its towers loved by rock climbers. RockStar decided she wasn't up to the side trip, but they were on my must-see list.

Tailwinds brought us our resupply boxes that night at Big Sandy, along with dinner: fried chicken, Caesar salad, watermelon, and the biggest chocolate chip cookies I'd ever seen. What more could a hiker want?

Heading off in the morning for an awesomely beautiful but progressively difficult day, I planned to meet RockStar two days later. Just before a beautiful meadow filled with purple asters (fleabane) and yellow daisies, I took my first break. Passing Big Sandy Lake, quite beautiful with towering granite peaks all around, I had lunch after the first steep climb with an amazing view back to the lake and meadow flowers.

Then it was *up*. Seriously up.

Working very hard and taking one slow step at a time, the flowers and towering rock faces kept getting more and more scenic. I needed boosts from other hikers for a couple high steps.

Many people were on the trail, a shock compared to our previous four days of almost complete solitude. Some 30-40 people were coming out of the Cirque and 30-40 more were going into this very popular destination.

Jackass Pass before Lonesome Lake was almost anticlimactic compared to the ridges hiding Fourth Lake and Arrowhead Lake. But from the pass, Lonesome Lake was revealed in the circle of towering peaks. Awesome.

Since it was illegal to camp near the lake, I and several other folks camped in the trees above and a respectful quarter-mile away. A patriotic array of flowers: red paintbrush, blue lupine and white bistort, as well as sheer rock towers, were the view from the door of my tent, clusters of white columbine and elephant heads nearby. (Elephant heads, a high-mountain flower growing in moist areas, has clusters of pink blossoms resembling elephant heads. Really. They look like tiny elephants.)

The challenge of the morning was getting down to the lake from the rock shelf, where I and others had camped. On the other side I wondered if there would be marked trail up to Texas Pass.

No.

At least there was none that I could find. There were cairns now and then, but following them took me obviously off track as they were climber cairns, not hiker cairns.

I struggled with altitude, struggled with no trail, and struggled with climbing over very large boulders, always moving at my familiar pace of a crippled slug. I thought I would never reach Texas Pass. For at least half of the ascent I couldn't even see Texas pass. I had rewards, though. Flowers grew everywhere, and looking back at towering spires of granite all around was stunning. I was in a truly beautiful place.

Eventually I stopped for a break and saw a couple guys ahead of me. Keeping them in sight, I had more assurance of where I was going. Cairns also became more reliable as I climbed higher.

After a view of lakes in a rocky bowl on the other side of the pass, I went down, no easy feat on the steepest trail tread I'd ever seen. (Appalachian rock doesn't count. Rocks aren't trail tread. Park

Mountain doesn't count; it had no tread.) I had to brace my poles forward to avoid sliding down the mountain when I was simply standing on it.

At the lake below the pass I chatted with Hike-aholic, a thru hiker having his lunch break.

After traversing another pile of boulders, I found trail tread past more lakes and had lunch at Shadow Lake. After that, it was just straightforward trail walking gently downhill to reconnect with the CDT.

"It wouldn't be the CDT without fording rivers every day."

RockStar had left her trademark stars drawn in the trail dust, so I knew she was ahead.

After loading water, I forded the river, upped the umbrella and donned my rain gear for a hard shower. I walked up to the campsite RockStar had chosen. We were glad to reconnect. We can both hike solo, but we also enjoy each other's company.

It was unpleasant to put on wet shoes in the morning, but they dried as the day went on. The trail was evenly graded, though rocky, over a high, open plateau near many beautiful lakes through meadows dotted with granite chunks. After meeting a couple of hikers and a group with horses, Bobcat, a NOBO thru hiker, passed us moving much faster than we could.

I managed to keep my feet dry all day, but wouldn't you know it, a mile before our destination we had to cross a very broad creek with no rocks. So I again had wet shoes for the night. We fell asleep listening to the falling of soft rain. (Wet shoes are quite annoying when making a middle-of-the-night potty run. You have to take bed socks off to stick bare feet into wet shoes, and then come back and reverse the process with the addition of having to dry your feet before putting on dry bed socks.)

The weather had been warm so far, in the high 40s when we woke up. By afternoon we were baking under hot sun before clouds gathered to give us shade and rain. Coming to more rugged country, peaceful and quiet, lakes reflected mountains and trees.

Views from 10,848-foot Hat Pass were glorious and flowers were quite showy most of the day. We forded one river, but I managed to find just enough rocks to rock-hop across the last one of the day, and my feet remained dry for the night. Yay.

It rained all night until miraculously stopping right after my alarm went off in the morning. Thank you, God. I hated packing up in the rain. We had two climbs of 500 feet or so in rugged, rocky country, where the views were superb, making climbs worthwhile even if we were slow. We walked by flower shows, picturesque lakes, and spectacular rugged ranges with snow on the peaks.

Creeks and rivers were beautiful, too, although I could have wished for a way to pass besides wading. It didn't seem that it would be the CDT without fording rivers every day. Turning at the trail junction before Pole Creek, we listened to water music as we climbed up and down the trail beside it, rockier than we had anticipated. When we did have to ford Pole Creek's wide and fairly swift current, the water was above our knees.

One of the hikers we met during the day was a priest in habit, muddy to the knees. I'd met priests before on US Wilderness trails, but never in habit. The long slog to Mary's Lake was more uphill than topography lines had suggested and slowed our already slow pace. We did not pass the lake until 4:00.

From the ridge above Eklund Lake, we had a picture-postcard view encompassing the lake and Wind River Mountains. Wow. Spectacular.

After getting water and one last snack break near Eklund, it was nearly 5:00. We pounded down the trail, which was, mercifully, better and mostly downhill, but it was long, and went through a generous amount of mud and standing water. We dubbed it *The Mud Pits of Wyoming*.

I should have remembered when planning this hike, that I was 73-years-old and just couldn't reasonably accomplish what I could have done more easily even a couple years previously. We did make it before dark, barely, arriving at the trailhead at 8:15, with umbrellas up.

Tailwinds had walked out to meet us. What a sweetie. She drove two very tired and scraggly hikers back to Cora for our blissful showers and fed us before we went to our lovely guest rooms and collapsed into heavenly beds.

Our planned rest day in Cora had very little rest in it. We organized the next three food boxes, did the laundry, and made our shopping lists for equipment and food. Then we were off to the Outdoor Store. I was able to replace the Steripen, get Aqua Mira, and a new platypus (water bag), so I was in business again with water purification and storage. We had lunch with a Camino hiker, who had arranged to meet me, peppered us with hiking questions, and brought us chocolate chip cookies and two palm crosses to bless our hike.

After that it was on to the grocery store. I found my one item and made phone calls to find out my daughter had just gone into labor. Back at Tailwind's we had more organizing and packing. Yellowstone (the hiker) and her two friends came by to pick up my car, which she would take to Yellowstone (the Park) after their backpack trip in the Winds.

After a quick shower, RockStar and I took Tailwinds and Fred out to dinner. Well, of course, they drove, as my car was already gone with Yellowstone. We wanted to reciprocate at least a little for all the incredible trail support they gave us. After dinner, still more sorting and packing needed to be done. We didn't do anything we didn't want to do on that busy day. It's just that we had much to accomplish. Rest days are not always restful. Well, we were not walking uphill with packs, so it was more restful than hiking.

News of the day: my daughter had twin boys: 6 pounds and 5 pounds, very healthy weights for twins. Mommy and babies were doing well, and I was Grandma once again, make that twice again.

The Central Winds

Up early, we left Pole Creek Trailhead by 7:00, and Yellowstone and her friends behind by five minutes, quickly passed us. We did pretty well on the trail—for us. After the gradual climb to Eklund Lake, we chose to take the trail to Seneca Lake instead of returning to

Pole Creek and going over Lester Pass. That saved us a few miles and gave us a lower campsite in case of thunderstorms. We passed Barbara, Hobs, and unnamed lakes, the trail gradually becoming rougher.

There were numerous backpackers. We played leapfrog with an older couple, Nonnie from Nowhere and Peter. Nonnie was a 73-year-old Triple Crowner. Let's hear it for us old ladies.

Seneca Lake was a large, granite-sided lake, my favorite lake of the trip. We camped above the north end in a secluded spot, and the view from above our tents was amazing. The water was almost as deep a blue as Crater Lake, and it was surrounded by granite reminiscent of Fontanelle and Aloha Lakes in the Sierra. I wanted to gaze longer, but the desire to be horizontal called me to my sleeping bag.

On a frosty morning, Nonnie and Peter caught up with us, and we all made our way past Little Seneca to the Highline Trail. (CDT) At Island Lake trail junction, we said *good-bye* to Nonnie, Peter, and their cute little dog Anza, an amazing hiker for such a small dog.

The trail was rugged most of the day; incredibly convoluted contour lines on the map depicted rough and rocky bumps over which we hiked up and down, between or around, moving at our regular snail's pace. The terrain, though difficult, was above timberline the whole day, beside numerous high and rocky peaks of the Wind River Range.

There were also numerous lakes of all sizes, named and unnamed and beautiful, rushing mountain creeks. Field after field was filled with flowers of yellow, red, purple, pink, and white. I'd never seen that particular combination of bright red paintbrush and purple asters with a pinkish cast. Elephant heads were a little past their prime but still noticeably fragrant. Bright, hot pink alpine primroses grew in a wet spot at high elevation. All of that color for foreground and rocky peaks for background surrounded sparkling blue lakes. Glorious. We took pictures of ourselves among the flowers at Upper Jean Lake, tall peaks in the immediate background, a favorite memory captured.

We didn't meet hikers until near the end of the day when we met Montana, hiking from his home in Bozeman, a 2008 PCT hiker. We searched for a campsite above a river crossing as I was getting pretty tired and had a small headache. With such a spectacular day, I didn't think a little headache was much of a complaint.

While crossing Pine Creek on an assortment of logs and rocks, I stepped on what looked like a very large and stable rock. Only it wasn't. It was a roller. I juggled to stay upright losing one foot to the creek. Initially I thought it was funny, but then I realized I'd tweaked my left knee, the replacement knee.

I quickly put on the knee strap to get some compression and then I babied the knee as we walked past Summit Lake to the Pass. Fortunately, the trail was smooth, but I was concerned as memories of a serious knee problem in Spain were quite fresh in my mind. I elevated the knee during break and lunch, took my regular pain killer after lunch, and walked gently and carefully.

The trail was smooth downhill the rest of the day as we descended to the Green River. It really was green, the color mixed to a light green by glacial silt and white rapids. We camped somewhat illegally close to the river but could find nowhere else to put a tent. We left no trace of our campsite, but previous campers had left two fire rings.

The next day, smooth and easy trail took us along the Green River, continuing to be a lovely green, sometimes mixed with white and sometimes darker green. Squaretop Mountain was impressive behind Green Lakes' dark green water. We were rather impressed with ourselves when we reached the trailhead at 12:30. Having no cell reception to tell Tailwinds we were early, we waited and lounged against our packs.

Eventually back at Cora, cell reception brought me pictures of my newest grandsons.

Weather Change and a Bailout

I woke a couple times in the night thinking, "What a lovely bed." In the morning Tailwinds took us out to the trailhead. Fresh and clean, we hit the trail. Entering deep fog through grass soaked with the night's rain, in less than five minutes, we were soaked from wet bushes and muddy from the trail. Our feet would be wet all day.

Climbing a thousand feet through gradually lifting fog, we listened to coyotes howl in the distance. After an eon, we reached the top of the ridge and descended a few hundred feet to Roaring Fork, where we met four people taking fish samples for the forest service. Besides going up at least another thousand feet, the trail insisted on going down every so often, so we climbed some of the elevation twice. Even crippled slugs eventually get to the top, and we finally crested Gunsight Pass and went down the other side.

Stopping to get water, Hawkeye, a NOBO, came by, and we chatted briefly. Our luck crossing creeks ran out towards the end of the day. I slipped in at one crossing, and we both ended up wading through a couple, so by the time we made camp we had really wet feet.

A beaver was swimming in a pond near our far-from-ideal campsite as we squished into tiny spots between two swamps, nothing else looking any better. We barely got tents up and dinner ready before it started to rain.

It rained and the wind blew the trees all night. We were not under widow makers, but I wondered if the charming beaver we had seen would come out at night and chew a live one down on us. We survived the night, and mercifully the rain stopped to let us pack.

Needing raingear and umbrellas the whole day, the rain wasn't a passing thunderstorm, but an extensive cold front with solid dark clouds over most of the sky. And RockStar's sleeping bag had gotten wet in the night.

We popped into the pretty open meadow of Fish Creek to share the scenery with cows.

Herding cows was not on our to-do lists for the day, so I talked a reassuring line of steady chatter in hopes they wouldn't just run down the trail in front of us for miles. Two legged critters with umbrellas no doubt looked strange to them. We were not making good time with constant rain, wind, and a cold 50 degrees, good hypothermia weather. Body cooling and wetness at 50 could potentially be a problem if we stopped moving and lost heat provided by exertion. Then we had to ford the creek. Already soaked, I just waded through. After grabbing some water from the creek, we went on, feet wet and cold.

Before we left Cora, we had heard the cold front was coming, forecast to be even colder over the next few days. We had hoped we might be lucky and the forecast would be wrong. We weren't that lucky.

As we came to the only likely bailout spot for the next three days, we knew we were in a potentially serious situation, especially for RockStar, with a wet sleeping bag and no way to dry it out.

Standing on a dirt road, we wished for a car, but all we saw were fairly fresh tire tracks. We hemmed and hawed for close to an hour wondering what we should do. Continue on the trail?

Walk down the road? Which direction? Standing in the rain staring at our GPS's wasn't getting us anywhere, and we were chilling from inactivity. As we were about to continue on the trail hoping for the best, a big SUV came around the corner. We bailed out thanks to two very kind and generous fishermen from Michigan.

For a 2 ½ hour drive on a bad jeep road, we bounced on the floor of the van, thankful to be going out. We returned to Tailwinds' house, joking about bad houseguests, who refused to leave. Tailwinds and Fred were very gracious and glad we were safe; we were glad to be warm and have dry feet. I'd lived through such weather before, but at 73 I was content to have both the good sense and good luck to get off trail.

Alternate Plans

I made everyone a pasta dinner, and in the evening looking at maps I made an alternate plan from Brooke's Lake to the Highway in Yellowstone with a bit of a slack pack before Brooke's Lake. We needed to keep our schedule going into Yellowstone as we had lodging reservations.

The alternate plan gave us an extra day to make up for our continually slow pace.

We made a good call to get off trail though I hated to skip a section. It rained all night, and the following day was stormy and cold, even in Cora. RockStar and Tailwinds both thought the proposed change in plans looked good. At any rate, it was the best we could do.

Yellowstone called when she and her friends came out of the Winds. They'd seen fresh snow and said it was very wet walking out. When Yellowstone got home, she posted a winter- weather advisory in Montana. It was only August 23,ʳᵈ but I was chilled in the house thinking how cold I would be on the trail. We hit the outdoor store for extra gloves and socks, and it was good to have two zero days to rest. Hopefully, we would have adequate gear and enough energy to carry out our revised plan.

Tailwinds drove us up to Togawotee Pass and dropped us off for a bit of a slack pack from a mile below the highway up to Brooks Lake. Below the highway was a pleasant walk; after crossing the highway, we were glad to have our GPS as the trail was indistinct, if it was there at all. We only had to walk a mile and a half through meadowland, but the tall, very wet grass, along with boggy marsh, wasn't pleasant. Our shoes, dried for two days in a house, were waterlogged again. Reaching the jeep road we found a sea of mud 6-8 inches deep. That wasn't pleasant to negotiate either.

The mesa above the lodge was pretty, with fresh snow in the cracks and below the sheer rock walls. The horses in the corral didn't look happy, standing mud-splattered in the cold. It felt like winter, and, of course, it rained. Tailwinds patiently waiting for us at the trailhead past Brooks Lake Lodge, took us to a motel in Dubois, and the weather forecast promised two more crappy days to be followed with nice weather.

"I think we're gonna die tomorrow."

The day we left Brooks Lake was better than expected but full of muddy challenges. Tailwinds drove us to Brooks Lake, and we said *good-bye* to our friend and wonderful trail angel. She and Fred had been extraordinarily hospitable.

Setting out in fog, we were not expecting good weather. Surprisingly, fog lifted before we got to the end of the lake. Although the day was overcast, it didn't rain. But the trail, a soupy mess of mud churned to slop by horses, was extremely difficult walking. We picked our way along, slowly balancing on the grassy edges of trail when there were grassy edges of trail.

Walking on the trail itself risked skidding severely or falling in mud and standing water. Mud caked on our shoes oozing out to the sides, like wearing tugboats or tanks.

Needless to say, we didn't make good time, though the trail would have been easy on a good day without the mud. We were glad we had rearranged our schedule to give us an extra day, even though we were carrying seven days food. We forded two creeks in our water shoes (I brought my sandals for this stretch.) and our feet almost dried out as we walked until, after the last ford, thunderstorms turned all the grass and bushes wet, so we again had wet feet.

Grizzly bear prints in the mud were all going in the opposite direction, and we hoped the bears didn't decide to come back. *Smellables* and food were in our big bear cans, and a few things like bug repellant and sunburn cream were in odor-proof bags and away from the tents at night. Bears like anything that smells, not just food.

The mountains had changed from the Winds, resembling the Sierra or Rockies to the Absarokas, shaped more like mountains in Glacier National Park. The only campsite we saw all day was fortunately near our water source for the evening.

In the morning there was ice on the bear cans, and right off the bat we had to ford an icy river. But the sky was blue. The trail was still mud, but icy cold mud was firm and much easier to walk on than squishy warm mud. Coming to a fork in the trail, we left the horse path, a relief to walk on a trail not chewed by hooves.

In a canyon thick with monkshood, a deep blue-purple flower and one of our favorites, we took an extended break to dry out wet tents and gear, and I sewed up a split seam in my pants while enjoying bright sunshine. The Tetons were visible through the Buffalo River gap as we forded the South Fork of the Buffalo River. Walking through burned timber in the afternoon, we saw 3-4 elk, as well as deer and bear tracks. Reaching the locked patrol cabin by 6:00 we set up our tents.

I left RockStar to defend our tents with bear spray should a bear appear and took our containers to the river for water. Worry about bears was then overshadowed by worry about tomorrow's river crossing. The riverbank was washed out, and trees lay tossed in a log jam, Walking back with our water, I told RockStar, "I think we're gonna die tomorrow." I was really spooked.

RockStar looked at me like I'd gone slightly crazy and just said we would worry about it the next day. I hoped the water level would go down a little overnight.

In the morning we packed up and went to face the beast, crossing Soda Creek. I might not have been so freaked out about the crossing if evidence of the rampaging river, probably from spring runoff, had not been so apparent. That cut away bank and the trees that had been uprooted and tossed in a log jam were such a clear demonstration of the power of water.

I was, quite frankly, frightened of crossing the fast flowing stream with obvious currents and small rapids. I'd forded many rivers over the past few years, but I just didn't like the looks of this one. I kept thinking of the headlines of day hikers or rafters in the Pacific Northwest, who had come afoul of fast water, pushing them under log jams with no way out. I might never be found under a log jam in this remote area.

RockStar took it in stride, helping me overcome my fears and being the rock of stability I could hang on to, literally. We didn't exactly use recommended river crossing technique, but discussed what would work best for each of us. We crossed together, she on the upriver side with her greater body mass protecting me on the downriver side. She wanted to use both her poles, so she didn't hold onto me. I held onto her waist strap with one hand and used one pole with the other, and RockStar moved more slowly than she usually did crossing rivers to accommodate my slower, uncertain footing.

The crossing wasn't too bad, though the water was mid-thigh deep and the current pretty strong. We made our way safely across. I have never been sure why that crossing freaked me out so much. I might have been the strong one calming RockStar down when she was near melt down in Colorado the previous year, but I was thankful for her support on the crossing of Soda Creek. Irrational fears can bite even an experienced hiker.

The icy water thoroughly abused my feet and legs, but they recovered walking the trail. We listened to bugling randy elk on our morning break. Halfway through the day we had another crossing, not too dissimilar to Soda Creek, yet I had no fear of that one.

On another horse-traveled trail, dry, horse-tromped mud turned into hard clods and made uneven footing to slow our walk even on level ground. Hard ground changed to meadows.

Grasshoppers, moths, butterflies, beetles, and frogs scurried and hopped away as I approached. An interesting ground bird warbled/gobbled at us, but we couldn't see it.

Two Ocean Meadow and Parting of the Waters

Hawkeye caught up with us in the meadow. He'd taken three days off while we had jumped ahead. After chatting a bit, he strode on ahead of our more sedate pace as we climbed to our campsite at the edge of another burn, warm enough now to have a Ziploc bath and wash a few things.

Before we descended to Two Ocean Meadow, a small pack train of five horses and three people passed us going the other way; they and Hawkeye were the only people we'd seen in four days. One end of Two Ocean Meadow drained to the Pacific Ocean, and the other end flowed to the Atlantic. After crossing the meadow and going a bit uphill, we came to the *parting of the waters*, a stream dividing to flow likewise to the Pacific the Atlantic.

A 2,000-foot climb was conquered with a steady rest step while looking at abundant flowers to take our mind off the effort. Views opened up behind us to the meadow and many mountain ranges. As we reached the high point, we saw the dramatic Tetons, the Winds, Absarokas, and other peaks in Yellowstone, a 360-degree view. Marvelous. A great reward for the effort of getting there.

Rain in the night gave us wet tents to pack in the morning. We crossed two rivers early in the day and another two before the day was over. Walking through broad valleys filled with willows, a reroute kept us out of a swamp. We passed two patrol cabins, one for the forest service and one in Yellowstone National Park, and we entered our biggest National Park through the remote southeastern border.

Yellowstone

At a small stream one rock shy for stepping across, RockStar picked up a giant rock and heaved it into the correct spot. Too bad we couldn't do that everywhere. Packs were lighter in food contents, but heavier with wet tents. My back was hurting earlier each day. Must be getting older. Yellowstone rules required us to stay in registered, assigned campsites. Arriving at 4:20, we were the only ones at the first backcountry campsite, so I could have a private Ziploc bath and be in bed by 7:30.

Many elk bugled in the night and in the morning. We might not see them, but they were amorously broadcasting their presence to the cow elk in the neighborhood and their potential rivals for dominance. RockStar and I joked that we didn't see much wildlife because we walked so slowly they had plenty of time to move away. True.

Walking through old Yellowstone burns, we observed new growth amid burned timber.

Flowers thrived in the burn area, a palette of colors: pearly everlasting and the autumn reddened leaves of fireweed adorned fallen and silvered old burn logs. Paintbrush added bright red color spots, blue-purple asters, lupine and harebells the blue, goldenrod and daisies the yellow and an occasional geranium or still- blooming fireweed the pink. Ground cover turning orange or yellow added to the mix. Above the low hills, silver logs and flowers, Mt. Sheridan called us to our campsite near Heart Lake.

For a trail that followed the Snake River downstream, we climbed a lot of steep hillsides and into and out of gullies. Earlier, we had stepped across the Snake River with a stride, but it was bigger now and required fording. Taking an early lunch before it rained, we then crossed a very large meadow, and the storm began in earnest, pelting us with rain driven by very cold wind. Walking with the curve of the umbrellas facing into the wind, we could have walked right into a grizzly without seeing him. We saw only the foot or two of trail in front of our feet below the edge of the umbrella. Lightning cracked and thunder peeled right above us as we walked on through storm and meadow.

Fording the Heart River in the rain, RockStar went first, and the water, opaquely brown with fresh silt, edged higher than her crotch. Shorter than RockStar, I found a way across a foot farther upstream and a few inches shallower. The water had a warm current from a thermal flow upstream.

On the trail once again, it rained some more. We made it to our campsite by 5:30, principally because we were too cold and wet to stop anywhere for rest. Just before our campsite, we had one more river ford with good water for the night, and the sun came out to cheer our soggy selves. But everything was still very wet. Chilled, I crawled into my sleeping bag before dinner to warm up.

Two other hikers occupied the backcountry campsite on that cold wet night close to the river. It rained all night long without letup. And it rained while we packed up. And it rained taking down the tent. And, did I say? It rained.

Hike Out and Go Home

My usual optimism completely deserted me. I told RockStar I wanted to hike out and go home. RockStar readily agreed.

We had planned for this to be a slightly long day but had figured on lighter packs with all food consumed. With rain-soaked tents and gear, I think they were heavier than when we began with seven days' food.

Hiking around the lake on a sandy beach, we reached a patrol cabin, Mt. Sheridan seen through breaks in trees, clouds, and fog. Sheridan now had snow, more than a dusting, extending down a thousand feet from the summit.

We stopped at the patrol cabin to have an early lunch on a dry bench under an overhang, the only dry place we saw all day. Some campers came over seeking Rangers, but found only two soggy women hikers. We headed up Witch Creek through a geyser basin with steam vents and pools that most tourists do not see, but I was mostly focused on the way out.

Out was a 5.5 hour hike from the cabin. We saw five or so hikers also going out and four hiking in. A big pack train of at least 10 horses passed us going out, and the lead rider seemed quite annoyed that we were on the trail with umbrellas. We followed trail etiquette by getting off the trail on the downhill side and talking to horses, so they wouldn't spook. But we didn't take down our umbrellas in the steady rain. We thought we had a right to be there, too, and to try to stay dry.

It was a hard walk out for me. Over the last three days my back had been hurting at the T-11 level, site of a compression fracture 20-25 years ago. I assumed my back was full of traumatic arthritis, as well as osteoarthritis. I couldn't get the pain under control, not with Tylenol, Percocet or Inflam-X. It felt like someone was sticking a shiv in my back and twisting. With nothing further to do for it, I just kept walking to the trailhead.

We were very lucky at the trailhead. After a number of tourist cars passed us by, one waved. A very nice young man from Idaho, who worked in the park turned around and came back for us and took us to Grant Village. We checked in, picked up our resupply boxes and caught a shuttle to the lodge and our room.

Showers were heavenly, and I tried to eat all the food in the Lakehouse Restaurant. Then, thoroughly spent, I became horizontal and in love with central heating. The next day we cancelled things: campsites, food and water drops and Old Faithful lodging. I was done.

After 2013 in Colorado and 2014 in Wyoming, I was tired of hearing locals say how unusually rainy and cold it was. I was bone tired. I suppose some of that had to do with being 73. The pain in my back was severe enough to make me consider stopping just on that account. The rain had added to our miseries. The constant river crossings had taken energy and contributed to slowness. Nights were cold, making breaking camp in the mornings less than fun. Freezing weather and snow were rapidly approaching. I'd dealt with each of those issues before on other hikes, but maybe not all at the same time.

Quitting this early into a planned hike was very unusual for me. We had more than 200 miles still on our hike itinerary for the year. Before this I'd hiked on even when my hiking companions bailed. I'd never before thought of getting off when not much more than half way through a planned hike.

A large part of long-distance hiking is mental. This time I didn't lack just the physical ability. I lacked that mental push, too. That was new for me. I'd left the trail early in Maine due to weather and safety concerns. I'd left the trail early in Pennsylvania due to a bowel obstruction. I'd never left the trail feeling quite like I did in 2014.

I felt discouraged and defeated. I thought to myself that I might never finish the CDT. I was pretty sure I would recover my optimism and be back out on a trail for another year, maybe two, but I was fighting a battle with time. Doing 400 miles a year on the CDT through the age of 75 had seemed a possible challenge. Doing only 200 miles a year would likely require more years than I could physically continue backpacking.

I was disappointed not to go on. But I just didn't want to take another step on the trail. I was done—at least for the year, maybe more. I'd not felt like that before.

Yellowstone (the hiker) came with my car. We had to pick up our resupply boxes from Old Faithful and take Yellowstone back to her home in Gardiner. After a night in West Yellowstone, we retrieved the box near Red Rocks Pass that had been such a challenge to arrange, and we decided to visit Glacier National Park as tourists before heading back to our homes.

Glacier National Park, even for a tourist, was a balm for wounded hiker souls. Fresh snow on the peaks was glorious. How could I even consider not hiking there some day? Plans for which part of the CDT to do next sprouted in my brain, definitely including Glacier. Trails would surely be in my future. I'd only walked 235 miles on the CDT that year. Trails remained. And I planned on walking them.

Chapter 42 Fall and Winter 2014-2015

Shoulder Replacement

By November, I could only raise my left arm about 15 degrees without pain, and I was very glad I'd scheduled a shoulder replacement before going to Wyoming. The MRI had shown something like a porcupine, which was supposed to be the smooth head of the humerus (upper arm bone) even before the hike. I had limited range of motion hiking, but it rapidly became worse after I left the trail.

The surgery wasn't that bad as surgeries go. The rehab was something else again. A large part of rehabilitation was pulling the arm in every direction possible with the help of rope and pulley hung over the door, self-inflicted, therapist-directed torture. It felt like I was trying to pull the arm out of its socket for many, many repetitions, three times a day. I also discovered I was more disabled without an arm than without a knee. I needed a knee for mobility, but I needed upper extremities for activities of daily living.

Rehab took a long time and was painful. I could see why some people discontinued therapy after a shoulder surgery. But I regained 90% of the range of motion in my shoulder, well worth the effort and the pain even if it didn't always seem like it at the time. I worked hard. I needed a shoulder to go backpacking. Your legs carry you on a trail, but not only do you need your arms for hiking poles, it was essential to have shoulder function to get up off the ground or into and out of a tent.

Besides rehab, I turned my mind to hike preparation. I wanted a spring hike, but not a hard one. I just wanted to walk a long ways. I chose the American Discovery Trail from near Cincinnati to the Mississippi, a flat part of the country with a lot of miles to walk. Great choice. That's another story. For this story it is enough to say it helped me get in hiking shape for the CDT.

Preparation for the second hike of the year, the one on the CDT, included training hiking companions. Ryan, a guy in the church I attend, was from Montana and had talked about wanting to do The Bob Marshall Wilderness. My pastor and his wife, Mark and Pam, were also intrigued by presentations I'd made about my hikes and wanted to come too. I'd taken day hikes with each of them and knew something about their hiking capabilities, but they were neophytes to backpacking. I was old, but had some skills to teach.

I took my role as hike leader and teacher quite seriously, writing down what they needed to know and helping them decide what to take for gear. I kept to a timetable, insisting they practice pitching their tents, walk to get in shape, and take overnight shakedown backpack trips with me. They learned what it felt like to carry weight over some miles, how to filter or Steripen their water, what they needed to do to modify their hiking shoes, how to hang their food, poop in the woods, leave no trace, and a myriad of small things that long-distance hikers take for granted because they are second nature to us.

They learned skills I had to teach, and the weather taught them more. I was glad it rained on one trip. They learned their tents worked to keep them dry, and so did their raingear. And there is nothing like forgetting to include gloves and hat on a cold and rainy trip to make you remember to include them the next time. We were going to hike into The Bob Marshall Wilderness, a pretty remote area, for 11 days. It wasn't exactly a beginning sort of backpack trip. Once we began, they had to continue. Bailout points were few.

RockStar and I would provide the experience of long-distance hikers, but they had to be able to do what would be required.

Chapter 43 August 1, 2015 CDT

Montana

RockStar and I hiked before and after The Bob, as The Bob Marshall Wilderness was commonly called. RockStar flew to SEATAC, and she and I drove to Montana in my car.

We started with a slack pack from Stemple Pass to Flesher Pass, our base the Sportsman's Motel in Lincoln, who would provide a shuttle. We walked through pine forests with hazy views of dry, golden grass on mountains and low hills. The 2013 and 2014 hikes had unusual rain. In 2015 forest fires and smoke were the issues.

The afternoon was quite hot, about 85. I went shirtless and to shorts an hour into the day.

After lunch we both put up our umbrellas for shade. Although in trees much of the time, we were still hot. Even if I were naked under that umbrella I would have been hot.

RockStar didn't have her trail legs so uphills were pretty slow, though she was a bit faster than me going downhill. At day's end back in Lincoln, we had showers, dinner, and beds, tired after our first day, my left knee complaining though the trail hadn't been unusually difficult.

I had the trail to myself the next day. RockStar was freaked out about elevation gains and losses for the day and her own state of conditioning or lack thereof. So she drove me to Flesher Pass and walked five miles of trail with 1,500 feet elevation gain as a training hike, and I did the planned section to Rogers Pass with a combined 3,000 feet of elevation gain.

The morning was nicely cool to begin. I saw ptarmigan, and a couple of deer, and I was on the Divide for a late lunch in a shaded spot under a very windblown and deformed fir. Along the Divide, I had 360-degree-views. Very nice. Raising the umbrella for a sunshade at about 10:00, it was worth its weight in gold as the day heated up, keeping the sun off while a gentle cool breeze blew over the Divide.

Before the day was over, the views were hazy with smoke. Something was burning to the west and south between Missoula and Lincoln, the western half of the US tinder-dry that year.

The two last climbs on south-facing slopes in the lowering sun were unpleasantly hot, but my knee did well, as did my shoulder, though the bottoms of my feet were tender. Half way down the switchbacks, I put a folded bandana under the ball of my right foot.

We ate a nice steak that night in Lincoln as a reward for my last hike at age 73. The next day we traveled to Benchmark, ready for a five-day SOBO section back to Rogers Pass, and, incidentally, my birthday. The old-lady hiker added another year to brag about.

Augusta was a cute little town. We had lunch with huckleberry ice cream. We had been doing a lot of eating, though we hadn't really *earned* it yet. It was time to put on our packs.

Scapegoat Wilderness

Taking the Straight Creek Trail from Benchmark, a lovely woods trail with such a gradual grade it was practically level, we headed into the Scapegoat Wilderness. Boy Scouts were the only people we saw all day. Umbrellas shed raindrops as well as the sun's rays during the day. Showers temporarily cooled the temperatures from 85 to 70, but the heat gradually again increased to make for a sweaty day.

Thimbleberry plants lined the trail, but the berries were long gone. In the afternoon we walked in an old burn area with seas and seas of fireweed's bright magenta, which was especially pretty against the bright green of new young pine trees growing among the black snags. Purple asters, goldenrod, and a sprinkling of other flowers also decorated the landscape.

After an uphill pull for the last two miles, we found water and a place for both tents, though finding an appropriate place to hang the food bags was a challenge in burn country. The new trees were not yet tall, and I hoped the bears were short, too. I'd decided we didn't need to carry bear cans as no one else we saw on the CDT was doing so. We would trust our bag-hanging skills.

While taking care of morning chores in our tents, a big thunderstorm hit. Hunkering down in tents, we waited for it to pass, giving us a late start. It was nearly 9:00 by the time we hit the trail. We forded creeks and streams at least 4-5 times during the day and had many wet bushes to walk through. I didn't mind it all that much, the cold water feeling good on hot feet.

After going up Straight Creek Pass, the rest of the day was downhill, except for all the little uphills that seemed to be part of even downhill days. We descended Welcome Creek and then Dearborn, and by afternoon we were out of the burn and into deep forest. Deer prints, moose poop, and one giant bear scat informed us of large animals, but we only saw chipmunks, hummingbirds, and other small birds. There were no big stands of flowers and no people.

We ended the day a couple miles ahead of schedule, hoping that would make the next day less brutal. Nearly 4,000 feet of elevation gain was planned, and we would be carrying a two-day supply of water. Ugh!

At Black Tail Creek Crossing, we loaded two gallons of water for RockStar and six liters for me, my requirements always less than hers, for which I was grateful. We then started out with a long climb in the forest. Leaving the forest and still climbing in the high country, ferocious winds increased in strength and distracted us from the effort of going up by seeking to hurl us back down the mountain.

Hunkered down behind some very short trees to avoid the gusts, we stopped for lunch before resuming our climb and battle with the wind. We might have made our planned destination with just the climb to worry about, but adding the wind and trying to keep from being blown over took more energy. We only made 8.3 miles after a lot of work, meaning we would have a longer day to reach Alice Creek, but we would have less water to carry.

Although we didn't get as far as planned, we had one of those *walking on top of the world* days with high mountain peaks surrounding us, most of them below our elevation, the rewards for our hard work. Amazing. We camped in a depression between hills on the high ridge to shelter us from the still-fierce wind.

It was a cold night, freezing condensation on tent walls by morning. Getting up first to take down the food bags, I was rewarded with beautiful morning light shining on the lower end of the north/south rock formation called The Chinese Wall, south of the iconic picture postcards but the same type of rock formation. The wall glowed almost orange in the early morning sunlight.

Within the first mile, we met PEOPLE. Section hikers Cassie and Tony passed us, and later, Problem Bear and Porter. We had met Problem Bear in New Mexico in 2013. After an on-trail chat, we continued in opposite directions.

RockStar had a very hard time, especially uphill in the morning, her legs fried from the 4,000-foot climb the day before under so much water weight. We took the Wolf option of the old road down to Alice Creek to find water, not arriving at our campsite until 8:00, but we had tents up, water stowed, and food bag line placed before dark. I took a Ziploc bath while sitting in my tent eating dinner, and we hung the food bags by headlamp.

Leaving first, RockStar saw a moose as she headed down the jeep road to Alice Creek Trailhead. Interpretive signs at the trailhead told us we were in a valley used by Shoshone coming down to their winter camping grounds, also the route of Meriweather Lewis coming back from the Pacific on the Lewis and Clark Expedition in 1806.

We hiked back up to the CDT at Lewis and Clark Pass, the principal path through the Divide before Rogers Pass was discovered. Half way up Green Mountain we met Beacon, whom we also knew from New Mexico in 2013.

After our trail chat, he continued NOBO and we SOBO. From the top of Green Mountain we could see ridges and mountains yet to walk on the way to Rogers Pass, down to a saddle, up a mountain, down to a saddle, repeat, repeat and repeat some more. RockStar had a very difficult day on completely worn-out legs before we reached Rogers Pass three hours later than anticipated.

Toni, our ride, wasn't happy about our lateness, but it was the best we could do with RockStar's fried legs. Toni was a friend we had met online, who had hoped to be part of our group in The Bob, but severe foot problems requiring probable surgery prevented her from joining us. She'd agreed to give us some very key trail support in transportation and lodging. But as a Montanan, she knew the highway from Rogers Pass was called suicide highway because deer frequently tried to be hood ornaments at dusk along that stretch of road. Toni had never been a trail angel before and had expected us to be there at the estimated time I'd given her. It was hard to be that precise over five days of unfamiliar trail, or maybe just because I was old and RockStar not in pristine hiking shape.

Toni drove us to her home in Big Fork with a stop in Lincoln to grab a remarkably good little pizza from a gas station convenience store, and bacon and eggs from the grocery for breakfast the next morning. Finally arriving at Toni's a little after 10:00, we were beat. Toni was glad the trip had not involved deer dashing onto the highway.

We took two rest days in a small house Toni and Frank had lived in while their big house was built. We needed the rest, and their *cabin* was a real house, not just a motel room, luxurious for hikers. Toni drove us around Kalispell so we could pick up various items of resupply or discovered need, and we dropped off one set of resupply boxes at the Moddermans, who would deliver them to us by horseback 3 ½ days into The Bob Marshall Wilderness.

The Bob

The section of the CDT through The Bob Marshall Wilderness was a long one, a real stretch for able-bodied thru hikers on one food carry. There was no way I, RockStar, and our three friends new to backpacking could have made it on one food carry. After a good deal of sleuthing, I'd found two sets of horse packers willing to bring us food at prearranged sites on the trail at a price we could split five ways. Moddermans were one of those horse packers. I talked to Mark, Pam, and Ryan by cell phone as they drove from Washington to Missoula. Soon there would be five in our group.

The second day, day Toni took us on a tour of Big Fork, a nice little artsy town, Toni herself an accomplished artist in paint and fabric. The tour included tales of many celebrities, who lived in or near the small town of Big Fork, including Johnny Dep, Wayne Newton, Charlie Sheen, Emilio Estevez and numerous others. Evidently Big Fork was a popular place.

Then a text from Pam told me they'd driven all the way to Montana before realizing they'd forgotten their hiking shoes, a little hard to walk The Bob without them. Lots of drama later, they replaced them at the REI in Missoula. At least they were in the right place to find more.

RockStar and I checked in with Forest Service Rangers about a fire in Glacier to the north of us and a fire west of the Divide. The reports said the fires were stable and not currently a problem; all trails we needed were open. Toni and Frank fixed us elk tacos for dinner before we came back to the cabin to pack. We looked at maps and elevations ahead, and I talked to my son and daughter by cell phone.

Oops. My alarm failed to go off in the morning, and we were awakened by Toni knocking on the door. RockStar and I scrambled to get ready and have breakfast, but we were still late. We left Toni with the impression we were *always* late. That wasn't true, but it was true for the short time we knew her.

Toni drove us to Kalispell to meet Mark, Pam, and Ryan, and Ryan's brother drove us all to the Marias Pass trailhead. Our little group was ready to hike into The Bob.

The day was a learning experience fording rivers for the three new backpackers as we took Wolf's route along the Two Medicine River instead of the Bear Creek route with numerous PUDs. (Hiker jargon for pointless ups and downs.) I liked walking straight through rivers with my hiking shoes on, and this route had almost as many river crossings in a day as the Gila, but RockStar and the new hikers changed to crocs at each crossing. We tried one high-water trail on the map, but the trail was so overgrown and difficult, we carefully made our way down a steep, overgrown hillside to the regular trail.

Smoke and Ashes

About 10:30 we looked behind us and saw tall, billowing smoke clouds, which were unnerving and somewhat scary. Going back toward the smoke didn't seem to be a good option, so we kept walking as planned, while we kept an eye on the smoke behind us. I encouraged my little group to think through what we would do if fire came toward us. Rolling in the river to get soaking wet or lying down under the water in deep pools seemed the best options. Having a plan helped to settle our nerves, though we didn't have to execute the plan.

At lunch we sat on a hillside in the shade above the river. Unfortunately RockStar lost her balance on the uneven ground, fell, and ripped out the rivet for the strap on her croc. Then as more and more bees appeared, I realized my pack was set on a ground nest of bees, and RockStar got stung. It wasn't the best lunch stop. It was very hot in the 90s.

The heat, the river crossings, and the newness of it all for Mark, Pam, and Ryan resulted in a very tired crew by the time we reached White Rock Creek, but we had a sense of accomplishment for completing the day together. Tents were set up, bodies cleaned, dinner eaten, water treated, food bags hung, and we turned in.

The next day everyone did a little better. The trail was good, and we moved steadily before lunch. Past the patrol cabin, we were temporarily slightly misplaced, but RockStar quickly located the trail change in the middle of the meadow we had just passed. Thundershowers passed by in the morning, but it only rained lightly.

I could still smell a whiff or two of smoke in the morning, but we no longer saw smoke in billowing clouds. We did see high peaks, though somewhat obscured by haze, and a few late- season flowers: pearly everlasting, goldenrod, and a scattering of paintbrush, geranium and cinquefoil. Gentian were drying up before they could bloom.

In the middle of the night, Mark and Pam saw a large rabbit, and in the day we saw a squirrel or two, and a few birds, and heard a loud bellow from a cow, who apparently didn't like us eating lunch by Kip

Creek.

In mid-afternoon, the trail gradually became less and less of a trail. We were happy to find campsites at the creek crossing, doctored Ryan's blisters, set up camp, and did camp chores.

Mark rigged a great food bag line.

RockStar and I were the experienced backpackers, but we learned a new way of hanging food bags from Mark. He threw a line high over a branch near the trunk of a tree and tied off one end close to the trunk. He then threw the other end of the line over a branch of a different tree a number of feet from the first. A fixed loop tied as high as we could reach on the line close to the first tree held carabineers with our food bags. Pulling the line over the branch of the second tree lifted food bags neatly suspended between the trees and far from the ground. That line was then tied next to the trunk straight down from the supporting branch.

I was impressed. In all my hiking years, I'd never seen it done quite like that, and it became my favorite method of food bag-hanging if appropriately spaced trees were available, a method especially useful in lodgepole pine forests without large branches. Old hikers can learn new tricks.

RockStar and I have never been particularly fast at getting on the trail in the mornings. Our backpacking newbies were only a few minutes behind us packing up. Overgrown trail in the morning slowed us down, but the trail improved as we passed Blue and Beaver Lakes.

We met thru hiker John Z heading North. He'd walked a bit west of the Chinese Wall and saw flames of the Three Sisters fire. He took some difficult alternate routes and made up a few of his own. And he was planning to head SOBO on the AT when he finished the CDT.

It was fun for the new backpackers to meet a thru hiker, who seemed a bit superhuman toward the end of his thru hike. We also met Cassie and Tony in the morning and Handy Andy and Twinkles in the afternoon. They had no trouble with the Three Sisters fire.

We experienced smoke all day. I thought it was coming from the north, maybe something started after we left Marias Pass. As we settled into camp beside Strawberry Creek, ash fell on us and on our tents. I hadn't experienced ash fall from forest fires before, although RockStar had on the PCT in 2008. Ashes carry a long way on the wind, and it was unnerving to have them fall on our tents days into the wilderness and far from any road.

I was the slowest one to be ready the next morning. Bad for me, good for everyone else. I could always use the excuse I was old, a nice excuse for pretty much anything whenever I needed one.

No smell of smoke lingered, and no ash fell in the morning. Walking down Strawberry Creek on good trail through meadows and trees beside the creek, we moved right along. Shortly before we reached the site of our rendezvous with horse packers, a ranger with a horse and two mules passed us heading NOBO. He was closing the trail we had just come over because lightning had caused a new fire in the Muskrat Creek drainage.

Shortly afterwards, we met our horse packers with our food boxes. They were early, and so were we, and the exchange of food for trash was smooth except for RockStar's squashed Doritos and Mark and Pam's moldy cheese. We all had plenty of food.

Next was a huge burn area with no shade, and my trail thermometer registered 94. Lunch was blessed with clouds that obscured the sun; without them we would have roasted.

After lunch, we forded Strawberry Creek, and the water was so inviting Mark and Pam became water sprites for a while as the rest of us went on to give them privacy.

Our burned trail turned uphill along Bowl Creek to wear us out before we reached Grizzly Park. We found pretty good camping in the meadow and were all tucked in as the sound of rumbling thunder threatened more rain.

Shortly after we went to bed, we were treated to a spectacular sound-and-light show.

Lightning repeatedly flashed closer than half a mile away, one flash closer than a count of one, with a deafening peal of thunder over our heads, and the fireworks were better than Disneyland's Electric Parade. Rain poured down on our tents while we remained dry inside. It was quite a show for new and experienced hikers alike.

The next morning our trail went through more burn, pockets of forest and wilderness that Mark said were all he'd imagined The Bob to be. A family of ptarmigans posed for pictures on the trail and the log next to it.

The best of the day was at the last, climbing to just below the towering face of the Northern Chinese Wall. Everyone expressed amazement and awe. The sub-alpine terrain was lovely as we made our way to Lake Lavale; the lake was a beautiful shade of blue-green below the rocky wall, though the water level was low. Considering the hot weather of the last few days, we were amazed to find a few patches of snow below the wall.

Fire Detours

As we ate our dinner, a beautiful doe circled our campsite in the trees below the lake. We didn't linger outside in the evening because a cold 47-degrees forced everyone to dive for sleeping bags.

We woke to a cold and foggy morning, but still went back to Lake Levale to take morning pictures; the lake sat behind a ridge above the campsite and was not visible from our tents. We wanted another view and were hoping for morning sun. Unfortunately the cliff walls were in fog, but the lake itself was still a lovely blue-green.

On the trail, fog lifted, giving us spectacular views of the North Wall as we hiked, an amazing, double, sometimes triple tier of cliffs extending for miles and miles to the south. We walked slowly below those cliffs, our mouths agape and cameras snapping shots.

After lunch, we were stopped by a newly placed sign saying our desired trail (Red Shale Creek) was closed, and tape stretched across the trail. An alternate on the North Fork of Lick Creek was suggested. After consulting our maps, (I carried three sets of maps plus my GPS and the guidebook) we decided to be law-abiding hikers even though we would miss a little of the North Wall.

The North Fork of Lick Creek trail wasn't bad although it had a few mud boggy spots. I managed to fall in the creek once, demonstrating my lack of gracefulness. We saw a trout in the creek; I might have scared it when I fell.

After taking a false start on a supposed short-cut trail on my map, we found it unmaintained and full of downed trees from an earlier burn, but we still made good time and were at our new trail junction by 5:30. We had time to clean up and wash clothes, which we hung on the willows surrounding our campsite.

Food bags were hung between new 20-foot pines, small trees to hold all our bags, but they were the highest trees in the burn. After dinner, we retreated to our tents. Mark, Pam, and I sang Holden Evening Prayer in our neighborly tents, after which darkness fell, and the melody of the nearby river brought sleep.

Our laundry didn't dry overnight. I left the campsite with wet laundry festooned over my pack. But no mater, the trail was a good one over a number of rises, through rolling hills and beautiful meadows, and we came out at Gates Park.

After fording one yucky stagnant stream, we were at the ranger cabin and found lots of pack horses and mules, our horse packer with our food, and a ranger. We had planned to come to Gates Park even though we had not planned to come down that particular trail. The good news was our food was there. The bad news was our trail to the South Chinese Wall was also closed.

There was lots of fire news. The Three Sisters fire had jumped the wall at Sock Lake near our planned campsite after the detour. The Rock Creek trail was closed all the way to the wall. There were two new fires on Moose Ridge, started by the sound-and-light show two nights previously. The Nyak Fire in Glacier National Park had grown from 1,000 acres to 11,000 acres the day we left Marias Pass and saw the billowing smoke behind us. The Nyak fire probably had been the source of the ash that fell on our tents nights ago.

So, there were four fires we knew about in The Bob and one in Glacier. We again had to reroute. We wouldn't see the Southern Chinese Wall, the Wall on all the picture post cards. We were very disappointed.

The other rangers were out checking on fires and would soon wrap the cabin at Gates Park with the giant roll of foil I saw on the porch.

We wouldn't take prohibited trails. We didn't want any ranger to risk their life for us. We followed directions. Besides, there was a $5,000 dollar fine for anyone caught on those closed trails. However, there was a route open to Benchmark from Gates Park. We were safe; we would just be finished with The Bob earlier than planned.

After enjoying our lunch, commiserating about the change in plans, and appreciating the *technology* of a sit-down outhouse, we headed out again. We were pleasantly surprised by a lovely valley with huge peaks around us everywhere we looked. It might not be the route anyone else would take for the CDT, but we found it beautiful, and we were also rewarded with four hawks circling overhead.

Fording Briggs Creek, we met two people with horses on the other side and set up camp south of theirs on an open bench. As we were almost through dinner, our horsey neighbors came by with wine and Jack Daniels and asked if we wanted some, so three of us had wine with dinner. How thoughtful and generous of our neighbors.

In the morning we continued down the Sun River Valley. The only untoward event of the day was Mark's drinking hose popping loose; it dumped three litters of water in his pack. Mark and Pam dealt with that and caught up with everyone else when we stopped to see four deer bound away, another standing on the trail. Later in the afternoon, we saw two more deer.

It was a good day for large birds, too: four hawks, three ospreys and 4-5 grouse, one of which puffed up his throat feathers and spread his tail wide, either to show off or to keep us from his harem. Our horse packer passed us going in with a mule-train load of planks for the forest service.

As we ate lunch, a pack train of dudes passed us going somewhere. The lady wrangler seemed to think the trail was her own possession, and we should have had lunch farther away. We hadn't known she was coming. Fording two rivers, Pam let me use her crocs, which Mark ferried back for her to use. So I kept my feet dry and Mark loved wading in the water both ways.

Reaching Bear Creek's open area for camping, we found it occupied by a large dude operation with outhouse, cook tent, numerous guest tents and lots of horses, some of which followed us a short distance. We found our own campsite at the next creek. An owl hooted in the gathering dusk as we tucked into tents.

Morning was cold and frosty, condensation on the inside of the tents had turned to ice. Anything wet outside was frozen solid, as were Mark and Pam's water hoses. Mark and Pam shook out their tent leaving a good-sized pile of snow cone material behind. Walking back to the trail, we saw very nice bear tracks clearly imprinted in the trail dust, looking quite fresh.

On a hot trail with no shade, we were happy to see the sturdy pack bridge and ate lunch in its shade by the West Fork of the South Fork of the Sun River. And after lunch we went on to another pack bridge leaving The Bob Marshall Wilderness. At the trailhead, we found my car, which I'd left there 18 days before.

We crammed five people and five packs into my Honda Fit along with the cooler, bags, and boxes that were already there, and we headed to the campground to set up camp with picnic tables and restrooms available for our use. What luxuries. Rather tired and punch-drunk silly, we washed up, had dinner, and laughed a lot.

Our Bob Marshall hike had not gone exactly as planned. We had missed the South Chinese Wall. But neophytes were now experienced backpackers with wilderness adventure memories. We were also probably the last hikers that year to get through The Bob on anything resembling the actual CDT, very lucky considering the fires surrounding us.

The sun rose, an eerie shade of red-pink through smoky haze, and we crammed everyone back in the car for the 30-mile ride on a dirt road to Augusta. Stopping once, we talked to thru- hiker Mark Trail, who was trying to get to Augusta as his food drop hadn't shown up at Benchmark. We could only have given him a ride if we had tied him to the roof. We did, however, give him my Bob Marshall Map with all possible trails on it to help him travel north.

Meeting Ryan's brother, Randy, in Augusta, we transferred three packs to his truck and all of us went to Mell's Cafe for traditional hamburgers and delicious ice cream, second only to Farson. Our group then split, with Mark, Pam, and Ryan headed to Missoula and thence to Washington, and RockStar and I headed to Great Falls and (we hoped) Glacier.

A protective plate under my car had jarred loose on those dirt roads. But the car was fixed in about ten minutes at the Honda dealership before we checked into the motel. Showers were wonderful. I was cleaned, shaved, lotioned, and my toenails clean, too. After dinner, clothes were washed and then we started getting all the bad fire news.

Highway 2 was closed both east and west of Marias Pass. Trails north of Two Medicine were all closed due to either the Thompson or Reynolds fires. Our planned lodging on Going to the Sun Road was closed. There was a fire between Goat Haunt and Waterton, Canada. A couple other trails were closed due to Bears. Poor bears, they had to go somewhere when their home was burning.

Our two support cars, driven by friends, were trying to get to East Glacier. David and Kathy were pulling a trailer and couldn't drive over Going to the Sun Highway. Jo and Carol *were* coming over Going to the Sun Highway. Everyone was punting and changing plans due to fires. There was also a fire north of Lincoln. All those fires made me very unsettled. Where could we hike? Where could we meet our friends?

Glacier

We woke up to a lot of smoke in Great Falls, blue haze coloring everything, even within a city block. The daily paper said airport visibility was four miles instead of the usual 12-14, and air quality in most of Montana was unhealthy. Besides Montana, fires raged in Washington and Oregon. Before walking the CDT, I never realized how badly the fires in the Cascades affected states to the east, smoke following the usual weather pattern west to east.

Since we were in Great Falls, we drove down River Drive to see two of the famous five falls and the Lewis and Clark Museum/Interpretive Center. The Interpretive Center was impressive, and we needed to stay longer to see it all. So RockStar wasn't too happy with me when I said we had to go, but I had friends, who were trying to support me, and they wanted to know our plans in this smoky mess. We needed to figure out what to do.

Grabbing a bite to eat, we headed to East Glacier and Two Medicine. We saw a herd of buffalo on the way, and RockStar saw a cougar as I slept while she drove through bare rolling hills. The smoke grew worse as we approached the park. Two Medicine is nestled down between strikingly steep mountains, but we could barely make out the outlines of the mountains when we were right beside them. One trail from Logan Pass to Chief Mountain was open, but the smoke was awful and the ranger couldn't say it was any better on that northern trail. I didn't think it wise to subject my old lungs to that much smoke, and we couldn't take cool pictures of mountains when we couldn't see them.

The tourist business was tanked, only 2-3 cars in the Two Medicine parking lot, not the hopping place one would expect in Glacier National Park in August. Hiking in Glacier was scrubbed for the year. The smoke widespread, both CDT and PCT were cut off from Canada by fires in 2015. We were just grasping how lucky we had been to get through The Bob with all the fires starting or spreading behind and around us.

Driving to East Glacier we checked into our tiny cabin. I was glad it had a heater as a cold front with rain and more thunderstorms descended. I figured out a NOBO version of a four-day hike from MacDonald Pass to Stemple Pass, not knowing if air quality would allow the plan to be used that year, or if it was for the following year. We still didn't know what we were going to do.

We woke up to brilliant blue skies, snow on the mountains, and ice on the car, smoke temporarily dissipated by the rain. Logistics extremely fluid, we got in touch with our two groups of support friends. Each group had their own desires and needs, and I was wishing to please everyone and also meet my own goals.

We met Jo and Carol at Saint Mary. It was good to see them. We found out the Waterton trail was open, but there were no openings for required campsites, nor did I have my passport as Kathy was bringing it. But she and David had not able to reach East Glacier and had gone to Missoula instead. We had no assurance the smoke wouldn't return to the currently clear sky.

After raiding the gift shop at Saint Mary, we all went to Browning to the Plains Indian Museum. We could at least play tourist. Although smoke was building again, I hoped to get two day hike sections done. Then we would head south to do a four-day section supported by Kathy and David. Flexibility and planning on the fly were the order of the day.

In the morning, Jo took us to Two Medicine, and RockStar, Carol, and I embarked on a 2,200-foot climb and descent back to East Glacier. Jo stayed with the car and Diogee (Jo's dog) for a relaxing day. RockStar had a very hard time though I wasn't sure why. A climb uphill is always hard, but even with well-graded trail, she struggled.

We had a beautiful day, towering peaks around Two Medicine were glorious now that we could see them. We could have done without the smoke coming down the valley though, which I am sure, didn't help RockStar. A dozen bighorn sheep descended the opposite canyon wall as we climbed.

RockStar chose not to make the little side trip to the scenic point, though Carol and I did. We talked to the ranger and a couple day hikers before catching up with RockStar for lunch. After lunch, it was 99% downhill. We could see the rolling plains of Eastern Montana, at least we could see as far as the smoke let us.

The ranger told us to beware of bears as we got back to trees and make lots of noise, so I sang Girl Scout camp songs all the way back to town. It must have worked as we saw no bears. We did see a pretty goldfinch on the way to our cabin where we greeted Jo, had a change of shoes, water, a bathroom break, and went out for dinner.

Jo and Carol then packed up to go to their campsite, more sightseeing, and the trip home to Washington. I took a 15-mile day hike on the CDT, though RockStar wasn't interested. I did whatever I could do, smoke or no smoke.

RockStar dropped me off at Marias Pass to walk back to East

Glacier. A train was hiding the trail. Ducking under a coal loader car, I crossed the next set of tracks to look for the trail five minutes before a westbound train went by on the tracks I crossed.

Since I was solo, and the ranger had warned us about bears on this trail too, I made lots of noise, usually by singing. I saw no bears and only a little scat on the trail. In spite of all my noisemaking, I saw a couple ptarmigan. It wasn't a particularly hard trail, but 15 miles was 15 miles and a bit much for an old lady. My feet hurt by the end of the day.

North of Helena

Finished with what little could be done in Glacier, we packed up the car and headed south to Helena, hoping for less smoke, but finding just as much in Helena. The Helena paper had lots of dire warnings about air quality. We were probably getting smoker's lungs without smoking. We also read that Benchmark, where my car had been parked for 18 days, had been evacuated. I was quite thankful our timing had been good and I still had a car.

We slack packed from MacDonald Pass NOBO to Mullan Pass, supported by David and Kathy. Purple thistles were the roadside flowers up to the cell towers. There might have been a view, but not through the smoke haze of that day. After Priest Pass, a red-tail hawk signaled his annoyance with our passing as he flew overhead, the hawk and an extremely lethargic snake our wildlife for the day. Passing the ruins of an old log cabin, we walked by the remains of a decrepit train trestle.

Rounding a hill, we could see out to the plains in the east. A freight train, probably two miles long, very slowly chugged its way among lower hills to the valley heading to the Mullan Tunnel beneath us. We stood watching for a long time and heard it pass through the tunnel below our feet. Then we were buzzed by what looked like an army helicopter. Mechanical transport of vastly differing speeds representing different eras of human invention were beneath our feet and over our heads, all shrouded by smoky haze as we used feet, the oldest form of human transportation on the trail.

A little farther on, we saw David and Kathy's white truck with our gear, food, and, importantly, our water. Kathy had already walked north a ways and brought us word of trees and a campsite in another mile. So they drove RockStar and gear to the trees, and I walked with a water bottle and poles, happy to walk an easy mile.

We set up camp, had dinner, and hung food bags on a long high branch of a convenient tree. Finishing our chores, we relaxed in our tents listening to the lonesome call of train whistles in the distance, probably another freight train headed to the tunnel.

In this section our plan called for short days under ten miles. As we traveled through ranchland, smoke cast a pall over everything. We chose the Dog Creek alternate for our route because it had water. It was not a particularly friendly route, and there were no-trespassing signs lining the road.

RockStar saw a couple white tail deer, and there were multitudes of cows. We got our water for the night and the next day and carried it half a mile uphill. At 2:30 it seemed too early to stop, even for lazy hikers like us, so we went around Round Top Mountain another mile and camped in a lodgepole pine forest. I hung the food bags by Mark's new method, perfect for lodgepole pines. We loafed at least an hour after setting up camp and doing camp chores. The sun had shone orange all day through the smoke, and we had seen a helicopter carrying a water bucket, but we were just two lazy hikers lounging in tents, waiting for darkness to fall.

In the morning we left our lodgepole pine forest for a mostly uneventful road walk. I saw one small bear print. More importantly we found Dana Spring behind its wooden stockade fence, an important water source in this dry country. Taking off the cover I found the water level two to three feet down inside the corrugated metal pipe. We had to lower my extra platy (Platypus water bag) with an attached wide mouth lid hung on our food bag rope to reach the water. RockStar held a bandana to filter the floaties as I poured water into her container ready for stirring with the Steripen to treat it. After treating with the Steripen, she filled various bottles and platys while I fished for more water. It was a production that took a while, but the water was clear (minus floaties) and cold, a good water source even in that dry year.

Loaded with water for the rest of the day, the night and a long walk the following day, we headed up a rocky jeep trail, climbing 1,250 feet higher. With that much water in the heat of the day, it was hard work. RockStar had been afraid we wouldn't find water and would die. I was afraid *since* we had found water and were so heavily loaded, *I* would die. I *hated* to carry large quantities of water.

We camped halfway between two saddles on not very choice real estate, but RockStar was too tired to go one step farther. I slid downhill all night. We were both surely tired of smoke. We had passed several useless view spots during the day from which we only saw the dim outline of smoky hills, and our campsite on the hill was no different. Tucked into our bags, we listened to the wind blow and the trees creak.

It sprinkled off and on during the night, not enough to leave anything wet in the morning, though the sprinkles did help clear a little of the smoke. As the day wore on, we had more sprinkles and ultimately thundershowers, bringing views as the air cleared.

The trail alternated between steep uphills and steep downhills. We didn't make very good time, though we had more distance to cover. Grouse flushed from the side of the trail as we walked, and we kept putting up our umbrellas for sprinkles and taking them down when real rain didn't materialize.

After lunch and more hiking up and down hills, the trail finally became easier. With additional showers, the views were nicer, too.

We were supposed to meet David and Kathy at 4:00 where the trail crossed a road.

Concerned we would be late, I tried to text, unsuccessful in sending, but successfully receiving. Kathy was in the hospital. She'd fallen from her bike and broken her ribs, the second bad bike fall for her over the last couple years. I was so sorry to hear she'd done it again.

Looking through the trees, we saw their white truck pull away on our jeep road, and RockStar was broken-hearted to see it leave. Shortly, another truck came by, and we asked the two guys in it if they'd seen the white truck. They cheerfully volunteered to go after it and tell David where we were. Soon David was there in the truck collecting my pack and RockStar. I walked the last four miles to Stemple Pass with my poles and a bottle of water. My feet hurt, but I completed the miles.

We visited Kathy in the hospital. She had four broken ribs, two of them broken twice. Six breaks. She was hurting. It seemed likely that RockStar or I would drive her car back to Washington when I finished hiking. For now, she was in the hospital on oxygen and in my prayers.

South of Helena

The rest of the day was spent resting and planning the next four days of walking. I would walk solo. RockStar was through with walking, had been mentally through ever since The Bob, but she would be my support person. I discovered my computer had not transferred this section of trail to my GPS, but RockStar loaded the Guthook maps into my phone. (Guthook (trail name) created an AP with the maps of the whole CDT. Many hikers now use Guthook exclusively.

Surprise. It was a lovely day. NO SMOKE. RockStar dropped me off at the pass under bright blue skies and gale force winds. Winds had blown away the smoke, but it was COLD. Pam had asked me in The Bob when we would wear rain gear since it was so hot, and we had only put up our umbrellas. I told her, "when it gets cold." This qualified as cold. I left the car at MacDonald Pass wearing my down jacket with rain gear of jacket and pants, gloves, head band, and two hoods. I needed it all.

Half a mile later, past the open knoll was much better. I walked in forest most of the day listening to the wind howl in the treetops but not feeling it at the level of the trail. By morning snack, I'd shed all cold weather gear. The day was beautiful. The high point, four miles into the day, had wonderful views I could actually see, all the way across the Helena valley to mountains on the other side of the basin. If Kathy had not mashed herself up, I would have recommended the walk for a nice day hike. I thought of her all day, praying for her pain to ease.

Quite a bit greener on the south side of MacDonald, a few flowers grew with a backdrop of *green* grass. It was such a nice change to have fresh air and blue skies with real clouds in them, not gray smoke and haze.

I met RockStar on Telegraph Creek Road. Walking to the turn, she gave me a lift back to the campsite, bringing pizza for dinner, which we ate while two whitetail bucks walked through the edge of our campsite. RockStar also brought the good news that Kathy was quite a bit better.

We heard elk bugling in the night rather close to us, making a late summer/fall hike feel complete. We ate breakfast in my nice warm car while defrosting the frozen windows. Then I set off up the hill on a good gravel/dirt road.

Moving well that day, I sent RockStar a text that I would make it out a day earlier than planned. Then I had a goal to shoot for. I met several NOBO thru hikers that day: Funk, OD, Mountain Spice, Dayman, and LaLa. I had nothing but bad news to give them about all the fires. They would have to do a lot of road walking to reach Canada. Some took the news well, others not so much. They all looked pretty tired.

By afternoon, I was pretty tired, too. My water source turned out to be just a mud puddle, so I was on short water rations until after the first five miles the next day. No Ziploc bath. Water was for drinking only. But I tucked in ready for bed listening to coyotes in the distance, almost as good as listening to elk bugling.

The elk bugled in the early morning. Although I heard them and saw their tracks often, they remained elusive and unseen. Looking chipper and ready for the day, Sheerah, a young woman NOBO thru hiker passed me while I finished breakfast.

My day was mainly a walk in woods up over Thunderbolt Mountain, much of the day strong winds tearing through skinny lodgepole pines making a forest of very long toothpicks sway in the wind rubbing on each other. Sometimes they blew down. I hoped none would fall on me.

Going with minimal water in the morning worked just fine. The pack was lighter, the morning cool, and I usually was thirstier in the afternoon. So filling my bottles at 11:00 and another liter and a half at 5:00 worked perfectly.

Some of the map-marked water sources were dry. Thunderbolt Creek wasn't running, but there were pools of standing water. I dipped and poured through a bandana to get out the floaties and then Steripenned. Just a bit farther was an unmarked running stream. Pools of water or running water, either way worked.

While finishing lunch, I met thru-hiker Dan, a cheerful hiker. I liked seeing cheerful thru hikers. I was really annoyed with whoever wrote "CDT sucks" on signs. My opinion was and is: If you don't like hiking the CDT, don't hike it. Nobody makes a person stay on the trail. Get off the trail, and do something you enjoy. Don't inflict others with your bad attitude by writing on signs that will last for years, although your mood will be temporary and is only related to you.

Hiking long-distance trails are not always unadulterated fun, and 2015 was kind of a miserable year with snow in the early season in Colorado and fires in the summer. But still, nobody is forced to keep hiking if they don't want to. No one forced me to be there. It was my choice to see where the trail would take me each day and discover whatever sights or adventures were disclosed.

So, what did I see? I saw the flash of tan as a deer bounded away, 3-4 startled ptarmigans, small birds, chipmunks, and squirrels. I liked seeing views and animals of all kinds, including thru hikers. I liked trees. I liked the wind singing in trees, at least most of the time. Stopping at 7:30, I snuggled into my tent and listened to the wind.

It was 37 degrees when I woke up and cold enough to make me wish I could stay snuggled longer. I left wearing my down jacket. A mile or so down the road, rain threatened, and I switched to rain gear and umbrella. The first three miles seemed endless. There was a new trail to the Divide bypassing Leadville. I wasn't sure whether to follow the new sign or Guthook and did a little of both, ending up walking through Leadville hoping there was something to see to make it worth my while. Nope. Nothing worth seeing in Leadville, and it was just more miles on rotten, very rocky road/trail. I should have kept with the new trail and saved myself some grief, not to mention miles.

Spending lots of energy on that little excursion, I was very tired. Stopping for a break at 11:00 I thought I would be lucky to meet RockStar by 8:00. But after break, walking went better.

I saw a whole field of the yellow flowers called butter and eggs, strange in that land of few flowers.

Wildlife consisted of about 100 cows spread out over the last five miles. They were stupid cows, wanting to stick to the road/trail ahead of me, so I kept herding cows down Long Park and beyond, no matter how I talked to them trying to persuade them to get off the road and eat grass in the meadows like happy cows should.

Great views in the second half of the day revealed mountains to south and east, the great valley and more mountains to the west. It rained off and on throughout the day and stayed cold, never reaching above 55. I used rain gear and umbrella most of the day.

About two miles from Champion Pass, I met Andy, another NOBO thru, and chatted with him. He had a great attitude even though he knew he had a long road walk around the fires ahead of him. Most thru hikers had good attitudes. They'd covered a couple thousand miles and surmounted many challenges by that time in their hike. The road walk was just another challenge to be overcome. It was disappointing to them to miss the Chinese Wall and Glacier National Park, but their goal was to reach Canada in one hiking season. They would do that, even if they had to walk roads a couple hundred miles. Section hikers can anticipate closed trails opening in another year, not needing to reach Canada in one.

RockStar was waiting in my car at Champion Pass, and I was very glad to see her. My *feet* were really glad to see her, one foot hurting quite badly that last day. We drove back to Helena, and my filthy body was transformed by soap and water to a somewhat normal person again.

Broken Ribs and a Broken Foot

In the morning, we loaded Kathy, hooked up to an oxygen tank, into Kathy's car, extra tanks in the trunk. RockStar drove Kathy's car. I drove mine. David would drive their truck home pulling their trailer, taking his time doing it. The goal of those in cars was to drive to Tacoma/Puyallup in one day.

My left foot was very sore on the top of the foot near the articulation of metatarsals. I was glad not to be walking on my foot, but it continued to hurt all day, even with natural pain meds and Tylenol. It was a very long day with frequent restroom stops, gas stops, and food stops, all complicated by moving Kathy's oxygen tank with her. She left her cane in one restroom while RockStar and I struggled with changing an oxygen tank. It hissed loudly, meaning a connection wasn't tight, and so startled us that we dropped the wrench needed to tighten it. A short comedy ensued until we had it fixed correctly. In the confusion and stress of hikers playing with oxygen tanks, the new cane was left behind.

Kathy did well. She was much more spry than I thought she would be. Her oxygen levels seemed to improve throughout the day even when not on the tank. But she (and we) were plenty tired by the time we delivered her to her home and their housemate for care. After she was settled in a recliner, RockStar and I drove to Puyallup.

The last stop was to get milk and bananas for breakfast. Walking to the far end of Safeway on my very painful foot seemed more difficult than any hiking I'd done. Once home, I fell gratefully into bed. But my swollen and red left foot hurt hike crazy.

The foot turned out to be a bit of a problem. I'd hiked nearly 300 miles but on the last day it seems I acquired a stress fracture of my third metatarsal about an inch below the tarso-metatarsal joint. (For non-medical types, that means it was on one of the long foot bones on the top of my foot.) The fracture was tiny. Until the Doc magnified the x-ray, it couldn't really be seen. Under magnification it looked like a tiny splinter split up from the main body of the bone. But it hurt and required wearing a boot for four weeks, rather inconvenient for gardening.

Another year on the trail had come to a close. The CDT had not been especially kind to me in 2013, 2014 and 2015. I had been bedeviled with lousy weather, forest fires, smoke and an unexpected stress fracture.

Montana was a big state. I had hundreds of miles yet to go. Whether or not I would finish the CDT was still an unsettled question. I would have to wait and see if I could complete the trail or advancing age and failing body parts would prevent that from happening.

But there were joys, too, in 2015. I was able to hike with RockStar again and greatly appreciated that she hung around to hike after getting out of The Bob. I enjoyed helping three friends learn about backpacking. Our little group in The Bob was quite compatible and had a good time in spite of reroutes and trail closures. They were now experienced backpackers with a nine-day trip under their belts. I enjoyed mentoring them.

We might not have seen the South Chinese Wall, but we did see the North Wall, more than many of the year's thru hikers could say. I still liked walking the trail, although each year I was a little slower and could go a little less far. I needed a different style of shoe. I didn't want another stress fracture. I needed more cushioning. The next year I would try Hokas.

Chapter 44 Fall and Winter 2015-2016

Another Replacement

Another aging body consideration was my right shoulder. The original x-rays of my shoulders a few years earlier had indicated severe arthritis in the left shoulder and moderate arthritis in the right. After my first shoulder replacement, my doc had told me I probably wouldn't wait as long to have surgery on the right one as I'd waited for the left. He was right. Although I still had pretty functional range of motion on the right, I'd developed a weird, sharp pain in one particular movement. I couldn't get my hand out of my pocket. That sounds nuts, but it was true. I could put the hand in the pocket with no problem, but there was something about getting it out that gave me a sharp stabbing pain in the joint. I didn't want to wait for it to get worse and scheduled the next replacement.

"So glad you are still able." Connie, March 6, 2016

Recovery from the shoulder replacement went more smoothly and quickly the second time around. I did have a problem during a conditioning hike in preparation for my spring hike on the ADT. The right knee seemed to be getting older faster than the rest of me. The x-ray said I had, a torn meniscus but it was unclear whether that was the old tear re-injured or just the old tear. The joint space was diminishing, but I knew something was different. The knee didn't rest well and would sometimes start hurting and wake me up from sleep. Connie, one of the people who signed my guest book, said she was so glad I was still able. *Able* was a very fluid category.

Yet I knew I was very fortunate to be able still to be backpacking. That knee with the new pain carried me 489 miles on the ADT in the spring with a bit more attention to prophylactic pain meds. I did have to work at staying healthy and active, plan and execute my hikes in a different fashion than younger folks and pay close attention to whatever the knee told me. I had no idea how long I would be able to hike. Once I reached my 70s, I considered every day to be a gift and every hike to be a spectacular gift. There would come a day when I couldn't hike. But while I still could, I would.

Time at home after my spring hike sped by at lightning speed. The CDT hike would be a scramble of differing sections, mostly NOBO but some SOBO. The reasons for the hodgepodge approach to assembling sections were the National Park lottery system for backcountry campsites at Glacier National Park and campsite reservations in Yellowstone National Park. The National Parks gave reservations when the National Parks decided to give them, and we needed more campsites than thru hikers. Other sections of the CDT were added around reserved times in National Parks to make the most of our available time, chosen for the number of days in the hike plan, not for consecutive miles on the trail.

Thru hikers recognize that hiking long trails is a marathon, not a sprint. Section hiking the Triple Crown was more like relentlessly making piles and piles of miles and days, accumulating over the years toward eternity. The piles of miles were growing, but the CDT is longer than AT and PCT. I wondered if I would find eternity before finding the end of the CDT.

RockStar, and I'd both turned in campsite requests for Glacier. My request was turned down. Half of hers was accepted. We would take what we could get. Tailwinds told us when she might be able to support us for that little section skipped in Wyoming. Both of us planned to be driving our cars, putting on lots of car miles, while we skipped around Wyoming and Montana, placing food and water caches, setting up starts and pickups. It was a logistical challenge.

To add to the logistical challenge, I was planning on taking a third long- distance hike in 2016. My friend Gwen, from Australia, whom I'd met on the Camino de Santiago in Spain, suggested we hike from the French town of Le Puy en Velay down to St Jean Pied de Port. I was planning that hike at the same time as planning the CDT, trying to learn French while I was at it. It was kind of nuts. But how could I turn down such an adventure? Having a friend from Australia ask me to hike in France wasn't an everyday occurrence.

Chapter 45 July 23, 2016 CDT

Centennials

Finally, logistical challenges behind, I met RockStar in Lima, Montana. Leaving one car in Lima, we purchased water and drove a long ways on dirt roads and set up two water caches and one food cache in our bear cans.

Caches set, we started out with full packs on the very first day going up 2,200 feet. We were not starting gradually. Ugh.

The trail seemed to have changed since the edition of Bear Creek maps in my possession. The Guthook AP on RockStar's phone reassured us we were in the right place, though the map indicated we were far from Bear Creek waypoints. We went *over* Lion Head instead of around it.

The change in route was worth the climb for the panorama on each side of the Divide, Tetons to the south, West Yellowstone in the distance, Lake Hebgen and the mountains beyond it, and other valleys and mountains on all sides. And the flowers were marvelous. It wasn't at all like the tinder-dry conditions of 2015.

Tons of flowers: hair bells, yarrow, lupine, paintbrush of shades from orange to magenta, four or five different kinds of yellow daisies, some covering whole hillsides, larkspur, some unusual white larkspur with purple centers, bright-blue penstemon, forget-me-nots, geranium, Lousewort, yellow columbine, stone crop, a purple fuzzy spiked phacelia, a creamy-colored flower with green centers, two or three white flowers whose name I didn't know, blue flax, alpine phlox, chiming bells and a four-foot-tall thistle.

We were quite enchanted by views and flowers and had plenty of time to see them as we slowly puffed up the hill. We also saw three SOBO women section hikers: Sweet Mama, Laurie, and Swan, Swan nearing the finish of her Triple Crown.

Late in the afternoon, two young boys, who were looking for a geocache, passed us hiking part way up Bald Peak. We then saw them on very steep snow slopes ahead, and returning to their car, they warned us not to go there. I told them we were CDT hikers and had no intention of going up Bald; we were smarter than that. They admitted to being young and dumb and reassured us they had flashlights if they needed them on the way out.

The trail reroute had eliminated some planned water sources, but we finally reached a stream as we rejoined the Bear Creek route. By the time we stopped at Clark's Lake for the night, we were two tired little puppies, both having breathing difficulties.

On the trail before 7:30 in the morning, we climbed another 1,000 feet to reach 10,000-foot Targhee Pass on the Divide for mid-morning snack, followed by umpteen bazillion switchbacks downhill, and we lost more than 3,000 feet in elevation. The last small elevation gain of the day, we were close to crawling up the hill. This wasn't a gentle start to a long hike.

The last week in July was prime flower season. More flowers included monkey flower, pussy paws, goldenrod, sulfur flower, lavender mallow, and fireweed.

During the day we met four SOBO thru hikers, who were our neighbors at the Lima Motel: Saint John the Baptist, JR, Grahams, and Blue Skies. They were doing 30+ mile days, taking three days to do what would be eight days for us. Nice to be young and buff. We were neither.

The trail is not just for the young, but it takes more planning and more time when you are older and can't whip off the miles so quickly.

We finally reached our first water cache at Reynolds Pass just before 7:00 that night, our plan to go past the highway a short distance to camp. The plan was thwarted as the *trail* was only posts hidden in knee and waist-high greenery, sometimes bent over by passage of other hikers, all on top of honeycombed gopher/mole holes and tunnels. Stumbling through vegetation over uneven ground, we eventually found what could pass for a campsite.

RockStar was still having breathing issues, though we were camped at only 6,920 feet. My knees were doing better than expected. But two hard days and stopping near a highway provided too great a temptation for a bailout. RockStar bailed. I went on.

The following day was much easier, a dirt road with nice views from high meadows. I met Knots, a NOBO hiker, and before Ant Hill Spring, I saw some very nice bear prints in the dust of the road. Yep. There be bear in these parts.

After washing my socks in the middle of the road by Ant Spring's pipe, two guys in a truck asked me if I wanted a ride to the pass. To their surprise, I turned them down. They thought walking a strange and unusual thing.

The afternoon was hot, and fluffy clouds that had been a saving grace the day before, now absolutely refused to get between me and the sun. Finding a very small tree casting just enough shade for one person, I took a good long break. Wildlife included several groups of cows, smart cows not running away from me on the road, no herding necessary.

When I reached Red Rock Pass, RockStar was there with my car and a nice footlong from Subway for my dinner. She knew how to support a hiker, even if she didn't walk all the trail with me. Eating in the air-conditioned car, we charged my phone. We found our previously placed food caches and tossed the bear cans in the car. Hooray. I wouldn't need to carry a bear can.

Camp chores accomplished, I became sparkling clean, by hiker standards.

RockStar hiked with me as far as Hell Roaring Creek with her full pack as a conditioning hike. We liked the striking rock cliffs at the entrance to the canyon. We'd seen this earlier while driving on the broad expanse of valley to the north.

Five SOBO thru hikers passed us. Both SOBO and NOBO CDT hikers hit this section of Montana at the same time of year. NOBOS start at the Mexican border in April or May. SOBOS usually begin at the Canadian border in July. I met many of both in Idaho and Montana.

After a snack break near the bridge, RockStar headed back to the car, and I continued up the creek, passing Lilian Lake, beautiful mariposa lilies and petal-less conehead. Topping the Divide about 6:00, I stopped to eat my previously hydrated dinner while admiring the flat plains to the south before crossing to the dry south side of the Divide.

The last water source on the trail was a very small trickle of a stream. I scooped a little pool under a tiny waterfall and eventually had enough water for my platy and the bottles carried on my shoulder straps. I'd carried more water in previous years, but I was older this year. The load was heavy. 4 ½ liters would have to last me two nights and a day and a half hiking. Ugh. SOBO hikers had informed me there was no more water until Odell Creek.

Stopping at 9:00, it was still light, and I quickly pitched tent and hung the food bag. I cleaned up with a pre-dunked soggy bandana. In the tent I treated my water and discovered a tiny hole in my platy. Bad. I could simply keep that hole up, so it wouldn't leak in camp, but I would have to carry it on the outside of the pack where it wouldn't be squeezed. The hole was tiny and seemed not to *want* to leak. Long hikes require continual problem-solving skills for whatever decides to go wrong.

In the morning I expected a climb over Taylor Mountain, a heavy pack and some nice views. I got so much more than I'd anticipated that lovely day. As I trudged uphill I met two thru hikers coming down through flowers, the fragrance of lupine thick in the morning air.

Travis came up behind me, a young local decked out in camo with his pistol on his belt. He was checking out the area for future hunting. Like thru hikers, he passed me as if I was standing still.

I kept steadily, if slowly, up the mountain more and more thickly covered with flowers. Lupine was the flower of the day but closely followed in numbers by thick stands of bright vermillion paintbrush boldly painting the sides of each ridge. Angelica and bedstraw added contrasting white. Travis stopped to sit and admire the view. "Absolutely beautiful," he said.

And I agreed. I'd seldom seen flower displays more glorious, rivaling Mount Rainier's flower shows in thickly covered beauty that went on and on. It was as if God had spilled all the paints in every color of the rainbow and the paint had not run together, each drop retaining its sparklingly clear color.

The top of the mountain was nearly anticlimactic. Oh, there were views aplenty, but they were slightly spoiled by smoky haze compared to the day on Lion's Head. The descent was on a long, gradually graded old roadbed. It had now become a place to continue the flower garden. It was a glorious day of flowers.

As I descended further, the trail became misplaced. *I* wasn't lost as I was always clearly on my GPS and usually on the magenta line indicating my route. But after following the bent grass trail to a trail post, there were no more posts, no tread, and no more grasses bent by other's passing. I crisscrossed the route on my GPS but didn't find trail. I crossed the creek bed (dry as expected) clearly seen on both maps and GPS, but there was no trail there, either.

I continued following my red line for a long time. That kind of walking, on the side of a mountain, even if mostly in open country, was slow and tiring from the exertion of clambering up and down hills while stopping every few steps to verify my position on the GPS. Worry lingered. Although I knew I wasn't really *lost*, I wasn't really *found* either. I didn't want to stop and camp until completely *found*, although I had my water and all I needed.

About 8:30, I saw a post and sign on the ridge ahead and above me directly in line with the setting sun. I climbed up that hill and positively identified the trail. A little to the side were two clumps of trees with enough ground to place my tent between them and a limb sticking out for hanging my food bag. The sun went down, but I was *found* again, so I was good with that.

I had only one bottle of water to last until the next water source, but I was good with that, too. I liked not carrying water and being on actual trail. T-minus and Buckeye, section hikers of my vintage, passed me in the morning heading SOBO. We had a nice trail chat, but I was sorry to give them the news there was no water until the other side of Taylor Mountain. They continued SOBO and I NOBO.

Reaching Odell Creek, I had an orgy of cleanliness. I washed myself, my bra, my shirt, and my socks. It felt SO good. Putting on a cold wet shirt was almost like diving into a cold swimming pool; it shocked tingling nerves but was delightfully refreshing to combat a hot day. I also had plenty of water to drink after treating it with Steripen.

When Dirt Wolf and Cheesy Snake came by, I told them the water info and my concern that T-Minus and Buckeye didn't have enough water. They would surely pass them. Was there any way they could take a little extra for them? Sure. They said they would just fill everything up.

Carrying extra water would kill me, but young thru hikers could do anything. I hoped they would find T-Minus and Buckeye.

Shortly after lunch, I came upon Rambler, an older hiker who remembered RockStar from 2009 on the PCT. He had a message for Beacon and Mermaid coming behind him, which I later delivered. RockStar and I had run into Beacon in New Mexico in 2013 and in Montana in 2015, the trail community spread out over miles and years.

Reaching the Aldous Lake trailhead, I found RockStar and cooled off in her air-conditioned car with a bottle of cold lemonade. Packed up, together we headed past Aldous Lake a few miles to make camp. RockStar would head back to the car in the morning, but it was nice to have company for a night. Her breathing problems were resolving thanks to Claritin and rest.

Aldous Lake was a family-friendly lake, only 1.3 miles from the parking lot. We saw a number of families coming out, one with pack goats and a number of children, including a baby. The wilderness is for all ages, including each end of the spectrum. Past the good trail from the parking lot to the lake, we negotiated a tangle of downed trees and new, steep trail before stopping for a leisurely evening, that tangle of trees a harbinger of things to come.

Waking to the smell of smoke and a red sunrise, we concluded the fire in Wyoming was growing. I left RockStar to make her way back to the car and headed out on the trail through another pile of blown-down logs. Good trail with a gentle grade made me feel I was doing well as I passed between two rocky cones, described in the guidebook and on the map. Then the trail promptly disappeared. I followed the bent grasses a little ways until they were not clear and seemed to be drifting farther away from my GPS route.

It was very difficult terrain for an old lady, an old burn area with lots of blowdowns from an old fire, now disguised and hidden in tall grass on a steep-sided hill under a hot sun, no shade, and no trail. I was seduced by an obvious trail above me with a cutout in the hillside. But that trail too petered out after about 50 yards. I carefully followed the contour of that horrid hillside toward the ridge my trail was supposed to pass, while looking below me for any sign of trail.

That tactic eventually worked as I rounded the bowl of the hillside and saw trail below me. Carefully making my way down to the trail, I stayed *found* the rest of the day.

But I'd lost an hour on an already challenging day. Worse, I lost far more than one hour's *energy* in that difficult terrain. My water source was a lovely stream with flowers and shade. But I was there at 11:30 instead of 10:30. I rested in the shade, ate my morning snack rather late, wet down my bandanas, hat and shirt, treated water to drink, and started off again.

Between the stream and Salamander Lake there was evidence of trail maintenance, fresh sawdust, blowdowns recently cut and even tall grass and weeds sheered back. I wished they'd gone a little farther with the trail maintenance around that horridly steep and overgrown hill on which I'd been misplaced.

After lunch at Salamander, I moved along fairly well for an old lady who had already expended much of her daily energy. I met SOBO thru hikers, Llama, DuPont and Steven. Nice young men. I had one last long steep climb at the end of the day before arriving at Rock Spring just as herd of sheep were leaving with sheep dogs and mounted sheepherders. I got my water at the slow trickle from a pipe carrying water from the spring to a 20-foot-long watering tank.

According to plan, I was supposed to go another mile or more. But it was late, and there was a metal bear box for my food beside the spring. I was tired. I searched for a place for my tent that was not covered with sheep poop and crashed. It had been a challenging day.

The last day of the section was 16-miles long and a long day for an old lady. I was more interested in covering those last miles than the views or the flowers. It was a long walk on a very hot day, mostly on a dirt road headed down out of the mountains to Highway 15. About a mile and a half from the end, RockStar met me in her car, and I gratefully walked the last part without the pack.

After a shower and a night's rest in a bed, we drove to West Yellowstone. There was no straight-line paved highway from Lima to West Yellowstone. On the dirt road, driving a good way behind RockStar's car to let the dust settle, I looked up at Mount Taylor and saw no sign of the magnificent flower show on its height. From the road, it looked like a barren ridge. Walking there had shown me the beauty hidden by distance.

On our way to West Yellowstone, we consulted with forest rangers about possibly passable backwoods roads on our maps. Then we drove RockStar's four-wheel drive to set two water caches for the section we would walk leaving Yellowstone. Not able to do the long days of a thru hiker, our trip would take more time, and we would need water. We finally arrived in West Yellowstone and did our laundry. We also changed our hike plan as the three days planned in Wyoming were closed by fire. I had an upset stomach for a birthday present. At least I didn't have to do a lot of driving.

After we parked my car at Targhee Pass, RockStar drove hers. I tossed my cookies in West Yellowstone and felt better, put the seat back and zoned out while RockStar drove to Old Faithful Village. We turned our backcountry reservation into a permit, dropped off a food box to pick up later, and played tourist with a few hundred previously unmet friends watching Old Faithful.

Then we drove to Grant Village campground. My stomach settled, and RockStar treated me to my birthday dinner, a light and delicious trout and Huckleberry brûlée. The wait staff sang to me for my B-day. RockStar said she hoped we would have "a restful and comfortable hike" through Yellowstone. I laughed and said not many people would put restful and comfortable in the same sentence with hike.

"A restful and comfortable hike"

Our trail from Heart Lake trailhead NOBO began with a long, nearly straight trail lined with young pine trees, meeting RockStar's wish for restful and comfortable, more up and down as we went along.

While taking our morning break, Tattu Jo came by and sat to chat with us. A well-known PCT hiker, he'd accompanied Scott Williamson on a speed-record hike. I'd met him on the AT in 2010, and now he was working on his double Triple Crown.

Fording the outlet on the southern side of Shoshone Lake, RockStar got some of the crushed obsidian sand in her crocs. She said it was very sharp. I waded through in my hiking shoes, the cold water blessing my feet. We had lunch beside the lake, and I could have stayed there all afternoon listening to the water lapping on the shore, blue water under blue sky. As we were packing up lunch, Beacon and Mermaid came down the trail (SOBO), and we talked with them for at least another half hour in that lovely spot.

Ok, time for serious walking. The trail delivered more ups and downs in the afternoon. We forded Moose Creek and pulled into camp at 6:00. There were pit toilets, thrones without walls, in National Park backcountry campsites. We appreciated the opportunity to sit.

The next morning dawned with a cold start, 40 degrees at 6:00 and 36 degrees a half hour later. Fortunately, the temperature then rose. Descending into Shoshone Basin at the west end of the lake, we met Dirt Wolf and Cheesy Snake, whom we'd seen in the Centennials a week earlier. We also saw super fresh bear scat. Mr. Bear might have gone by as we stopped for snack. Pearly everlasting, monkshoods, fringed western gentian, and brushy cinquefoil were pleasing to the eye, along with the blue of the lake and the light and dark greens of basin meadows and trees.

After a sandy beach, we waded by yellow pond lilies in standing water, which smelled like a swamp. Some of the smell had been contributed by active geothermal areas a few hundred feet on both sides of the trail.

Geothermal Fun

Once out of the marsh, we came to another geothermal area with numerous pools of hot red or blue water bubbling like witches' brews.

Our favorite feature was a very accommodating small geyser that went off every three minutes, allowing multiple opportunities for picture taking. The leader of a group of kayakers said it was Minuteman, though that name wasn't on any of our maps.

Hoping to see Lone Star Geyser that evening, we followed Shoshone Creek and then Firehole River and stopped to get water from the river as our campsite would be dry. When we reached our campsite, we quickly put up our tents and unloaded everything but food and smelly, bear-attracting things. Those we took with us as we hurried to the geyser, where we sat to wait a long time before RockStar discovered from notes in the geyser journal we had missed the eruption.

Back at our campsite, I tried to wipe accumulated trail dust from my body with a wet bandana. RockStar was too tired for another look at Lone Star, almost half a mile from our campsite, but I walked back for another look. Going off pretty regularly every three hours, Lone Star is a very large and long geyser with a 40-foot high plume. Starting at 7:52, the last bursts of steam clouds didn't subside until 8:18. Very impressive.

In the morning we packed up and walked out to Lone Star Geyser again, so RockStar could see the show, a much different show in the morning but equally grand. First it bubbled and burbled, coy and camera shy, for about half an hour. We wondered if that was all. Then it did its grand major blow like the night before for 15-20 minutes, 40-feet-high and steady like a fire hose, changing from actual water to steam for another 10 minutes. Since the morning was sunny with a blue sky above, the pictures were better than the night before. To top off the show, a rainbow danced in the water drops around the base of the geyser. Nice way to start a day.

Four miles later, we were at Old Faithful Village having burgers at the grill. After showers, washing clothes, and organizing food, we enjoyed quality resting time and received a phone call from Jellybean, who was driving down from Helena after completing her Triple Crown. Yay.

Congrats. We had met Jellybean on the PCT in 2008 and 2009 and had seen her in New Mexico, too. She was hiking with Smurph, a 73-year old, now also a Triple Crowner. They just happened to be driving through Old Faithful and would stop to see us.

We had a wonderful time catching up on adventure tales. Jellybean was also an accomplished sailor, who had sailed to Antarctica. After completing the Triple that year, she went to Alaska and built a log cabin. What a wonderful adventuress. It was great fun to meet Smurf too. Viva la 70+ -year-old hikers.

It seemed ridiculous, and possibly dangerous, for them to attempt to drive late at night to Dubois with nowhere to stop until then. We quietly smuggled them into our room, so they could sleep on air mattresses on the floor.

After breakfast, we said *good-bye* to Jellybean and Smurph. They drove off to Denver, and we hoisted packs and umbrellas to stroll through a light rain down Biscuit Basin. We had it pretty much to ourselves due to leaving early and rain, while steaming geyser vents throughout the basin put on a nice display in the cool air. Steam clouds made it difficult to get pictures of hot pools of bright blue water, but we took them anyway.

Heading up the ridge past Firehole River and Little Firehole River were two relatively short, but steep climbs. NOBO thru hikers, Third Monte and 76-year-old Fixit, passed us going uphill. Yay again for 70+ hikers. Fixit was the oldest hiker I'd seen on the CDT and a thru hiker at that. If he had an interest in completing the AT, he could easily be the oldest Triple Crowner, or at least the oldest one I knew, but he claimed no interest in that achievement.

By this time in my hiking life, I'd begun to say I might be the oldest woman Triple Crowner if I completed it. The statement was mostly a way to joke about my slow speed. I could brag about being old, but I certainly couldn't brag about being a *better* hiker than the multitudes who had passed me over the years.

We had two periods of thunderstorms through the day, lots of rumbling and crackling of thunder and some lightning less than a mile away. In between the noisy weather, the sun came out for lunch. Summit Lake was lovely, and we had plenty of time for camp chores and visiting with SOBOs Lee and Jay. RockStar said this had been a day that reminded her why we liked to do "this silly-ness of backpacking."

We woke to fog on the lake and frost on grass and logs in open areas, although it was quite a bit warmer in our sheltered spot under trees. Leaving on a trail with very minor changes in elevation, we passed the last thermal area and said *good-bye Yellowstone; hello dry-and-dusty trail.*

"A strange hobby for someone who liked to be clean"

The trail wasn't too eventful, although there was always something to admire. Obsidian was mixed with something bright and made the rocks under our feet and beside the trail sparkle. A bright and shiny caramel-colored rock mixed with the obsidian for contrast. The forest, mostly lodgepole pine, also had spruce, looking like Christmas trees. Leaving the National Park, we walked on old roadbed.

The only problem with this section was the lack of water. We had left Summit Lake with a full load of water, except my full load was nearly a liter short since I had to fold the top of my platy to prevent it from leaking.

We met lots of SOBO hikers on the trail: Stephen, Cullen from the UK, Orbit, and Tick Tock, Wiseman, Simple Soul, Susie and Michael from Australia. The trail is an amazing place to meet amazing people from anywhere and everywhere, and I loved the endless invention of trail names.

I was dirty from the dusty trail, but in that notoriously dry section, all water was reserved for drinking. I didn't like going to bed dirty. RockStar said I had "a strange hobby for someone who liked to be clean."

We walked with minimal water to find our first water cache, and the trail consisted of old roadbeds followed by Black Canyon Loop Road, a few views of Black Canyon, Taylor Peak, and the peak above Henry's Lake. Flowers were few, but all the more appreciated. We liked the fluffy look of barberry ground cover beneath the trees and met no hikers as most thrus went to Mac's Inn, while we were headed to Targhee Pass.

From our second cache, we loaded the water we'd need until mid-morning the next day, and I used left over water for a quick bath. It felt heavenly. My fingernails came clean, and I put on my clean bra, Yay. It felt so good to be clean. The night before I'd used hand sanitizer three times, but I was just sterilizing dirt and moving it around. I'd even used sanitizer on a bandana to wipe off my dusty feet. Water worked much better. Being clean improved my attitude immensely. I even had a wet bandana around my neck the last four miles, comfortable under my umbrella in the sun as I sang my way down the trail, and RockStar listened to her iPod as we covered the miles.

The first order of the next day was a road walk to the ridge and our second water cache, only 6 ½ miles from the first one. We had used the only two points we could access by road to place water. Loading up for a day and a night, I washed my socks in the leftovers and put soggy wet bandanas in Ziploc bags for the night's cleanup. Folks in a passing ATV agreed to take our empty water jugs so we didn't have to hang them on the outside of our packs.

Shortly after lunch, we met SOBO hikers Bubbles and Holden. They were surprised to find the reports of waterless walking to be true. We told them where there was supposedly water off trail not far from where we had camped, though we had not checked out the veracity of that source. They'd been counting on waypoints marked for water on Bear Creek maps.

Unfortunately, all of those except the one we didn't check had been dry. I hoped they would find water, but they were young and strong enough to deal with their situation.

In the afternoon we looked down on West Yellowstone and saw smoke rising from a fire 20 miles north of town. RockStar said she liked the views a lot. She just didn't like the climbing up to see them. She may have had difficulty going uphill, but, as usual, I had a hard time keeping up with her on downhills.

We passed some areas with columbine and lupine long past blooming, leaving their signature leaves. Calling it a day at 5:00 with four miles to go in the morning, it seemed early to stop, but RockStar liked to stop when planned, helping me not push rashly past our limits.

Eager to reach the car the next morning, I reveled in carrying only one bottle of water and virtually no food. We rewarded ourselves with brunch in West Yellowstone. I had a Grizzly Bear Omelet with lots of yummy extras added. Then it was off to drive through Yellowstone to get RockStar's car, which we had left at the Heart Lake trailhead. We finally drove back to West Yellowstone and saw elk and buffalo from the road. RockStar thought she saw a wolf. We rarely saw wildlife while hiking, but Yellowstone roads were good for wildlife. Cars move faster than feet, and wildlife doesn't have time to move away. After dinner in West Yellowstone, I played Grandma buying shirts for my nine grandchildren, since I had a car to put them in.

Yellowstone reservations now used, it was time to set up another section of hiking. Fires had eliminated our plans for Wyoming, so we headed to the site of the first crossing of the Continental Divide by Lewis and Clark at Lemhi Pass to drop my car. Back down the dusty road we hopped into Dillon, one of our favorite Montana towns, for a late lunch, a trip to Safeway to purchase food for dinner, a stop at Starbucks for RockStar and Dairy Queen for me. I'd found a hot fudge sundae every time we went through West Yellowstone, as well as one in Dillon. Lucky me.

Off again, we drove north to Jackson and down the dusty road to Miner Lake. Checking out the nearly three miles of jeep road after Miner Lake Campground toward the CDT, we verified that we could meet there in three days within .2 mile of the trail. We found five other vehicles at the trailhead, but the road definitely demanded high clearance and four-wheel drive. I was glad RockStar had such a car and drove such roads well. That confirmed, it was out to the highway again past Wisdom and up Gibbonsville Road to Big Hole Pass. After all-day driving, we reached the pass at 7:30, set up tents and ate our Safeway dinners of salads, fried chicken, and watermelon.

Big Hole Pass to Lemhi Pass

RockStar had decided to sit out the next three days, a good decision for her. I would begin at 7,050 feet, go up to 7,200 feet, down to 5,700 feet, up to 8,800 feet, and drop to 8,600 feet to camp, a very up and down day.

As the jeep road dropped precipitously into Bradley Gulch, I saw a trail paralleling the road at a much more reasonable grade. There were no signs, but not liking the looks of the extremely steep and rocky road, I chose the trail. Checking my GPS and Guthook, the road was the correct path. But I was feeling perverse, and the trail looked recently made. Maybe maps on electronic aids hadn't been updated.

It turned out to be a good choice, adding about half a mile but saving what was left of my knees. It appeared to be made solely to avoid the road's steep descent, but signs would have been nice. A SOBO could take a chance on it like I did, but I a NOBO would likely miss it entirely as it connected perpendicularly to the trail in bushes, again without a sign.

Once in Bradley Gulch, I continued downhill beside the creek lined with sweet and tasty Thimbleberries. Eventually I passed a cabin and forded the creek. After that it was uphill. The Wolf book said it climbed, sometimes steeply. Edit: for the first 600 feet up it was very, very steep, and my replacement knee developed an audible click. Pretty certain that wasn't a good thing, I stopped for lunch, relieved the click didn't return again.

Beside running water all day, I took short rests to fill a bottle and to mix my dinner. Two cedar waxwing in a tree beside me provided entertainment when my aching knees needed another rest. Four hikers, youngish dudes, Soju, Bambi, Buttercup and Maverick, all guys, passed me NOBO. At the top of a big switchback, a group of 13 mountain bikers stopped, waiting for two more. They had to have come on a different trail than the one I went up. I asked them what they were doing in the middle of nowhere. Laughing, they asked me the same thing.

I ate my dinner at a little creek and pushed on, slowly chewing up elevation. As shadows lengthened, I wondered if I would make it to my stopping point before dark. I did, but not with a lot of time to spare. It was after 8:30 before I had the tent up and the bear rope ready. After clean up, I hung my food bag with the last rays of light and walked back to my tent by headlamp.

The next day was my reward for all the climbing of the day before. With water from the little creek flowing from a spring, whose banks were lined with pink monkey flower, I had a short climb to the other side of the Divide, where the trail entered a high bowl. My trail stayed high, just below cliffs and talus slopes, as I traversed the bowl. The peaks around me were amazing, the views across the bowl and the high meadows equally so. I could even see the broad valley of Big Hole proper.

Passing a few lakes and high tarns on the other side of the bowl, I went up and over the Divide again to another high valley, Squaw Mountain dead ahead. Through the notch between Squaw Mountain and the Divide, yet another vista lay before me, this time revealing Lower Slag-a-Melt Lake and peaks still splotched with snow. Upper Slag-a-Melt Lake was tucked below a high peak with snow patches on its side. Lena Lake was only a mile distant from Upper Slag-a-Melt for crows, but it was a long three miles around a mountain for me. It rained lightly half the way there, but the view walking into Lena Lake was magnificent: jagged peaks all in a row with snow in the gullies.

One of the hikers I met that day was John, a NOBO in his 50s. He told me he was trying for a record. He'd already done both the AT and the PCT *that year*, each in 60-something days, and he planned to finish the CDT in about 78 days. Yes, some hikers on these trails are near superhuman.

Leaving Lena Lake in the morning, I headed down the trail, which turned into *up* trail on a very beautiful, high-country day, with every stream lined with pink monkey flower, yellow daisies and a variety of other flowers. I went over three high points in the day, the last at 9,200 feet. Each ridge or Divide revealed new views of ruggedly grand peaks, as well as the distant Big Hole Valley. The peaks, some with snow lingering, usually had rocky cliffs on the northwest side and were smooth and barren on the southeast side.

The meadows were green, and the streams coursing down the mountains were lovely as I passed many lakes and tarns. Photo opportunities provided excuses for many short rests. A few elephant heads still bloomed, and one last bunch of pink heather. Bright-yellow alpine St John's wort grew thickly on stream banks along with monkey flower on a joyfully dazzling day. In the talus before the last climb, four furry marmots shrilled at me and posed for pictures.

The afternoon was a very long downhill past Rock Island Lakes all the way to Miner Creek to meet RockStar. She brought Subways for dinner. Charging my cell phone and Steripen with her car charger, we decided to add another day to our plan to Lemhi Pass. The three days from Big Hole Pass to Miner Creek had required walking late. RockStar couldn't have covered the distance I did in three days, and we would both be happier if we didn't push so hard to Lemhi Pass.

We started out with a thousand-foot climb walking through pine forests and a few scattered firs in the cool morning with distant views of the Divide and a few flowers. Tattu Jo and All Good passed us headed NOBO. We chatted with them and took pictures, one of the advantages of hopping around on different parts of the trail.

Flat tent space was at a premium that night, only one log separating our tents. I took my Ziploc bath standing naked on a one-foot square of grass not far from my tent. The rushing creek made soothing white noise as we relaxed well before hiker midnight.

After a good night's sleep, I didn't feel so trail-worn, and knowing we had a short day, we took a leisurely lunch with a bit of shut-eye. In the afternoon we crossed paths with several NOBOs, Thermometer, a Korean hiker, and Sketchy, Stop and Go, Veg, Hiker Box, and Zorro. Zorro, from Barcelona, Spain, wasn't feeling well and hoped to see a Doc in Anaconda or Hamilton, both quite a number of miles ahead. Thru hikers are made of very stout stuff and keep on walking, whatever the need.

The last of the climb was hard on RockStar. I insisted we go to Lake Janke, another high- mountain gem a half mile and 100-feet up from the trail. Flowers appeared again: daisies, paintbrush, lupine, monkey flower and some unusual white monkshood. We found a place to camp on a bench above the lake at the edge of a meadow filled with blue bog gentian. The sunset over the lake from my tent was worth the climb and shaded the hills and water a delicate pink.

Rain sounded on the tents as we snuggled in for sleep.

Leaving Janke Lake, we met Early Bird and Squirrel, young NOBOs who had already come more distance that morning than we would go in the whole day. Ah, youth. They both carried small stuffed animals. Squirrel's was deep in his pack as he was afraid of losing it. Early bird's was an owl tucked in her backpack pocket with beak and eyes sticking out. She said, "Alfred keeps a watch on things as we walk."

Very cute.

Crossing a ridge, we descended a little, circled a bowl above a small lake and crested the Divide again before lunchtime. Then it was up and down with nice views of the Divide looking north, a peek at Big Hole, a look at the Salmon Valley, and ahead to Goldstone Mountain. We also looked down on Darkhorse and Cowbone Lakes, former routes of the CDT with very steep climbs back up to the Divide, glad we were not on them.

There was no water at Goldstone Pass. Our choices were to go down nearly half a mile to Goldstone Lake or a quarter of a mile on the west side of the Divide to a spring, the start of Pratt Creek. We set up tents, hung our food and walked to the creek, finding it a challenge to get water from a spreading, shallow flow through marshy ground. After dinner we watched the pink sunset as the birds became quiet, and stillness descended with the dark.

As I delivered RockStar's food bag to her tent in the morning, I told her the day was clear and beautiful, but I could see the valley was all fogged in. Before we finished packing, the fog engulfed us, too, icy-cold fog accompanied with a strong and steady 20-30 mile-an-hour wind. Brr. Even in my gloves, my hands were so cold they could hardly function.

The trail went steeply straight up Goldstone Mountain. We should have had great views, but all we saw were a billion water droplets of fog, though we could tell we were on the edge of steep drop-offs. Later on, the sun broke through, providing us views of Swift Lake and the Salmon River Valley, but we were cold all morning.

We met Fixit and Third Monty again. Fixit might have been 76-years- old, but he and Third Monty were thru hikers making at least 20 mile days, far more than I could have done in that terrain even if I'd been ten-years younger than my 75. Yay for 70+ hikers. Especially for Fix-it.

Going so slowly through the cold and windy fog over Goldstone, we were afraid we would be hiking in the dark. But after lunch, we zoomed on gentle trail. At least we did *our* interpretation of a zoom.

After passing Popeye and Olive, a cute couple from Belgium headed NOBO, we followed Wolf and Ley maps to Patty Creek. Most thru hikers wouldn't go a mile off trail for water. But we couldn't do 20+ mile days and Patty Creek met our needs. Finding a nice flowing stream through a high-meadow cow pasture, we avoided the cow pies and set up our tents.

We knew we were going to be cold in the open meadow and probably have condensation but glad to have water, we settled in before sunset. The morning turned out not to be a little cold with a little condensation. It was 27 degrees, condensation was frozen solid, as was the top inch of my platypus. I couldn't even unzip the top to pour water until sun heated it.

My knee objected to so many days without a day off. Between its complaining, the cold, and my neck and shoulder hurting, I didn't sleep well. Packing up in the cold was the pits.

However, on the trail once again, we found it easy to take the shallow gulley from the turn in the road up the short distance to catch the CDT, short barberry ground cover easy to traverse.

Twigg (NOBO) told us there was a fire north of us, which had closed the trail, and other NOBO hikers were road walking around it. He'd found an alternate way on the map to stay on a trail as long as possible. Though we had been hoping to run into Illusive (another 70+ NOBO), he was now probably road walking past us, and we would miss him.

After looking at Beaver Head Mountains and other ranges farther away, we could see all the way down to Lemhi Pass, a steep descent to which both of my knees strenuously objected.

Reaching the pass, we found an annual memorial run/walk of the Shoshone Tribe from Tendoy to Lemhi Pass, memorializing the expulsion of the Shoshone. They told us there would be a big celebration in Salmon, Idaho with lots of dancing and food and all were welcome, including us. Unfortunately we were headed for Dillon on the east side of the Divide.

We found my car all safe and sound at Lemhi Pass and were happy to take off packs and hiking shoes, ready for a break. We read all the Sacajawea signs and stood astride the water flowing in a tiny stream, which was the source of the Missouri River. In Dillon, we dried tents, took showers, did laundry, and ate a steak dinner, as well as kibitzing with a local woman about ultra-light backpacking.

Waking up in beds was wonderful. After breakfast, we set out in my car to Jackson and up the Miner Creek Road to Miner Creek Campground. There we had to leave my non-four-wheel drive vehicle and walk up the jeep road toward RockStar's car, which we'd left six days earlier. After walking 1.5 miles we got lucky. A couple driving to the upper trailhead gave the two lady hikers a lift for the last mile or so, and we told them about long-distance hiking. Climbing into RockStar's car, we drove back to my car. Setting up for hikes and retrieving cars were part of the drill to make the CDT work for us, even if it meant an extra hike.

Montana is a big state. We drove as far as Helena that day and the next to Great Falls for another shot at the Lewis and Clark Interpretive Center, stopped in Cutbank, the closest lodging we could find to Glacier National Park and Saint Mary, which left us a 75-mile drive before a 15-mile hike the next day.

Piegan Pass

On the road at 5:00, we left RockStar's car at Saint Mary and drove mine to Jackson Glacier Overlook. Since we couldn't do the Wyoming section, which had been closed by fire, we decided to do the Piegan Pass section in Glacier as a day hike. RockStar booked a cabin at Swift Current and a shuttle back to Saint Mary the following day. Sweet.

Starting on our 2,000-foot climb north of the overlook, we saw peek-a-boo views of pointy mountains between the trees. Foam flower, bead lily, purple fleabane, and pearly everlasting made appearances beside the trail. More prominently, the trail was thickly lined with ripe thimbleberries. As we gained elevation, thimbleberries changed to huckleberries, and we proceeded to munch our way up the trail with breakfast fruit.

Reaching the Siyeh Bend Junction, our solitude and berries came to an end. Siyeh Bend was a popular trail that avoided the thousand feet we had just climbed. Everyone passed us: families, tourists, hiking clubs, and serious hikers. Lots of people were on the trail, and we were the slowest. RockStar had challenges going uphill, and I'd become old somewhere along the years. We might be long-distance hikers, but we were definitely not *fast* long-distance hikers.

No matter. We chatted a bit with Nancy and David from Portland. They had guessed we were backpackers from our packs, though we didn't have most of our gear. Learning we were CDT hikers, Nancy asked if we had done AT and PCT, too, and were working toward Triple Crowns. Cool. Rarely did anyone know what that was, but Nancy was a long-distance-hiker wannabe.

We were slow for more than age or the state of our bodies. We were slow because we took a billion pictures. Stupendous, spectacular, awesome, jaw-dropping pictures. Glacier's mountains require all the superlatives. Towering mountains formed by glaciers carving immense cliffs surrounded us. Everywhere we looked was another view, flower, or field *and* hillside covered with flowers. Hanging glaciers clung to the mountains, and waterfalls plunged down the canyons.

Glacier had been the *carrot* ever since we bailed in 2014 due to bad weather. Sheer sides of Glacier's mountains reached to the sky and lured us back on the trail after first seeing their grandeur. RockStar had hung in with me for the other CDT hikes for the chance to hike in

Glacier. Climbing to Piegan Pass lived up to our expectations and then some.

Emerging from trees to the meadows of Preston Park, we saw even more flowers. The early bloomers were mostly done, but substantial numbers of others made an adequate show. Yellow Daisies were the dominant flower, especially in the high country. But valerian, yarrow, harebells, paintbrush, gentian and others chimed in.

It was a long walk above timberline to the top of the pass. The changing views of mountains and layers of cliffs laden with snow patches and glaciers were breathtaking. A ranger- led group passed us, and the ranger explained the bright turquoise color of the lake below the summit to the north was a result of rocks ground to powder by glaciers.

Descending opposite craggy cliffs and mountain walls with more hanging glaciers, we eventually stopped for a very late lunch as we reached scrubby, nearly wind-flattened trees. I fell and sat on one of the trees, and the fragrance of crushed needles was so sweet, I didn't mind falling.

Two girls from Taiwan, almost as slow as we were, passed us when we stopped for lunch. Watching them walk, I thought they were having more fun than the speedy hikers we had seen earlier. Our languages were different, but our enjoyment was the same. As we came to Morning Eagle Falls, which we'd first seen in the distance downhill, I took way too many pictures of it tumbling over maroon-colored rocks. I was afraid each view would be the last one, so I had to capture it. After the falls, it wasn't far to the valley floor past bushes loaded with huckleberries. How could we make any time when we were being tempted by luscious dark-blue goodness begging to be eaten on every step of trail?

Passing Lake Josephine after a long, nearly level haul through the bottom of the valley, we took the short cut between Josephine and Swift Current Lakes on a bridge. The view of Many Glacier Hotel across the lake was classic.

That day was everything we could have hoped for. The only mar besides our slowness, was a paucity of blue sky; it was cloudy and cold all day. No rain fell beyond a few half-hearted spitting drops. Walking in such gorgeous scenery made it hard to complain about anything.

We made it to Swift Current about 7:30, not a great time speed-wise, but we *had* a great time. The cabin at Swift Current was cute, the beds superior. We exhaustedly fell into them and slept like logs.

After breakfast at the Swift Current Restaurant, we caught the hiker shuttle to Saint Mary and RockStar's car. After looking at campsite information for the next year, RockStar drove me to the St. Mary Falls trailhead, so I could walk up to Jackson Overlook. Slack packing that short hike would change our last day of hiking from 15.1 miles to a more do-able 12.6.

I enjoyed pretty Deadwood Falls while munching on trail snacks and an apple. Back at Jackson Overlook I found my car and moved it down to the St. Mary Falls trailhead. I and all food and gear we needed for the next five days, were loaded into RockStar's car, and after a stop for a late lunch, we headed to East Glacier for the night.

In the morning we picked up our backcountry permits and watched the compulsory bear/park rules video. After our late breakfast, lunch for me consisted of two very big cinnamon rolls, while doing our laundry and writing a few notes about age records for a Triple Crowner.

Records are made to be broken. Having joked the last couple years that I was trying for the old lady record for completion of the Triple Crown, it looked like I might actually achieve that. Many caveats accompanied that statement. To begin with, no one keeps such records, and for all I knew, an 80-year-old woman might already have received the Triple Crown.

I was basing my *sort of claim* on the fact that Susan Alcorn, who kept an unofficial record of women's age of completions for the PCT, had told me I was one of the oldest to do that, completing the PCT a week before turning 71. I assumed no one older had come along since then. I further assumed the CDT would be the last trail a Triple Crowner would complete. I also assumed I would have heard about an older woman, or man for that matter, on the CDT. If all those assumptions *happened* to be correct, I *might* turn out to be the oldest, if

I was able to complete the CDT in 2017. Those were a lot of assumptions, the truth of which I had no way of knowing. Who knew?

Any musing about being the oldest was theory anyway, until the trail was complete. At 75, a failing body part could complicate life. With two shoulder replacements, one knee replacement, and another knee close to needing a replacement, plus various other age-related problems, I was quite aware complications were possible.

I had a rival for the supposed record. Barbara was a 74-year-old CDT section hiker, who had completed AT and PCT. Pretty cool. I am all for old ladies still on the trail. One of us may be the oldest woman Triple Crowner in a year or two, and any supposed record would be likely to stand only briefly, as increasing numbers of older women and men are doing this crazy thing of long-distance hiking. Pretty cool, that. Yay for the older set. I would be quite OK with being *one* of the oldest hikers to complete the Triple Crown.

Our dinner at Glacier Lodge was less than stellar, but we rescued the culinary adventure by getting huckleberry pie back at Luna's. Best huckleberry pie in town.

After breakfast at Luna's, having walked the half-mile from the Ranger Station to the trailhead the day before, we began at the trailhead for an uphill sort of day. Crossing the creek above Pray Lake we walked around Rising Wolf Mountain up the Dry Fork Valley between Rising Wolf and Red Mountain. Flinsch Peak and Mount Morgan were in sight most of the day.

Some of the ground cover was turning red. Berries were abundant: red Thimbleberry, orange mountain ash, red kinnikinnick, purple Oregon grape, and green to purple juniper, decorating the trail with color. And, of course, huckleberries asked us to munch them as we walked, leaving me with a purple mouth.

We had 1,500-feet elevation gain, and the last 500 feet seemed to take forever. Not a high- mileage day, we reached Oldman Lake about 2:30. A couple and their adult daughters camped at Oldman, too, and we enjoyed talking with them. The lake, at 8,700-feet elevation, was beautifully set in a large cirque comprised of Flinsch and Morgan's shoulders. There was plenty of grand scenery, though not quite as breathtaking as Piegan Pass. Debating Glacier scenery is quibbling over hairs.

After dinner and a few chores, we snuggled in our tents for a chilly night. I'd brought my leg warmers and fleece, as well as my down jacket and extra gloves, not liking the extra weight, but glad to have the warmth. The wind roared all night long, waking me several times.

Oh well, up and at 'em. We started out with a 1,000-foot elevation gain as we climbed the walls of the cirque to Pitamakin Pass. In spite of the wind, I was in a good mood, and the climb went well. Spectacular mountains, valleys, and lakes on both sides of the pass, we said *good-bye* to Oldman Lake and Flinsch Peak, starting down toward Lake of the Seven Winds and Pitamakin Lake. I misread the name on my GPS as Lake of the Severe Winds. Severe or seven, the wind was fierce, nearly blowing me off my feet and trying to hurl me into the lakes below us. I was glad for the weight in my pack and often crouched low, hanging on to my poles to brace against the wind. We finally made it down to tree line.

Descending 2,277 feet, we had a very late lunch before Morning Star Lake. Our campsite neighbors from Oldman Lake passed us to camp there. Our trail wound through foliage composed of yellows, browns, and a few reds. Although the flowers were few, strikingly bright red king's crown was on that very windy trail above Pitamakin and Seven Winds Lake.

We met a Back Country Ranger, who had been a thru hiker on the PCT. He thought Mother Goose, an 81-year-old woman, had to get off trail in the Great Basin in Wyoming, but would probably finish next year. Wow. Huzzah. Huzzah for Mother Goose. I could settle for being *one* of the oldest women Triple Crowners. (Later in the year while talking to Billy Goat, he said didn't think Mother Goose was that old. Maybe there were two hikers named Mother Goose.

Huzza either way, for all older women, and men too, who walk long trails.)

Turning up Atlantic Creek, long, wispy waterfalls fell on the sides of mountains beside us and a bigger, close-up one at Atlantic Creek just before we reached our campsite. Campsites in Glacier National

Park are often a communal affair, all eating together in a *kitchen* area near a food-hanging bar set between trees. Not enough privacy for Ziploc baths, so cleanup was sketchy. I was going to be really dirty after four days.

Best Ever

The next day we had a 2,000-foot climb, the most incredibly grand and glorious climb ever. It was 2,000 feet up with a view at every step. The ranger had said it would be "a slog, but pretty, though." We thought it was spectacular, our new favorite day in Glacier. "Best ever," said RockStar.

The nicely graded trail cut through red/maroon-colored rock, a sedimentary rock with streaks of white, sometimes tinted blue or green. The rock alone was interesting. Across the grand valley were towering mountains, and at the head of the cirque was Medicine Grizzly Lake below more towering mountains, whose snowbanks released water tumbling down to the lake. A smaller lake was higher up across the valley. Everywhere we looked were amazing views.

Flowers covered the color spectrum even though late in the season: blue harebells, yellow daisies, cinquefoil, and suffer flower, red paintbrush, purple asters, penstemon and unopened gentians and white yarrow, bedstraw, angelica, and pearly everlasting.

As we approached Triple Divide Pass, clouds boiled over down into the bowl on our side.

Standing on the pass, we were suddenly in thick, foggy clouds with no view.

Water falling on Triple Divide Peak separates three ways. One way becomes Atlantic Creek, eventually making its way to the Atlantic Ocean. Another becomes Pacific Creek headed for the Pacific Ocean, and the third becomes Hudson Bay Creek, flowing to Hudson Bay and the Arctic Ocean.

We headed down through the fog, and the mountains teased us with fleeting views of their tops behind moving cloud banks. Eventually the sky cleared and revealed Triple Divide Peak, Split Mountain, and the craggy ridge between. We ate lunch with all that splendor laid out before us. We saw marmots, too. I'd discovered, on an interpretive sign near Swift Current, that the marmots in Glacier came in a very small variety. They looked more like oddly shaped squirrels, coats flecked with white. We glimpsed a mountain goat from a distance, as a white dot moved up one of the mountains.

It was a long way down. 2,500 feet and 8 miles. It took us a long time, walking through an old burn, silver trunks contrasting with the yellow and orange foliage of spent thimbleberries.

The trail seemed to go on and on, broken only by a bit of excitement of crossing two bouncy suspension bridges.

Eventually we reached Red Eagle Lake. Our friends from Oldman Lake had passed us on our descent and stopped at the head of Red Eagle. It looked like it would be difficult to get water there due to a big mud flat on that end of the lake. We reached our camp area at the foot of Red Eagle in a fairly open area of old burn. But the water was easily accessible, and a group with Glacier Guides provided company around a fire while we ate our dinner.

On our last morning, it felt colder than the thermometer said as we packed up and climbed the little hill by the lake. We had no major climbs that last day. I wanted to hike to sunshine in the cold morning, but the temperature quickly passed from cold to hot. Another suspension bridge swayed side-to-side, as well as bouncing up-and-down as we crossed. Fun, as long as it was only me on the bridge.

Fall color seemed to have as much to do with dryness as season or altitude. Valleys and hillsides with southern exposure had the most fall color. Reaching St. Mary Lake we encountered more green. Mirrored mountains in the peacefully calm lake were stunning, but vegetation overgrew our trail. RockStar said pushing through bushes was worse than going uphill. Willow and alder added to overgrown thimbleberries and guaranteed scratched legs. Four guys passing us had camped at Red Eagle Head the night before. They'd seen two moose as a reward for having a mudflat for a water source.

It took us a long time to reach Virginia Falls, and we passed many more short falls as we proceeded down the trail toward St. Mary Falls on a broad tourist trail, which was quite a contrast to the overgrown trail before the falls.

After St. Mary Falls, we trudged to the trailhead and passed a young deer losing the spots of fawnhood. One last pull to the shuttle stop and I walked down and got my car. CDT was finished for the year.

After dinner at Rising Sun, we drove to RockStar's car at Two Medicine. On the way, weather drastically changed to a thunderstorm with black clouds. We thought about all the hikers we had met, who were being pelted with the cold rain trying to be snow hitting our windshield. Our timing to get off the trail had been perfect. Reaching RockStar's car, both of us drove to our little cabin at East Glacier. The day was done. The CDT for 2016 was over. The next day was a long drive home.

2016 had included some relatively boring parts from Rock Spring to Highway 15 and some of the section to Targhee Pass from Yellowstone. It also included unexpected flower shows on Lion's Head and Mount Taylor, great high country with beautiful lakes from Big Hole Pass to Miner Creek and the sublime hikes of Piegan Pass and Triple Divide. We had not been chased by forest fires, although fire had prevented from us from finishing Wyoming. We had not had horrid weather. We had not quit early. It was a great year.

Chapter 46 Fall and Spring 2016-2017

Grandma Again

September 15, the day I started hiking the GR65 in France, my tenth grandchild was born. Total hiking on long-distance trails in 2016 had been 1,256 miles. I enjoyed all three hikes, but three hikes in a year were a bit much for a 75-year-old grandma. I met my newest grandson on the way back to Washington and looked forward to doing less in 2017.

Faceplant

Indeed, I did do less in 2017, even less than I planned to do. My spring hike was on the ADT (American Discovery Trail) in Nevada, and I took the only serious fall I have ever had. Don't fall downhill. Always fall uphill. You build up momentum exponentially as you fall and even three feet from a standing position straight down a steep hill means you hit with considerable impact.

I skinned my face, broke my nose, scratched my glasses, smashed the nosepiece into my nose and cut it, got two of the most amazing shiners ever, and tried to dislocate a rib. Then I walked another four days, not because I had to, but because it seemed like I'd done everything in first aid than anyone else would do. Caveat on my behalf, the rib didn't start hurting until 30 hours after the fall. In retrospect, I probably had a concussion, too, but as far as I knew I'd not lost consciousness and was making reasonable decisions. When asked by the ER Doc four days later about possible loss of consciousness. I answered, "If you are alone, would you know?"

I was cleared to continue hiking but told the rib would continue hurting. I threw in the towel and decided to hurt at home as I healed there instead of on the trail. So ended my spring hike.

RockStar and I again applied to Glacier National Park for permits to finish the CDT. Again, I was turned down, but RockStar awarded the much sought-after permits. That set the end dates for our 2017 hike. I just had to plan the other assorted sections to work out before we were in Glacier. RockStar reminded me the Eclipse was coming, and it would be ideal to be in Wyoming then. Well, OK then. I included the eclipse in the plan.

RockStar bought a car camping tent, as she definitely didn't plan on hiking every step with me. She was having trouble with a knee had started rounds with Docs and physical therapy.

I decided on the Anaconda cutoff to enable me to complete the trail in 2017. It seemed a good idea to start off with a mostly level four-day walk for both of us to get in better shape.

After reflection on my age and recent fall, I purchased an inReach device. It clipped on my chest strap just as my Garmin Oregon had done, and the inReach had an even better GPS map with the CDT already indicated on it. Not just replacing my older GPS, it would record my progress in real time to anyone to whom I gave the connecting information. Every 10 minutes a little dot recorded my location.

My children could see what their mother was doing, and where she was. In a macabre sense, they would know how to find the body. In a more hopeful sense, I could press the SOS button, and help would come no matter where I was in the world. I hoped neither of those uses would ever be necessary. But I would carry the device for a GPS, and as a concession to old age and safety. The inReach also had the capability for limited two-way communication, which turned out to be very helpful for RockStar supporting me.

Chapter 47 July 25, 2017

The Cutoff

RockStar and I met in Anaconda. She would take short walks to get in better condition, and I would take longer ones to complete the section between Storm Lake and Champion Pass, all slack packs.

Storm Lake was beautiful, the hills thick with a profusion of wild flowers. Parrot's beak, miner's candle, western saxifrage, rock jasmine, and bear grass joined all the usual high elevation flowers. RockStar sprayed me with OFF to discourage mosquitoes, and I headed out.

Those first four days on the Anaconda cutoff I had no paper map. The Guthook AP on my phone and the maps on my inReach device worked in tandem to give me needed information as I walked to my previously placed car. The next day RockStar dropped me off at the Twin Lakes Road and drove a few miles closer to town before she started her shorter hike back to the motel. I pretended I was home doing my usual neighborhood walk, and the miles went by in good order. The trail routed through the town of Anaconda. I stopped at a grocery store to eat lunch in air-conditioned comfort and stopped at the Dairy Queen for a hot fudge sundae, which I ate as I walked. There are perks on a road walk through town.

After stopping at the motel to compare notes with RockStar, I doffed my pack and a few minutes later was out again for a quick walk with just water and umbrella to my previously placed car at the junction north of town. Reaching my car at 14 miles for the day, I drove back to the motel, and we retrieved RockStar's car. Each of us were meeting our goals and having a good time. Since it was still early, and I'd had such a good day, I drove out to the junction again and hiked 3.3 more miles of very pleasant walking, even on a highway with traffic. Following the old rule, "Walk on the left facing the traffic, and step off the road when cars approach," I had no problems.

The next day we did the usual early-up drill and placed my car where I left off the day before. RockStar drove me 14 miles up Cottonwood Road and dropped me to walk back to my car. She chose a spot to do an out-and-back hike to her car. She had a 700-foot elevation gain; my hike was downhill or flat, but longer.

My umbrella was up most of the way, and hazy clouds disappeared into intense sunshine. I stood in the road getting three blasts from farm sprinklers overshooting the field. It felt good, but wet coolness didn't last long in the hot sun. I was overjoyed to finally find a farmhouse with shade trees and lawn by the road. Murphy and Movin' On—SOBOS, whom I'd met earlier—caught up with me and sat in the shade as we chatted.

Highway 48 was brutally hot highway walking. Sun shining directly on the device on my chest strap said it was 110. It probably wasn't really that hot, but it felt like it in the sun.

RockStar drove by with a carload of thru hikers, passing me about a mile before my car. They were properly impressed with the old lady who was *"crushing it."* Actually, I was walking fast because I was terribly hot and wanted to reach my car as soon as possible.

Catching up with Murphy and Movin' On resting in some shade, we walked on together to my car. Hallelujah. I took their packs to town so they could walk the last five miles without them. After dinner, we drove my car to Cottonwood Road and left it so we would have less driving in the morning.

During those first three days, RockStar gradually increased her conditioning: 4, 6, 8 miles. So the next morning we decided to go together for 8.7 miles. Driving to Champion Pass, where I'd stopped in 2015 required driving through Deerlodge and a lot of miles on a bad gravel/dirt road.

I explored a possible short cut road to use later, but the other road, though on my GPS, fruitlessly ended at a locked gate. RockStar had gone ahead while I was exploring, and I caught up with her just past Four Corners. RockStar then went ahead while I was eating lunch. By the time I caught up with her, she was done, and her knee was hurting. I walked the last 3.6 miles as quickly as I could to bring the car back to her, as both of us were very concerned about her knee.

After the long drive to retrieve RockStar's car, we drove to Deerlodge for dinner. By then, she could barely walk leaning on poles and walls. RockStar's knee didn't recover overnight. Her chances of hiking didn't look good for at least a few days. I would be a solo hiker with a great friend, who supported me and found things to do by herself while her knee rested.

"What ya gonna do?" Plans change.

After laundry and stopping at a CVS and a gas station, we drove to Butte and a Walmart, had breakfast for lunch at Perkins, then moved on to Wisdom, left my car, and finally drove to

Big Hole Pass. Setting up for section hiking took time and car miles. I jumped into hiker clothes, said *good-bye* to RockStar, set up my tent, and ate dinner. I fed the left overs to one of the tons of SOBO thru hikers, who walked through Big Hole Pass that evening. The previous four days had been warm ups. The next day I would carry a full pack and have nearly 3,000 feet of cumulative elevation gain.

As I packed up in the morning, a dark grey, nearly black fox came very near my tent. I wondered if it knew campers were good for a handout or if it was rabid. It showed very little fear, and I had to yell at it and toss little rocks at it four times to drive it to away. I didn't like the unnatural behavior.

Flowers and views south to the section I'd completed the year before gave me opportunities to stop and take pictures on steep uphill climbs, of which there were many. The afternoon was more difficult, and I stopped a half-mile short of my goal. I was tired and had found flat ground. That was good enough for me.

RockStar brought me orange juice and watermelon chunks at Chief Joseph Pass the next day, along with water. Great trail angel treats. Since we were going to camp together at Gibbons Pass, I dumped most of my gear in her car and slack packed the rest. The hike wasn't too exciting, but I was happy for an easier day.

Arriving at Gibbons, I found RockStar's wonderful car camping tent and lawn chairs, luxuries on the trail, which I shared.

Since RockStar wasn't hiking, I slack packed another day through old burn areas in various stages of regrowth. SOBO thru hikers, who had been in RockStar's car near Anaconda: Salt Lick, Sonic, Puma, Red Bass, and Lavender, passed me in a new forest of lodgepole

pine. Arriving at Schultz Saddle by 3:15, RockStar picked me up in a half hour.

We had to change my hike plan for more reasons than RockStar's knee. Though I hadn't planned to do the Pintlers until late August, two fires had started. I was concerned they might burn their way across the CDT by late August, so I needed to complete that section of trail before it was closed. That changed everything. We hadn't planned to do that section in six days. But the road access midway was already closed by fire. So two three-day sections became one six-day section. Six days of food weighs more than three days, but *what ya gonna do?* Plans change.

It took nearly an hour to drive out to the highway and into Wisdom to the Forest Service. We were lucky they were still open. Though concerned about a big smoke plume in the sky, the ranger said it wasn't threatening the CDT. A new fire had broken out to the west, and Big Hole Pass was to be closed. Good thing I already had done that part.

I organized to leave the next day, had a shower, ate dinner, did a little hand wash, brushed my teeth, and fell into bed. The fire hadn't closed the Pintlers. RockStar was still supporting me, and our revised plan would work. After 12 busy hours in town, some spent sleeping, RockStar drove me back to Schultz Saddle, and I was on the trail again.

"Thank you that though I am old, slow, and forgetful, I can still be here."

I missed hiking with RockStar, but I was profoundly grateful she was giving me car support. At least I could see her on town stops. My pack was heavy with six days' food, and I needed to eat it lighter.

As I packed up after lunch, the wind shifted, and the air filled with smoke. A lot of smoke.

The ranger had reassured me I wouldn't be burned up, but I wondered if that covered asphyxiation from smoke inhalation. I walked for a while with my bandana bandido style and hoped that might help. Wind shifted again in the next hour, and blue sky and more breathable air returned. Passing Surprise Lake, with Johnson Peak behind it, I went on to the saddle a half-mile farther.

The next morning I celebrated my birthday by losing my socks. Hey, a 76-year-old forgets things. I was ready to take down my tent when the first NOBO of the year came by, Thai Stick, a tall, skinny guy from New Zealand, who lived in Thailand. Distracted from my routine by talking, I forgot to put my wet socks on the back of my pack, and left them hanging on a branch. Oh well.

I told Thai Stick my age, and he went on at his usual 26-27 mile-a-day pace and told every SOBO he met on the trail to tell me Happy Birthday. What a sweetheart. I was greeted all day by people telling me Happy Birthday. Meeting Hummingbird, a young woman SOBO, I asked her to look for my socks and walk them out of the wilderness for me. I felt bad about forgetting them, but couldn't add miles to my day to return for them. Phil and Julia (NOBOs) came up and chatted while I was talking to Hummingbird. They'd hiked 2/3 of the CDT the year before and were on a quest to finish. Merlin, Hummingbird's partner, wished me Happy Birthday, too, as did Old Gear (OG).

I was sorry to have to tell all these CDT hikers about trail closures. RockStar had sent me a text saying the latest closure was from Lost Trail to Miner Lakes, another section I'd completed the year before. Farther up the trail, Continental Drifter wished me Happy Birthday.

The first water source was a marsh, not ideal for drinking water. At the second I met Star Fish, who recommended I go farther. She and Diesel gave me another Happy Birthday, and I found a place for my tent on a small-game trail.

After lunch the next day, I headed up Pintler Pass, flowers blooming the whole way. Most high-country flowers were represented, including shooting stars on foot-long stems. Rock jasmine were thick, and there were even a few late-blooming bear grass. A few weeks earlier, a solid profusion of bear grass and heather would have lined the trail, which was now a forest of dry bear grass stalks thickly standing sentinel. I wondered if the locals hiked these trails to see the bear grass like Washingtonians climb Bandera Mountain in the early summer.

Before I reached Johnson Lake, sun shone red through smoke. I walked past the nice campsite by the lake, continuing to a stream crossing where I stole a deer's bedroom of flattened grass. As I bathed inside my tent to avoid the mosquitoes, a deer came nibbling greenery about 10-feet away. Although I shooed it, it returned, peering quizzically through the trees, perhaps wondering why I was in its bedroom.

The next day wasn't one of flowers but of grand mountain peaks. I forded the West Fork of the La Marche, though the log for crossing was unusable—broken and turned on its side.

Another big log with its branches still intact had fallen across the water, but was 25-feet across and 3-feet above the river. I might have trusted it for a 5-foot stretch, but not for 25. If old ladies fall three feet onto rocks, they break. I safely waded.

Before Warren Lake, I got worried about my foot as it felt reminiscent of the stress fracture I'd had a couple years before. So I developed a new gait for uphills: a long step with the left and a short step with the right, preventing the stress of pushing off with the left. Hopefully, I could control the problem without a full-blown stress fracture. Old lady hikers have to discover solutions for problems with old bodies.

Going up Cutaway Pass, the views were marvelous, better than from the pass itself. After lunch, I passed the Richter family from Michigan, heading to Warren Lake, though they admitted they might not make it that night because they were carrying old, very heavy gear. As we chatted and went our separate directions, I wished I could have consulted with them to save them some grief on their gear choices. But learning through mistakes teaches lessons, too.

It was hard to get up in the morning. Hiking nine days straight will do that to an old lady. I forgot to treat the water in the platy at night, and the Steripen charge was dead. I still had 1/2 bottle of treated water to hike with, and I put Aqua Mira in the platy for later, but it wasn't a good start for the day. And it was cold. I glumly wondered if I was getting too old for this sort of thing.

A tenth of a mile later I came to the water source, surrounded by bank after bank of bright- pink monkey flower. Beautiful. All I could say was, "Thank you, God that this 76-year-old lady can be on this trail to see beauty that so fills my soul with gladness. Thank you that though I am old, slow, and forgetful, I can still be here." After that, the day went much better.

On the long climb up Rainbow Mountain I saw two grouse. Lunch was in a gully filled with corn lily. Food gone, the pack was lighter going up the last climb to Goat Flats, where I talked to two Forest Service guys who told me the section from Johnson Lake to Rainbow Lake was now included in the fire closure, although they thought it was still OK for CDT hikers.

It would be a shame to eliminate the Pintlers for that tiny square corner of the map. But perhaps it was on the closure list for a sliver of old burn with dead trees easy fuel for a new fire. Every year fires somewhere keep thru hikers from seeing a slice of magnificent scenery on the trail.

The Forest Service guys kindly pointed out posts indicating trail over the tundra-like high country toward Storm Lake Pass, and I headed up. In bad weather, it might have been difficult to see those posts, but the day was still good, though smoke haze was building. White gentian bloomed from Goat Flat to the pass and paintbrush, valerian, sulfur flower and others made displays as I traversed a steep cut around a bowl. Stopping to take many pictures I should have taken even more for I would never be that way again. I have often had that thought on my treks. I don't repeat long trails, and each year I am more aware of advancing years and the reality that I can't keep hiking forever.

Down from the pass, the trail was surprisingly good, but at least a mile longer than anticipated. I pounded down the trail in good fashion, but it was an hour later than I'd estimated I'd be. An hour off schedule is not a large difference for six days of travel. Since I was using inReach, RockStar knew where I was when she looked at her cell phone at 2:30 and figured I would be later than 4:00.

We drove down to Anaconda for a shower. Clean clothes. And a huge chicken-fried steak smothered in gravy. My belly stuffed, I was ready for a soft bed.

RockStar still wasn't hiking. The diagnosis of Drs. Quack and Malpractice (Me and another 70-year-old hiker) was a torn meniscus. It wasn't getting better. We ordered Inflam-X from the Your Health Store in Washington as a last ditch effort to help. I was very sorry she couldn't hike and exceedingly lucky to have such a good friend to stick around to support *my* hike. I wished for a magic potion to fix her knee.

We drove to Lemhi Pass for a picnic at the Sacajawea Memorial and to see if RockStar's car could manage the jeep road I soon would be traveling NOBO. She actually *liked* driving rough jeep roads. We drove in 5 ½ miles before deciding that was far enough, and we hid a gallon of water behind some way-marked stumps.

Returning to the pass, we chatted with a NOBO from the Netherlands named Franklin and a support friend of Continental Drifter. I grabbed the appropriate food box from my car and a few odds and ends. Leaving my car at the pass, we drove to Dillon to hit the Dairy Queen for sundaes. Yum. Then it was organization, packing, and bed.

"Bet I'm older than you."

RockStar drove me to Bannock Pass and stopped to take a picture of the red sunrise behind us. I started out lacking high expectations for the section. The Pintlers had a reputation for rugged beauty and flowers. But this section did not. I anticipated just a trudging couple of days to get the section done, days that had to be completed but not likely to hold much excitement.

My first excitement was being seduced by the lovely road, not seeing the trail heading up the hill. I had an inReach, Guthook on my cell phone, Bear Creek Maps, and Wolf's book. None do much good if you don't look at them. (My son later told me and enjoys rubbing in that he knew I was off trail before I did as he'd happened to be looking at the inReach information in real time on his computer.) But it was *such* a lovely road for walking. Sigh.

Oh well. I went over the sagebrush hill, rolled pack and self under a fence and connected with the CDT, adding a half-mile to my day. It could have been worse. At least I looked when I did.

Stopping at the fenced spring, I filled my water bottles and hydrated my dinner. Later, I found the head of Black Canyon Creek flowing nicely across the trail, meaning I'd carried more water than needed. I HATED to carry water, but it was better to be safe than sorry.

The Pintlers had been more scenic, yet I took more pictures on this little section. When you are not expecting much, what you do see stands out more. There were many kinds of flowers, though I'd had to have sharp eyes for some. Squirrels and chipmunks abounded. So did moose, deer and elk poop, cows, and cow pies.

For several miles an old log fence separated the states of Idaho and Montana. Putting up that fence must have taken a lot of work in days before barbed wire. In the afternoon, open country with interesting views of sun and shadow playing on the grassy mountainsides entertained me. Ponds in various stages of drying up dotted the Idaho side of the trail.

While I was still quite exposed on open jeep road, a thunder squall caught me just before I reached trees. I couldn't seem to reach my umbrella without taking off my pack, although I'd done so nearly every day for sun shade. I got quite wet in the shuffle. Eventually, pack cover on and umbrella up, the storm moved on to give the lowlands a nice dump of rain. Continental Drifter passed me after road walking around trails closed by burns, one of the last SOBOs to start that year but now passing many.

Trekker, a 74-year-old section hiker came by as I was setting up my tent. As we chatted, he said, "Bet I'm older than you."

I said, "I don't know. How are old are you?" He proudly said, "74."

I chuckled and told him I was 76.

He, however, would be getting his Triple Crown at the ALDHA Gathering, when he finished his section in Yellowstone. He had all his paperwork in and would finish before the deadline. I wouldn't finish until Sept 8, after the deadline to be recognized in 2017. He could have the glory this year. Yay anyway, for all septuagenarians.

Again the sun shone red through smoky skies. For a few miles I was on a lovely plateau at about 9,400 feet, views filtered by smoke haze from Washington or Oregon fires. Cows shared the trail with me, and I talked and sang to them that I was OK, and they shouldn't get excited. Flowers were few and dusty except for one bright patch of harebells.

Humming Bird, Merlin, OG and Starfish passed me SOBO. Hiking five miles before mid- morning snack, I reached my water cache for a late lunch. After lunch, I trail pounded on, the increasingly smoky skies preventing views into Idaho or Montana, and I reached Lemhi Pass and my car at 5:03. Good job, old lady. I drove to Dillon for my shower and steak. Leftovers would be the next day's lunch. Bone weary, I headed for sleep.

A Steak-Sandwich SlackPack - What a Good Way To Do the Trail.

In the morning we drove from Dillon to Lima, our next base of operations. Checking into our motel, we chatted with One of Us. He wanted his picture taken with the old lady on the trail, my claim to fame.

Then we were off to a trailhead west of Monida Pass for a 7.8-mile slack pack to fill the rest of the day. I set off with my slack pack system of detachable lid from my pack as waist pack and multiple things in pockets and dangling from my belt. RockStar gingerly walked a mile on her recovering knee.

I met a group of five NOBO hikers: Treeman, J-peg, Quick Silver, Apache, and Flip Flop.

Treeman was from Germany, the son of Evangelisch Pastors.

(Evangelisch is a unification of Protestant groups including Lutheran and Reformed.)

Lunch was left-over steak strips in left-over dinner roll, with extra strips rolled up in a tortilla. Eating steak sandwiches while strolling along a good dirt road, my umbrella shading me from the sun, observing the rolling land before me and not carrying a pack—what a good way to hike the trail. Eventually my steak was consumed, and I resorted to serious trail pounding, walking a slack pack always easier than walking with full pack.

RockStar passed me after talking with the NOBO hikers not eager to begin their uphill climb from the trailhead. She headed back to Lima and I to my car a few miles further. On the last two-mile stretch I met Abba, Moise, and Mack. As we talked, the black sky to the north decided to become a thunderstorm. Mack got his camera out to try to catch the lightning, and I traveled on wondering if the storm would miss me. Nope. The last .8 mile I walked in thunder and lightning, rain and hail. My umbrella and rain jacket worked well, but my legs and feet got wet and beaten with wind-driven stinging hail. I was glad to reach my car.

Next up: An honest-to-goodness zero day. No driving, no walking, just cleanup, camp chores, and hanging around with other hikers. Lima is the principle civilization on Highway 15, where NOBOs and SOBOs cross past each other in their quests to complete the trail in one year. Puma, Red Bass, Sonic, Stomper, and Funny Bone were all there. Lavender had gotten off the trail, bought a bike, and was planning a bike trip to somewhere on the East Coast. There are many ways to engage in an adventure.

Rain, Hail, and Runny Cow Poo

After my rest day, RockStar and I drove out to find Bannack Pass. (one letter different than Bannock Pass) Unfortunately, a wide creek about knee-deep stopped the car 2.7 miles from the pass, so I had a creek ford and 2.7 miles added to my day.

Saying *good-bye* to RockStar, I forded the creek and headed up the road to the pass. It rained on the way, making the dirt sticky. Even a little mud changes the weight of shoes.

The views were amazing. There were ranges yet to go over to the north, and a huge valley reminded me of South Park in Colorado. More showers fell before mid-morning snack and four more times in the afternoon. While I ate a snack sheltered slightly from the wind by a single gooseberry bush, a red tail hawk swooped within 10 feet. Past my snacking spot, the trail climbed past remarkable white chalk-like rock formations. Recalculating came toward me across open meadows, and we both commented on the beauty of the vistas. He hoped his wife could hike with him in Glacier.

Seeing threatening clouds over open meadows, I looked for a sheltered place for lunch, but didn't find one. So I sat down in the meadow under command of my stomach. I HAD to eat.

Preparing lunch to take with me, a parade of NOBOs started with Big Sauce, Prophet, and Gentle Spirit, followed by Fainting Goat, Acorn, and Sheriff Woody. Then the rain began, and I hurriedly stuffed my food in my waist-belt pouches to eat while walking under my umbrella.

Lunch Box, Save the Party, Bones, Jeremy, and Spice also passed in the wave of NOBOs. The trail, a bit sketchy in the high meadows, alternated pleasantly with thick forest.

Winding in and out of forest and meadows, I climbed higher. In spite of the rain, I enjoyed views dominated by Garfield Mountain. I pitched my tent at the edge of the forest, a meager shelter on a rainy night.

Drive On, Thor, and Scrapbook walked by me NOBO as I readied to go in the morning. They'd camped in a higher meadow and were quite wet, hoping for a dry-out spot later in the day. I had my doubts they would find one.

I steadily climbed upward through thick, wet greenery, my shoes soon re-soaked. Views still lovely and interesting, red Conglomerate Mountain had a different structure and color than the talus-covered slops of Garfield. I passed them both and made it over another pass to see valleys stretched out on the other side. Little was dry in the rain-soaked forest, but I found just enough space for me and my pack under a tree, which held off the deluge.

Going down the other side of the pass, I ran into an AmeriCorps Work Crew looking for downed trees to remove from the trail. They were from St. Louis and looked like this was all new to them. They seemed to enjoy the views if not the climb. Trail maintenance is another way to enjoy wilderness, and hikers are quite beholden to trail crews.

In the afternoon I met NOBOs Jo and Joel from London, whom I'd seen in Lima, and I stopped at the Sawmill Trailhead to hydrate my dinner. Only four more miles to go for the day, but they turned out to be wet and muddy miles with confusing or absent signs.

Although I couldn't see them, I was following a group of equestrians. The horses were making mush of the trail in boggy areas, and I could hear protesting whinnies ahead. Apparently, horses didn't like crossing boggy areas, and they thrashed in the soggy ground, leaving few solid hillocks for a hiker to use.

The horsey protests ahead of me sounded louder and more frantic just before I came to an especially bad boggy area. For 40-feet up and down the stream, the banks were totally churned to deep boggy mud. Searching for a place to cross, I stretched as far as I could and moved quickly on the last collapsing hummocks of grass. The mud reminded me of bogs in Maine, and my poles sank as if there were no end to the goo. I didn't think the horses had crossed there in spite of having tried so hard. I heard one snort in the trees above me, but never saw them.

Coming to Little Beaver Creek, I found a downed sign on the ground near a river crossing. By this time it had also rained and hailed a few times, so I carefully made my way down a very slippery and steep slope to the creek and walked through. The cold stream water washed mud from my shoes.

On the other side, I found CDT markers, which led me back to cross the creek again. Huh? Maps didn't show two crossings. What was going on? I followed the cow trail on the north bank until I was certain it wasn't my trail, and I returned to cross the creek to the south bank yet again. I concluded I was just seeing an old and a new crossing, not two separate crossings. There was no sign of trail up the hill. I believed my GPS and went up the hill anyway, eventually finding trail and cows. The cows, having eaten so much green grass, left runny, wet cow pies all over the trail. Tread briefly went missing another time or two, and as I stood under a tree and my umbrella eating a KitKat bar, I watched the ground turn white with hail. It was a miracle I didn't fall anywhere that day to be coated with mud and fresh, nearly liquid, cow poo.

It was after 8:00 when I reached the low point on Shineburger Creek in the rain, following a hailstorm. I had to find a place to camp. The cows knew where to stand out of the wind. I could tell because every single place even slightly sheltered was recently signed with runny piles of slop. I couldn't simply kick dry cow pies away as I'd done in New Mexico.

I finally found a not-so-level piece of short grass by a hill. That would have to do. With difficulty, I set the food bag rope on Aspen in tall, wet bushes, but didn't use it as rain poured by the bucketful, and I was dry and eating dinner. Nope. Not going out in that again.

It had been a beautiful day until the challenges of the last four miles. The rain had taken away the smoke, and the views had been expansive. You can't have everything. I was dry and warm in my tent and sleeping bag, and life was good even as clouds unleashed a flood on my tent.

"...out-hiked everyone my age"

The next day was a planned long and hard day, as opposed to the unplanned difficulty of the day before. Day dawned with clear skies, though the hill beside me blocked the sun from my wet tent. I walked up the valley, sometimes finding the trail, sometimes not. After wet meadows, I was glad to go uphill on a line of rocky ridges to stay out of the grass. Ridge walking on the Divide the rest of the day, I only had to be sure I was on the correct ridge.

I stopped at the top of the second large ridge top for a snack break, while I admired spectacular views in many directions. I heard them before I saw them. Elk. Big creatures, whose everyday communication sounds like electronic beeps and squeals. Looking down on one of the valleys, I saw a herd of 30 or more going over a pass on a ridge extending down from the Divide. A lovely moment to hold in memory: sitting on an open ridge with elk moving over a ridge below me.

A bit later Merlin, Hummingbird, OG, and Starfish came by. Since they were at least three times faster than I was, and I'd last seen them below Lemhi Pass, I'd anticipated seeing them again. Route finding was easy for a while; I just followed the rapidly receding figures of four hikers ahead of me.

Hikers looking at their feet on the trail see rocks. On ridges of the Divide I saw unique Easter Egg-shaped rocks, fist size to bigger than a football, black, pinkish quartz, tan and even, rarely, white. They were distinctly oval and polished like river rock. One looked like it had glacial striations. Were these tops of the Divide once river rock? Why all the distinctive oval, egg shapes? A curious question to ponder while trudging on and around them.

Passing the four SOBOs as they stopped for lunch, I told them I was hiking solo because finding similarly paced hikers was difficult for someone old and slow. Hummingbird, or maybe Starfish, said that I'd just "out-hiked everyone my age." That had a grain of truth to it. Yet I knew other 70+-year-old hikers were out there hiking. There were just fewer of us than younger hikers. I hiked on, and several ups and downs later they passed me again, saying, "See you in Lima." They would be there at least a couple hours before me.

The ridges went on and on. Up and down and up again. Black clouds were building behind me. Bare ridge tops are not the safest places to be in thunderstorms. But ridge tops were where the trail went, so I did too. And I saw rain pour over mountains to my rear. I listened to thunder, and hoped the main storm would miss me, which it did. Thank you, God.

Only 2-3 miles from the end of my trail, I missed a turn. As I exchanged umbrella for rain jacket to break the wind raging like a hurricane at the edges of the storm, I quickly looked at Guthook and thought it indicated the next hill as the trail. In the howling wind trying to pluck me off the ridge, I made my way up that hill and followed the trail up the next hill as well to find somewhere out of fierce wind. Once out of the wind, I looked at Guthook again and discovered I wasn't on the right trail.

Drat and horse feathers. I had to go out into the howling wind once again and retrace my steps, climbing up and down two hills. More carefully looking at Guthook on the ridge saddle, even as the wind tried to knock me over, I started down a steep, trail-less meadow. I checked Guthook several times on the way those last 2.5 miles. I was on the wrong side of a teepee-style barbed-wire fence, not an easy one to roll pack or self under with its double barbed wire strands 3-feet apart horizontally at the base. Eventually, I found a place with single vertical strands and rolled to the side that more resembled trail.

The last 2.5 miles contained many sections of extremely steep descents. I kept thinking of my face plant in Nevada on similar steepness, making me very careful, therefore even slower. It was 8:00 before I reached RockStar and her car. The last 2.5 miles that day and the last four miles the day before had been the most difficult of the year. Fourteen miles and more than 3,000-feet elevation gain plus lots of steep descent were a lot for an old lady. Getting misplaced in howling wind plus those multiple steep descents had added an extra hour onto an already challenging day.

Limitations and RockStar's Hike

After driving back to Lima and dinner, I managed to stand up long enough for my shower before collapsing into bed. Everything hurt—feet, knees, shoulders. But I hadn't been hit by lightning, and I did get to the car. I loved seeing the elk herd and that series of high, bare ridges overflowing with spectacular views. I thought the pain and effort worth the grandeur of the wilderness. Saying good-bye to Hummingbird, Merlin, and OG, at breakfast in Lima, the last time I would see them, we exchanged hugs and wished each other well on our respective hikes.

Then we drove from Lima to Dubois for the short section in

Wyoming I'd skipped in 2014. Seeing two hikers looking for a hitch where we crossed the highway below Brooks Lake in 2014, we stowed their packs in RockStar's car and cleared the seats in mine so they could ride. Dassie was from South Africa, but lived in Switzerland. She'd started at the Mexican border in April, but she needed to get off trail and fly home to work. Mud Slide was from Missouri and planned to continue the trail after a stop in DuBois.

Their plans contributed to my musings on limitations, as I sat doing my laundry. Even young, very strong hikers have limitations. Dassie's limitation was time. She had to leave the trail and go to work. Weather could be a limiting factor. SOBOs needed to get through the San Juans in Colorado before deep snow hit the high country. For NOBOs, early limitations could include lingering snow in the San Juans in spring and onset of snow in Glacier in the fall.

I, of course, had limitations regarding age and joints. Every year it was more difficult to cover enough miles in a day to make significant progress on a section of trail.

When Big Sauce passed me, he said he would like to be a section hiker, so he could take it easy and enjoy it more. No, that may not be the case. Section hikers probably work just as hard as thru hikers; some of us simply have more limitations with which to deal.

Due to my limitations: I sometimes hiked *more* miles *off* trail because I couldn't cover as many *trail* miles in a day to reach usual food drops sites. I had to discover more complicated resupply arrangements to meet my limitations, sometimes walking more *total* miles than other hikers. Example: I had to add 2.7 miles due to a creek blocking the road. I might walk fewer miles per day at a slower speed, but thru hikers not needing to start where I did wouldn't need to walk that particular 2.7 miles. Who worked harder? Unanswerable.

So what was I getting at?

We all have limitations of some kind or another. They differ. Life requires us to learn to deal with limitations. Adjusting expectations, accommodating limitations, and searching for creative solutions can enable reaching goals in a different way.

Advice for myself and other older hikers: Don't try to be younger, stronger hikers. They have their own set of limitations. Yours are different. Discover how to adapt new methods to accomplish your goals. Take more days; arrange more food drops, even walk more miles if necessary. Adapting to limitations is an ongoing life lesson as our limitations change.

RockStar would hike the next day, and we would try to adapt to our limitations. We left my car below Highway 287 and drove RockStar's car to Union Pass, where we had bailed in 2014.

The coming eclipse had already brought scads of people. Bailing in bad weather at Union Pass in 2014, we had stood on that dirt road for nearly an hour hoping for a car. Now, some kind of vehicle passed every 5-10 minutes. We parked near a group, who had been camping near Union Pass for days, holding the area for 30 family members on their way to see the eclipse.

50,000 people were expected in Jackson and 200,000 in Casper. It was just nuts.

We only planned to go 3.9 miles after placing cars. RockStar decided her knee was feeling good enough to go. If she could complete this section, she would have bragging rights for walking all of Wyoming. It was the first time RockStar had picked up a fully loaded backpack in 2017. She was quite slow. But she was tough, and she was moving.

Lake of the Woods was pretty, a number of campers already around the lake. Lupine, fleabane and many color shades of buckwheat cheered our path. After getting water at the creek, it was RockStar's decision to walk farther for better camping.

After stopping, almost ready to snuggle into bed, two SOBOs, Governor and Somo, and one NOBO, Rabinath, from the Netherlands passed us. Rabinath came over to talk. Finding I was a pastor, he asked for a blessing. I readily complied with a prayer before he went on. We slept that night in a high, open meadow, mountains topped with snow around us, coyotes yapping nearby.

We woke to cold, icy tents at 34 degrees. RockStar struggled throughout the day, partly due to the knee injury, partly due to lack of conditioning because of the knee injury and partly due to added weight on pack and body. She panted even on downhill walking.

It was a pretty day with an assortment of views and flowers, high mountains south of the Tetons and Tetons too in full view. Purple fleabane, a tall stemmed cinquefoil, the ubiquitous many shades of buckwheat, pale larkspur and yarrow lined the trail and filled the meadows.

I took over getting water as I could get there first and fill and treat containers before RockStar arrived. The trail was pretty good save for a few boggy spots, but we still fell short of our goal. Shortly before stopping, we met Jasper and Margolin from the Netherlands. A tenth of a mile short of water on top of a bunch of molehills was as far as RockStar could manage. No good trees for hanging, we needed to have only short bears in the area that night.

It was again cold in the morning, but the sun was bright in a clear sky, vastly different than the last time we had been in Wyoming. Near the middle of this four-day trip, we contemplated going back to the car because of RockStar's knee. But RockStar didn't want to go back and moved pretty well in the morning.

Two SOBO section hikers in their 60s passed us, and I chatted with them, immediately forgetting their names. RockStar didn't chat. Slowly and determinedly, step by step, she continued up the hill. While I attended to nature's needs, RockStar continued to Sheridan Creek, always slow, but always moving. A herd of cows followed her slow walk, attracted to her slow amble like a cow's Pied Piper.

Fording the creek, water was a little too cloudy to use with our treatment systems, so we went on to the next spring and left the cows happily wallowing in the creek behind us. I went ahead to get water, RockStar barely moving. She was one tough woman to keep moving even at a crawl.

While at the spring, Oil Can and Phantom, whom I'd met at Big Hole Pass, came SOBO. We watered up, climbed to the top of the ridge near a dirt road, and found our campsites before dark. Rusty passed us and told us eight more SOBOs were coming—the large group I'd seen back at Big Hole Pass.

Over the next hour, headlamps came through the forest twice, getting directions about marshy meadows, and going on in the dark. I thought they were nuts to walk in the dark, but they were young and no doubt reached their goal.

RockStar's knee was toast. I wondered if I should hit the SOS button on the inReach, but thought I should pursue other avenues of help first. We were camped beside a road, but tracing it on our device maps through many changes of elevation and creek crossings, we concluded that my car couldn't reach our campsite. RockStar wasn't going anywhere. Besides her knee, her breathing was terrible. Having seen the metal shine of a camper farther down the creek we had forded, I planned to check it out in the morning, setting the alarm for 5:00. Leaving my pack with RockStar, I walked .8 miles down the road assuming it went to the camper.

I'd gone only a short ways when a cute, small dog, and two riders on horses met me coming up the road. Bona fide cowpokes, they were headed to *push* the herd where they wanted them to graze. I told them of RockStar's plight, and they assured me they would get her to DuBois if folks in the camper by the creek could not. Much relieved at a possible solution for RockStar, I continued down the road to the creek and forded across. Addressing the camper with a loud good morning, I woke them up, and they were not terribly receptive. I heard the woman wondering why I didn't just press my SOS button for search and rescue.

Apologizing for waking them and thanking them for listening, I said the cowboys would get her out. Returning to RockStar, I told her she had a way out if she could go .8 mile and ford a creek not even the cowboy's truck would cross. I was confident she could get that far. She was ready to go and limped slowly down the road. She told me later it took her an hour.

She actually had a good day, many thanks to Eli and Ashly, cowboy and cowgirl. After taking care of their cows, they took RockStar to town, and RockStar learned about pushing cows and cattle operations, which she enjoyed.

A solution found for RockStar, I had a lot of miles to cover and a late start. Stopping short of our planned mileage for two days, I had to make up that mileage plus hike the distance planned for the day. The first couple miles had difficulties I was glad RockStar had not faced—blowdowns and fording a wide creek. A spring spread its rivulets broadly over a whole hill, I had to climb, though cows had trampled it to a muddy mess.

After keeping my feet dry by taking the time to switch to crocs, the next several meadows were boggy with unavoidable large stretches of wet marsh. Wet feet became inevitable; it had been pointless to have bothered with crocs earlier. I met Happy in the meadow, a 60-something NOBO. He warned me about two tricky left turns in a burn area, but I missed them both anyway, though because I checked Guthook on my phone frequently, I didn't get too far off trail either time.

The burn was very fresh-looking, with lots of black char, last year's fire. This year's flowers were loving the openness of the forest to the sun, bright yellow daisies and fireweed happy in black char. Four miles of my day were on fairly good dirt road on which I made excellent time.

I heard from RockStar by inReach satellite text. She was OK and had made it to the motel.

RockStar didn't quite finish Wyoming, but if there was ever an "A for effort," she earned that and then some.

The next day was the eclipse. We drove out to Union Pass to get RockStar's car and find a place to view the eclipse. On a five mile stretch of road on a high open plateau, a zoo of people were camping or had driven out to see the eclipse like us, a *camping show,* passing tent and camper rigs of all kinds. We chose our ridge for watching the eclipse, an event RockStar and millions of people across the USA had been anticipating. RockStar had eclipse glasses, and we had chairs she'd brought for car camping.

I made myself a bagel with cream cheese, and we sat in style viewing the eclipse and taking pictures with four different cameras with mixed results. RockStar got a gorgeous picture of Totality. Someone in a group near us called Totality a wedding ring in the sky. The drastic drop in temperature was a stark reminder of how much we need that sun to have life on earth. After the eclipse, we joined the cavalcade of cars down the dirt road to the highway to DuBois.

Bedbugs and Deadman

The next day we went back to Lima, and RockStar was still limping badly. In the morning, I discovered bedbugs don't only live in France and Spain. Though we had stayed in that motel many times over three years, this was the first time there were bedbugs. Travelers bring them.

Travelers suffer from them. I was sorry for the owners as they were nice people who helped hikers. I was sorry for me because I had lots of bites. Seeing one crawl on my white nightshirt, we knocked it into the sink and sent it down the drain with lots of hot water. It was about three times bigger than the variety I'd seen in France, but it was a bedbug, and I had the bites to prove it.

Bedbugs or not, I was hiking. I didn't want to place my car by the creek where RockStar had dropped me off several days ago as the forecast was for rain, and I didn't want to risk trouble driving up a muddy hill. Parking at the top of the hill added another .5 mile.

RockStar then drove me to Nicholia Creek. I didn't go very fast on my steady uphill climb, but I made reasonable time over sagebrush hills, walking by flowers past their prime, red spots added by the leaves of spent buckwheat. Flying grasshoppers whirred and popped around me. It had become late summer in Montana, while we were in Wyoming.

Completing the climb, I headed down to Deadman Creek for water and Deadman Lake for camping. I wondered who the Deadman was? Who'd found him? Did he have a name? Whose son was he? Who grieved for him? Did they ever know he'd died?

A few flowers bloomed on the lake-side of the ridge, larkspur, rabbit brush, a greenish yellow paintbrush, a few blossoms of shrubby cinquefoil, yellow monkey flower. A cloudy day, the views disappeared in the haze.

In the morning the still lake perfectly reflected the few pines on the sagebrush hills. Starting up a 900-foot climb out of the canyon, I saw a pretty whitetail deer. Even though the hills were dry, the views were interesting. According to posted signs, there were two Bannack Passes about three miles apart—odd. I reached the second one about 12:30. Time for lunch? Nope. Clouds were building, the sky was turning black, and thunder was booming. There were no sheltering trees, and my car was 3.3 miles off trail in open country. Halfway there I had to hoist the umbrella and put on the pack cover. Walking through the creek, I continued up the hill to the car. Nice car, sitting there waiting for me. As I drove back, I began getting messages from RockStar on the inReach.

They'd changed her room. In the new room she been eaten alive by more bedbugs. Refunded for the next two nights, we drove to Dillon for bedbug-free lodging. I gobbled cashews, jerky, and dried pears in lieu of lunch and drove to Dillon and met RockStar at the laundromat.

We washed all our clothes in hot water and dried them on hot, the only thing that kills bedbugs for sure. We probably shrunk some things. We sprayed permethrin on duffle bags, my sleeping bag, and my down jacket, all before we checked into the motel. It was more difficult to get bedbug-free than it had been in France because we had more stuff and we had cars. Our stuff had been sitting in our cars. How could I guarantee the critters had not crawled somewhere, now hidden in the car? Bedbugs can live a whole year without feeding, and very little kills the nasty critters. We did everything we could think of as a precaution against being carriers.

Unsuspecting travelers carrying bedbugs from place to place is how they spread. I knew more about bedbugs from my trip to France than I'd ever wanted to know, and I hoped I'd never need that knowledge again.

Between hiking and extensive laundry and bedbug precautions, I felt like I'd done two days' work in one day. Finally checked into the motel, I had my shower and sealed my hiking clothes in a plastic bag until I could wash them too. We had dinner at a little Mexican place with excellent food, came back to the motel, and crashed.

Nicholia Creek North

The next day I was back out on the trail in another set of hiking clothes. Originally planning to hike the section in four days, I'd looked at the elevation changes and added another day. My first day was short, but it had 1,700-feet elevation gain as I ambled along the trail.

At Bear Creek, the stepping stones didn't work for me, so I changed to crocs and went wading, rearranging rocks, thinking RockStar, even with a bad knee, could have crossed on my improvements, my small bit for trail maintenance.

Harkness Lakes had at least 20 ducks on pretty ponds tucked in folds of sagebrush hills surrounded by shrubby cinquefoil. I walked under my umbrella for shade, and a big Spruce provided better shade at Cottonwood Creek.

The next morning didn't start well. RockStar had told me an update on Guthook said it was easy to lose the trail at a creek crossing. No lie. I couldn't find the trail for half a mile, though I was crisscrossing Guthook's red line many times while climbing a steep hill in the woods.

Numerous cows on multiple cow paths wondered what I was doing there.

After frustrating, hard, slow work, I finally found a CDT post 45 minutes later. There was little tread for much of the first 6 miles. Climbing 2,300 feet to the Divide, I walked cross- country looking for posts or cairns. Sometimes trail was discernible in bent grass. Sometimes not.

Checking Guthook frequently and walking cross-country takes longer than walking on even poor trail. While carving my own way on open uphill steepness, a NOBO passed me. But he was closer to the next cairn than I, and we never talked. Watching him speed ahead uphill, I felt my age in comparison.

It took until nearly 4:00 to cover only six miles. Mercifully, after the Coyote Creek junction the trail had tread again. I saw a deer with a mangy coat and one of the giant gray bugs called Mormon

Grasshoppers, inspiration for nightmares or sci-fi horror shows.

There were few flowers. What gentians still bloomed were quite small though still their familiar bright blue. Passing the top of Tex Creek, a NOBO from Germany named Horst caught up with me. I'd climbed to the Divide in the morning and then almost back down to the flat valley we'd driven in on. Arriving at lower Tex Creek, I found Horst ready to cook his dinner. After my tent was up and the food-bag rope hung, I ate my dinner with him as he had his coffee, and we chatted.

In the morning I arranged stepping stones again at the second Tex Creek crossing, then meandered through sagebrush foothills on a jeep road, under sun hot enough to need the umbrella. Tired by the time I reached Morrison Lake nestled below Baldy Mountain, I sat in the shade by the lake eating lunch and looking at lady's thumb, water smartweed. I had no problem getting water. My problem was *carrying* a full load up 800 feet on steep jeep road. Lugging that load to 9,000-feet was almost more than I could do.

Well, I did do it, but I chose to stop early for the night, my age showing again. Putting up the tent, I crawled inside and didn't move for an hour. Gradually I came to and entertained myself by flicking ants off my mosquito netting. Must have set the tent near an anthill. I cleaned up with the sloppy wet bandana I'd carried from the lake, all the water I could spare in a dry country. I was glad my pack would be lighter in the morning.

I talked to a thru hiker passing my tent in the morning and set out for a high country day walking over hill after rounded hill of high Divide above the tree line. I looked at Idaho on one side or Montana on the other. I followed an old jeep track and watched clouds and storms around me but avoided rain. Sun directly overhead, I was hot under my umbrella.

A young hunter at the end of a jeep road was surprised to see an old lady on the trail. The last chunk of trail real trail, not road, I toiled upwards in the sun, while the young hunter breezing by me headed to his camp on the other side of the Divide. Near the top, just short of a low spot on the Divide, a beautiful spring flowed into a metal tank.

Watering up, I promptly lost the trail. After stumbling around a little, I was *found* again and pitched my tent by some trees providing shelter from the wind.

That night as darkness fell, I crawled out of my tent to pee and saw the young hunter, who had come back for water. He pointed out the coyotes I could just barely make out as moving shapes in the almost dark as they ran over the meadow, both of us smiling to see them. Saying goodnight, he trudged on with his water, and I tucked in for the night listening to coyotes.

In the morning, coyotes still noisy, I woke early, a little short of breath. Since I was awake, I had an early start and was on top of Elk Mountain at 8:15. The trail didn't quite go to the summit, but I scrambled to the top over talus, to superb views in all directions. From the summit I could see the Bannock Pass Road and parts of my trail reaching it 11 miles away. Carefully picking my way over the talus back down to the trail, I resumed my job for the day: reaching Bannock Pass.

The long downhill trail was evenly graded until the jeep road began. Even this late in the season there were flowers: lupine, yarrow, rabbit brush and sorrel. Buckwheat had dried up, leaving leaf mats turning red. The sky was cloudy much of the day, for which I was thankful, amazed how hot the sun was when it cleared the clouds, like a switch flipped to preheat an oven.

Jeep tracks went straight up and straight down hills. Deadman Pass was the worst—another dead man, whose unknown history rattled in my mind.

Clouds turned menacingly dark and threatened rain. There were no trees for cover, and the wind blew fiercely, but I needed lunch. The sharp notch that was the pass had a two-to-three-foot drop on the east side by the border fence, and it was all the shelter I could find. My break was short. I gobbled cheese and crackers and fixed the rest to stuff in pack pouches to eat along the way. Raindrops told me I might as well walk and eat under my umbrella, its handle jammed in my bra to keep the wind from ripping it away. I had my Dri Ducks on to ward off icy cold wind on the jeep road going straight up from Deadman

Pass.

Shortly after that bit of drama, the squall went elsewhere, whipped away by the wind. I took my jacket off but kept the umbrella up to keep from frying in the sun. I went from icy cold to blazing heat in a few minutes. The rest of the day was up and down interminable hills until finally I came over the last rise to see RockStar's car.

Canada

It took us three days to drive to Waterton, Canada. We toured Butte while waiting to get my air conditioning fixed. After a night in Lolo for inexpensive lodging, I got out of bed and my knee hurt—my good knee—for no reason whatsoever.

It wasn't too unusual for me to have something stiffen for a little while. After all, I was 76. I thought a shower and moving around a bit would help. Nope. I'd been moving just fine before I went to bed. I'd been very happy that both knees had felt so good in 2017, better than I had any right to expect. I'd done nothing the day before but sit and drive my car. I'd done nothing to hurt that knee, even a little bit. But I got out of bed that morning, and the knee hurt all day.

Driving up the east side of Flathead Lake and into Glacier National Park, we heard the Sperry Chalet had been lost to fire the night before. Driving by Lake McDonald, we could see smoke billowing up the mountainside from the fire. The west side of Going to the Sun Road was only mildly smoky. But as soon as we reached Logan Pass we saw where all the smoke had been blown by the strong-and-gusty wind. The east side all the way to Saint Mary was very, very smoky, fresh smelling smoke.

We drove on to Babb, a town, as the saying goes, so small, if you blinked you would miss it. But we considered it a real find. The motel was newly remodeled and quite nice. The swelling in my knee went away overnight, though it still hurt. We left my car at Swift Current, where I hoped to see it in a few days if my knee would cooperate. Then we drove to Canada.

Glacier and Waterton Lakes National Park span the border between two countries. The little town of Waterton, Canada swelled with tourists for Labor Day Weekend, the last weekend of the summer, bustling with humanity below the large and stately Prince of Wales Hotel on the hill.

Smoke rose from a fire to the north, but it was fairly clear to the south. But before the afternoon was over, the pall of smoke in town had thickened, and wind whipped fires in dry forests.

We napped. We checked on boat rides for the next day. We rested. We played tourist. I played Grandma, buying small presents for my grandchildren. Dinner and big ice cream scoops completed the evening. My knee was better than the day before, but still a concern.

Playing tourist one more day, we rode the boat up Waterton Lake to Goat Haunt. The mountains were glorious rising from the lake— layer after layer, both sides of the border beautiful. Returning to Waterton, we drove to the Visitor Center, picked up our permit, and watched the mandatory back-country movie, which we'd seen a couple times before.

The fire in Glacier had now closed Going to the Sun Road, and the fire we saw driving into Waterton had also grown. But all our route and campsites were open. I was a little nervous about this last section with all the fires, and, of course, it was *Glacier,* and there could be bears, both grizzly and black, though most hikers never see them.

A black bear in the middle of the road near the Visitor Center looked a little confused and overcome at all the cars and people. He just wanted to eat the tender shoots of at the ends of little Aspen trees. The tourists leaped from their cars for pictures; RockStar and I tried for one, too.

I would have felt better about this last hike if my knee had been as good as it had been the rest of 2017. It just didn't feel 100%, or whatever percent an old lady usually had. I drowned my concerns in two large scoops of ice cream. Later, I remembered I had a medication I'd been carrying in my kit for a few years. My doc had told me it wouldn't expire, and I could use it someday if I needed it to get out of the back country. Now might be the time. The thought gave me reassurance. In the morning the knee felt great. I didn't know if that was due to healing or to the medication I'd decided to take. I was just thankful it felt good enough to hike.

Stopping to take a picture of Cameron Falls, there were no other people in the picture at that hour in the morning. I began walking at the Bertha Lake trailhead. The first folks I saw were a Canadian couple at the trailhead and an older American couple from Nebraska. They were a shade faster than me, but they stopped often enough that I caught them to chat as they stopped for breaks. They and a younger couple went on to Bertha Lake, while I continued toward Goat Haunt.

Others I met included day hikers from or to the boat landing at Goat Haunt. Some were impressed I was traveling alone and were totally freaked out worrying about bears. Others were interested in the CDT, and one group of four from San Francisco had many questions about walking long trails, light-weight equipment, and other trail talk. Four NOBOs were completing the trail that day: Navi, Coach, and Phil and Julia whom I'd met on my birthday a month before below the Pintlers.

The vegetation was very dry. A ranger at Goat Haunt said they'd not had measurable rainfall for 90 days. No wonder fires were burning from lighting strikes. I felt sorry for the bears as there were few berries left for them to eat. At the border obelisks, no one was there to take my picture so I took a selfie. Good-bye Canada. Hello USA.

RockStar, having walked from the boat, was already at the campsite when I arrived, hydrating her dinner in the kitchen area of the campground. Rangers had urged me to go through customs before putting up my tent. I did so, leaving gear with RockStar and fording the river for a shorter trail, then legally in the US as well as physically.

Our permit for campsites assigned by the Park gave us a short second day. As it turned out, that worked well for us, as RockStar could manage a short day. Leaving the campground late in the cold morning, after crossing a suspension bridge, I took the side trail to see Rainbow Falls, which RockStar had seen walking in from the boat. It was a nice little falls cut through rocks tilted on edge, deep blue pools below them. I caught up with RockStar at Goat Haunt, and we off-loaded a little trash in the trash can and visited the real bathroom with running water even though we had to walk an extra tenth of a mile to do so. Old ladies like real bathrooms.

From Goat Haunt, we walked through forest thick with dry thimbleberry undergrowth. Corn lily plants had their tops snapped off by bears and white snowberries lined the trail. According to a ranger I overheard, Native Americans called them ghost berries, saying they were food for the dead, the white berries poisonous to humans. I wondered if they were poisonous to bears, and if so, how would bears know not to eat them? They were the only berries left.

We talked to a couple Border Patrol guys on the way to Kootenai Lake for a day hike, and five other day hikers and a couple women backpackers passed us. A woman ranger walked in with us to Kootenai Lake, checked things out and left. Two cow moose were in the lake along with two swans and numerous ducks.

Kootenai Lake was a lovely spot (except for smoke and flies) at the foot of the Citadel, a portion of the tall spires of rock making up Porcupine Ridge. Smoke had been building all day, and we could only make out the spires' dim outline. Flies at Kootenai Lake were almost as bad as those near the horse camp on the North Puyallup on the Wonderland Trail many years ago.

Three hikers from Colorado/Germany chatted with us as we ate our dinner, where the group food-prep sites encouraged socializing. After we were in our tents, NOBOs Fainting Goat and Sheriff Woody, whom I'd met south of Bannack Pass, hiked in and said *hello*. Darkness descending, we listened to the ducks on the lake.

In the morning, thru hikers of the night before were already gone when we woke up, but we enjoyed breakfast with the Colorado/Germany folks. RockStar took a perfect video of a mama moose and her baby in the lake grasses close to shore, perhaps bringing her enough joy to redeem her whole trip.

RockStar turned north, back to Goat Haunt and to the boat to take her to Waterton and her car. I turned south toward Fifty Mountain, in the heart of the high country. Supposedly 50 mountains could be seen from there. Not that day.

After hiking mildly uphill through thick forest with lots of thimbleberry past its prime, I passed hikers coming down from Stoney Indian Pass and then met three guys coming from Fifty Mountain: Gideon, Disco and Star Gazer. They had ultra-light equipment but were not CDT thru hikers that year. Having a long-distance hiker look about them, I thought Disco and Star Gazer might have done the CDT in earlier years. Gideon was excitedly learning about backpacking from the other two, and he did most of the talking, although Sky Gazer told me he was going to the ALDHA-West Gathering in Colorado.

After a snack at the patrol cabin, I started uphill, 2,700 feet of uphill in three miles. Stopping for lunch at a little waterfall, I loaded up with more water. Then the uphill grade increased. It was hot and smoky, and I seemed to crawl up that hill. There should have been beautiful views of many mountains to encourage me, but there was just a gray sea of smoke. It was like hiking in Washington in a cloud, but the smoke wasn't wet. Vegetation was very dry, huckleberry leaves turning red. As I climbed higher, a few huckleberry plants had berries—not many—but enough to keep my mouth interested as I plodded uphill.

Frank, a NOBO, came running down the trail trying to get to Goat Haunt as a sign said the last boat from Goat Haunt would be the next day at 5:00, and access to Waterton would then be closed due to the fire in Canada. I hoped all would go well for RockStar as she would be in Goat Haunt in the afternoon.

Finally reaching open, high country on the shoulder of a mountain, ground cover was dry browns and reds. A half mile from Fifty Mountain, after passing several dry streambeds, I was surprised by a lovely stream, yellow daisies next to rushing water. Treating my water bottles, I gulped one down right there. A little farther on I arrived at Fifty Mountain.

Setting up my tent, I bathed with a small baggie of water from the last creek. A bear-proof food box meant I didn't have to hang food. Unfortunately, there were no Fifty Mountains to be seen, and campsites and trails were powdery dust making it difficult to stay clean after my bath and ruining the zipper on my tent. But the company that night was lovely as couples from Seattle, Michigan, and Cleveland exchanged hiking tales, one a fairly harrowing bear tale.

In the morning, the trail went straight to the mountain wall and diagonally up the wall to the first pass. I was up high all day. Well duh, it's called the Highline Trail. I knew I was surrounded by tall and rugged mountains, some with snow, but I could see nothing except the ridge above me, and that dimly.

After the first 6-700 foot climb, the trail went gradually downwards coming to a little stream with a tiny faucet-like waterfall where I decided to treat another bottle of water, but I dropped the Steripen, breaking a filament inside, ending its life. I switched to treating water with Aqua Mira.

Sean and Mathinya, the young couple from Cleveland going to the same campsite, caught up and passed me. We leapfrogged each other during the day, and I enjoyed getting to know them. Sean wasn't feeling well, or they would have quickly left me in the dust. Joining the wet t- shirt club at the waterfall on Cattle Queen Creek to combat the heat, I reached Ahern Creek quite a bit before Sean and Mathinya, beginning to worry about them. When they arrived, I fed Sean Jolly Ranchers. Getting sugar in him seemed to help.

The bottom fell out of my bear spray holster. It was a good thing I was almost finished.

Gear was falling apart: tent zipper, Steripen, and now bear spray holder had croaked. I pretended the smoke was Washington fog and concentrated on beauty nearby and within sight, enjoying huckleberry leaves turning red, corn lilies turning yellow, and a few odd flowers and nearby rock cliffs.

Snow would have covered Ahern Drift early in the season. Wolf's book talked about the need to cut new paths through snow as gravity and melt pulled the Drift down hill in the summer. Now, very little snow was left, and that high above us. The trail was cut, not through snow, but up the edge of cliffs. A long day for Sean, Mathinya, and me, and we were very ready to reach camp.

The campsite at Granite was down a hole from the trail. Mathinya and I spent almost an hour looking for a supposedly treated water source before we gave up, and she pumped our water from a puddle left in the streambed. We were tired and dirty, but it was my last night on the CDT. After a long unfolding quest, the next day I would be a Triple Crowner.

I started the descent from Swift Current Pass. I'd hoped smoke would be cleared. Other hikers had told me it was clear from Many Glacier to the pass, but they'd left Many Glacier two days earlier. Today, smoke from the fire, which had consumed the Sperry Chalet, had spread even over Swift Current Pass. Smoke also followed me from the Canadian fire near Waterton. Still, the haze was slightly less than the day before.

I wanted to take it all in. Who knew how many more trails I would be able to walk? I intentionally looked at everything, trying to soak it all into my vision and memory.

In spite of smoke, the high country was still beautiful, all shades of brown, yellow, and red ground cover on that very dry September day. I could still see a few banks of snow and rocky crags gradually became more visible as I neared them. Smoky haze didn't obscure everything, though no pictures I took would show the clear beauty of a blue sky. Trees, bushes, rocky crags, ground cover, everything was grayed with smoky haze.

As I descended, I could see two moving white dots on the opposite hill. Goats. Mountain goats. As I got a little closer I could make out heads too, reaching down to graze, barely seen legs moving across dry forage between rocky cliffs. Seeing goats made me excited and happy, a special gift on my last trail day.

The best was yet to come. Turning a corner of the trail around the shoulder of a ridge, singing old Girl Scout songs at the top of my lungs as a warning to bears, WOW. A grizzly bear popped out of the trees on the lower side of the trail, 50-75 feet in front of me. The griz didn't even glance at the walking singer, just lumbered across the trail, powerful yet graceful, as he moved up through the gulley of rocks. Magnificent.

I stood in awe watching, the bear in no way interested in me or a threat of any kind. I also saw another griz farther up the gulley. These were not small bears. They were mature grizzlies. Two of them. I'd seen no grizzlies ever before, though I'd been walking in grizzly country ever since Northern Colorado five years ago. I was thrilled.

It was amazing how quickly the griz covered ground, though he seemed in no particular hurry. Big boulders and a few trees kept getting in the way of a clear camera shot, and I didn't want to spend precious moments trying to focus. I only wanted to see all I could see, until they turned the corner out of sight in a rocky cleft above the trail.

What an amazing gift for my last day on the Continental Divide Trail.

After the grizzlies disappeared, I continued down the trail, turned another corner, and Swift Current Basin opened before me, trail cut along cliffs, switch-backing down to the valley below. Four thin waterfalls plunged hundreds of feet from cliffs forming the high mountain bowl. Even through smoky haze, I could look above waterfalls to glaciers. Yes, there was smoke. No, the pictures wouldn't be as spectacular as they would have been without smoke. But even a smoke- filled valley couldn't completely obscure the grandeur of the view. In the valley below, I could see the outline of Bullhead Lake.

Smoke or no smoke, it was an awesome way to end the Continental Divide Trail. I walked the rest of the way to Many Glacier on a personal high: Last day on the trail and two magnificent grizzly bears. Pretty hard for a 76-year-old lady to find any way to beat that.

Chapter 48   Walk As You Can

"Medicare Pastor, when people suggest that I'm getting too old to thru hike, I mention you. They don't argue after that." ~Transient, August, 8, 1015

If you are an older hiker, you are not *finished* unless you or your body truly says you are. It is perfectly all right to say so. No one *has* to hike. But if you wish to extend joys and challenges of the trail, and your body agrees, get some light-weight equipment to extend your hiking life.

Do not compare yourself negatively with younger, more able hikers. You are the person you are now and, at any age, you are probably capable of more than you realize. If you are in your 70s, you won't hike the same way you did in your 20s, 30s, 40s, or even 60s. Still, a guy named Cimmaron hiked most of the AT in his 90s in 2013. He wasn't the hiker he had been in his younger years, but he was on the trail. Billy Goat, four years my senior, still walks long trails, though he has had heart bypass surgery. He too, walks differently than he did in younger years.

Perhaps you can, too.

My friend Grapevine Kate and I took a walk around Deep Lake near Enumclaw several months ago. It wasn't a long walk, but it went through a small patch of forest wilderness around a lake. We met another walker, who shared with us her recovery from severe injuries sustained in an automobile accident. That she could walk at all was a miracle. But by dint of the marvels of medicine plus determination and effort on her part, she was on a hike. Her son had told her Deep Lake couldn't be called a *real* hike. We emphatically contradicted her son. Of course it was a hike. It was the perfect hike for *her*. It was the perfect hike for my friend, Kathy, too. She now has extensive back fusions and knees that complain. Her dog carries what she needs for a day hike. Yet while she can walk at all, she loves to be out in woods and mountains, and I love walking with her. It was a hike for *us*.

Find a hike that fits your abilities and interests. Get outdoors. See the beauty around you. Walk in whatever way you can. There *will* come a time for each of us when we can no longer walk. Walk while you can.

I am still able to get up and down from the ground. That means I can still get in and out of a tent. I am blessed to be able to walk at 76. My story of the Triple Crown ends here. I need to plan my next long hike.

"Medicare Pastor…keep on going until you find the edge of the

Earth. It is out there somewhere next to the horizon."

Transient - August 8, 2015

If you enjoyed Old Lady on the Trail, please leave a review on Amazon and/or Goodreads to help other readers decide on this book. Telling your friends would also be wonderful.

Acknowledgements

Acknowledgements are difficult to write, not because I have no gratitude for so many people having helped me on my journeys and with the publication of this book. It is difficult to know where to start and where to stop,

Should I start at the creation itself? Without such an incredibly beautiful and captivating world to explore, I would never have begun hiking trails. Without the trails themselves I could not have traversed the miles. Without the vision of those who imagined National Scenic Trails and the work of hundreds of thousands of people who work to create, preserve and maintain them, this old lady would not have walked them. Without other hikers and trail angels to encourage and support me over the years I would not have been able to hike these miles. I am especially grateful for my friends Kathy O'Toole and Karen Keller who walked with me many miles and other friends and total strangers who walked with me for shorter times or supported me along the way. Many are named in this book.

I know, acknowledgements are primarily for those who have helped make the *book* possible. But the *book* was not possible without first having trails through creation and friends along the way.

The book was sparked by people along the years who said I should write one and specifically those who talked to me that last day hiking into Many Glacier. Those who signed my trail journals along the way kept me writing them and their comments made me think perhaps I could tell the story to a broader audience.

One winter of intense work resulted in a draft of a book. Many thanks to my friend, Kathy O'Toole, who helped me see that a draft is only a beginning as she ruthlessly made editing suggestions and filled some pages with red ink. Five edits of my own later, I searched for a professional editor.

A friend from church suggested her mother, Teresa Crumpton of Authorspark.org. Teresa did far more than edit. She encouraged me, volunteered help in formatting and answered endless dumb questions

most authors already know the answers to from writer's groups, classes or their own research. I was (and am) a babe in the woods regarding the book writing business, having devoted my life to other pursuits. I severely tested her patience with my ignorance and questions. There would have been no book without her help and time, large portions of which she gave without remuneration.

I try to pay attention when God puts people in my path. On a rainy day walking in Virginia while visiting my daughter, Lindsay Heider Diamond stopped her car to talk with me as I walked under my umbrella with my pack. She became my Cover Artist with her talent of Graphic Design – Illustration – and Fine Art, www.lindsayheider.com

Technology itself has been key to writing. Technology is great … when it works. I am grateful to my son, David, who tries to keep his mother's computer working.

My son, David, and my daughter, Sara, along with their spouses and my grandchildren put up with my life being absorbed both with hiking and then the writing of this book. They all fill my life with joy and love. My friends too, have put up with my one track mind and focus.

Susan Alcorn, author of *We're In the Mountains, Not Over the Hill,* and newly released *Healing Miles: Gifts from the Caminos Norte and Primitivo* gave her time to read the book and write the blurb for the back cover.

In spite of the conflict of her own canoe adventure, Julianne Baker, Naturalist/Guide Yellowstone Forever, Yellowstone national Park/Nature journaler on Writing the Wild.com, found time to read the book and write a blurb for the back cover.

Many, many people encouraged me to write this book and even more sent notes on Facebook or wrote the old fashioned way or spoke to me in person to encourage me. Their encouragement daily made a difference.

And now I thank my readers, without which there is not much point in writing. I hope you have enjoyed the journey to the Triple Crown at 76 with the Old Lady on the Trail.

About the Author

Mary has been a lot of places and done a lot of things. After all, she is 77 years old. Besides turning her hand to writing of her hiking adventures, this Triple Crowner has been in the Peace Corps, a Physical Therapist with a specialty in Pediatrics, an Army wife, a Pastor of a church for 16 years, a gardener and retired. She is the mother of two and grandmother of 10. (the outdoor grandma) In her spare time she preaches and plays the cornet.

Trailjournals.com (Medicare Pastor)
Facebook.com/MaryDavison
Website – maryedavison.com